"A DREAM OF STONE"

André Gill, *Émile Zola* (from *Les Hommes d'aujourd'hui*). Photo M. Garval.

Frontispice   Les Grands Hommes font bien dessus.
     —Gustave Flaubert, *Dictionnaire des idées reçues*

[Frontispiece   Great Men look nice there.]
     —Gustave Flaubert, *Dictionary of received ideas*

"A DREAM OF STONE"

Fame, Vision, and Monumentality in Nineteenth-Century French Literary Culture

Michael D. Garval

DELAWARE
Newark: University of Delaware Press

(Excerpt) pp. 27–29 By Jean-Paul Sartre, translated by Lloyd Alexander, from NAUSEA, copyright © 1964 by New Directions Publishing Corp. Used by permission of New Directions Publishing Corporation.

From Jean Paul Sartre's *The Words* translated by Bernard Frechtman. English translation copyright © 1964 by George Braziller, Inc. Reprinted by permission of George Braziller, Inc.

Excerpts from Jean-Paul Sartre, *La Nausée* and *Les mots*, © 1938 and © 1964, Éditions GALLIMARD. Reprinted by permission of Éditions GALLIMARD.

Art Object:
Felix Tournachon Nadar, French, 1820–1910
Preliminary study for the projected lithograph "Pantheon Nadar" 1854., 1854
Graphite pencil and charcoal drawing, on tan paper.
68.58 × 88.26 cm (27 × 34 3/4 in.)
Museum of Fine Arts, Boston
Lucy Dalbiac Luard Fund and Abbott Lawrence Fund
1984.769

Associated University Presses
2010 Eastpark Boulevard
Cranbury, NJ 08512

The paper used in this publication meets the requirements of the American National Standard for Permanence of Paper for Printed Library Materials Z39.48-1984.

Library of Congress Cataloging-in-Publication Data

Garval, Michael D., 1963–
    "A dream of stone" : fame, vision, and monumentality in nineteenth-century French literary culture / Michael D. Garval.
        p. cm.
    Includes bibliographical references and index.
    ISBN 0-87413-862-0 (alk. paper)
    1. French literature—19th century—History and criticism.   2. France—Intellectual life—19th century.   I. Title.

PQ283.G37 2004
840.9'007—dc22   2004002542

PRINTED IN THE UNITED STATES OF AMERICA

Contents

Illustrations

Acknowledgments

MONUMENTS RAISED IN NINETEENTH-CENTURY France, while commonly seen as the work of one sculptor, were often sponsored by public subscription. The artist would thus receive credit for what a host of supporters had made possible. So too a book like this, while signed by one, can only come to fruition with help from many. But with no more impressive pedestal for inscribing benefactors' names, this preface will have to suffice, to express my thanks.

So many friends and colleagues have left their imprint on this project as it evolved, but I would like to thank in particular Janet Beizer, Claus Cluver, Dario Gamboni, Isabelle Naginski, Jonathan Ribner, Peggy Waller, Alex Wettlaufer, and Barbara Wright for the insights they have shared. It goes without saying—but needs saying nonetheless—that while responsibility for any flaws is mine, the book would be much the poorer without their contributions. Above all, I would like to thank Larry Schehr for his belief in my ability to carry out a study of this magnitude, for his constant encouragement and advice along the way and, in particular, for his prompt, generous, and perceptive readings of each chapter.

I am likewise indebted to the teachers who, at each stage in my education, made a difference: in particular, the late Virginia Anastassoff, my French teacher at Fair Lawn High School, who sparked my love for French language, literature, and culture; Ilse Hempel Lipschutz, my undergraduate mentor at Vassar, who taught me to pay attention to details; and Richard Sieburth, my thesis advisor at New York University, who urged me to consider the larger picture as well.

A number of grants have helped me carry out the research for this project: a 1993 Summer Research Travel Grant from Vassar College; a 1996 Summer Stipend for Research from the North East Modern Language Association; a 1996 Research Fund Grant, a 1998 Summer Stipend, a Fall 1998 Off-Campus Scholarly Leave and, most recently, a 2003 Publication Subvention (underwriting the permission and production costs for the book's many images), all from the College of Humanities, Arts & Social Sciences at North Carolina State University. In particular, I would like to thank Matt Zingraff, my college's Associate Dean for Research & Engagement, for his support and guidance over the years.

Many others at North Carolina State University have helped in important ways, notably: Debora Godfrey, Administrative Assistant in the Department of Foreign Languages and Literatures who, along with her husband Wayne, always made sure that my images looked their best; my friend and colleague Dudley Marchi, who was a bastion of support during his tenure as Interim Department Head, while I was finishing work on this project; and, Herman Berkhoff, Managing Director of the university's Digital Media Lab, who gave generously of his expertise in helping me prepare the book's illustrations.

I am grateful to Miron and Sandra Hunt, whose extraordinary hospitality during my stays in France made it possible for me to complete my research. I also thank the University of Delaware Press, and the Associated University Presses for recognizing and helping to realize the book's potential.

Earlier versions of parts of this book appeared in articles: "The Rise and Fall of the Literary Monument in Post-Revolutionary France," in *The Pictured Word. Word & Image Interactions 2*, Martin Heusser et al., eds. (Amsterdam: Rodopi, 1998): 183–99; "Visions of the Great Woman Writer: Imagining George Sand through Word and Image," in *Le Siècle de George Sand*, David A. Powell, ed. (Amsterdam: Rodopi, 1998): 213–34; and, "'A Dream of Stone': Fame, Vision, and the Monument in Nineteenth-Century French Literary Culture," in *College Literature*

30.2 (Spring 2003): 82–119. I am grateful to Rodopi, and to *College Literature*, for permission to reprint this material.

My wife Alina, and my children Stefan and Emma, endured the interminable hours I worked on this project. I thank them for their patience, and beg forgiveness for time not spent with them.

Finally, this book is dedicated to the memory of my father, Herb Garval. I hope that it reflects at least a little of his humor, skepticism, love of language, and passion for ideas.

"A DREAM OF STONE"

Introduction: Literary Greatness and the Monument

Colosse de bronze ou d'albâtre,
Salué d'un peuple idolâtre,
Je surgirais sur la cité
Comme un géant en sentinelle,
Couvrant la ville de mon aile,
Dans une attitude éternelle
De génie et de majesté!
　　—Victor Hugo, "À M. David, statuaire"
　　　　　　(1828) [1964–1967, 1.734]

[Colossus of bronze or alabaster,
Hailed by an idolatrous populace,
I would loom over the city
Like a watchful giant
Covering the town with my wing,
In an eternal attitude
Of genius and majesty!]
　　—Victor Hugo, "To M. David, sculptor"

Et l'objection que l'on peut faire, qu'il y a des grands hommes qui sont d'une petite taille, n'est pas un argument sérieux pour moi, parce que je sais que l'imagination donne, tout naturellement, à ces hommes une proportion colossale et que la statuaire n'est pas la représentation matérielle de l'homme, mais son apothéose, l'essence de son âme divine, devenue forme, pour être saisie par l'âme des générations.
　　—Pierre-Jean David d'Angers, *Carnets* (2.143)

[And I would not consider as a serious argument the potential objection that there are great men who are small, because I know that our imagination quite naturally gives these men colossal proportions, and that statuary is not the material representation of a man, but his apotheosis, the essence of his divine soul, given form, to carry on to future generations.]
　　—Pierre-Jean David d'Angers, *Notebooks*

In 1881, perhaps for fear the old man would not reach his next birthday, the beginning of Hugo's eightieth year was declared a national celebration. On the *avenue d'Eylau*, where he lived, a temporary triumphal arch was erected and, on February 26, his seventy-ninth birthday, six hundred thousand admirers paraded beneath his window. In July, the street was renamed *avenue Victor Hugo*, an honor once reserved for kings, and now for dead luminaries (Bournon 1909, 183–84). This telling rededication assumed immortality in life—indeed, from this point on friends would address mail "A monsieur Victor Hugo, en son avenue": Victor Hugo in his avenue, like Mausoleus in his tomb. With the morbidly commemorative zeal of a premature burial, the eightieth-year fanfare prefigured the great man's passing four years later.

Hugo's grand state funeral marked, in many ways, the apogee for the monumental vision of literary greatness that had evolved, across the nineteenth-century in France, toward an ever-closer identification of writer and monument, flesh and stone. In an elaborate, commemorative petrifaction, organized around two symbolically charged monumental structures, Hugo lay in state beneath the *Arc de Triomphe*, then was enshrined in the *Panthéon*. On June 1, 1885, two million spectators, more than the population of Paris at the time, watched the funerary procession bring him to his final resting place. Throughout much of his long career, Hugo had been considered France's greatest living writer, his literary accomplishments already seen in monumental terms. Now this farewell extravaganza appeared to confirm his passage from the animate to the inanimate. The great writer seemed to fuse with the monument; to become what Pierre Nora has called a "lieu de mémoire" [realm of memory] (Nora 1997, passim); indeed perhaps to become the figure he himself had prophesied nearly six decades earlier, in a poem dedicated to sculptor David d'Angers: the "Colosse de bronze ou d'albâtre, / Salué d'un peuple idolâtre," poised to lord, eternally, over the city. Yet, amid the monumental pomp and circumstance of Hugo's funeral, there were elements that paint a different picture, that tell a related but divergent story. Unprecedentedly extensive press coverage, the event's prodigious attendance, the proliferation of manufactured Hugo memorabilia, and the temporary *mise-en-scène* of the wake beneath the *Arc*, point to the emergence of less monolithic, less eternalizing, more mass-media, mass-market modes of fame. And maybe there had always been at least a *soupçon* of fragility or impermanence underlying the period's seemingly confident vision of monumental glory. After all, in the late 1820s, when Hugo was rapidly emerging as the leader of the blossoming Romantic movement, he nonetheless chose to portend his eventual, monumental apotheosis, not in the certitude of the future tense, but in the more tentative conditional: "je surgirais."

As all this suggests, Hugo's spectacular state funeral was emblematic of the complex interrelations among fame, vision, and monumentality in nineteenth-century France. The wide-ranging socioeconomic, political, cultural, and technological transformations in this postrevolutionary period were at once exhilarating and troubling, prompting both delight in novelty—avant-garde agitation in the arts, commercial and media innovation, utopian schemes for a better world, positivist faith in "progress"—and a desire to slow things down, to seek respite from the howling winds of change. In this respect monuments offered a soothing illusion of solidity and stability, a vision of cultural permanence, as a nation in flux strove to define itself, its relation to the past, and anticipated survival into the future. Imagination, as David d'Angers put it, naturally lent greatness "une proportion colossale," a suitably grandiose form for projecting into the future, "pour être saisie par l'âme des générations." Paradoxically, greatness was increasingly seen as the result of innovation, yet celebrated through would-be immutability—with flights of creative fancy frozen into cultural artifacts for posterity, like bronzed butterflies.

Born of desire, hope, and imagination, such commemorative fervor was deeply compensatory. Impressive and solid as they might seem, nineteenth-century France's burgeoning monumental constructions, whether sculptural, architectural, or even—as we shall see—textual, perched precariously upon the sands of absence, displacement, and negation. They substituted marble and bronze for cardboard and plaster, leather-bound complete works for newsprint ephemera, durability for impermanence, solidity for insubstantiality, national unity for political chaos, secular apotheosis for religious transcendance, resplendent glory for mass-cultural mediocrity, virility for impotence, heroic distinction for vain aspiration, and so on, their imposing presence compensating for such individual and collective demons as uncertainty, failure, impermanence, ignominy, anonymity, obscurity, emasculation, desecration, revolution, regicide and, post-1815, France's relative lack of military and political power. Emblematically, the *avenue d'Eylau*, named for a great Napoleonic victory, became the *avenue Victor Hugo*, a tribute to a different kind of greatness, as earlier traditions of honoring royal, imperial, or martial might were supplanted by increasing commemoration of great men, based upon an ideal of collective glory through cultural accomplishment. In the broadest sense, nineteenth-century France's visions of monumental grandeur cut straight to this society's deepest concerns, over change and continuity, individual striving and national prestige, the lure of the here and now, and the promise of a hereafter.

Not surprisingly, within this larger context, and in a nation with such a long-standing and vibrant literary culture, there evolved an influential ideal of great writers and their work as immortal, that saw literary glory in monumental terms. This envisioning of grandiose possibilities for writers and their work might best be called "un rêve de pierre" or "dream of stone"—an oxymoron that Baudelaire used to evoke the nature of beauty (Baudelaire 1975–76, I.21; 1991, 47), but that also captures the curious mix of material and ideal, concrete and imaginary, ephemeral and eternal, within the period's conception of literary greatness.[1]

The "dream of stone," while now largely forgotten, was a central, organizing force in nineteenth-century French literary culture. Cutting across genres, periods, and movements, it pervaded the world of letters, informing the lives, work, and reception of literary figures from obscure but ambitious scribblers to such touchstones of greatness as Honoré de Balzac, George Sand, or Victor Hugo; from popular hacks like Pierre Alexis, vicomte Ponson du Terrail to cerebral aesthetes like Stéphane

Mallarmé; from dignified Germaine de Staël to outrageous Alfred Jarry; and, from François-René de Chateaubriand in the early years of the nineteenth century, to Marcel Proust at the beginning of the twentieth. In recent years, historical and art historical scholarship has dealt extensively with nineteenth-century France's monumental art and architecture, and especially its commemorative statuary, an abundant legacy long-disparaged by the modernist tradition that succeeded it. Attention has focused on the interrelated iconography and ideology of the monument, particularly with respect to questions of individual renown, national identity, and cultural memory (Janson 1976, Agulhon 1978, Nora 1997, Hargrove 1990). There have been a number of exhibitions conceived along similar lines, at the fertile crossroads of word and image, high and low culture, literary and cultural studies, intellectual history and what the French call *histoire des mentalités*, including: *La Gloire de Victor Hugo* [The Glory of Victor Hugo], at the *Grand Palais* in 1985; *Rodin et la caricature* [Rodin and Caricature], at the *Musée Rodin* in 1990; *Mémoire de marbre: la sculpture funéraire en France, 1804–1914* [Memory of Marble: funerary sculpture in France, 1804–1914], at the *Bibliothèque historique de la Ville de Paris* in 1995; at the *Musée d'Orsay, Nadar, les années créatrices: 1854–1860* [Nadar, the creative years: 1854–1860], in 1994, and *En collaboration avec le soleil: Victor Hugo, photographies de l'exil* [In collaboration with the sun: Victor Hugo, photographs from exile], in 1998–99; and, at the *Maison de Balzac, Benjamin Roubaud et le Panthéon charivarique* [Benjamin Roubaud and the Panthéon charivarique] (1988), *Dantan jeune: caricatures et portraits de la société romantique* [Dantan jeune: caricatures and portraits of romantic society] (1989), and *Nadar: Caricatures, photographies* [Nadar: Caricatures, photographs] (1990). There has also been excellent scholarship on the history of fame (Braudy 1986); on the rise of the "great man," and particularly of the great writer, in eighteenth-century France (Bonnet 1998); on the interconnectedness of literature and architecture in nineteenth-century France (Hamon 1992); on nineteenth-century French literary culture (Clark 1987); on the period's mythologizing of the great writer (Georgel 1985, Porter 1995); and, on the links between litera-

ture, biography, and the "death of the author" in late nineteenth- and early twentieth-century literary culture (Boym 1991). Despite all this, and despite the general trend toward contextualization in literary studies, there has been scarce research into the rich confluence between nineteenth-century France's culture of monumentality and its literary culture.

This study thus seeks to reconstruct nineteenth-century French literary culture's pervasive "dream of stone"—to uncover its salient features, trace its far-reaching implications, and chart its rise and fall—by drawing not only upon an array of authors and works, but also upon diverse sorts of evidence, from journalism to poetry, caricature to statuary, postcards to public monuments, while focusing on the lives and work of three of the period's most celebrated writers: Honoré de Balzac (1799–1850), George Sand (1804–76), and Victor Hugo (1802–85). In so doing, the analysis that follows historicizes questions about the "death" and subsequent "return" of the author, by resituating nineteenth-century literary figures within the period's own view of the links between life, letters, and posthumous glory. At the same time, it expands word and image studies into the realm of literary fame by tracing the complex interweaving of word and image through which the author constructs himself and is constructed as a public figure; and, by delineating as well the vital interrelations between different kinds of verbal and visual representations of literary greatness. Finally, it also tackles a largely unexplored aspect of nineteenth-century gender studies, by examining the deep-rooted gendering of literary fame itself; and it seeks, along the way, to refine feminism's critique of the literary canon by contending that certain representations of nineteenth-century women writers actually helped French culture "envision" the very category of the great woman writer. In this connection, I must add a word about gender neutrality—or the lack thereof—in my prose. I shall always, unless the specific context deals with women, use "he," "him," and "his" to refer to the nineteenth-century author, assuming the same male norm as the period itself. The point, in this respect as in all others, is to evoke the nineteenth-century French literary world, not as we might like to see it, but rather as it liked to see itself.

**Fig. 2. Marcelin, *Les romans populaires illustrés par Marcelin (Popular novels illustrated by Marcelin).*
Cliché Bibliothèque nationale de France.**

A brief look at two emblematic images shall further introduce the broad lines of this inquiry.

Marcelin's caricature, "Les romans populaires illustrés par Marcelin" [Popular novels illustrated by Marcelin], which appeared in the satirical *Journal pour rire* on September 10, 1853, depicts novelists George Sand, Eugène Sue, Honoré de Balzac, Victor Hugo, and Alexandre Dumas *père* as commemorative marble busts (fig. 2), though all except Balzac were still alive at the time. The title already plays with viewers' expectations: instead of illustrated novels here, it is at once the author and novel, or better yet the author as novel, that Marcelin "illustrates"—both renders, and renders illustrious. Indeed, the caricaturist casts his newspaper and himself as arbiters of fame, for he wears a newsprint vest emblazoned "JOURNAL POUR RIRE," and proffers the conventional laurel wreaths of fame above the writers' statufied heads. On the lower part of each bust, though, where we would expect to see the writer's name, we find instead the title of his or her most famous work. Similarly, on each pedestal, there is a heraldic shield that displays not the author's coat of arms, but instead a witty emblem of the work in question, pointing to a broader preoccupation at the time with the genealogy of genius, the worthy *oeuvre* here supplanting a distinguished lineage as the source of the author's greatness. Thus, for Sand's *François le Champi*, we find the woolen stockings, wooden clogs, and bagpipe of the novel's *berrichon* peasants; for Sue's *Mystères de Paris* [Mysteries of Paris], a ladder leading into the sewers of the Parisian underworld that the novel explores; for Balzac's *La Comédie humaine* [The Human Comedy], a bag of gold stabbing a heart, evoking the work's dual—and dueling—obsessions with money and love; for Hugo's *Notre-Dame de Paris* [The Hunchback of Notre-Dame], Quasimodo ringing the cathedral bells; and, for Dumas' swashbuckling *Les Trois Mousquetaires* [The Three Musketeers], a half-dozen cadavers skewered on a pair of swords. In these ways, Marcelin's caricature equates and integrates, through the monument, each writer's life, work, and projected literary afterlife. Oddly, moreover, George Sand seems for once to be depicted on a par with her male counterparts; perhaps such an unusual representation is made possible by her masculine appearance here, by the use of a male character name to designate her, even by the fact that these are mere busts, not more prestigious full-length statues. In this connection, Marcelin's text beneath the drawing begins "L'Égypte a eu ses pyramides, la Grèce a eu ses sept sages, Rome a eu le monde; nous, nous avons les romans à quatre sous" [Egypt had its pyramids, Greece had its seven wisemen, Rome had the

world; we have four *sous* novels] and continues in this vein, contrasting the great French classical authors Corneille, Racine, and Molière with their current-day counterparts. Like the drawing, in which foregrounded contemporary luminaries are surrounded by shadowy statues of past greats, the accompanying article seems to lament the shabbiness and commercialism of the moderns compared with the grandeur and monumentality of the ancients. Yet, drawing and text also self-consciously promote modern celebrities, and modern celebrity culture, through the contemporary medium of the press. More subversively perhaps, by equating statues of current-day stars with this modern, commercial, media-driven brand of celebrity, the drawing invites us to see contemporary statuary as a vehicle, not for permanence, but for impermanence.

In his 1854 lithographic *Panthéon*, the caricaturist and pioneering photographer Nadar (pseudonym of Gaspard Félix Tournachon) depicts a serpentine procession of literary celebrities, lined up in order of relative prominence (fig. 3).[2] This is the contemporary literary pantheon according to Nadar for, as in the Marcelin drawing, the artist is fame's arbiter. In the foreground, moreover, at the head of the procession, stands a small cluster of deceased writers represented as statue busts and medallions. Like the very idea of a modern "pantheon" of letters, the way in which the great men are immortalized here—transformed from caricatures into statues when they die—links the nineteenth-century writer and the monument, casting the author's death as a passage into monumentality. The fact that George Sand and a handful of other living women writers are also included as statues, yet thus excluded from the crucial *process* of immortalization, points at once to the increasing prominence of women in the world of letters, and to their broader exclusion from the pinnacle of literary greatness, as we shall see later on.

Nadar was an important producer and purveyor of images of the famous, playing a role not unlike that of Andy Warhol a century later, as the recent *Nadar, Warhol: Paris, New York* exhibition at the J. Paul Getty Museum contends: "As men and portrait photographers, . . . [they] have more in common than might be supposed, particularly as adroit manipulators

Fig. 3. Nadar, *Panthéon Nadar*. Courtesy George Eastman House.

of the media of their day in simultaneously promoting their own reputations and those of their subjects" (Baldwin and Keller 1999, 11). Nadar's emblematic career spanned much of the nineteenth century, during which time he portrayed virtually all the literary eminences of his day, from Baudelaire, to Flaubert, to George Sand. He published the *Panthéon*, moreover, at a watershed both in the history of visual culture and in his own career. It offers a rare, revealing conjunction of monument, caricature, and photography, representational modes that, as we shall see, embodied divergent views of fame itself. With the continual expansion of the press in nineteenth-century France, and concurrent improvements in printing and paper-making, caricature flourished. At mid century, however, the abundant political caricature of the July Monarchy was curtailed by the Second

Empire's stricter censorship, and artists like Nadar turned to popular but less controversial subjects—in particular, as here, to the depiction of contemporary celebrities. At about the same time, the French literary world was adding to its vision of the literary work as monument a complementary vision of the writer as monument that would be manifested most spectacularly in an unprecedented proliferation of statues to writers under the early Third Republic. While Marcelin's "Romans populaires" monumentalizes the writer and his work simultaneously, Nadar's *Panthéon* focuses instead on the writer's transformation into a monument. Both images, however, with their public display of statue busts and medallions, and mix of living and dead writers, reveal a visual culture in transition, on its way toward the Third Republic ideal of full-length public statuary figuring posthumous glory. Finally, these were also the early days of photography, a medium that, as it developed, would offer ever more accurate, abundant, inexpensive, and instantaneous likenesses to—and of—an ever-broader spectrum of the population. Toward the end of Nadar's work on his satirical *Panthéon*, he first tried photography as a means of documenting faces, and soon afterward largely abandoned caricature to dedicate himself to the new medium. It seems that Nadar's experience with the *Panthéon* propelled him toward photography: his obsession with documentary accuracy, as well as the sheer number of effigies crammed into his lithograph, exhausted caricature's potential for depicting a significant number of contemporary celebrities expediently and faithfully, compelling him to explore instead the representational possibilities of photography. Nadar the photographer picked up where Nadar the caricaturist left off, continuing his cultural pantheon of contemporary France through individual photographic portraits. In these ways, both through the details of its composition and through the circumstances of its creation, the *Panthéon Nadar* urges us to consider how the period's literary "dream of stone" evolved amid shifting iconographical possibilities.

These two drawings already raise many of the complex ideological, cultural, and aesthetic questions intertwined with the development of a monumental vision of literary greatness in nineteenth-century France. Why did Balzac's, Sand's, and Hugo's contemporaries come to understand greatness in general, and literary greatness in particular, through the monument? How did such an ideal of greatness emerge, and what were its implications, both within the literary realm in particular, and within the culture at large? What, for example, was the impact of political systems and beliefs on society's conception of greatness and means of representing it? More broadly, what relationships obtained between power and the monument? How did this nation in transition negotiate tensions between an increasing democratization of fame, and continued need for fame to signify some kind of distinction? How did visions of greatness differ for men and women? What relationships existed among different visual and verbal media, as vehicles of fame? How did new technologies trans-

form the collective vision of greatness? Amid change, what traditional elements persisted, and why? How might one reconcile contemporary celebrity with lasting renown, temporal realities with longings for the eternal? In this context, what sort of posterity might the monument be thought to embody? How did writers and artists, creators and critics, make sense of, and foresee a future for, the rich and varied cultural legacy that they were shaping? How, in the largest sense, did they understand nineteenth-century France's place in the world, and in world history?

Oh! quand il bâtissait, de sa main colossale,
Pour son trône, appuyé sur l'Europe vassale,
    Ce pilier souverain,
Ce bronze, devant qui tout n'est que poudre et
   sable,
Sublime monument, deux fois impérissable,
    Fait de gloire et d'airain; . . . .
C'était un beau spectacle!
    —Victor Hugo, "À la colonne" (1830)

[Oh! When with his colossal hand he built
Like a throne, dominating Europe,
This sovereign pillar,
This bronze, before which all is but dust and
   sand,
A sublime monument, doubly immortal,
Made of glory and brass; (. . .)
It was a great spectacle!]
    —Victor Hugo, "To the column"

L'avenue [de Neuilly] est décorée ou plutôt déshonorée dans toute sa longueur par d'affreuses statues en plâtre figurant des Renommées et par des colonnes triomphales surmontées d'aigles dorés et posés en porte-à-faux sur des piédestaux en marbre gris. Les gamins se divertissent à faire des trous dans ce marbre qui est en toile. . . .

Un médiocre décor d'opéra occupe le sommet de l'arc de triomphe, l'empereur debout sur un char de Renommées, ayant à sa droite la Gloire et à sa gauche la Grandeur. Que signifie une statue de la grandeur? Comment exprimer la grandeur par une statue? Est-ce en la faisant plus grande que les autres? Ceci est du galimatias monumental.
    —Victor Hugo, "le retour des cendres"
    (*Choses vues*, 15 December 1840)

[The Avenue (of Neuilly) is decorated or rather dishonored along its entire length by horrid plaster statues representing Renown, and by triumphal columns topped with gilded eagles and installed precariously upon grey marble pedestals. Kids are having fun poking holes in the marble, made of canvas . . .

There is a mediocre opera set atop the triumphal arch, with the emperor standing upon a chariot of Renowns, on his right Glory, on his left Greatness. What does a statue of greatness mean? How can greatness be expressed by a statue? By making it bigger than others? This is monumental rubbish.]
—Victor Hugo, "the return of (Napoleon's) remains"

Whether constructed, imagined, excavated, restored, preserved, consecrated, desecrated, or destroyed, monuments mattered in nineteenth-century France. From the Revolution through the First World War, a period of unprecedented flux, monuments not only commemorated specific people, accomplishments, and ideals, but also provided French culture with a powerful—yet slippery—metaphor of permanence. Emblematic events and trends included: the razing of the Bastille and Revolutionary vandalism; the rise of modern archaeology and of the Romantic obsession with ruins; the founding of Alexandre Lenoir's *Musée des monuments français* and of the *Père-Lachaise* cemetery; a new-found concern for the plight of "historical monuments"; urbanization in general and "Haussmannization" in particular; five *Expositions Universelles* in Paris in less than a half-century; the repeated metamorphoses of such ideologically charged structures as the Vendôme Column and the *Panthéon;* and, throughout all this, a growing desire to establish a collective, cultural heritage or *patrimoine*, in particular by designating structures like tombs, triumphal arches, museums, and birthplaces as repositories of a larger national consciousness (Nora 1997). An extraordinary number and variety of monuments, both sculptural and architectural, were inaugurated or consecrated. These range from the *arc de triomphe du Carrousel* (1806–8), to the equestrian statue of Henri IV on the *Pont-neuf* (1819), to David d'Angers' pediment for the *Panthéon* (1831), to the Obelisk of Luxor on the *place de la Concorde* (1836), to Napoleon's tomb in the *Invalides* (1842), to the *Opéra-Garnier* (1862–75), to the *mur des fédérés* in the *Père-Lachaise* cemetery (1871), to the Eiffel Tower (1887–89), to the 150 statues of great men erected in Paris

alone, in the first four decades of the Third Republic. While these far from exhaustive litanies favor Parisian examples, both for their familiarity and significance, much the same forces were at work in the provinces, in everything from the vogue for amateur archaeology earlier in the century (satirized by Mérimée in *La Vénus d'Ille* [The Venus of Ille]), to the "statufication" of local heroes in countless town squares, around the *fin-de-siècle*. Amid the historical ruptures of the Revolution and its prolonged aftermath, monuments focused French culture's attempts to define, to situate its protean self in relation to both the past and the future. Ironically, the stasis that this commemorative penchant sought to establish was undermined, not only by neglect, vandalism, or demolition, but also by the feverish pace of construction. The proliferation of new monuments, designed to showcase stability, instead made a public spectacle of change.

Wishing to confer distinction and would-be immortality, to convey ideals of excellence and immutability, monuments were predicated upon a belief in greatness, not only of individuals and of their works, but of the nation as a whole. "Greatness" may be a notion anathema to our relativistic age, but in nineteenth-century France there prevailed a faith in hierarchies of value, in superlatives, in the superiority, transcendance, eternity, of certain creators, works, or nations. Greatness was seen as the measure of all human endeavor, and terms like *gloire* [glory], *grandeur* [greatness], and *génie* [genius] defined, identified, and rewarded greatness in all its forms. By foregrounding such a preoccupation with greatness, this book neither yearns for lost standards (like the canon), nor wishes to debate fruitlessly what is and is not great in the nineteenth-century cultural heritage (Staël yes? Nodier no?). The point is instead to consider on its own terms a period in which, even in humorous contexts like Marcelin's *Romans populaires* or Nadar's *Panthéon*, this ideal of greatness was taken very seriously.

While the French Revolution was a crucial turning point in the development of French ideas about greatness, and monuments, and how these were interrelated, such notions did not somehow spring full-grown from beneath Marianne's phrygian cap. Rather, they emerged out of a long historical evolution that reached back to antiquity. Substantial new developments from the Renaissance onward, and particularly in the eighteenth century, lay the groundwork for the pervasive culture of monumentality that took shape in the nineteenth.

In his seminal essay on the public monument, H. W. Janson asserts that " 'Monument,' derived from the Latin root monere, means simply a 'reminder'"(Janson 1976, 1). He is right, of course, to underscore the monument's commemorative function for, beginning in antiquity, pyramids, triumphal arches, and statues perpetuated the renown of a select few. Janson neglects to mention, however, that *monere* also means "to warn" (as in "admonition" or "premonition"), suggesting a preternatural, even vatic quality about the monument. Indeed, as we shall see, secular and sacred elements, homages to worldly greatness and ones to greatness of a higher, divine order, are so often interlinked in the history of the monument, and vestiges of the devotional have continued to inform the Western monumental tradition well into recent times. To be sure, the earliest monuments were often associated with religious practices. Pagan idols, the graven images of Old Testament proscriptions, could be conceived not just as tributes to the godhead (as in later Christian statuary), but as its incarnations, embodying absolute greatness. With the spread of a Judeo-Christian worldview, such idolatry was strongly discouraged, but never entirely died out. A seventeenth-century bronze of Louis XIV or, for that matter, a nineteenth-century monument to Victor Hugo, whatever else it might be, is also in some sense a sacred image, that participates in a cult of its subject. A great man statue, as David d'Angers contends, is "son apothéose, l'essence de son âme divine" [his apotheosis, the essence of his divine soul].

The first major flowering of Western civic sculpture dates from Roman antiquity, starting in the Republican period, and reaching its apogee under the Empire:

We know from literary accounts that, from early Republican times on, meritorious political or military leaders were honored by having their statues put on public display. The habit was to continue until the end of the Empire a thousand years later. Its beginnings may well have derived from the Greek custom of placing votive statues of athletic victors and other important individuals in the precincts of such sanctuaries as Delphi and Olympia. [Janson 1977, 166]

Something of this original, devotional attitude persisted throughout the history of Roman civic statuary. For example, the famed *Augustus of Primaporta* (Janson 1977, 166) represents the emperor not only as both political and military leader, but also as both human being and divinity, reflecting the ruler's desire to be venerated as a demigod. Specifically, while his features are clearly individuated enough to provide a distinct human likeness, they are idealized as well, like his body, making him appear superhuman. His bare feet suggest, moreover, that he walks on hallowed ground. Yet a statue like this would have been installed in a secular, public setting. Unlike imperial effigies on coins or paintings, a statue of this sort

associated the entire human body with the civic space of a public square. Instead of being privately venerated by the viewer, it must be approached as a monument, an embodiment of the power to impose oneself on others. Civic sculpture is primarily *there*, standing proudly in the viewer's path. (Braudy 1986, 198)

Imperial Rome also saw the first large-scale, public commemoration of cultural figures, as Augustus decorated libraries with busts and medallions of great writers.[3] While limited in size and scope, compared with the period's grandiose and abundant commemorations of its rulers, these portraits did at least recognize writers as worthy subjects for public statuary and thus constituted an important, initial step toward the full-sized, free-standing monuments to writers that would invade public space in nineteenth-century France.

First, however, the rise of Christianity would deal civic sculpture a substantial, and long-lasting blow:

From the triumph of Christianity through the Middle Ages rounded civic sculpture went into a definite decline. When churches began to include statues of the saints, they were firmly attached to the structure. What would it mean to be able to walk around God or Christ or one of the saints? They stand beyond perspective and beyond realistic description, just as they stand beyond the world of the senses in general.

To whatever limited extent medieval leaders were also represented in statuary, they too appeared "flattened and hieratic," for they were subject to the same theological imperatives: "As Christianity theologically focused on the world in heaven, so even on earth its adherents, whether priestly or political, were depicted as men and women in touch with divinity, gazing beyond the present into eternal life." In the Renaissance, however, civic sculpture did revive somewhat, "because of the simultaneous reassertion of the importance of the state, its leaders, and those artists who celebrate them." Yet only much later—most notably in France and America, between their revolutions and the first World War—would there be "a revival of civic sculpture to an extent unparalleled since imperial Rome." (451)

As in Imperial Rome, civic monuments from the Renaissance through the late eighteenth century remained largely the privilege of the country's rulers. They extended the sovereign's temporal power, and exalted his divine prerogative, through their iconographical programs and imposing presence. This tradition reached its apogee in France with the reign of Louis XIV, and particularly with a series of royal equestrian statues (Martin 1986). During the Renaissance the French court had remained largely ambulatory, and the king exercised power over an ever-expanding territory with regular visits throughout the realm, accompanied by the pageantry of elaborately orchestrated *entrées royales*—an ongoing road show of monumental extravaganzas (Graham and Johnson 1974, 1979). In the seventeenth century, though, the French court settled at Versailles and, increasingly, the monarch tried instead to exert his influence on the populace through a sort of monumental visual proxy. Under Louis XIV, many statues of the king were erected in provincial centers, and many more were planned but never executed. These statues were often equestrian, and designed to be the centerpieces of newly created *places Royales*, framed by harmoniously identical facades. As their symbolic role in war and conquest suggests, moreover, Louis XIV's statuary likenesses ruled in the king's physical absence, from the provincial cities of his realm to his latest acquisitions abroad:

Pour Louis XIV, confisquer le cheval de la statue nancéienne de Charles III revient à annexer la Lorraine; lui ajouter un cavalier à son image c'est interrompre une lignée vaincue. Inversement, imposer à Besançon un arc de triomphe, envisager de contraindre les villes soumises des Pays-Bas à accepter sa statue, c'est régner par effigies interposées. (Gardes 1994, 15)

[For Louis XIV, confiscating the horse of the statue of Charles III in Nancy is the same as annexing Lorraine; making himself the horseman is a way of shortcircuiting a defeated royal line. On the other hand, forcing a triumphal arch on Besançon, or trying to get the vanquished towns of the Netherlands to accept his statue, is a way of ruling through images.]

Under the reign of the Sun King, the colossal size of much royal statuary not only buttressed the absolute monarch's hold on worldly power, but also (at least iconographically) legitimated his larger claims to divine right, for sculpture of this magnitude had, in the classical tradition, been reserved for deities. In addition, monuments to Louis XIV set an important precedent, in France, for the compensatory use of public statuary, trying to command space in the sovereign's absence, much as nineteenth-century monuments to great men, raised after their death, would seek to transcend time.

From the seventeenth century onward, there began to take shape profound changes in the nature of fame that would help transform the monument as an embodiment of greatness. The forces underfoot included the rise of capitalism and bourgeois individualism, followed by a relative decline in the monarchy and traditions of patronage, all leading to greater opportunity and social mobility. This trend was spurred on as well by a certain blurring of boundaries between theatrical representation and politics:

After the visually confined hierarchies of the Middle Ages, when willful ostentation was limited to a very few and only the well-born could be remembered through monuments or tombs, the way was now open for others to present themselves profusely to the world. . . . More and more people were getting into the act. Merchants, tradesmen, and lawyers put on festivities as elaborately theatrical as those of royalty.

[Meanwhile,] monarchs in England, France, and in other parts of Europe were wholeheartedly accepting the connection between the structure of the playhouse and the structure of the nation, between the plot of a play and the plot of history, between what they did on the throne and what actors did on the stage. (Braudy 1986, 317–18)

Actors playing kings convincingly, and kings playing like actors to affirm their authority: this sent a powerful message to the rest of society, that greatness was not inborn but could, even needed, to be achieved. While the common man could not yet aspire to rule his nation—Napoleon would come later—he could indeed attain greater prominence than ever before.

Over the course of the eighteenth century in France, there evolved an influential new ideal of the great man or *grand homme*. Progressively, an earlier model of military, aristocratic, or royal heroism and prestige was supplanted by that of the man of genius, of talent, the creator, inventor, explorer and, above all, writer—exemplified by the figure of Voltaire. Ultimately, the *grand homme*, the cultural hero, would replace the monarch as the principal object of adulation, glorification, and commemoration. Honoring great men and their deeds manifested an Enlightenment ideal of human perfectibility, marking a shift from an *ancien régime* vision of glory in which all revolved around the absolute monarch, to the new republican model of a nation built on the strengths, talents, and virtue of its citizenry. Elevating great men undermined the monarch's ostensible monopoly on greatness and, by extension, heralded the eventual ruin of the monarchy.

In *La Naissance du Panthéon* [The Birth of the Pantheon], Jean-Claude Bonnet traces the complex, interwoven threads of this evolution, identifying as the first major development the transition from the earlier *oraison funèbre* à la Bossuet—with its conventional moralizing about greatness and vanity, and adherence to the status quo of aristocratic and military glory—toward the novel genre of the eulogy or *éloge*. The *Académie française* provided a catalyst for this in 1758 by deciding to "proposer désormais pour sujet du prix d'éloquence l'éloge des hommes célèbres de la nation" [offer from now on a prize for eloquence in praise of

the nation's famous men] (Bonnet 1998, 64), and the now-forgotten academician Antoine-Léonard Thomas (1732–85) rapidly emerged as the master of this new rhetorical exercise. The nascent cult of the great man was accompanied, moreover, by a shift in society's prevailing conception of death and the afterlife. Emblematic in this respect was André François Deslandes' *Réflexions sur les grands hommes qui sont morts en plaisantant* [Reflections on great men who died while joking] (Deslandes 2000). Death was no longer to be seen as fearsome, meant to spur sinners to Christian repentance; rather, it was to be welcomed, as a joyous passage into immortality. For the great man in particular, confronting his impending posterity, death offered a sort of neo-pagan apotheosis, a journey into latter-day Elysian Fields.

This ideal of the great man evolved in concert with abundant images of the great man. As Bonnet remarks, "Loin de promouvoir le règne exclusif de la raison, comme on le croit trop souvent, les Lumières ont produit, dans une intense fébrilité idéologique, tout un répertoire d'images" [Far from promoting the exclusive reign of reason, as it too often is believed, the Enlightenment's intense ideological ferment produced a wealth of images] (Bonnet 1998, 113). Over the course of the eighteenth century, there was a succession of projects, private galleries, public installations, and theoretical tracts, all dedicated to the commemoration of great men (Gardes 1994, 96). In the first decade of the century, Titon du Tillet's curious project for a monument called the *Parnasse françois* took a first step toward the grand, public commemoration of great men that would occur later on (Titon du Tillet 1971, Colton 1979). The project featured Louis XIV as Apollo, brandishing a lyre and flanked by great writers of his reign, represented in the guise of the three graces and nine muses. For nearly a half century, Titon strove in vain to have his monument built, updating the project several times and even, on the eve of his death, trying to include Voltaire, who remained unimpressed. As Bonnet explains, Titon's project failed because it was both behind and ahead of its time: on the one hand, glorifying the Sun King; on the other, honoring great men alongside the king (Bonnet 1998, 118).

From 1758 on, the new practice of the academic *éloge* gave rise to considerable debate over how to honor great men publicly, yet in 1765, in his study of *Monumens érigés en France à la gloire de Louis XV* [Monuments raised in France to the glory of Louis XV], architect Pierre Patte could still affirm that, "Il n'est pas d'usage d'élever en France des monumens aux grands généraux ou aux hommes célèbres; les Rois seuls obtiennent cette distinction" [It is not customary in France to raise monuments to great generals or to famous men; only kings are accorded this distinction] (Patte 1765, 93). Still, the inauguration two years earlier of the central statue of the monarch in the *place Louis XV*—later named the *place de la Révolution*, then *place de la Concorde*—reveals some movement away from earlier modes of glorifying the sovereign. Edme Bouchardon's statue is equestrian, yet the king rides not upon the conventionally fiery, rearing stallion of the military conqueror (as in François Girardon's equestrian *Louis XIV* for the *place Vendôme*, destroyed in 1792 [Gamboni 1997, 34]), but rather upon an older, gentler mount. Whereas earlier royal statues represented slaves, chained and prostrate, at the sovereign's feet, this pedestal displays allegories of Justice, Prudence, Force, and Love of peace. This iconographical program was meant to demonstrate the Enlightenment monarch's greatness, not through his military conquests, but through his extraordinary virtue, although this particular king's reputation for vice moved observers to remark cynically, "Les Vertus vont à pied, le Vice est à cheval" [Virtues are on foot, Vice is on horseback] (Bonnet 1998, 119). While it might still have been difficult to imagine great men honored alongside the monarch in such a central, strategic location as this—aligned with the Louvre, Tuileries, and Champs-Élysées—Patte does describe another project, to be located at "une des extrémités de Paris," in which a central statue of Louis XV would be surrounded by a "multitude" of statues honoring great men, and even by a number of empty pedestals, meant to fuel the "zèle des citoyens" [citizens' zeal] to aspire to such honors themselves: "Instruits de la route qui devoit conduire à ces places glorieuses, ils auroient fait les plus grands efforts pour se signaler" [Apprised of the path that would lead to such glorious recognition, they would make the greatest efforts to stand out] (Patte 1765, 210–11). Despite the protorepublican ring of these remarks, Patte is careful to explain, at the end of this section, that the king's glory would remain the focal point:

Élevé au milieu de cette arène immense, [la statue de Louis XV] auroit paru comme la source d'où tout dérive, & le centre où tout aboutit. Les statues des grands hommes, distribuées avec méthode dans ce superbe monument, n'y auroient été placées que pour annoncer l'influence du pouvoir de Louis sur leur émulation, & le concours de tous les talens pour l'illustration de son règne. (212)

[Raised in the middle of this huge arena, (the statue of Louis XV) would have seemed like the spring from which all proceeds, & the center to which all leads. The statues of great men, arrayed purposefully in this superb monument, would only have been placed there to publicize Louis' power to inspire their emulation, and the concurrence of all talents in illustrating his reign.]

Along similar lines, from mid century onward there began to form plans for a museum in the *Grande Galerie* of the Louvre, with the king represented amid portraits and sculptures of great men. Under Louis XVI, between 1775 and 1789, a number of paintings and twenty-eight statues of great men were commissioned for this purpose. The majority of the subjects for the statues were men of letters and thinkers, including Descartes, Fénelon, and Montesquieu, but no living *philosophes*, with a noteworthy predilection for figures whose reputations had suffered injustly during their lifetime. A number of military heroes were also honored—not, however, for their martial prowess, but rather for their admirable serenity, humanity, and patriotism (Bonnet 1998, 129).

In another revealing development, there were issued between 1783 and 1785 a series of porcelain statuettes reproducing the statues of great men from the *Grande Galerie*: twenty-one in all, they each stood forty to fifty centimeters high, and were conceived as decoration for private homes. In this respect, they followed the example set by the Englishman Josiah Wedgewood who, in 1760, had begun selling throughout Europe his cameos and "heads of illustrious moderns from Chaucer to the present time," a group including Voltaire, Rousseau, and a number of other eighteenth-century French writers (131). Such collectable mini-monuments were but one of the visual means through which the evolving cult of great men was disseminated among a broader public. In France, printmakers sold abundant engravings, both idealizing and satirical, of contemporary cultural luminaries—indeed satire, as Bonnet argues, provided a necessary counterpoint to the gravity of the period's veneration of great men: "l'imaginaire du culte des grands hommes, la nouvelle vulgate . . . , menacée de devenir trop assoupissante, avait besoin de s'enrichir de formes antagoniques. Seul cet apport essentiel de la dimension critique put lui assurer une étonnante pérennité" [the imaginary of the great man cult, the new scripture, in danger of becoming too dull, needed to be enriched with antagonistic forms. Only by taking on this essential critical dimension could the cult enjoy such astonishing longevity] (145). Theater also provided a vital arena for propaganda and ideological ferment, with plays like Mercier's *Molière* and *Montesquieu à Marseille*, or Sauvigny's *Mort de Socrate* offering up heroic images of great men to appreciative audiences. "Le théâtre . . . permit . . . d'illustrer, et d'entretenir, avec ses moyens propres, toute une part rituelle du culte des grands hommes, en mettant en scène des visites auprès des personnages célèbres et des apothéoses" [Theater offered its own means to illustrate, and maintain, rituals particular to the cult of great men, by staging visits to famous people, as well as apotheoses] (126)—the apotheoses, that is, of the plays' venerable heroes, and of current-day greats like Voltaire, honored in commemorative ceremonies onstage, even figuring in plays that reenacted contemporary consecrations occurring offstage, or rather on a grander national stage (359 n. 57). The second half of the eighteenth century saw as well the beginnings of interest in the great man's house transformed into a museum (244), a trend that would blossom through the nineteenth century, and on to the present day (Lacambre 1994, Georgel 1994). Along similar lines, during the Revolution streets started to be renamed in honor of great men—for example, *rue Plâtrière*, where Rousseau had resided, transformed into *rue Jean-Jacques Rousseau*—anticipating the con-

version of the *avenue d'Eylau* to the *avenue Victor Hugo* a century later, and figuring a broader desire to recast the city itself in the image of the nation's heroes.

The single grandest commemorative project of the Revolutionary period, as revealing in its ambitions as in its shortcomings, was the transformation of the *Église Sainte-Geneviève*, intended by Louis XV to honor the saint for his recovery from a desperate illness, into the *Panthéon*, meant to be a national temple of renown, honoring great men (Bonnet 1998, Muray 1984, Nora 1997, *le Centre canadien d'architecture* 1989). In this respect, such eighteenth-century British commemorative practices as dilettantes' elaborate private collections of great man effigies, exemplified by the *Temple of British Worthies* at Stowe or the burial of great men alongside royalty at Westminster Abbey from 1734 onward, provide instructive comparison. The *Panthéon* embodies characteristically French tendencies, heralded by earlier developments but reaching fruition in the Revolutionary period: the penchant for official, secular commemoration of great men, within a grand national context; and the divorce between the ideal of great men and the country's royal heritage—an evolution, in less than a century, from the monarchy glorified exclusive of great men, to great men commemorated exclusive of the monarchy.

The successive reconsecration and deconsecration of the entire edifice, as well as the induction and eviction of so many honorees points, at once, to a yearning for monumental commemoration, and to the precariousness of the immortality ostensibly bestowed. Similarly revealing are those monuments from the Revolutionary period that, unlike the massive if mutable *Panthéon*, only existed in the frenzied minds of contemporaries. The feverish years leading up to and including the Revolution were marked by a profusion of grand monumental projects imagined but never realized because of general unrest, the inability of unstable regimes to support and carry out building projects, and the utopian, even chimerical nature of the projects themselves. Particularly noteworthy in this respect are monuments to genius, greatness, and republican ideals by visionary architects like Jean-Jacques Lequeu or Étienne-Louis Boullée

(Jacques and Mouilleseaux 1989, Leith 1991). Grandiose but imaginary, these projects set a powerful precedent for the nineteenth century's prolonged dream of stone. Likewise, the impressive yet temporary installations concocted for the *fêtes révolutionnaires*, honoring Reason, Equality, or the Supreme Being (Leith 1991), both hark back to earlier *entrées royales*, and look forward to Charles Garnier's spectacular *mise-en-scène* for Hugo's wake beneath the *Arc de Triomphe*. Perhaps though, as Victor Hugo contends in *Quatrevingt-treize*, the French Revolution also offered the real—though paradoxically immaterial—monumental legacy of *La Convention*:

> Les royalistes commencèrent par rire de ce bonnet rouge gris, de cette salle postiche, de ce monument de carton, de ce sanctuaire de papier mâché, de ce panthéon de boue et de crachat. Comme cela devait disparaître vite! Les colonnes étaient en douves de tonneau, les voûtes étaient en volige, les bas-reliefs étaient en mastic, les entablements étaient en sapin, les statues étaient en plâtre, les marbres étaient en peinture, les murailles étaient en toile, et dans ce provisoire la France a fait de l'éternel. (1965, 151)

> [At first the royalists laughed at this greyish-red bonnet, this phoney chamber, this cardboard monument, this papier-mâché sanctuary, this mud and spittle pantheon. How fast this would disappear! The columns were of barrel planks, the vaults of cladding, the friezes of mastic, the entablatures of pine, the statues of plaster, the marble of paint, the walls of canvas, and from such impermanence France made something eternal.]

What Hugo considers the grandest and most enduring heritage of the Revolution took root in the flimsiest of physical settings. Lasting institutions, he thus suggests, could be built in people's minds, rather than in stone.

As great men reached new heights of glory in eighteenth-century France there evolved, in particular, a radically new role for the man of letters. Once seen largely as subservient, dependent upon the whims of powerful royal and aristocratic patrons for support and sustenance, writers increasingly took on new authority, prestige, and clout. As Alexis de Tocqueville contends in *L'ancien régime et la Révolution*, over the course of the eighteenth century, France's men of letters—its *philosophes*—rose to unprecedented political power, undermining, indeed supplanting royal authority, and thus preparing the Revolution (Tocqueville 1967, 229–41). Of particular interest is Tocqueville's evocation of how this development was accompanied by a prodigious, imaginary construction, as writers led the populace away from "la société réelle" [real society], with all its irregularities, inequities, contradictions, and confusion, toward "une société imaginaire, dans laquelle tout paraissait simple et coordonné, uniforme, équitable et conforme à la raison. . . . On se désintéressa de ce qui était, pour songer à ce qui pouvait être, et l'on vécut enfin par l'esprit dans cette cité idéale qu'avaient construite les écrivains" [an imaginary society, in which all seemed simple and harmonious, uniform, just, and subject to reason. People lost interest in all that was, to dream of what could be, and finally they lived in their minds in this ideal city that had been built by writers] (238–39). Concurrently, within the world of letters, there evolved a new, and in some sense analogous conception of the complete works or *oeuvres complètes*. On one level, the construct of the complete works implied new ways of reading and thinking about literary production and formed, as Bonnet argues, the basis for the nascent field of literary history, predicated upon the idea of *l'homme et l'oeuvre*. On another, as writers promulgated a vision of society as unified and coherent, and came themselves to be seen as monumental figures, so too might a writer's work be understood as massive, cohesive, and worthy of commemoration—a possibility exemplified by the procession bringing Voltaire's remains to the *Panthéon*, which featured a carriage displaying the Kehl edition of Voltaire's complete works, an edition Voltaire began to prepare in the the last months of his life, and which opens with a *Vie de Voltaire* [Life of Voltaire] by Condorcet (Bonnet 1998, 251). Already here we see overlapping elements—the writer's biography and his literary production, the end of the writer's life and the beginning of his posterity, the writer's complete works and the monument to his glory—that would fuse further in the years ahead, to form what I shall call the "ideal synthesis" of writer, work, and monument in late nineteenth-century French literary culture.

Paradoxically, the writer's fame could be so extraordinary that it became divorced from the writings that had made him famous in the first place, as Rousseau noted with perplexity in his *Confessions*:

J'avais à Môtiers presque autant de visites que j'en avais eu à l'Ermitage et à Montmorency, mais elles étaient la plupart d'une espèce fort différente. Ceux qui m'étaient venu voir jusqu'alors étaient des gens qui ayant avec moi des rapports de talents, de goûts, de maximes les alléguaient pour cause de leurs visites et me mettaient d'abord sur des matières dont je pouvais m'entretenir avec eux. À Môtiers ce n'étaient plus cela, surtout du côté de France. C'étaient des officiers ou d'autres gens qui n'avaient aucun goût pour la littérature, qui même n'avaient jamais lu mes écrits, et qui ne laissaient pas, à ce qu'ils disaient d'avoir fait trente, quarante, soixante, cent lieues pour venir voir et admirer l'homme illustre, célèbre, très célèbre, le grand homme etc. (Rousseau 1968, 384)

[In Môtiers I had almost as many visitors as in l'Ermitage and Montmorency, but most of them were of an entirely different sort. Those who had come to see me until then were people who, having talents, tastes, and principles similar to mine, offered these as the reason for their visits and from the outset chose subjects that I could discuss with them. In Môtiers this was no longer the case, particularly among the French. They were officers or other people who had no taste for literature, who had never even read my writings and who, they claimed, never tired of traveling 30, 40, 60, 100 leagues to come see and admire the illustrious, famous, very famous man, the great man, etc.]

Rousseau filtered such occurrences through his burgeoning paranoia, imagining these people to be spies, sent by enemies plotting against him. Seen from a less personal and broader historical perspective, what Rousseau observed were the beginnings of a modern fame culture—rife with distortions, contradictions, transformations, and the frenzy of exuberant if ill-informed fans. Particularly important in this evolution was the development of journalism, which increasingly turned its attention to great men, and particularly great writers, critiquing their works; scrutinizing their actions, motives, and foibles; publicizing their names and faces; making and unmaking reputations; and heralding the yet greater influence the press

would acquire over the course of the nineteenth century.

No eighteenth-century literary figure received more of this attention than Voltaire. As the monarchy's star faded on the eve of revolution, "le Roi Voltaire" shone with extraordinary vigor. After early literary successes that established his reputation as a writer, Voltaire emerged, around mid century, as the undisputed leader of the ever-more influential *philosophes*. His exile in Ferney only added to this luster, the visit to Ferney becoming a requisite stop on the grand tour, and the narrative thereof a popular para-literary subgenre. Newspaper accounts of Voltaire's every movement and *bon mot*, prints that idolized and others that mocked him, statuettes of the *philosophe* strolling or writing at his desk, commemorative plates, even paper cutouts featuring his familiar features and garb (Apgar 1995), all abounded. Shortly before his death in 1778, a very old, sick, and tired Voltaire returned in triumph to Paris where, amid intense anticipation of his imminent passage into posterity, he posed for the sculptor Houdon, and attended the performance of his tragedy *Irène* at the *Comédie Française*. On March 6, on the occasion of the play's sixth representation, there took place a revealing, double apotheosis, which intermingled the living author on the brink of eternity, his ostensibly immortal work, and the sculptural tribute to his everlasting glory: the frail old man was crowned by laurels in his box offstage, while a Houdon bust of Voltaire was similarly honored onstage. This public spectacle was further disseminated through a number of contemporary engravings, accompanied by heavy-handed glosses like this:

Aux yeux de Paris enchanté
Reçois cet hommage,
Que confirmera d'âge en âge
La sévère postérité.
Non, tu n'as pas besoin d'atteindre au noir rivage
Pour jouir de l'honneur de l'immortalité;
Voltaire, reçois la couronne
Que l'on vient de te présenter;
Il est beau de la mériter
Quand c'est la France qui la donne.
(Desnoiresterres 1970, 95)

[Before Paris' enchanged eyes
Receive this homage,

That severe posterity
Shall reaffirm for the ages.
No need to reach the dark shore
To bask in the honor of immortality
Voltaire, take the crown
That has just been offered you.
How fine to have earned it
When it is given by France herself.]

Meanwhile, Voltaire continued posing for Houdon. Supposedly, at the last moment of the last sitting, the Marquis de Villevielle, who had arranged the sessions, staged a scene calculated to spark a livelier expression in the face of the weary *philosophe*—perhaps the same indescribable expression in Houdon's effigy that, not unlike the Mona Lisa's smile, continues to fascinate viewers. Villevielle apparently leapt forth and placed on Voltaire's head the laurel crown from the ceremony at the *Comédie Française*. "Que faites-vous, jeune homme" [What are you doing, young man], objected Voltaire, pushing Villevielle away, "jetez-la sur ma tombe qui s'ouvre" [throw it upon my beckoning tomb]. He rose, turned toward the sculptor, and uttered, "Adieu, Phidias" [Farewell, Phidias]. Then, taking Villevielle by the arm, he said, "Mon ami, allons mourir" [Let us go die, my friend], at which point Villevielle threw himself at the master's knees, asked to kiss once more "la main qui écrivit *Zaïre*" [the hand that wrote *Zaïre*], amid copious tears from both parties. "Ses douleurs cependant devinrent intolérables" [His pain became intolerable, however], concludes Villevielle, "nous rentrâmes et quelques jours après il n'était plus" [we returned home and several days later he was no more] (Gielly 1948, 27–28). While perhaps apocryphal, the anecdote's survival attests to its appeal, and specifically to its engaging *mise-en-scène* of the great writer's death as a passage into the posterity of the monument. Houdon did in fact produce a number of posthumous effigies, including a variety of widely reproduced busts and two full-length, seated marbles of superior quality, one for Catherine the Great (now in the Hermitage) and the other for the *Comédie Française*, installed in its lobby in 1780. Along similar lines, Voltaire's remains were transferred to the *Panthéon* in 1791, in an elaborate and revealing public ceremony. After his death, the remains of the controversial *philosophe* had been secreted

out of Paris; now, they made a triumphant return, reminiscent of an *entrée royale*; after a wake upon the ruins of the Bastille, where Voltaire had once been imprisoned,

douze chevaux blancs tirèrent un char monumental de quarante pieds de haut dessiné par David, au sommet duquel était un simulacre de Voltaire sur un lit de repos et couronné par une allégorie de la Renommée. Derrière une étonnante statue du patriarche d'après Houdon, dorée et en carton pâte, défilaient les hommes de la halle, des sociétés fraternelles, des clubs. Les académiciens, surtout, furent à l'honneur: ils accompagnaient les oeuvres complètes de Voltaire dans l'édition de Kehl portées sur une sorte de châsse. Louis XVI et la famille royale, retenus aux Tuileries depuis l'épisode de Varennes quelques semaines auparavant, auraient regardé passer le convoi à travers une ('jalousie') qui, selon Villette, n'avait jamais été si bien nommée. (Bonnet 1998, 308)

[twelve white horses pulled a monumental chariot, forty feet high, designed by David, atop which was a slumbering figure of Voltaire crowned by an allegory of Renown. Behind an astonishing gilded cardboard statue of the patriarch after Houdon paraded merchants, fraternal organizations, clubs. Above all, the academicians stood tall, accompanying the Kehl edition of Voltaire's complete works, borne upon a sort of reliquary. Louis XVI and the royal family, held in the Tuileries since the events of Varennes several weeks earlier, would have seen the passing procession through a "jalousie" (both venetian blind and jealousy in French) which, according to Villette, had never been so well named.]

These final honors, as well as the writer's precocious success, leadership of the contemporary literary world, paradoxically profitable exile, much-anticipated passing, and morbidly pre-posthumous commemoration, as well as the mix of adulation and vilification by the populace, both before and after his death, prefigured much of Victor Hugo's trajectory as a great man a century later. Indeed, Hugo and his contemporaries became all the more aware of such parallels toward the end of his life, as the newspaper *Le Siècle* mounted a highly publicized campaign to erect a parisian monument to Voltaire in 1867, and as France celebrated the centenary of Voltaire's death in 1878.

These developments in the history of fame, literary fame, and the monument, which gained momentum through the eighteenth century, crystallized with the dramatic political, socio-economic, and technological transformations of the late-eighteenth and early-nineteenth centuries, as there emerged what Braudy describes as the powerful, volatile, and ubiquitous "marketplace of fame in which all might sell their wares" (Braudy 1986, 342). The democratization of fame, and of literary fame in particular, was made possible not only by the general egalitarian thrust of the Revolution, but also by "the great expansion of the reading and viewing public as well as the means of reaching them which marks the nineteenth century" (476). In more specific terms, the emergence of a substantial bourgeois audience of readers, viewers, spectators, and fans, together with a veritable explosion of new media technologies—from lithography, to photography, to mechanized printing—permitted an unprecedented dissemination of words and images, names and faces. A variety of new cultural forms evolved and flourished, while older ones developed and expanded their scope in novel ways. These diverse vehicles for fame included: an abundant journalistic discourse on renown (e.g., gossip columns, success stories, celebrity obituaries); a profusion of memoirs, biographies and other popular publications on the famous (e.g., anthologies of mini-biographies about renowned writers, criminals, actors, courtesans, etc.[4]); innumerable "galleries," "pantheons," and "series" of caricatures, lithographs and, later on, photographs depicting famous personnages (e.g., Achille Devéria's lithographic portraits of romantic writers and artists; Benjamin Roubaud's *Panthéon charivarique,* Nadar's *Lanterne magique,* Pierre Durat's *Photobiographies,* Adolphe-Eugène Disdéri's *cartes de visite*);[5] and new legal and commercial modalities, including literary "property," "brand" names, and paid advertising that protected and promoted the fame of both people and products. Such developments were all part of a burgeoning "fame culture" which, as it spread, brought both promise and pain; an obsession with fame tempered by wariness. Celebrity might be easier for the common citizen to obtain, yet harder to retain; tempting, yet slippery, perplexing, misleading. With the rise of the democratic, increasingly technologized "marketplace of fame," celebrity became at once more alluring and more elusive. Mean-

while, change and incertitude lent new appeal to the monument as a commemorative vehicle. Although the spread of new visual and print media flooded a fame-hungry public with portrayals of the latest celebrities, the monument alone seemed, however mistakenly, a vehicle for lasting renown.

Beginning with the Revolution, as kings and potentates were toppled, restored, and replaced with unprecedented frequency, monuments to them suffered much the same fate: the erection of lasting monuments to conventional embodiments of political authority thus became an ever more dubious proposition, making cultural figures all the more attractive as vehicles of national glory. In addition, a new romantic sensibility privileged cultural figures of a less civic, more private nature—paradoxically, thrusting them into ever more public view. A precursor of Romanticism in so many other ways as well, Jean-Jacques Rousseau was the first to be afflicted by this peculiarity of modern fame culture:

> [son] choix de faire sécession en se retranchant de la société, irrita un peu plus une curiosité grandissante à son endroit, et l'on n'hésita pas à le traquer dans ses retranchements où sa vie devint un spectacle. . . . Comme le lui déclare le prince de Ligne, avec beaucoup de perspicacité, à l'occasion de sa visite rue Plâtrière: "M. Rousseau, plus vous vous cachez, et plus vous êtes en évidence; plus vous êtes sauvage, et plus vous devenez un homme public." (Bonnet 1998, 199–200)

> [(his) decision to break loose by retreating from society provoked even more the growing curiosity about him and, as people did not hesitate to hound him wherever he sought refuge, his life became a public spectacle . . . As the prince de Ligne remarked insightfully upon visiting him rue Plâtrière, "M. Rousseau, the more you hide, the more you are noticed; the more unsociable you are, and the more you become a public figure."]

As a text like Vigny's "Moïse" [Moses] suggests, Romantic mythology evolved further in this direction, favoring lone, tragic, promethean heroes: prophets, explorers, discoverers, inventors, and other *chercheurs de l'absolu* in diverse fields, but particularly in the creative arts. Typically, the hostility, neglect, or indifference that such solitary figures endured during their lifetimes was thought proof of their ultimate worth to posterity, intensifying the perceived need for their posthumous commemoration. Conversely, contemporary fame was thought no guarantee of everlasting glory—perhaps even proof to the contrary. In the largest sense then, there seemed a profound disjuncture between contemporary and posthumous renown. Whereas earlier, statues of the monarch had been erected in public squares during his lifetime, as an extension of worldly power, nineteenth-century monuments to cultural heroes were necessarily a posthumous apotheosis, a last judgment upon worthy lives, an embodiment of posterity. Lesser tributes like medallions and busts could pay homage to the great man in life— could offer, as it were, a premonitory dream of stone—while only in death might one receive the ultimate consecration of the free-standing, full-length public monument.

The work of Pierre-Jean David d'Angers (1788–1856) links the keen interest in great men that the early nineteenth century had inherited from the eighteenth, with the explosion of commemorative activity later on. France's most enthusiastic sculptor of great men during the first half of the century, David was also an important early theoretician of the genre who, in his extensive correspondence and *Carnets*, argues for sculpture's durability and commemorative potential, anticipating much of the later philosophical, ideological, and aesthetic orientation of the later nineteenth century's commemorative fervor. "Les statues sont les glorieuses archives du genre humain" [Statues are the glorious archives of humankind], he affirms in the *Carnets*, "Quand une génération est entièrement endormie dans la poussière, il reste encore un peuple de grands hommes debout sur les autels de la patrie" [When an entire generation slumbers in eternal dust, a few great men still stand tall upon the nation's altars] (Huchard et al. 1990, 36). The sculptor thus has a mission: "Je poursuis toujours ma galerie des grands hommes" [I am still compiling my gallery of great men], he explains, "On me voit avec ma petite ardoise, courant, comme si j'allais voir de près l'immortalité. Un statuaire est l'*enregistreur* de la postérité; il est l'avenir" [You can see me running with my little slate, as if coming face to face with immortality. A sculptor is the *recorder* of posterity; he is the future] (David d'Angers 1958, 1.99–100). He dwells,

moreover, on how not simply to "record," but rather to frame the great man's posterity. How, he ponders, might iconography best provide a vehicle for immortalization? What might be the proper shape, size, material, and placement for commemorative statuary? Proportions, to be sure, should be colossal, and use of marble or bronze is essential. What though of costume? While he would at times use modern dress in his sculpture, in his writings he remains skeptical about it, finding that classical dress (like classical nudity) better embodies his ideal of immortality: "Le costume ancien est poétique porté par les hommes de notre époque dont nous voulons honorer la mémoire. Il semble les mettre dans une atmosphère différente de la nôtre. Il les recule dans la postérité. Il complète pour eux l'apothéose" [Ancient garb is poetic when worn by men of our time whose memory we wish to honor. It seems to place them in a different atmosphere from our own. It sends them back into posterity. It completes their apotheosis] (181). Here, as throughout his writings, David's reflections on his craft expose his broader ideas about greatness: the great man, it seems, might best project his renown into the future by retreating into the comparably "poetic" and "different" atmosphere of the past. With the established timelessness of the past thus substituted for the as yet only imagined timelessness of the future, he would be lifted out of the ignoble present and, playing the role of the precursor, appear immortal. As we shall see, this is a strategy that Victor Hugo would use, with particular virtuosity, during the Third Republic.

Across the nineteenth century, France witnessed an increase in monuments to Enlightenment-style *grands hommes*. According to Jacques Lanfranchi (1979), in Paris alone, 26 new monuments were erected between 1815 and 1870, and an astounding 150 between 1870 and 1914. The vast majority of these statues commemorated cultural heroes, including artists, musicians, scientists, and explorers, with writers forming by far the largest group. Out of the 176 public monuments inaugurated in Paris between the fall of Napoleon and the start of the First World War, Lanfranchi counts 67—nearly forty percent—that honor literary figures. The veritable boom of commemorative activity under the early Third Republic, a phenomenon known at the time as "la statuo-manie" [statuemania], needs to be explained on both practical and ideological grounds. Hauss-mann's reconfiguration of Paris under the Second Empire created an abundance of new spaces and perspectives—wide boulevards, welcoming parks, sweeping vistas—that virtually cried out for monuments to be placed there, at least until the rise of the automobile further transformed the urban landscape. While the ideological underpinnings for "statuemania" had been in place since the late eighteenth century, until now no republican regime had lasted long enough to see through a substantial number of projects honoring the nation's great men. Significantly, in this respect, the great man who would most frequently be honored was none other than the great precursor, Voltaire: "All told, no fewer than six representations of Voltaire were to figure in the public realm of the capital before the turn of the century; no other person was commemorated so vigorously in this period" (Bird 2000, 98).

Over the course of its long history, the monument evolved not only from ancient origins in the sacred toward increasing secularity, but also from a political toward a more broadly ideological role. While nineteenth-century regimes no longer dared fill public space with statues of their current ruler, they did nonetheless pay frequent sculptural tribute to significant precursors: Napoleon I and Napoleonic war heroes for the Second Empire; Vercingétorix, Joan of Arc,[6] Thiers, or Gambetta for the Third Republic. Increasingly, moreover, the Third Republic would use civic statuary to appropriate cultural figures in support of its broader ideological program. As June Hargrove observes, this was a time when "Public homage [through monuments to Great Men] became a statement of national identity and an ideological weapon, both of which accelerated its popularity" (Hargrove 1990, 7). Haunted by the memory of earlier civil unrest, the Third Republic tried its best to rally diverse elements of the populace around common goals, ideals, and accomplishments, particularly through public commemoration of the nation's great men. As shining embodiments of France's greatness, and of the "genius" of the French people, statufied grands hommes appeared fundamentally beyond reproach: what self-respecting French citizen would not honor

compatriots who had created Les Contemplations or discovered a vaccine for rabies? The ostensibly unobjectionable nature of such statues served a double purpose, fostering national unity, but also camouflaging the transmission of specifically republican values (i.e., Victor Hugo as the champion of Liberty, or Pasteur as the beacon of Scientific Progress). Thus, despite their benign appearance, Third Republic statues to great men urged on potent, self-serving civic lessons. Like the plethora of civic-minded textbooks published at the time, for public schools that were being secularized, statuemania was a form of republican propaganda, and an especially effective one, not only because of its visibility and seeming neutrality, but also because it was difficult for those in the political opposition to combat on its own terms. The government exercised substantial control over the funding and placement of monuments, making it nearly impossible for opponents of the Republic to erect statues of their own heroes. Moreover, those rare statues actually raised to antirepublican figures (e.g., the 1899 statue of Joseph and Xavier de Maistre in their native Chambéry [Gardes 1994, 76]) were not only all but lost amid the forest of prorepublican effigies; their form also worked at ideological cross-purposes to their subject matter. In other words, the medium of the monument to great men became synonymous with a republican message: a vision of a nation built not upon the power of a sovereign, but upon the extraordinary accomplishments of its citizens. "Aux grands hommes, la patrie reconnaissante" [To great men, the grateful fatherland], as proclaimed the motto atop the Panthéon, inscribed below David d'Angers' pediment. Third Republic statuemania thus marked the apogee of an idea that had begun to emerge a century and a half earlier, with the Parnasse françois: that of commemorating the collective glory of the nation through individual great men.

The disproportionately large number of literary figures honored through statuemania epitomized the extraordinary veneration of the writer in nineteenth-century France—what Paul Bénichou (1973) calls "le sacre de l'écrivain" [the crowning of the writer], the apogee of what Dennis Porter (1995) describes as the emergence and eclipse of a heroic ideal of the writer in modern French literary culture.

Between the formative years of the Enlightenment and the *ère du soupçon* of the twentieth century, the ideal—indeed the *idée reçue*—of the great writer flourished in nineteenth-century France. Whether in the guise of demiurgic romantic creator, high priest of *le mot juste*, or virtuous conscience of the French nation, the great writer was seen as the greatest of great men. This cult of the author was energized, moreover, by a boom in popularizing visual technologies: lithography, photography, mechanized printing. In a general way, like the proliferation of supposedly permanent great man statues, the nineteenth century's voluminous production of more ephemeral celebrity galleries, "pantheons," illustrated biographies, and print or *carte de visite* series played upon the public's seemingly insatiable desire to contemplate its cultural luminaries, especially its writers. Whether in the public square or on newsprint, images spread literary celebrities' fame in ways words alone could not: once known only to a lettered elite, writers became cultural icons, whose effigies haunted the collective imagination, not unlike show business stars today.

Such images, I contend, were at once "visions" in a *literal*, and in a *figurative* sense. Literally, they were visual depictions—likenesses—of a particular writer. Figuratively, they were also interpretations, conceptions of that writer's fame and, more broadly, of fame in general. Each caricature, portrait, or statue thus functioned, on the most basic level, as a portrait of the writer in question, of more or less documentary value, while helping as well to define that writer's stature within the collective imagination and, ultimately, to define and refine society's understanding of fame itself. What, such images asked—through their potent mix of earnestness and jest, reverence and satire—did it mean to be famous? What, they urged, in an ongoing process of renegotiation and redefinition, were the possibilities and limitations of fame, in this life and beyond?

Within nineteenth-century French culture, there was also remarkable interpenetration between visual depictions of literary celebrities and writing by or about the writers in question: to wit, portrait galleries accompanied by descriptive prose, written descriptions evoking famous portraits, or caricatures alluding to the writer's published work. In addition, there was a tendency to see the writer and his work, *l'homme et l'oeuvre*, as a coherent whole, and ideally as something greater than the sum of these parts. This culminated, later in the century, in an "ideal synthesis" of writer, work, and monument (cf. chapter 1), but was manifested from earlier on as well, through the persistent phantasm of the author as character: Chateaubriand as René; Staël as Corinne; Constant as Adolphe; Musset as Octave; Sand as Indiana or Lélia;[7] Balzac weaving substantial parts of himself into such characters as Louis Lambert, Rastignac, Lucien de Rubempré, or Balthasar Claës; Hugo cast in caricatures as Jean Valjean; even Huysmans as des Esseintes and Rachilde as Raoule de Vénérande. Similarly, Flaubert is reported by his niece to have said, "Madame Bovary c'est moi." He may have meant the novel, or his words may be his niece's fabrication, yet the line's continued familiarity attests to its resonance with readers, attuned to the dynamics of identification peculiar to the author-character pair in nineteenth-century fiction. "L'histoire du roman au XIXe siècle" [The history of the 19th-century novel], contends Nicole Mozet, "pourrait se décrire comme une sorte de ballet gigantesque entre les écrivains et leurs personnages" [could be described as a sort of gigantic ballet between writers and their characters] (Mozet 1990, 175). To be sure, this interplay can seem a hypocritical "jeu de cache-cache" [game of hide and seek] of authors identifying themselves with or distancing themselves from their characters, as it suited them. Yet this also produced an intermingling of life and art, in which the author seemed to be larger than life, and the character to transcend the work of art. In the fullest sense then, the collective "vision" of specific literary figures, and of literary fame in general, emerged from a combination of authorial self-fashioning and broader societal construction, from an elaborate web of visual and verbal representations, with complex patterns of harmony and dissonance, consensus and contradiction, between the documentary and the imaginary, life and art, text and image.

Cutting across authors, genres, periods, and movements, the "dream of stone" pervaded the entire world of letters in nineteenth-century France and, recognizing this, the next chapter shall range broadly from Ponson du Terrail to Mallarmé, Sainte-Beuve to Proust, Delphine de

Girardin to Villiers de l'Isle-Adam. Within this mix though, certain literary figures—like Chateaubriand, Staël, Vigny, Baudelaire, Zola—did matter more than others and, whenever possible, I shall suggest how these illustrious peers fit into the problematics being discussed. For a number of reasons, though, the subsequent chapters shall narrow in on Balzac, Sand, and Hugo. As their collective foregrounding in both Marcelin's and Nadar's drawings suggests, each one, in his or her own way, was a touchstone of greatness for the period. Born within five years of each other at the dawn of the nineteenth century, they all achieved substantial renown in Paris by the middle of the 1830s. They moved in similar literary circles, knew each other personally, and commented extensively on each others' lives and work. They were moreover among the first writers whose entire lives, literary work, and reputations (both before and after death), would be shaped by the rise of this dream of stone. They achieved distinction however through different genres—and genders. Balzac and Sand triumphed in narrative fiction, and Balzac in particular cultivated his fame by excluding all but narrative from *The Human Comedy*, whereas Hugo pursued glory by ranging over as diverse a literary terrain as possible, from poetry, to prose, to plays, to political satire. While two were emblematic "grands hommes," the other was "la grande femme," the great woman of the day, whatever this might mean. During their lives, all three excelled at promoting themselves and their work, shaping the public's vision both of them in particular and of literary greatness in general, however each did so in distinct ways. Finally, while their lives and renown seemed to follow much the same timeline at first, they died at significantly different points in the century, and in substantially different circumstances. In sum, these three form a coherent yet divergent group, whose similarities and differences foreground broader questions about the dream of stone, its evolution, and implications.

The purpose of the first chapter, "The Dream of Stone," is therefore to set the stage for the focus on individual figures in the subsequent chapters. It traces the development of this dream, from seeing the literary work as a monument; to also seeing the writer as a monument; and, ultimately, to imagining an ideal synthesis of writer, work, and monument. Throughout all this, I contend, the monumental vision of literary greatness was fundamentally male, even phallic and, above all, deeply compensatory, suppressing the individual and collective demons of an uncertain age through monumentality. Chapter 2, "Balzac: The Literary Work as Monument," examines how Balzac's *Human Comedy* exemplified the vision of the literary work as monument, both in scope and design. Conceived as at once a vast, totalizing whole of interlinked stories, and an immense textual mausoleum, this monumental construct served to raise Balzac from the ignominy of his origins and obscurity of his early career, to substantial contemporary renown; over time, this prodigious "fame machine" has continued to promote its own reputation and memorialize its characters, its age and, above all, its creator. Chapter 3, "Sand: Visions of the Great Woman Writer," explores how George Sand challenged contemporaries to think of her as a great writer in the monumental mode usually reserved for men. In particular, extensive yet neglected visual evidence reveals how nineteenth-century France saw the possibilities and limitations of women's literary greatness in the image, indeed largely through images, of George Sand. Chapter 4, "Hugo: The Writer as Monument," contends that Victor Hugo exemplified nineteenth-century France's vision of the writer as monument, and largely defined its scope. Throughout Hugo's long career, particularly from mid century on, as the "dream of stone" increasingly monumentalized writers, his multifaceted monumentality—at once heroic, comic, visual, spatial, temporal, and libidinal—embodied both present renown and enduring glory. After Hugo's death, though, the scarcity of actual monuments raised in his honor, together with the rise of Hugo memorabilia, heralded a broader shift from the period's heroic, monolithic conception of literary glory, toward the beginnings of modern mass-media, mass-market celebrity. Finally, the conclusion, "The Dream Crumbles," considers the dream of stone's disintegration in the twentieth century, the vestiges that survive, and the further cultural transformations that emerge out of the rubble.

But for now, we need to understand better how this dream evolved in the first place.

1

The Dream of Stone

comme un rêve de pierre . . .
—Charles Baudelaire, "La Beauté" (1975–76, 1.21)

[like a dream of stone . . .]
—Charles Baudelaire, "Beauty" (1991, 47)

The Literary Work as Monument

—Pas de réflexions! Copions! Il faut que la page s'emplisse, que "le monument" se complète. . . .
Finir sur la vue des deux bonshommes penchés sur leur pupitre, et copiant.

[—Don't think! Just copy! The page must be filled, "the monument" must be completed. End on the sight of the two chaps bent over their writing desk, copying.]
—Gustave Flaubert, "scénario" for projected final chapter of *Bouvard et Pécuchet* (1979, 443)

What might it mean for a literary work to be considered a monument? According to the *Trésor de la langue française* (1971–94), the word "monument," in addition to its other usages, designates an "Oeuvre artistique, littéraire ou scientifique imposante par ses dimensions, ses qualités" [Artistic, literary, or scientific work, imposing in its dimensions, its qualities.] This definition outlines the main ways in which the literary work's monumentality was understood: in terms of both magnitude ("ses dimensions") and excellence ("ses qualités"). Likewise, the word "imposant," at once synonym of "considérable" and "majestueux," suggests both the work's quantitative and qualitative aspects, its sheer size and aesthetic refinement—with, as well, undertones of undue force, intrusion, imposition, as we shall see in the case of Victor Hugo's progressive "conquête d'un siècle en quatre-vingts livres" [conquest of his century in eighty books] (Roy 1958, preface), perceived by his contemporaries as both triumph and subjugation.

In the most basic sense then, monumentality meant quantity, the volume of work produced by such prolific authors as Balzac, Hugo, Dumas *père*, Sand, Zola, or Proust. The ninety titles of Balzac's *Human Comedy* were written in less than twenty years. Dumas' production was even more astounding, totaling nearly 250 titles, though at least some of this can be attributed to *l'atelier Dumas*, rather than to Dumas himself. In 1844 alone, Dumas published thirteen works, nine of them novels, including *Les Trois Mousquetaires* [The Three Musketeers] and *Le Comte de Monte-Cristo* [The Count of Monte-Cristo]. In another sense, beyond sheer physical quantity, monumentality involved conceptual magnitude; that is, the scope of the author's project, the breadth of his vision. Individual works could cover ample ground in various ways: geographically (e.g., Verne's *Le Tour du monde en quatre-vingts jours* [Around the World in Eighty Days]), historically (e.g., Sue's *Les Mystères du peuple, ou histoire d'une famille prolétaire à travers les âges*[1] [The Mysteries of the people, or history of a proletarian family across the ages]), sociologically (e.g., Balzac's *Splendeurs et misères des courtisanes* [Harlot High and Low]), politically (e.g., Balzac's *Le Médecin de campagne* [The Country Doctor]), philosophically and spiritually (e.g., Sand's *Spiridion* or Flaubert's *La Tentation de Saint-Antoine* [The Temptation of Saint-Antoine]), psychologically (e.g., Stendhal's *La Vie de Henry Brulard* [The Life of Henry Brulard]), aesthetically (e.g., incursions into music, like Sand's *Les Maîtres sonneurs* [The Master Pipers], or into the plastic arts, like Balzac's *Le Chef d'oeuvre inconnu* [The Unknown Masterpiece], or Zola's *L'Oeuvre* [The Masterpiece]), as well as synaesthetically (e.g., Huysman's *À rebours* [Against the Grain]). Authors achieved even greater amplitude by uniting individual works in larger series or cycles. Such overarching projects included: Balzac's *Human Comedy*; Madame Amable Tastu's four-volume *Chroniques de France* [Chronicles of France] in verse; Pierre Alexis, vicomte Ponson du Terrail's *Rocambole* ("un roman qui ne finirait jamais" [a novel that would never end; XLVI]); Paul Féval's *Les Habits noirs, ou la mafia au XIXe siècle* [Black Clothes, or the mafia in the Nineteenth Century]; Gérard de Nerval's *Les Filles du feu* [Girls of Fire]; Hugo's *La Légende des siècles* [The Legend of the Centuries]; Jules Vallès's *Jacques Vingtras*; Zola's *Les Rougon-Macquart* ("Histoire naturelle et sociale d'une famille sous le Second Empire" [Natural and social history of a family under the Second Empire]), followed by *Les Trois Villes* [The Three Cities] and *Les Quatre Évangiles* [The Four Gospels]; Maurice Barrès's trilogies *Le Culte du moi* [The Cult of the Self] and *Le Roman de l'énergie nationale* [The Novel of National Energy]; Alfred Jarry's *Ubu* plays; and, Proust's *À la recherche du temps perdu* [A Remembrance of Things Past].

No subject was too vast for the nineteenth-century author to tackle, even the history of humanity which, as Léon Cellier observes, was the central preoccupation of the romantic epic: "L'épopée romantique est humanitaire et religieuse. Il n'y a qu'un héros épique: l'Homme; il n'y a qu'un sujet épique: le progrès de l'Humanité" [The Romantic epic is humanitarian and religious. There is but one epic hero: Man; there is but one epic subject: the progress of Humanity] (Cellier 1954, 77). Dumas *père*'s *Isaac Laquedem*, for example, was to be "l'oeuvre capitale de [s]a vie" [the great work of his life], as he explained in a letter of March 16, 1852:

un immense roman en huit volumes . . . qui commencerait à Jésus Christ et qui finirait avec le dernier homme de la création. . . . Les héros principaux sont le Juif errant, Jésus Christ, Cléopâtre, les Parques, Prométhée, Néron, Poppée, Narcisse, Octavie, Charlemagne, Vitikind, Velléda, le pape Grégoire VII, le roi Charles IX, Catherine de Médicis, le cardinal de Lorraine, Napoléon, Marie-Louise, Talleyrand, Le Messie et L'Ange du Calice. (Biet, Brighelli, and Rispail 1986, 112)

[a vast novel in eight volumes . . . that would begin with Jesus Christ and end with the last man in creation. . . . The main heroes are the Wandering Jew, Jesus Christ, Cleopatra, the Fates, Prometheus, Nero, Poppaea, Narcisssus, Octavia, Charlemagne, Vitikind, Velleda, Pope Gregory VII, King Charles IX, Catherine de' Medici, the Cardinal of Lorraine, Napoleon, Marie-Louise, Talleyrand, the Messiah and the Angel of the Grail.]

As the authors of *Alexandre Dumas ou les Aventures d'un romancier* remark, "Dieu avait dicté la Bible, Balzac a rédigé la Comédie humaine, Dumas projette l'histoire de l'humanité: c'est la spirale des ambitions" [God had dictated the Bible, Balzac wrote the Human Comedy, Dumas plans a history of humankind, as ambitions spiraled ever higher] (Biet, Brighelli, and Rispail 1986, 112). Along similar lines, in his unfinished epic triptych of *Dieu*, *La Légende des siècles*, and *La Fin de Satan*, Victor Hugo planned to elaborate his own comprehensive vision of human history. Not surprisingly, neither of these projects was completed, yet the authors, like so many of their peers, dared conceive of them (Cellier examines similarly ambitious works by Pierre-Simon Ballanche, Edgar Quinet, Alphonse de Lamartine, Alexandre Soumet, Victor de Laprade, and Alphonse Louis Constant). "Le génie," remarked Hugo, "c'est l'omnifaculté" [Genius is all-doing] (Hugo 1985–90, 12.575). As we shall see, moreover, in describing such overreaching, totalizing literary aspirations, contemporary commentators often evoked the Tower of Babel—the ultimate and ultimately unrealizable monument.

Prolixity and ambition alone, while often equated with monumentality, were no guarantee of quality. Accordingly, another powerful current within French literary culture, particularly from mid-century onward, identified monumentality instead with formal excellence. Sainte Beuve's seminal essay, "De la littérature industrielle" [On industrial literature] (1839) marked an important first step in this direction. Sainte-Beuve is alarmed here by what he sees as the rising tide of bad literature, a "débordement" [overflowing] (676) that, like a river basin, "ne tend que trop naturellement à s'agrandir" [all too naturally tends to grow larger] (691). Through commercialization, he maintains, the entire literary world is being engulfed "dans un vaste naufrage" [in a vast shipwreck] in which "le niveau du mauvais gagne et monte" [the level of what is bad triumphs and rises] (675) and "le bas fond remonte sans cesse" [the dregs rise relentlessly] (691). There are then, he concludes, two literatures: "la bonne et . . . l'autre" [the good and . . . the other], the latter being a grave threat to the former. This other bad, "industrial" literature he constantly associates with chaotic and dangerous excess, through aqueous metaphors of floods, torrents, and shipwrecks. Sainte-Beuve is reacting here to a turning point in literary history. What he calls "l'invasion de la démocratie littéraire" [the invasion of literary democracy] (681)—the rise of both the literary marketplace and of Braudy's "democratic marketplace of fame"— had been aggravated by several recent developments, discussed at length in his article. These included: the creation of the modern newspaper and of modern newspaper advertising, with the founding of Émile de Girardin's tremendously successful *La Presse,* in 1836; controversy over literary property and foreign counterfeiting of French texts, in which Balzac found himself embroiled (cf. his 1834 *Lettre aux écrivains du XIXe siècle* [Letter to nineteenth-century writers] and his 1839 *Lettre sur la propriété littéraire* [Letter on literary property]); the founding of the *Société des gens de lettres* in 1838 (Balzac was elected president in 1839); and, in particular, the birth and rapid success of the serial novel or *roman-feuilleton* (the first, Balzac's *La Vieille Fille* [The Old Maid], was published in *La Presse* in 1836). The romantic tendency for verbal overabundance was exacerbated by the serial novel's new incentive system of payment per line—rewarding, in Sainte-Beuve's view, "des pages écrites pour fournir le plus de colonnes avec le moins d'idées" [pages written to yield the most columns with the least ideas] (684–85). Commercialization breeds prolixity, and prolixity, triviality.

Clearer about what he dislikes than about what he likes, Sainte-Beuve does, however, make passing reference to "seriousness" and "good taste," discusses briefly the "belles oeuvres" [fine works] or "monumens majestueux" [majestic monuments] (677) of seventeenth- and eighteenth-century literature, and simply mentions that "quelques vrais monumens" [some true monuments] (676) were written more recently. While Sainte-Beuve consistently associates "bad" literature with excess, verbosity, and chaotic overabundance, he associates "good" literature instead with such aesthetic qualities as beauty, majesty, or refinement. We infer that, in his view, a literary work is a 'true' monument not because of its gigantic proportions, but rather because of its aesthetic merits. While it does so indirectly, Sainte-Beuve's essay turns the prevailing view of literary monumentality on its head.

Following Sainte-Beuve's lead, many others would further develop and promote this idea of excellence, not magnitude, as the basis for literary monumentality. Flaubert, apostle of *le mot juste,* compared books to pyramids (cf. below), but less for their immensity than for the arduousness and precision of their construction. Similarly, "L'Art pour l'Art," "Parnasse," and Symbolist movements in poetry generally prized formal difficulty and aesthetic refinement, preferring smaller, denser, more intensely concentrated works to larger, but less focused, more disparate ones.[2] Gautier's 1852 collection of poems, *Émaux et camées,* is emblematic in this respect. The title already casts the poems as carefully wrought art objects that combine jewel-like delicacy and meticulous craftsmanship with extraordinary hardness and durability. In particular "L'Art," the key final poem in the collection, and really an *art poétique,* elaborates upon this vision:

> Oui, l'oeuvre sort plus belle
> D'une forme au travail
> Rebelle,
> Vers, marbre, onyx, émail . . .
>
> Tout passe.—L'art robuste
> Seul a l'éternité.
> Le buste
> Survit à la cité . . .
>
> Les dieux eux-mêmes meurent;
> Mais les vers souverains
> Demeurent
> Plus forts que les airains.

Sculpte, lime, cisèle;
Que ton rêve flottant
        Se scelle
Dans le bloc résistant!
                (Gautier 1970, 3.128–30)

[Yes, the work emerges more beautiful
from a form
        Hard to fashion,
Verse, marble, onyx, enamel

All passes.—Only steadfast art
Is eternal.
        The bust
Survives the town.

Gods themselves die;
But sovereign verse
        Remains
Stronger than brass.

Sculpt, file, chisel;
May your evanescent dream
        Be sealed
Within the resistant block.]

The writer, like the sculptor, must seal his evanescent "dream" within "le bloc résistant"—impart his creative vision to posterity through a medium at first "resistant" to the artist's manipulation of it, then, once transformed, "resistant" to the passage of time itself. For Gautier, just as for his less austerely aesthetic peers, the literary "dream of stone" was, fundamentally, a dream of permanence. Thus, while those who, like Gautier, understood literary monumentality as formal excellence might seem at first to stand at opposing ends from those who understood it as magnitude, Gautier's poem demonstrates how their views converged. What these divergent perspectives shared was their common desire for literature to rival, even transcend, the durability of the public monument, of an "Ouvrage d'architecture ou de sculpture édifié pour transmettre à la postérité le souvenir d'une personne ou d'un événement" [A work of architecture or sculpture built to transmit to posterity the memory of a person or event] (*Trésor de la langue française*, 1971–94). Literature, seen as a monument, was supposed to last.

Exegi monumentum aere perennius
regalique situ pyramidum altius,

quod non imber edax, non Aquilo impotens
possit diruere aut innumerabilis
annorum series et fuga temporum.

[I have erected a monument more durable than bronze and loftier than the Pyramids' royal pile, one that no wasting rain, no furious north wind can destroy, or the countless chain of years and the ages' fight.]
                —(Horace 1964, 278–79)

While preponderant in nineteenth-century France, the idea of the literary work as monument was a venerable one. Horace's *exegi monumentum* topos, as Roberto Campo remarks, "would advance that monuments in words endure the ravages of time better than monuments in bronze and stone," and it has proven to be "one of the most popular literary topics of all time" (Campo 1998, 138). Renaissance poets in particular, returning to and striving to surpass their classical precursors, echoed Horace's claims for the superior durability of literature. Ronsard informed both kings and lovers that they would only be remembered because he had sung their praise. Poetry that is, not the plastic arts, would preserve their memory:

Les Colonnes elevées,
Ne les marbres imprimés
De grosses lettres gravées,
Ne les cuivres animés,

Ne font que les hommes vivent
En images contrefais,
Comme les vers qui les suivent
Pour témoins de leurs beaus fais.
(Ronsard 1914–75, 2.150)

[Columns raised,
Nor marbled carved
Engraved with bold letters,
Nor inscribed copper,

Can make men live on
Through their distorted images
As can verses that follow them
Bearing witness to their great deeds.]

Du Bellay, while more reserved in his pronouncements, sought nonetheless to "defend and illustrate" the French language as an appropriate vehicle for enduring literary greatness, like Greek and Latin before it. In *Antiquités de Rome*, for example, he may have lamented the modern fall from the grandeur of ancient Rome, but did so in a volume with its own designs on posterity and architectonic title that helped transform French versification and survives as a tribute to du Bellay's poetic achievement.

In the nineteenth century, however, Horace's metaphor became more than a popular topos. At the confluence of so many major trends—including the increasingly broad-based veneration of literature, the generalized preoccupation with monuments and monumentality, the democratization of fame and secularization of the afterlife, the popularization and dissemination of authors' *oeuvres complètes*—it became an obsession, repeated insistently, and with great variety, both within literary discourse and beyond, in popular journalism, caricatures, speeches, and so forth. From as early as 1819, for example, and through the 1820s, Balzac began to develop the idea for the monumental literary project that he would realize in the 1830s and 1840s (cf. chapter 2). Chateaubriand conceived of his *Mémoires d'outre-tombe* (1804–41) in similarly monumental terms. Indeed, the familiar last sentence of the work—"Il ne me reste qu'à m'asseoir au bord de ma fosse; après quoi je descendrai hardiment, le crucifix à la main, dans l'éternité" [All that remains for me is to sit down beside my grave; then I shall descend boldly, my crucifix in hand, into eternity] (Chateaubriand 1951, 2, book 44, chapter 9)—is preceded, in the same chapter, by an important, related assertion: "Grâce à l'exorbitance de mes années, mon monument est achevé" [Thanks to my advanced years, my monument is finished]. In other words, the several thousand pages leading up to this conclusion form a monument, ready to perpetuate the author's memory as he descends into the grave. The literary work is a mausoleum.

As Balzac or Chateaubriand's examples suggest, a vision of the text as monument was generally predicated upon the author's role as heroic monument builder. In certain works of the 1830s, 1840s, and beyond, though, the author or sometimes, particularly in the fantastic tale or *conte fantastique*, the first-person narrator instead played a closely related role: that of the archaeologist who discovers, excavates, deciphers, or preserves the object that is the central focus, and well-spring of the fiction. This could either be a still-intact monument, or a fragment that evokes or stands in for a larger, monumental construct. Notable examples include: Mérimée's 1837 "La Vénus d'Ille" [The Venus of Ille], which revolves around the discovery, interpretation, and eventual destruction of a Roman statue of Venus (Mérimée 1982);[3] Gautier's 1840 "Le pied de momie" [The Mummy's Foot] (1981, 177–93), whose narrator purchases a mummy's foot that launches him into an elaborate Egyptian reverie, set in a veritable forest of obelisks, sphinxes, pylons, columns, and thrones, where the kings and pharaohs of antiquity meet to pass judgment on his retrospective love for the princess to whom the foot belonged; and, similarly, Gautier's "Arria Marcella" of 1852 (235–72), in which the narrator's contemplation of the imprint left in the Pompeian lava by a beautiful woman's breast resuscitates not only the woman, but the whole of her Roman town—while the enchanting vision lasts. In each of these examples, the author or narrator, who acts not only as an archaeologist but also as an admirer or lover, is male. The artifact itself, however, either already fragmented or destroyed by the end of the story, is identified as female. In these works then, the male lover's gaze on the fragmented female body also points to the period's difficulty in honoring women with a full-fledged monument, a problem we shall look at in greater detail vis-à-vis George Sand.

Works such as these were informed by a growing fascination with archaeology and concern for the preservation of "historical" monuments. From the mid-eighteenth century onward, notably through the work of Winckelmann, visits to the great monuments of antiquity became a standard feature of foreign travel; fodder for the recounting (and pictorial representation) of innumerable real or imagined *Voyages en Orient*; and (so the rationale went) an opportunity to enrich burgeoning European collections with artifacts that indigenous peoples, lapsed into barbarism, no longer appreciated or deserved. In early nineteenth-century France in particular, in the wake of Napoleon's campaigns and Champollion's discoveries, fascination with things Egyptian was much more than a fad, figuring the broader "allure of empire" (Porterfield 1998), and specifically a vision of ancient Egyptian grandeur revived and assumed by modern

France—a vision complicit with both a burgeoning national consciousness at home and colonial expansion abroad, informed by the presumption of France's cultural, scientific, and technological preeminence. Likewise, there also evolved a new awareness of France's own architectural heritage, especially that of the Middle Ages, stimulated not only by romantic writers' and artists' exoticism in time as in space, but also by a broader yearning for native monumental art to rival that of antiquity. Emblematic of these cross-currents, and of their persistence through the period, is Albert de Korsad's caricature of Gustave Eiffel (fig. 15), his left hand reaching down to the tip of an Egyptian pyramid, his right extending toward the top of his tower, while in between the cathedral of Notre-Dame dangles from his watch fob: Eiffel's stance traces a peculiarly French genealogy of grandeur, from the monuments of Egyptian antiquity, to gothic cathedrals, to the exploits of modern French engineering.

Through the middle years of the nineteenth century, two men in particular promoted the ideal of a French architectural *patrimoine*. From 1834 to 1860, Prosper Mérimée (1803–70) worked tirelessly to fill the newly created post of Inspector General of Historical Monuments, criss-crossing the country on extensive inspection tours, writing up endless reports, making well-founded recommendations for maintaining the nation's architectural treasures;[4] this serious, dedicated functionary led a strange, double life, however, concurrently enjoying substantial literary renown, as he published tales of passion and fantasy, in which the scholarly, erudite traveler gets pulled into wild intrigues of jealousy, revenge, or murder, amid ruthless brigands, enchanting gypsies, vendetta-bent Corsicans, an animated statue, even a Lithuanian nobleman who turns out to be half-man, half-bear. In close collaboration with Mérimée, architect Eugène Viollet-le-Duc (1814–79) undertook major, if controversial restorations of such medieval sites as Carcassonne, Mont Saint-Michel, and Notre-Dame de Paris.[5] By the latter part of the century, it would seem inevitable that Bouvard and Pécuchet, Flaubert's fictional embodiments of contemporary received ideas, also succumb to the lure of old stones and try their hands at archeology (*Bouvard et Pécuchet* 163–64).

Victor Hugo's *Notre-Dame de Paris* [The Hunchback of Notre-Dame], published in 1831, was the first major literary work informed by—and instrumental in popularizing—concerns about the fate of France's historical monuments. Like his 1825 and 1832 articles entitled "Guerre aux démolisseurs" [Down with demolishers] (Hugo 1974, 648–61), Hugo's prefaces of 1831 and 1832 proclaim his preservationist position and herald his novel as a forum for pleading "la cause de notre vieille architecture" [the cause of our venerable architecture] (34). More subtly, though, they also negotiate a complex relationship between the text and the monument it evokes. The 1831 preface opens with the Greek inscription "ΑΝΑΓΚΕ" [fate], which the author had supposedly found on the cathedral wall several years back, but which had vanished—suggestively—in the interim:

hormis le fragile souvenir que lui consacre ici l'auteur de ce livre, il ne reste plus rien aujourd'hui du mot mystérieux. . . . L'homme qui a écrit ce mot sur ce mur s'est effacé, il y a plusieurs siècles, du milieu des générations, le mot s'est à son tour effacé du mur de l'église, l'église elle-même s'effacera bientôt peut-être de la terre.
C'est sur ce mot qu'on a fait ce livre. (29–30)

[aside from the fragile remembrance accorded it here by the author of this book, nothing remains today of this mysterious word. The man who wrote this word on this wall vanished, centuries ago, from amid the generations, the word in turn has been erased from the wall of the church, the church itself shall perhaps soon be erased from the earth.
This is the word that gave rise to this book.]

Stone inscriptions, and even whole cathedrals can disappear, hence the need for the author to accord the inscriptions the "fragile souvenir" of his attention and, more broadly, to transfigure the monument into a text called *Notre-Dame de Paris*. What though of *this* work's durability? No direct answer to this question is offered; however, in the 1832 preface to the "édition définitive," which included three chapters left out of the original one, Hugo asserts (referring to himself as author in the third person), "Voici donc maintenant son oeuvre entière, telle qu'il l'a rêvée, telle qu'il l'a faite, bonne ou mauvaise, durable ou fragile, mais telle qu'il la veut" [Here then is his entire work, as he dreamed of it, as he made it, good or bad, durable or fragile, but as he wants it] (32). Hugo's formulation cuts to the heart of the contradictory dream of stone, as parallel structure sets dreaming against making, good against bad, durable against fragile, and, implicitly, aligns the three first and three second terms: what is dreamt would be good and durable; what is made, bad and fragile. Discounting Hugo's false modesty, though, we might infer that the author intended his work to be both good and durable ("telle qu'il la veut" [as he wants it]). Later in the same preface, moreover, Hugo writes, "en attendant les monuments nouveaux, conservons les monuments anciens" [while waiting for new monuments, let us preserve the old ones] (33). At this point, he has already voiced serious doubts about there occurring an architectural renaissance in the nineteenth century, for he fears that "la sève ne se soit retirée de ce vieux sol de l'architecture qui a été pendant tant de siècles le meilleur terrain de l'art" [architecture's old soil has lost its former vitality, which for so many centuries made it art's most fertile ground] (33). If architecture is disqualified, then what should take its place as modern monumental art?

Hugo's comments here open up the possibility that, in a work like *Notre-Dame de Paris*, the preservation of old monuments and the search for new ones could converge: in other words, that "conserving" architectural monuments by writing about them could, in turn, create new textual ones. In a broader sense, contemporary monuments could—perhaps necessarily would—be textual, regardless of their subject matter. This idea receives much ampler treatment in the chapter "Ceci tuera cela" ["This shall kill that"] (237–54). Hugo explains thus the archdeacon's curious turn of phrase, which has given the chapter its title: "le livre de pierre, si solide et si durable, allait faire place au livre de papier, plus solide et plus durable encore" [the book of stone, so solid and so durable, was going to give way to the paper book, more solid and yet more durable] (238). From the historical vantage point of the novel's setting in the late fifteenth century, "L'imprimerie tuera l'architecture" [Printing shall kill architecture] (238). According to Hugo, since the Renaissance, architecture has declined whereas, thanks to the printing press, the written word has flourished, replacing ar-

chitecture as the leading manifestation of monumental art. (Balzac also reflects extensively on the transformative power of printing technology in *Illusions perdues*, however with a much more pessimistic view of recent developments.) While in earlier times architecture had been a form of writing ("jusqu'à Gutenberg, l'architecture est l'écriture principale, l'écriture universelle" [until Gutenberg, architecture was the main form of writing, universal writing; 244]), writing has now become a form of architecture: thus, "Il faut admirer et refeuilleter sans cesse le livre écrit par l'architecture; mais il ne faut pas nier la grandeur de l'édifice qu'élève à son tour l'imprimerie" [The book written by architecture must be admired and perused endlessly; but the greatness of the edifice raised in turn by printing must not be denied] (252). Individual works stand alone as separate monuments: "Depuis la cathédrale de Shakespeare jusqu'à la mosquée de Byron, mille clochetons s'encombrent pêle-mêle sur cette métropole de la pensée universelle" [From Shakespeare's cathedral to Byron's mosque, one thousand little steeples crowd pell-mell into the metropolis of universal thought] (253). Together, the entire production of the printing press is a colossal work-in-progress, a "prodigieux édifice . . . toujours inachevé" [prodigious edifice . . . always unfinished] (253), built by all humanity: "le genre humain tout entier est sur l'échafaudage, chaque esprit est maçon" [all humankind is on the scaffolding, every mind a mason] (253). In short, the printed word is forming no less than "la seconde tour de Babel du genre humain" [humankind's second Tower of Babel] (254). Hugo argues for the superior staying power of the textual monument, compared with its stone predecessor, for human thought ("la pensée") becomes indestructible when expressed in print: "De solide qu'elle était elle devient vivace. Elle passe de la durée à l'immortalité. On peut démolir une masse, comment extirper l'ubiquité?" [Once solid it became alive. It passed from mortality into immortality. A mass can be destroyed, how can ubiquity be eradicated?] (247). This evolution from "solid" to "alive" reflects an earlier, romantic vision of literary monumentality as the inanimate becoming animate, whereas the tendency in the later nineteenth century would instead be to envision the animate becoming inanimate. Moreover, as the novel became increasingly popular and as the period's conception of literary fame evolved, there occurred a slippage from the initial identification between text and monument toward one between author and monument: in the public's eye, Hugo became inseparable from the cathedral he championed (cf. chapter 4). Hugo's use of "ubiquity" also urges us to look ahead to the later nineteenth century when, through a profusion of press coverage and memorabilia toward the end of his life and beyond, he became increasingly ubiquitous, an unavoidable cultural icon. Yet, as we shall ask in chapter 4, does such ubiquity bolster monumentality, as Hugo's remarks here might suggest, or rather diminish it through dispersion? In any case, while Hugo's ideas in "Ceci tuera cela" transcend the novel in many ways, they also reflect back upon it. The original equivalency between text and monument, posited by the title *Notre-Dame de Paris*, is supported in turn by Hugo's broader reflection on the interrelationship of literature and architecture.

The metaphor of the literary work as monument proliferated during the 1820s through the 1840s and, by the middle of the century, had become inescapable. In his 1850 funerary oration for Balzac, for example, Hugo describes the novelist's *oeuvre* as a public "monument," repository of his literary immortality (cf. ch. 3). Alfred de Vigny's "L'Esprit Pur" [Pure Spirit] (1.166–68)—completed in 1863, but begun two decades earlier—proclaims, "Aujourd'hui, c'est l'ÉCRIT, / L'ÉCRIT UNIVERSEL, parfois impérissable, / Que tu graves au marbre ou traces sur le sable, / Colombe au bec d'airain! VISIBLE SAINT-ESPRIT!" [Today, WRITING/ UNIVERSAL WRITING, sometimes undying, / You engrave upon marble or trace in the sand / Brass-beaked dove! MANIFEST HOLY SPIRIT!] Through the complex image of the dove's beak as stylus, the literary work is construed as both divine writ and monument, and the writer as at once messenger of the sacred Text and sculptor of its inscription. As in "Une bouteille à la mer" [A bottle in the sea] though (Vigny 1986–93, 1.153–59), Vigny remains fatalistic about the transmission of the literary message, described as only "parfois impérissable" [sometimes undying]: perhaps graven in marble, yet perhaps just traced in sand. Published at about the same

time as "L'Esprit Pur," Baudelaire's "L'Esprit de M. Villemain" [M. Villemain's Mind] posits the monument as aesthetic paragon. Villemain's writing suffers from a "Phraséologie toujours vague; les mots tombent, tombent de cette plume pluvieuse, comme la salive des lèvres d'un gâteux bavard; phraséologie bourbeuse, clapoteuse, sans issue, sans lumière, marécage obscur où le lecteur impatienté se noie" [Chronically vague phraseology; words fall, fall from this drizzling pen, like spittle from the lips of a doddering blubberer; a muddy, sloshy phraseology, labyrinthine and lightless, a murky marsh in which the impatient reader drowns] (Baudelaire 1975–76, 2.197). Much as in Sainte-Beuve's aqueous metaphors of bad writing, Baudelaire condemns Villemain's prose as drizzly, salivary, muddy, sloshy, murkily marshy (cf., along these lines, Segal 1998; Schehr 1997, esp. 104–7 and 196–209; and Serres 1980). In contrast, "toute phrase doit être en soi un monument bien coordonné, l'ensemble de tous ces monuments formant la ville qui est le Livre" [each sentence should be a coherent monument unto itself, the whole of these monuments making up the city that is the Book] (2.197). Well-crafted sentences can stand alone as monuments and, together, compose the book, a form analogous to the larger, urban "monument" of the burgeoning nineteenth-century city.

Conceiving of the literary work as a monument implies a distinct, recognizable, architectonic "structure." In many cases, authors themselves announce such a design (as in Balzac's prefaces); in others, it is instead ascribed to the works by commentators. In 1896, Barbey d'Aurevilly writes, in metaphorical terms, of the structure organizing Baudelaire's *Les Fleurs du mal* [The Flowers of Evil], "il y a ici *une architecture secrète*, un plan calculé par le poète, méditatif et volontaire" [there is *a secret architecture* here, a carefully calculated structure willed by the poet] (*Le Tombeau de Charles Baudelaire* 1979). Similarly, in his inaugural address for the Falguière Balzac monument, Abel Hermant declares,

L'édifice d'idées que ce romancier présente à la critique est harmonieux, massif et stable. Il peut contrarier nos goûts d'architecture et nos théories de la construction; mais il tient debout par sa cohésion et par son poids. La besogne ne serait

pas moins malaisée de le démonter assise par assise que de le renverser d'un bloc: car le ciment
qui lie les pierres mêmes, et les outils de fer s'y
briseraient comme aux joints des indestructibles
ruines romaines. (Hermant 1903, 48)

[This novelist offers criticism a harmonious, massive, and stable edifice, made of ideas. It may
upset our taste in architecture and our theories of
construction; but it stands by virtue of its cohesion
and its weight. No less arduous a task would it be
to take it apart layer by layer than to overturn
the whole structure: for the blocks are joined with
cement, and iron tools would break upon them, as
upon the joints of Rome's indestructible ruins.]

The underlying assumption in these examples
is that, whether he actually claims to or not,
and whether his means are orthodox or not,
the great writer willfully, deliberately structures his work. Accordingly, the writer is often cast as a monument-maker: variously, as a
mason, builder, architect, or sculptor. Félicien
Champsaur's article on Zola in the *Hommes
d'aujourd'hui* caricature series—accompanied
by an André Gill drawing of Zola saluting a
bust of Balzac—concludes, "Émile Zola est un
grand maître maçon" [Émile Zola is a great
master mason] (Champsaur 1879, 3). Likewise,
in another typical Gill caricature, Victor Hugo-
as-sculptor hammers away at busts of Robespierre, Danton, and Marat, shortly before the
publication of *Quatre-vingt-treize* [*Ninety-three*]
(fig. 4). Hugo too stands upon a pedestal—
the monument-maker appears to be a monument, more prominent even than the "work"
he promotes—yet his apparent stature, and the
seriousness with which he sculpts the subject
matter of his novel, are undercut by the parallel
activity of an infant who, unbeknownst to the
Great Writer, traces scatological phrases on the
base of Marat's bust. Louis Reybaud's *Jérôme
Paturot* displays similar irreverence toward
Hugo's preponderant monumentality. A thinly
disguised Hugo figure (called "le Génie" [the Ge-
nius]) is said to be composing a play, *Les Durs
à cuire* [The Tough Nuts], by carving his heroes
out of the Pyrenees and making pedestals of
the Alps. The accompanying Grandville illustration, which shows him finishing his sculpture, is captioned with mock grandiloquence,
"Il avait fendu les Pyrénées pour y sculpter ses

héros" (Reybaud 1846, 260–62). In a more serious vein, Baudelaire's "Rêve parisien" evokes an
oneiric escape from "l'horreur de mon taudis,"
to an imagined world of gleaming metal and
luxurious marble structures:

> . . . peintre fier de mon génie,
> Je savourais dans mon tableau
> L'enivrante monotonie
> Du métal, du marbre et de l'eau.
>
> Babel d'escaliers et d'arcades,
> C'était un palais infini,
> Plein de bassins et de cascades . . .
>
> Et des cataractes pesantes,
> Comme des rideaux de cristal,
> Se suspendaient, éblouissantes,
> A des murailles de métal.
>
> Non d'arbres, mais de colonnades
> Les étangs dormants s'entouraient, . . .
>
> C'étaient des pierres inouïes
> Et des flots magiques; c'étaient
> D'immenses glaces éblouies
> Par tout ce qu'elles reflétaient! . . .
>
> Architecte de mes féeries,
> Je faisais, à ma volonté,
> Sous un tunnel de pierreries
> Passer un océan dompté;
>   (Baudelaire 1975–76, 1.101–3)

[I gloated in my reverie,
Proud of my genius as a painter,
Drunk with the monotony
Of metal, marble, even water.

Stairways of Babel and arcades
Joined endless palaces to hold
Uncounted basins and cascades. . . .

Huge and heavy waterfalls
Hung motionless like crystal shrouds
Suspended on the metal walls,
Silent within their dazzling clouds.

Not by trees, by colonnades
Were sleeping pools marked in their places, ...

And there were stones of sorts unknown
And magic floods and plates of glass
Immense and gleaming wherein shown
The mirrored selves of all who'd pass! . . .

HUITIÈME ANNÉE. — N° 357.   PARIS ET DÉPARTEMENTS : 15 CENTIMES   DIMANCHE 29 AOUT 1875.

FONDATEUR
F. POLO
—o—
ABONNEMENTS
PARIS
52 numéros................ 6 fr.
26 numéros................ 3 —
Les abonnements partent du
1er de chaque mois
—o—
BUREAUX
16, rue du Croissant, 16

L'ECLIPSE

FONDATEUR
F. POLO
—o—
ABONNEMENTS
DÉPARTEMENTS
52 numéros................ 8 fr.
26 numéros................ 5 —
—o—
ANNONCES
Fermage exclusif de la publicité
ADOLPHE EWIG
10, rue Taitbout, 10

ADRESSER LES ABONNEMENTS ET RÉCLAMATIONS A L'ADMINISTRATEUR DU JOURNAL

VICTOR HUGO, PAR GILL

Fig. 4. André Gill, *Victor Hugo*. © Photothèque des musées de la ville de Paris.

An architect of fantasy,
By domination, by my will,
Through tunnels formed from jewelry
I bid obedient oceans spill.]
                      (Baudelaire 1991, 193–95)

In this poem dedicated to Constantin Guys, celebrated elsewhere as "le peintre de la vie moderne" [the painter of modern life] (Baudelaire 1975–76, 2.683–724), Baudelaire's "je" would be the artisan, not of ugly modernity, but of a glistening classical fantasy replete with colonnades, fountains, and mirrors, a "Babel d'escaliers et d'arcades, / . . . un palais infini" (literally a "Babel of stairways and arcades, / . . . an infinite palace") that figures monumental ambitions—appropriately, through the period's familiar Babel metaphor. Water is not associated with the "muddiness" or "sloshiness" of bad writing, as in the later critique of Villemain, but rather provides a massive and powerful building material, like metal and stone—as in the gardens at Versailles, the French exemplar for the kind of "palais infini, / Plein de bassins et de cascades" (literally, "infinite palace, / Full of basins and cascades") that Baudelaire is trying to envision. The "architect" of reveries bathed in "un silence d'éternité" [an eternal silence] thus leaves behind the quotidian misery of the *poete maudit* for a self-made, architectonic Elysium: a premonitory *rêve de pierre*, portending immortality for the creator of monumental imaginative works.

In his essay on Balzac in *Les Romanciers naturalistes* [Naturalist Novelists], Zola uses the monument-maker conceit as a point of departure for his assessment of *The Human Comedy*. Balzac has built an extraordinarily ambitious monument of verbal profusion, which Zola likens—of course—to the Tower of Babel:

> *La Comédie humaine* est comme une tour de Babel. . . .
> [C]'est . . . la tour aux mille architectures, la tour de plâtre et de marbre, que l'orgueil d'un homme voulait élever jusqu'au ciel, et dont des bouts de muraille couvrent déjà le sol. Il s'est fait des trous noirs, dans cette série d'étages superposés; çà et là, une encoignure a disparu; les pluies de quelques hivers ont suffi pour émietter le plâtre que la main hâtive de l'ouvrier a trop souvent employé. Mais tout le marbre est resté debout, toutes les colonnades, toutes les frises sont là intactes, élargies et blanchies par le temps. L'ouvrier a élevé sa tour avec un tel instinct du grand et de l'éternel, que la carcasse de l'édifice paraît devoir demeurer à jamais entière; des pans de mur auront beau crouler, des planchers s'effondrer, des escaliers se rompre, les assises de pierre résisteront toujours, la grande tour se dressera aussi droite, aussi haute, appuyée sur les larges pieds de ses colonnes géantes; peu à peu, tout ce qui est boue et sable s'en ira, et alors le squelette de marbre du monument apparaîtra encore sur l'horizon, comme le profil immense et déchiqueté d'une ville. Même dans un avenir lointain, si quelque vent terrible, en emportant notre langue et notre civilisation, jetait par terre la carcasse de l'édifice, les décombres feraient sur le sol une telle montagne, qu'aucun peuple ne pourrait passer devant cet amas, sans dire: "Là dorment les ruines d'un monde." (Zola 1906, 3–5)

> [The Human Comedy is like a tower of Babel.
> It's a tower fashioned of a thousand architectural styles, a tower of plaster and marble, that one man's pride wanted to raise skyward, but already fragments of wall are strewn across the ground. Dark holes have poked through the succession of stories; here and there, a corner has disappeared; several winters' rains have sufficed to crumble the plaster that the workman's hasty hand too often applied. But the marble stands proud, all the colonnades, all the friezes remain intact, and the passage of time has made them seem grander, and shine whiter. The workman raised his tower with such an instinct for the great and eternal that its frame seems as if it should always remain whole; it matters not that sections of wall shall crumble, floors shall collapse, staircases shall break, the stone foundation shall always resist, the great tower shall always stand as straight, as high, supported upon the large feet of its giant columns; little by little, all that is mud and sand shall drift away, and then the monument's marble skeleton shall still appear on the horizon, like a huge, jagged cityscape. Even in a distant future, if some terrible wind, sweeping away our language and civilization, would knock down the structure's frame, the remains would leave such a mountain upon the ground that no distant people might pass before this pile, without saying, "There slumbers a world in ruins."]

Anticipating the exceptional staying power of Balzac's textual "monument," Zola imagines its eventual transformation into unforgettably impressive rubble: a place of memory, still recognizable to the distant future as "a world in ruins." The choice of vocabulary here ("the large feet," "the skeleton," "the frame" [la carcasse]) also suggests human remains, and the end of the passage recalls Horace's claim that even if a great epic poem had only survived in fragments it would still be possible to recognize these as the scattered limbs of a poet—"disiecti membra poetae" (*Satires i*, 4, 62). By implication then, not just the work but the writer himself would endure: here, as ruins, or elsewhere, enshrined in his self-made monument. Indeed, Zola's tribute to Balzac resembles the Gill caricature of Hugo sculpting busts of revolutionary heroes, in that both cast the man of letters as at once monument-maker and monument. Balzac creates his own textual mausoleum, *The Human Comedy*, and Hugo carves out his own place in history through his writing. They are the "authors" of their works, but also of their own posterity. Along similar lines, in an 1857 letter, Flaubert likens books to the pyramids:

> les livres ne se font pas comme les enfants, mais comme les pyramides, avec un dessin prémédité, et en apportant des grands blocs l'un par-dessus l'autre, à force de reins, de temps et de sueur, et ça ne sert à rien! et ça reste dans le désert! mais en le dominant prodigieusement. Les chacals pissent au bas et les bourgeois montent dessus, etc.; continue la comparaison. (Flaubert 1973, 2.783)

> [Books are not made like children, but like pyramids, with a premeditated design, by putting great blocks one atop the other, back-breaking, time-consuming work, and it's useless! and stays out in the desert! but towers over it impressively. Jackals piss on the bottom and bourgeois clamber up it, etc.; continue the comparison.]

While perhaps "useless" to the incontinent jackals and dull-witted bourgeois who beset them, the literary work and the pyramids are nonetheless still formidable and enduring works.[6] They not only share the rigor and deliberateness of their design, and the vastness and difficulty of their execution, but also both commemorate and entomb their creator. To continue Flaubert's comparison, as he requests, is indeed to uncover the writer himself who, as latter-day Pharaoh, both builds and is enshrined in his own monument. A similar vision of the

author informs Gautier's *Roman de la Momie* [The Mummy's Tale], published in spring 1857, just a few months before Flaubert's letter, and dedicated to the egyptologist Ernest Feydeau, Flaubert's nephew and also the addressee of his letter. The female mummy here is at once the central figure buried in the tomb that a pair of contemporary archaeologists excavate, and the ostensible author of the novel's central, embedded narrative, which the archaeologists find, on papyrus, attached to her petrified body (Gautier 1966). While the *Roman de la Momie* partakes of a certain nineteenth-century convention of the female body as an archeological artifact subjected to the authoritative male gaze, it also raises the interesting possibility of a "monumental" female author, a possibility we shall take up again later, with the case of George Sand.

Like so many vulgar, contemporary travelers to the orient, confronting the mysterious grandeur of the pyramids, Flaubert's hypothetical bourgeois reader appears both perplexed and enthralled. Literature renders him at once bewilderedly gape-mouthed or *béant* (a favorite Flaubertian adjective) and spiritually transfixed, or *béat*. Flaubert's comparison points, that is, toward a powerful devotional strain in the view of the literary work as a monument. With less sophistication perhaps, but no less zeal than the period's self-conscious literati, the bourgeois public venerated the monumental literary work. As the long-standing devotional tendencies of the public monument intersected with sacralization of the literary work (cf. e.g., Vigny's "L'Esprit Pur," discussed above), the bourgeois readership's fervor bordered on religiosity. According to Sartre in *Les Mots*, this was a view of literature characteristic of the nineteenth-century bourgeoisie and inculcated in him as a child by his belletristic, hugophilic grandfather:

> Je ne savais pas encore lire que, déjà, je les révérais, ces pierres levées: droites ou penchées, serrées commes des briques sur les rayons de la bibliothèque ou noblement espacées en allées de menhirs, je sentais que la prospérité de notre famille en dépendait. Elles se ressemblaient toutes, je m'ébattais dans un minuscule sanctuaire, entouré de monuments trapus, antiques, qui

m'avaient vu naître, qui me verraient mourir et dont la permanence me garantissait un avenir aussi calme que le passé. (Sartre 1964a, 29–30)

[Though I did not yet know how to read, I already revered those standing stones: upright or leaning over, close together like bricks on the book-shelves or spaced out nobly in lanes of menhirs. I felt that our family's prosperity depended on them. They all looked alike. I disported myself in a tiny sanctuary, surrounded by ancient, heavy-set monuments which had seen me into the world, which would see me out of it, and whose permanence guaranteed me a future as calm as the past.] (Sartre 1964c, 40–41)

The young bourgeois-in-training reveres books here in much the same way as distant ancestors might have revered the prehistoric monuments at Carnac: fervently, devoutly, and uncritically. As with Flaubert's thick-headed pyramid-climbers, the youthful initiate's devotion is born of incomprehension. He misconstrues the literary work as the source of bourgeois wealth, stability, and continuity. In nineteenth-century French society the literary work, cast as a monument, came to be seen as an anchor of bourgeois cultural values, guarantor of a broader bourgeois consciousness and, ironically, all the more for those who (like young Sartre) could not read, or did not bother to do so. "[Le] bourgeois de Paris" writes Balzac in *César Birotteau*, "admire Molière, Voltaire et Rousseau sur parole, . . . [et] achète leurs oeuvres sans les lire" [The Parisian bourgeois admires Molière, Voltaire and Rousseau on faith, . . . and buys their works without reading them] (CH 6:690). Thus Césarine Birotteau, the perfumist's daughter, marks her father's ascension to a higher realm of bourgeois mediocrity by purchasing for him an exquisitely leather-bound collection of great French writers:

> Césarine avait jeté toutes ses économies de jeune fille dans le comptoir d'un libraire, pour offrir à son père: Bossuet, Racine, Voltaire, Jean-Jacques Rousseau, Montesquieu, Molière, Buffon, Fénelon, Delille, Bernardin de Saint-Pierre, La Fontaine, Corneille, Pascal, La Harpe, enfin cette bibliothèque vulgaire qui se trouve partout et que son père ne lirait jamais. (6:166)

[Césarine had plopped down all her girlhood savings on a bookseller's counter, to buy her father: Bossuet, Racine, Voltaire, Jean-Jacques Rousseau, Montesquieu, Molière, Buffon, Fénelon, Delille, Bernardin de Saint-Pierre, La Fontaine, Corneille, Pascal, La Harpe, in short the most ordinary of libraries, that one finds everywhere, and that her father would never read.]

Balzac critiqued such simple-minded bourgeois appropriation of literature, yet did not doubt the ideal behind collecting great authors' works in complete editions—indeed, as a young, aspiring printer, he produced *oeuvres complètes* of both Molière and La Fontaine; later, he would strain to construct *The Human Comedy* as his own preposthumous complete works. For Sartre, though, the disabused, mid twentieth-century intellectual who, with hindsight, denounces a young literary acolyte's absurd illiteracy and scoffs at "heavy-set" monuments worshipped from within a tiny sanctuary, such a heroic, reverential view of literature had clearly become untenable.

The Author as Monument

First the literary work was seen as a monument; then, the concept of the text as mausoleum helped make the transition toward a vision of the writer himself as a monument. This vision did not blossom until later in the period for, in large measure, it contradicted an earlier Romantic aesthetic, characterized by a privileging of the natural and desire to animate the inanimate. Around mid-century, though, there emerged a new aesthetic that, in its privileging of the inorganic and tendency toward reification helped, as it were, to turn the writer to stone.

This aesthetic shift also informed how the crucial relationship between the writer and his work was understood. Throughout the period in question, *l'homme et l'oeuvre* were construed as essentially indissociable, however such consubstantiality was first expressed in "natural" terms. As Hugo wrote in a fragment apparently composed in preparing *Les Contemplations*, "Ce que nous écrivons est notre propre chair. / Le livre est à tel point l'auteur, et le poème / Le poëte;" [What we write is our own flesh. / The book is to such an extent the author, and the poem / The poet;] (Hugo 1964–67,

2.853).[7] Here, the inanimate is animated, with the text becoming flesh. As in so much romantic literature, with its strongly confessional and autobiographical bent, the text is understood as an organic extension of the writer. Later on, however, the living author was instead seen as becoming the inanimate text, an idea still prevalent in Sartre's youth:

A mes yeux, [les auteurs] n'étaient pas morts, enfin, pas tout à fait: ils s'étaient métamorphosés en livres. Corneille, c'était un gros rougeaud, rugueux, au dos de cuir, qui sentait la colle.... Flaubert, c'était un petit entoilé, inodore, piqueté de taches de son. Victor Hugo le multiple nichait sur tous les rayons à la fois. (Sartre 1964a, 50)

[In my sight, they were not dead; at any rate, not entirely. They had been metamorphosed into books. Corneille was a big, rugged, ruddy fellow who smelled of glue and had a leather back.... Flaubert was a cloth-bound, odorless little thing spotted with freckles. The multiple Victor Hugo was on all the shelves at once.] (Sartre 1964c, 64)

Great writers become their works, and live on through them; Victor Hugo, the most imposing, haunts all the shelves at once, in multiple volumes. Along the same lines, as time passed, and his autobiographical project evolved, Chateaubriand changed its title from *Mémoires de ma vie* [Memoirs of my life] (1826) to *Mémoires d'outre-tombe* [Memoirs from beyond the grave] (1848). This change is indeed emblematic of the period's broader aesthetic shift from the animate to the inanimate: no longer the record of a life, Chateaubriand's memoirs became instead a pre-posthumous textual afterlife. Similarly, Flaubert's assertion that "books are not made like children, but like pyramids" is informed by a view of the author's posterity, not as biological reproduction, but as immortalization in stone.

The 1833 caricature of Victor Hugo, entitled "Hugoth," is an early attempt to see the author as a monument (fig. 5). The relationship appears though to be a natural one, with the author of *Notre-Dame de Paris* seeming an organic outgrowth of the Gothic masonry. Stone, that is, becomes writerly flesh. By mid-century however, a commentator like Barbey d'Aurevilly would instead see the living author turning to stone: "Goethe, ce favori du destin, a passé

marbre de son vivant, dans une vieillesse qui était comme l'avance de son immortalité. Mais Balzac a été frappé dans le milieu de sa vie, dans l'empire agrandi de ses facultés et de ses projets." [Goethe, whom destiny favored, turned to marble during his lifetime, his old age like the prefiguration of his immortality. But Balzac was struck down in the middle of life, in the full bloom of his faculties and projects] (Barbey d'Aurevilly 1850). The assumption here is that the great man normally turns to stone after death, concretizing his immortality. This notion is illustrated as well by Nadar's *Panthéon* and by André Gill's caricatures of Zola. In one of the latter, the novelist salutes a bust of Balzac, clasping a copy of his own answer to *The Human Comedy*, *Les Rougon-Macquart* (frontispiece); in another, he tries in vain to pull a statufied Hugo from his pedestal, no doubt in order to take his place, while next to Zola lies the true instrument of attack, his pen, metonymy of his own monumental work-in-progress (fig. 6). Both of these Gill drawings depict ambitious Zola playing the would-be statue, with his work serving as the means to this most ardently desired end.

In *Le Peintre de la vie moderne* [The Painter of Modern Life], Baudelaire also holds up the statue as an ideal: "Qui ne voit que l'usage de la poudre de riz . . . a pour but . . . de créer une unité abstraite dans le grain et la couleur de la peau, laquelle unité, comme celle produite par le maillot, rapproche immédiatement l'être humain de la statue, c'est-à-dire d'un être divin et supérieur?" [Who does not see that rice powder is used to create an abstract unity in the skin's color and texture, a unity like that created by a bodysuit: straightaway it makes a human being appear like a statue, in other words like a divine and superior being] (Baudelaire 1975– 76, 2.717). Significantly, the living human approaches the statue's divine superiority through the artifice of makeup. Whereas an earlier reluctance to think of the author as a monument was consonant with a general aesthetic of the organic and, more specifically, with a Romantic conception of genius as inherent and natural, the later nineteenth-century preference for the "statufication" of authors meshed instead with a newer vision of the artist as construct, as self-consciously self-made dandy. Seen thus as artificial in life, the later nineteenth-century writer

Galerie
des fous contemporains.

La Charge, N° 4.
(2me année)

Journal Satyrique
paraissant le Dimanche.

HVGOTH.

Evoque tant écrite
Ca Victor Hugo seul porte la tête droite ;
Et croie le plafond de son crâne géant !
Pierre B.

Fig. 5. Anonymous, *Hugoth*. © Photothèque des musées de la ville de Paris.

Fig. 6. André Gill, *Loisirs naturalistes* (*Naturalist pastimes*). Photo M. Garval.

could, in death, pass more easily than his predecessors into the monument's stony permanence, privileged site of the literary afterlife.

This was the case not only for the writer's body, but for his consciousness as well. In the poem "Spleen—'J'ai plus de souvenirs que si j'avais mille ans'" ["Spleen—I couldn't hold more memories in a thousand years"], Baudelaire mourns,

> mon triste cerveau....
> ... est une pyramide, un immense caveau,
> Qui contient plus de morts que la fosse
> commune....
>
> —Désormais tu n'es plus, ô matière vivante!
> Qu'un granit entouré d'une vague épouvante,
> Assoupi dans le fond d'un Sahara brumeux;
> Un vieux sphinx ignoré du monde insoucieux,
> Oublié sur la carte, et dont l'humeur farouche
> Ne chante qu'aux rayons du soleil qui se couche.
>
> (Baudelaire 1975–76, 1.73)

> [my melancholy brain....
> ... is a pyramid; it is an open drain
> Containing more cadavers than a pauper's
> tomb....
>
> —From this time forth, O stuff of life, you are no
> more
> Than blocks of granite compassed round by some
> vague fear,
> Dozing in the depths of a Sahara's dust;
> An ancient sphinx, lost in the world's disinterest,
> Lost on the map, your wild caprice was never
> sung
> Except beneath the luster of the setting sun.]
>
> (Baudelaire 1991, 139)

The writer's brain, described as a pyramid, is a repository for his memories ("J'ai plus de souvenirs que si j'avais mille ans"—literally, "I have more memories than if I were a thousand years old"); as a monument, though, it is also potentially a repository for the broader cultural memory of his literary accomplishments. Baudelaire's portrait of the writer as pyramid and sphinx recalls Flaubert's exactly contemporary (1857) comparison of books and pyramids. Like Flaubert's letter, moreover, Baudelaire's poem suggests that the writer will live on in stone, outlasting contemporary neglect and incomprehension ("lost in the world's disinterest / Lost on the map,") to perhaps, at some point

in the future, be recognized for his true greatness. Baudelaire's perspective here provides an extreme example of what Braudy calls "the posture of reticence and the sanction of neglect" (Braudy 1986, 390–449), a willfully paradoxical stance central to nineteenth-century fame culture. Informing the lives and work of such diverse literary figures as Byron, Baudelaire, Dickinson, and Poe, this stance was predicated upon the belief that contemporary failure, rejection, and isolation offered fame's highest, most enduring consecration.

Literary Statuemania and the Ideal Synthesis of Writer, Work, and Monument

> La forme, ô grand sculpteur, c'est tout et ce n'est
> rien.
> Ce n'est rien sans l'esprit, c'est tout avec l'idée!
> —Victor Hugo, "Au statuaire David"
> (1840; Hugo 1964–67, 1.1069)

> [Form, o great sculptor, is all and nothing.
> Nothing without ideas, and all with them!]
> —Victor Hugo, "To the sculptor David"

The dream of stone culminated in the late nineteenth and early twentieth centuries, with French society in the throes of an unprecedented literary "statuemania," and increasingly convinced that literary glory resided in an ideal synthesis of writer, work, and monument. Literary statuemania marked an exceptional moment in the long history of civic statuary, and the ideal synthesis it embodied had evolved out of a complex of interrelated sociohistorical and aesthetic factors, including new conditions in the world of letters, changes in society's conception of fame, and a shifting horizon of iconographical and commemorative possibilities.

From the beginning of the century onward, France had indeed witnessed the emergence of a substantial, new literary marketplace, a phenomenon that Balzac called "l'accroissement progressif de la masse lisante, ce.... monstre à soixante million d'yeux" [the progressive growth of the reading masses, this monster with sixty million eyes] (Balzac 1955–63, 27.252). While Balzac is exaggerating for effect here, the gist of his remark holds true, for before this period, literature had generally been a more intimate undertaking, among a smaller, lettered elite. Especially in court circles, writers and readers tended to know each other, and to know what to expect of each other: within a largely familiar public's eyes, the author was inextricably linked to his writing, much like the baker to his bread. With the advent of a modern literary marketplace, however, there arose the potential for profound disjunctions, not only between the writer and his public reputation, but also between the writer and his *oeuvre*, as dramatized through the figure of Canalis in Balzac's *Modeste Mignon*. Similarly, in the preface to *La Peau de chagrin* [The Wild Ass's Skin], Balzac laments the way in which readers conjure up images of the author: "involontairement, ils dessinent, dans leur pensée, une figure, bâtissent un homme, le supposent jeune ou vieux, grand ou petit, aimable ou méchant" [involuntarily, in their minds, they draw a face, construct a man, imagine him young or old, big or small, likeable or mean] (CH 10.48). In his case, particularly outlandish speculation had resulted from the anonymous publication of *La Physiologie du mariage* [The Physiology of marriage]: readers had supposed it the work of an elderly doctor, a debauched courtier, or a disillusioned misanthrope, conjecture symptomatic of what Balzac sees as the current sorry state of the literary world. As an antidote, he not only offers a corrective to the public's image of him—painting himself as a sober, serious young man—but also indulges in a nostalgic fantasy. He imagines a return to the less confusing way things used to be: he, the author, "s'est promis d'en finir avec un nombreux public qui ne le connaît pas pour satisfaire le petit public qui le connaît" [promised himself to be done with the large readership that does not know him, in order to satisfy the small one that does] (10.49)— what Stendhal, in the envoi to *La Chartreuse de Parme* [The Charterhouse of Parma], calls "the happy few."[8]

This is just wishful thinking for, through the century, the reading public, the means for reaching it, and the potential for distortions as a result all grew. In addition to anxiety over disjunctions between the writer, his work, and his public, there arose substantial anxiety over the perceived fragility of literary renown. This stemmed in large measure from a more general perception that fame itself was becoming increasingly transitory. The 1839 "Balzac" issue of the popular *Galerie de la presse, de la littérature et des beaux-arts* [Gallery of the press, literature, and fine arts] refers, for example, to "toutes les fumées et bulles de savon de la gloire" [all the smoke and soap bubbles of glory], much as Achille Laffont's "Un jeune homme de lettres" [A young man of letters] laments "l'ombre trompeuse de la fortune littéraire" [the deceitful shadow of literary fortune] (Laffont 1853, 1). Similar sentiments are echoed by Flaubert's *Dictionnaire des idées reçues* [Dictionary of received ideas], which defines "gloire" [glory] as, "N'est qu'un peu de fumée" [Just a bit of smoke] (Flaubert 1979, 523), and by Abel Hermant's 1902 inaugural speech for the Falguière Balzac monument, which muses that, unlike the author of *The Human Comedy*, "toutes les immortalités ne sont pas à l'épreuve d'un demi-siècle" [all immortality is not up to the test of a half century] (Hermant 1903, 44).

In reaction to such anxieties over discontinuity and impermanence, French literary culture evolved, from about 1850 onward, a vision of lasting literary glory as a seamless fusion of writer, work, and monument. Culminating in the early decades of the Third Republic, this was a profoundly compensatory vision. It counterbalanced the reality of an increasingly volatile and unpredictable literary marketplace with a retrograde phantasm of the whole literary enterprise as inherently unified, orderly, and durable. Within late nineteenth-century French literary culture, there prevailed this curious double vision, almost a collective schizophrenia, with a keen awareness of the vagaries of change existing alongside an equally powerful dream of purposefulness, solidity, and immutability—an imagined, ideal world of letters that never was, and never would be.

Of the iconographical and commemorative options available at this time, the monument was perceived as the way to represent enduring fame, the vehicle for articulating both the author's and literary work's crucial passage from the present to the hereafter. The two representational modes that most clearly embodied the period's opposing conceptions of fame were caricature and the monument. While caricature expressed a more recent view of renown as momentary celebrity, the monument embodied

the more traditional vision of renown as enduring fame. Caricatures appeared in ephemeral
media, thrived on contemporary detail, and
were critical and irreverent: while elevating
their subjects to a certain public notoriety, caricatures also debunked them by highlighting
their flaws and foibles. Monuments, however,
rendered in durable marble or bronze, were
reverential, idealizing, and often classicizing,
seemingly "timeless": designed, in short, to perpetuate their subjects' fame. Public and commemorative, they were intended to last, as H. W.
Janson establishes in his seminal essay on the
public monument. Such installations were indeed "meant to be permanent—as permanent as
the means available could make them" (Janson
1976, 1).

Despite such fundamental oppositions between them, caricature and monument coexisted, and were to some extent interdependent,
during much of the nineteenth century. Indeed,
the monument's extraordinary vitality derived
in part from its antithetical relation to caricature, which acted as a necessary comic foil to
its solemn gravity. At the time moreover, these
modes of visual representation were paralleled
by analogous modes of writing: faddish journalistic *prose du jour*, rapidly consumed, easily
forgotten, barely outlasting the paper on which
it was printed, versus the ponderous literary
oeuvre, solidly leather-bound in voluminous
complete works, meant to be read and reread
with reverence, clearly intended to last. In this
connection, a preparatory sketch for Nadar's
Panthéon is emblematic (fig. 7). Dozens of tiny
demons carry flimsy, individual sheets of paper,
each bearing the name of a mortal destined
for literary immortality. This furious activity,
reminiscent of a scene from Hieronymus Bosch,
swirls toward the center of the composition,
where an allegorical figure of Death records
the names in a massive, bound volume (Hambourg, Heilbrun, and Néagu 1994, 22). Death
plays a pivotal role, not only in the preliminary,
but also in the final version of the *Panthéon*
(fig. 3), as a passage from the ephemeral to
the everlasting: from newsprint-like sheets to
a monumental tome in the sketch; and, from
caricatures of contemporary writers to statues
of deceased literary glories in the completed
lithograph. Both versions thus foreground the
process of immortalization itself: in the first,

this is a transformation from one textual mode
to another; in the second, an analogous transformation from one plastic medium to another.

While caricature and monument embodied
the extremes, there was also a continuum of
iconographical possibilities that defined the
shades of renown in between. From the less to
the more permanent, this included lithographs
and engravings within publications, free-standing prints, paintings, bas-relief medallions, and
busts. These visual forms correlated with textual ones, along a similar continuum, delimited
by daily journalism on one end and leather-
bound complete works on the other. Again, from
less to more permanent forms, the continuum
in between included weekly, monthly, or occa-
sional periodicals; inexpensive paperback publications; and more carefully produced hardback
editions. Toward the lower end of both the visual
and the textual gamuts, works became increasingly insubstantial, inexpensive and, through
mechanical reproduction, multiple; toward the
higher end, they became more carefully crafted,
precious, and singular; they retained, or at
least cultivated, what Walter Benjamin calls the
"aura" of the traditional, nonmechanically reproduced art object (Benjamin 1969, 221). This
was clearly the case for painting and sculpture,
but also for texts with, for example, a nonre-
producible original edition worth far more than
an eminently reproducible facsimile edition, as
an 1839 article in the *Revue des Deux mondes* contends.[9] Along similar lines, impressively
leather-clad literary *oeuvres* sought, through
their painstakingly hand-wrought bindings, to
redeem the mechanically printed texts they contained as unique works of art.[10] The widespread
fetishism of fine bookbinding was indeed a
largely compensatory disposition: thus, Balzac
emblazoning his book bindings with the arms
of the Balzac d'Entragues', a double imposture
that pairs his own imagined nobility with the
imagined singularity of a work so distinguished;
or, his character Césarine Birotteau seeking to
raise her father out of petty bourgeois ignominy
by bestowing upon him the double distinction
of great writers' *oeuvres* cloaked in the masterful work of the "célèbre relieur Thouvenin,
un artiste" [famed bookbinder Thouvenin, an
artist] (CH 6.166). Such bookbinding artistry,
and the prestige it confers, did have its price. In
Césarine's case, notes Balzac, "Il devait y avoir

Fig. 7. Nadar, preparatory sketch for the *Panthéon*. Photograph © 2003 Museum of Fine Arts, Boston.

un terrible mémoire de reliure." The value of a book could thus be conflated with that of its cover: Edmond de Goncourt, for example, confided, "J'aime les livres dont la reliure coûte cher" [I like books with expensive bindings] (1989). In a broader sense the binding, like the literary work itself, and like the monument that commemorated the work and its creator, aspired to posterity both through the exquisiteness of the raw material used (the morocco and gold-leaf of the binding, like the rich "stuff" of the author's existence, or like the marble and bronze of monumental statuary), and also through the skill with which such material was rendered (the "craftsmanship" or "artistry" of the binder, writer, or sculptor).

The extent to which material considerations might thus figure into the perception of a literary work's enduring value suggests that renown could be bought or fabricated, a possibility Villiers de l'Isle-Adam (1986) explored in *La Machine à gloire* [The Fame Machine], first published in 1874. Villiers' satirical sketch offers an incisive, even prescient reflection on the period's burgeoning fame culture, and especially on the impact of fame-making "machinery." Here, as in *L'Ève future* [The Future Eve], Villiers appears ambivalent about technology: while fascinated with its novelty and ingenuity, to the point of indulging in lively science fiction writing himself, he also laments technology's general dehumanizing and leveling effects. More specifically, Villiers's satirical sketch pretends to hail the invention of an elaborate, mechanized version of *la claque*, the widespread nineteenth-century practice of guaranteeing a play's success through paid applauders. This ingenious "machine à gloire," installed in the theater, combines mechanical clapping hands, hidden phonographs, and ducts for laughing and tear gases to secure the desired audience reaction, thus fame for the play and—by extension—for its author, no matter how undeserving he might be. While fanciful, Villiers's machine does stand in for a host of real, emergent fame-making technologies in nineteenth-century France, with the specifically theatrical audience providing a *mise-en-abîme* of the easily manipulated, fame-hungry public at large. Villiers even anticipates such twentieth-century innovations as the laugh-track (with recordings of "tous les Bruits publics PERFECTIONNÉS" [all the audience noises, PERFECTED; 591]), the press release, and even word-processing: "les Articles critiques, confectionnés à l'avance, sont aussi une dépendance de la Machine: la rédaction en est simplifée par un triage de tous les vieux clichés, rhabillés et vernis à neuf, qui sont lancés . . . à l'instar du Moulin-à-prières des Chinois" [reviews, concocted beforehand, are another of the Machine's functions: writing them is made simple by recombining the whole stock of old clichés, dressed and shined up for the occasion, and cast out in the manner of a Chinese Prayer-mill] (595).

Beneath Villiers' satire lies disdain for the contemporary celebrity fostered by new technological means, and this is made clear from the outset. The text is dedicated to a like-minded soul, Stéphane Mallarmé, the most hermetic and cerebral of nineteenth-century French poets, certainly no easy crowd-pleaser. The fame-making machine itself is said to be created by a certain Bathybius Bottom, whose name suggests the lowness and asininity his invention engenders. The spectators it targets are indeed undiscerning, even illiterate: unable to distinguish Shakespeare's worth from Scribe's, and "[in]capables de lire quoi que ce soit, voire des étiquettes de pots à moutarde" [incapable of reading anything, even mustard jar labels] (585). Critics fare no better in Villiers's assessment. The machine's idiotic, ready-made reviews are "[le] choix et lessivage des plus décrépités, tortueuses, nauséabondes, calomnieuses et baveuses platitudes, gloussées au sortir de l'égout natal" [the bottom of the barrel of the most decrepit, convoluted, nauseating, slanderous and salivary platitudes, ever to emerge, cheerfully, from the birth canal]

(594)—exhibiting precisely the mucilaginous sogginess that Baudelaire's critique of Villemain identified with bad writing (cf. above). Yet leading contemporary critics could not help admiring such mastery of their art: "nos plus spirituels critiques . . . en soupiraient et en laissaient tomber la plume d'admiration" [our cleverest critics . . . sighed and dropped their pens in admiration] (595).

Early on in the text, moreover, Villiers poses the fundamental, broader question already inferred by his title: how can "[un] moyen physique" (584), "une pure machine" (586) be used to attain something as intangible, as ineffable as fame, "un but purement intellectuel"? This in turn raises the question of what kind of fame the *Machine à gloire*—and fame-making technology in general—can produce? Through most of the text, the machine seems able to secure only contemporary success, although it can do so without fail ("infailliblement"), using even the poorest of raw materials: "avec [cette] Machine, l'acteur n'eût-il pas plus de mémoire qu'un linot, l'auteur fût-il l'Hébétude en personne et le spectateur fût-il sourd comme un pot, ce sera un véritable triomphe!" [with (this) Machine, even if the actor had no more memory than a brick, if the author were Dullness incarnate and the spectator were deaf as a post, it will be a great triumph] (590). Near the end, though, along with a bill for services rendered, the playwright is said to receive material evidence of a more enduring sort of fame. He is given, "au nom de la Postérité, . . . à titre d'offrande, un buste ressemblant, garanti, nimbé et lauré, le tout en béton aggloméré (Système Coignet). Tout cela peut se faire à l'avance! Avant la représentation!!!" [as a gift, in Posterity's name, a guaranteed, haloed, laurel-crowned bust, sporting his likeness, all done in aggregate concrete (Coignet's System). This can all be done in advance! Before the performance!!!] (595). But how can such a bust consecrate an author's supposed achievement, if it can just as well be prepared before his play's first performance? What sort of posterity, moreover, could be embodied by a statue made not of the traditional noble materials—marble, bronze—but of concrete, the vulgar, industrial material *par excellence*? Having thus questioned the Machine's ability to create enduring fame, Villiers now reveals one last design feature, to drive home his larger critique of modern celebrity, and of the fame-making technology that promotes it:

> Si l'auteur tenait même à ce que sa gloire fût non seulement présente et future, mais fût même *passée*, le Baron [Bottom] a tout prévu : la Machine peut obtenir des résultats rétroactifs. En effet, des conduits de gaz hilarants, habilement distribués dans les cimetières de premier ordre, doivent, chaque soir, faire sourire, de force, les aïeux dans leurs tombeaux. (505)

> [Even if the author insists on being famous not only in the present and future, but even in the past, Baron (Bottom) has foreseen all: the Machine can yield retroactive results. Indeed, laughing gas conduits are placed skillfully in the most exclusive cemeteries, in order to make our ancestors smile, nightly, in their tombs.]

The grotesqueness of the image argues for the absurdity of such "retroactive" fame and, by extension, the broader impossibility of fabricating fame for any time other than the present. In short, fame-making technology, no matter how powerful or ingenious, can generate only present-day popularity, not enduring renown. Yet the idea of thus pursuing "retroactive" fame is not as far-fetched as it might first appear, in light of the emergence of the modern cemetery over the preceding three-quarter century, which included a strategic manipulation of such noteworthy "ancestors" as Molière, La Fontaine, and Héloïse and Abélard, whose tombs were relocated to the Père-Lachaise as a marketing ploy (cf. chapter 2). Moreover, as we shall see later on, at the time Villiers wrote this, Victor Hugo, the most famous writer of the day, sought to enhance his glory by conquering the past, positioning himself as the spiritual "ancestor" of the Third Republic. Even at its seemingly most fanciful point, with this image of laughing gas piped into tombs, Villiers' critique aims at the real excesses of modern fame culture, of a yearning for celebrity that knows no bounds.

A "dream of stone" is an oxymoron, an uneasy mix of the impalpable and the palpable. Indeed, the dream of stone's culminating ideal emerged amid the materiality of mid nineteenth-century France's real and fictional fame-making machinery. For example, the preliminary and 1854 versions of Nadar's *Panthéon,* when juxtaposed,

provide a revealing, early example of this penchant for synthesizing writer, work, and monument. In the former, the writer becomes a book, whereas in the latter the writer becomes a statue. The substitution of one process for the other reveals their imagined equivalency, and that of the three elements involved. In both cases, death is the crucial moment of transformation, when the author accedes to lasting fame. Along similar lines, on June 20, 1853, at about the same time as Nadar was drafting his *Panthéon,* Charles Matharel de Fiennes, literary columnist for *Le Siècle,* imagined a more appropriate tomb for Balzac than his current, modest grave: "Un beau mausolée portant une table d'airain sur laquelle on gravera ces simples mots: L'Auteur de La Comédie humaine" [A handsome mausoleum displaying a brass plaque upon which shall be inscribed these simple words: Author of The Human Comedy] (Schopp 1981, 246). While never realized, Fiennes' project is noteworthy for attempting, with its pithy epitaph, to consolidate the author and his complete works in the space of the monument. In this way, it anticipates many later monuments to authors. Particularly under the Third Republic, the literary monument typically blended representation of the writer with reference to his works. The author might be depicted composing works, pen in hand, or instead just appear to be composing his thoughts, in a contemplative attitude all the more suggestive for simply pointing toward the depths of literary creation beneath the surface. Literary monuments also often included titles of works, typically on the pedestal, close to the author's name, but sometimes incorporated in the statue itself. For example, Carrier-Belleuse's monument to Alexandre Dumas, *père,* in the novelist's native Villers-Cotterêts, depicted him leaning on a podium upon which is inscribed a list of his novels, ending emphatically with, "Etc. Etc. Etc."[11] While other monuments would evoke the author's *oeuvre* through a global title, a full list of individual titles, or a partial list of representative works, Carrier-Belleuse attempted instead to capture the scope of Dumas' production, by suggesting that a complete enumeration would not fit, that the monumentality of the *oeuvre* surpasses the bounds of the monument itself.

Like the Dumas memorial, many other late nineteenth-century monuments were raised in their subject's birthplace: "Les portraits des grands hommes doivent être édifiés dans les lieux qui les virent naître" [Portraits of great men should be raised in their birthplaces], prescribed David d'Angers (Huchard et al 1990, 14). Yet this practice can be explained only in part as home towns honoring their native sons. In a larger sense, hometown monuments—like birthplace plaques or such popular publications as *L'Enfance des enfants illustres* [The Childhood of famous children] (cf. Sartre 1964 a, 167)—telescope birth and death, expressing a teleology of greatness central to the period's ideal synthesis. This idea of inexorable destiny propelling the predestined child toward immortality had long been a fixture of Christian martyrology and iconography (e.g., baby Jesus pricking His chubby finger portentously on a thorn). It became integrated into a pervasive romantic myth of the writer as a doomed promethean figure, a martyr to literary creation, that, as we shall see, remains so central to our understanding of Balzac in particular.

The ample verbiage that generally surrounded the inauguration of a monument in late nineteenth-century France can also provide valuable insights into the period's ideal synthesis. Such discourse ranged from public debate and fundraising pleas beforehand to official ceremonies and critical assessments afterwards. Some of the forms it took, however, may be unfamiliar for the modern reader. On one level, the 1896 *Tombeau de Charles Baudelaire* recalls the venerable tradition of the *tombeau*, "recueil de vers et proses à la gloire du défunt" [volume of verse and prose to the glory of the deceased] (Dupriez 1984, 105); on another, it is a particularly elaborate example of a genre Chantal Martinet describes in her essay on how monuments were funded through subscription:

Parfois, le comité [de souscription] fait imprimer une brochure, petit livret illustré, qu'il vend, bon marché, ou distribue gratuitement aux souscripteurs, à titre de récompense-souvenir. Ces modestes imprimés rappellent la vie et les mérites du futur statufié. (Pingeot 1986, 233)

[Sometimes the (subscription) committee prints a small illustrated booklet, sold at a nominal price, or distributed for free to subscribers, as a souvenir and token of gratitude. These humble publications recall the life and accomplishments of the honoree.]

Much more than a simple booklet like, say, the 1887 *Statue de Honoré de Balzac à Tours* [Balzac's Statue in Tours], the 125-page *Tombeau de Charles Baudelaire* [Tomb of Charles Baudelaire] was an ambitious fund-raising endeavor for the "Comité pour ériger un monument à Charles Baudelaire" [Committee to raise a monument to Charles Baudelaire], published in a limited, luxury edition of 250 copies, such exclusiveness in itself conferring distinction upon the subject. The committee was organized and led by Stéphane Mallarmé, and its membership included such leading literary figures of the day as Paul Bourget, Anatole France, Edmond de Goncourt, J.-M. de Heredia, J.-K. Huysmans, Maurice Maeterlinck, Catulle Mendès, Octave Mirbeau, Algernon Charles Swinburne, Paul Verlaine, Émile Verhaeren, and Émile Zola. Contributors included Mallarmé, François Coppeé, Léon Dierx, Stefan George, Gustave Kahn, Pierre Louÿs, Nadar, Henri de Régnier, and Verhaeren. Following a frontispiece by Félicien Rops, the volume consists of a title page, with a list of prominent contributors; a "Justification du tirage, désignation des papiers & des prix" [Detailing of printing, papers, and prices], followed by a "Liste des souscripteurs" [List of subscribers]; a committee roster; an "Étude sur les textes des 'Fleurs du mal,' commentaire & variantes" [Study concerning the texts of the "Flowers of Evil," with commentary and variants] by Prince Alexandre Ourousof, that includes a section on "L'architecture secrète des 'Fleurs du mal'" [The secret architecture of the "Flowers of Evil"] (with tables of contents from the three principal editions, for comparison), a detailed discussion of "Les trois textes des Fleurs du mal" [The three texts of the Flowers of Evil] and their variants, as well as an "ERRATA des éditions posthumes" [ERRATA of the posthumous editions] based on the poet's corrections for the first two editions; thirty-two poems and nine brief prose pieces that deal with Baudelaire's life, *oeuvre*, and projected monument; a dozen pages containing the "Oeuvres posthumes de Charles Baudelaire, inédites ou non recueillies dans les éditions des oeuvres complètes du poète" [Posthumous works of Charles Baudelaire, unpublished or not included in editions of the poet's complete works]; and finally, some "Notes pour une iconographie du poète Charles Baudelaire" [Notes for an iconography of the poet Charles Baudelaire] (*Le Tombeau de Charles Baudelaire* 1979).

From the outset, the title *Le Tombeau de Charles Baudelaire* announces the volume's general goal of memorializing the dead poet. The more specific, stated goal is to raise a public monument. This, however, is intertwined with the closely related, but unstated goal of preserving and promoting his work and, to this end, establishing what exactly constitutes this *oeuvre*, hence the extensive discussions of variants, editorial concerns, and textual "architecture." The assumption here is that the great author lives on, simultaneously and analogously, through the sculptural monument erected in his honor and through the textual "monument" of his *oeuvre*. To brave posterity, both of these should be properly "constructed," remaining true to the spirit of the author himself. For the *oeuvre*, this involves rectifying typographical errors or determining the proper order of the poems. But what might this involve for the projected monument to Baudelaire? Several of the poems and prose pieces in the volume do attempt, however obliquely, to imagine such a monument. Émile Blémont's contribution, typical of these efforts, begins and ends with:

Sur l'idéal tombeau que je rêve à ta gloire,
O sombre et grand poëte ami, je dresserais,
Parmi le vert laurier, le myrte et le cyprès,
Une belle Africaine en sa nudité noire. . . .

Et sur sa gorge pure aux seins durs et pointus,
En ses yeux imprégnés d'amour et de souffrance,
On croirait voir flotter des paradis perdus.

(45)

[I dream of the perfect tomb to your glory,
O my great, somber, poet friend, upon which I
    would raise,
Amidst the verdant laurel, myrtle, and cypress,
An African beauty, in all her ebony nakedness.

And upon her pure bosom, her hard, angular
    breasts,
And in her eyes filled with love and suffering,
Would sparkle a vision of paradise lost.]

As Blémont's use of the conditional and of exotic and dream motifs suggests, this is not a pragmatic but a poetic reflection, an ideal vision of literary glory. Given the context, one would imagine a Baudelaire monument to be the focal point here, but this is completely absent Instead, Blémont's poem focuses on the "belle Africaine"—a reference, perhaps, to Jeanne Duval, Baudelaire's *belle Créole*, which provides an appropriately Baudelairean aura of mystery, exoticism, and somber "volupté," to frame the missing monument. This pattern repeats, yet more emphatically, in Jacques des Gachons' "Décor pour la Statue de Baudelaire (Maquette)" [Décor for the Statue of Baudelaire (Model)]. This prose piece opens with only the vaguest evocation of a monument:

Un front énorme que la lune blafarde
lugubrement, et des yeux aux regards altiers
de Créateur. . . .

Sentiment d'une puissance géniale . . .

De ce front, de ces yeux, s'élance un
merveilleux poème, un magique paysage.

(93)

[The moon lights lugubriously a
prodigious brow, and eyes with a haughty,
Creator's gaze (. . . .)

A feeling of genius's power . . .

From this brow, and these eyes, springs forth a
marvelous poem, a magical landscape.]

The rest of the text turns to the "Décor" surrounding this shadowy presence:

D'abord, aux pieds du Poète, un précipice qu'aucun oeil n'a mesuré, et qu'il domine, hautain.

De l'autre côté, en avant, un lac immense et calme, sans barque, sans vol d'oiseau, un lac où s'ensommeillent les nénuphars aux racines longues commes des pensées tristes, les nénuphars et les songes qui s'y viennent baigner, mystérieusement. Le ciel est immensément bleu. Il n'y a pas d'étoiles.

[First, at the Poet's feet, a precipice that no eye has measured, and that he commands mightily.

On the other side, in front, a huge, calm lake, with no boats, nor birds in flight, a lake where there slumber waterlilies with roots long as sad thoughts, waterlilies and dreams that float there mysteriously. There are no stars in the immense, blue sky.]

This continues for three more paragraphs of lyrically synaesthetic, self-consciously "Baudelairean" description. While purporting to be a "maquette," a text like this clearly does not function as any kind of practical model. How indeed could one reproduce a precipice "that no eye has measured," or roots "long as sad thoughts"?

A few pages later, Louis Ménard imagines a conversation between Baudelaire and the recently deceased Parnassian *chef d'école* Leconte de Lisle: "Je viens d'assister, par le téléfone, à un dialogue entre Baudelaire et Leconte de Lisle dans le paradis des poètes" [I have just listened, by telefone, to a dialogue between Baudelaire and Leconte de Lisle, in the poet's paradise] (99; throughout, as part of his long-standing campaign to reform French "ortografe," Ménard uses strange, alternate spellings[12]). Learning that there are plans to erect a monument to him, Ménard's Baudelaire objects that Gautier, his "maître inpeccable" should be so honored first, then—recalling his *Salon* of 1846—adds, "je n'aime pas la sculpture, c'est un art des Caraïbes" [I do not like sculpture, it is primitive art] (100). But a monument, counters Leconte de Lisle, was the only way of consecrating the poet's "gloire éternèle," to which Baudelaire retorts, "Si, il i avait un autre moyen: il falait rééditer mes oeuvres, qi doivent être épuisées. C'est cela qi était moi" [Yes, thair waz another way: bi reissuing my works, wich must be out of print. That was reely me] (100). Paradoxically then this volume, despite its contributors' ostensible goal of erecting a monument to Baudelaire, repeatedly points up the inadequacy, even impossibility of such an endeavor—to the point of having the great poet himself opine, from beyond, that his works are the best "monument" to his everlasting glory.

The phenomenon of statuemania does provide some of the most striking, tangible evidence of how literary fame was envisioned in late nineteenth-century France. Yet many contemporary commentators, like the contributors to *Le Tombeau de Charles Baudelaire*, came to see actual monuments as flawed vessels for the monumental ideal they sought to embody. In an 1893 article commemorating the thirty-third anniversary of Balzac's death, Arsène Houssaye asserted, "Mais à quoi bon un autre monument que celui de ses oeuvres. En ce siècle de statuomanie, le marbre n'est plus assez pur, le bronze n'est plus assez fier pour représenter l'homme de génie" [But of what good is a monument other than his works. In this age of statuemania, marble is no longer pure enough, nor bronze proud enough to represent a man of genius]. In "Une Statue pour Balzac" [A Statue for Balzac], Zola is appalled that, when there was not yet a public statue of Balzac, Paris was planning to erect one of Alexandre Dumas. He explains that first, "Au lendemain de la mort d'Alexandre Dumas, il y a dix ans, on songea, m'a-t-on dit, à faire une de ces éditions qui sont comme le monument de bronze d'un grand écrivain" [Right after Alexander Dumas' death, ten years ago, I heard of plans to make one of these editions that are like a great writer's bronze statue] (Zola 1888, 88). Zola already supposes the author's *oeuvres complètes* to be the equivalent of his monument; by using the phrase "une de ces" [one of these], he also supposes this to be a familiar notion for the reader. The Dumas project was abandoned though, Zola presumes, because even the best of his work was not sufficiently worthwhile: "les meilleurs de ses romans n'avaient pas assez de consistance pour supporter la publication solennelle d'une édition définitive" [the best of his novels had not the substance to justify the solemn publication of a definitive edition]. "Consistance" and "supporter" have architectonic as well as literary critical connotations here: from the point of view of posterity, Dumas' work appears structurally unsound.

Zola continues his analysis, affirming that "L'idée d'une édition complète abandonnée forcément, le projet d'une statue devait tôt ou tard se produire" [With the idea of a complete edition abandoned, it was inevitable that sooner or later a project for a statue would surface]. The statue is an inferior substitute for a complete works. Perhaps, though, muses Zola, Parisians are justified in not honoring Balzac with a monument because they have been thinking, "c'est un homme de génie, il a le temps d'attendre; il obtiendra bien sa statue tout seul; tandis qu'il faut se hâter de couler en bronze les amuseurs, si l'on veut que le temps ne les mette pas en poussière" [he's a man of genius, he's got time to wait; he'll get his statue all by himself; however, we must hurry and cast jokers in bronze, if we don't want time to reduce them to dust] (89). Zola is, of course, ironic about the Parisians' attitude toward Balzac and Dumas. Yet beneath the irony lies a telling mindset. The truly great writer accedes naturally to statufication; he is transfigured "all by himself," as if by magic. In contrast, the popular hack disintegrates into nothing ("to dust"), and thus demands a positive effort to transform him into a statue. Seen in this light, statuemania seems largely a campaign on behalf of mediocrities who would otherwise be forgotten. Zola's comments thus far present works as better, more appropriate "monuments" than monuments themselves. In conclusion, he pushes this argument even further:

Si l'on veut savoir le fond de ma pensée, je dirai que je suis d'avis de n'élever de statue à personne. Pour les écrivains surtout, les oeuvres sont là qui suffisent comme monument. Si vous laissez des oeuvres grandes, à quoi bon une statue qui paraîtra toujours plus petite; et si vos oeuvres sont médiocres, si vos flatteurs pensent les hausser en mettant un bronze dessus, ce bronze, trop grand pour vous, vous rapetissera encore devant les générations.

(94)

[If you want to know what I really think, I'll say that I believe in raising statues to no one. Particularly for writers, their works suffice as monuments. If you leave behind great works, of what good is a statue that always shall seem ever smaller; and if your works are mediocre, if flatterers try to exalt them by placing a bronze above, this bronze shall be too big for you, and shall shrink you for generations.]

Great works are monumental in themselves, and can stand alone in commemorating their author. Conversely, an unjustified monument, one not rooted in great works, is antimonumental, shrinking its subject for eternity.[13] Zola's remarks are useful as well in providing the measure of his own ambitions and, in our conclusion, we shall examine the extent to which Zola's public would also hold him up

to such monumental standards. His remarks might, however, give the mistaken impression that late nineteenth-century France's commemorative options were limited to complete works and monuments. At this time, though, an abundance of interrelated cultural productions venerated the writer and his work. Partaking of the spirit of the monument without actually being or even containing one, these forms incarnated as well the period's pervasive dream of stone. They included such traditional tributes as eulogies, obituaries, biographies, or reverential portraits in diverse media. The collective commemoration offered by such structures as the *Panthéon* or the cupola of the *Académie Française* was joined, in the late nineteenth and early twentieth centuries, by museums dedicated to individual writers. The *Maison de Victor Hugo*, for example, was opened in 1903 (Georgel 1985, 293), and the *Maison de Balzac* in 1908 (Sarment 1980, 7). The period's commemorative zeal also took to the streets in the form of signs and plaques. As Bournon's 1909 study of *La voie publique et son décor* [Public thoroughfares and their surroundings] notes, "La préoccupation d'honorer les hommes célèbres en donnant leur nom aux voies publiques est . . . chose relativement récente. De même que pour les statues, le privilège en fut d'abord réservé au seul souverain" [The concern for honoring famous men by giving their names to public thoroughfares is . . . a relatively recent thing. As with statues, the privilege was first reserved for the king alone] (183). Significantly, naming streets after great men is seen here as analogous to the erection of statues in their honor. The study explains as well that in 1879, "[afin de] multiplier ce genre d'hommages et les rendre plus précis et significatifs," an administrative commission had been established in Paris to deal with "l'apposition de plaques commémoratives" [the placement of commemorative plaques] (184). Over the preceding forty years, about 120 such plaques had been placed around Paris, and at least as many similar projects were considered but rejected. "Plaquemania" paralleled the rise of statuemania:

Tout le monde les connaît, ces discrètes plaques de marbre blanc, marquées de l'estampille municipale qui les authentique. La plupart signalent au passant la maison natale ou mortuaire d'un homme illustre, ou son emplacement, ou simplement le logis parisien qu'il habita longtemps.

[Everyone knows of these discrete white marble plaques, bearing the official, municipal stamp. Most indicate to passersby the birth or deathouse of a famous man, or its location, or simply his longtime Paris residence.]

Such efforts mark the great man's passage, through the here and now of the modern city, into some kind of eternity. In conjunction with statuemania, they also convert that urban space into a veritable gallery of renown, realizing a vision David d'Angers had already expressed in an 1847 letter, declaring: "Il faut que . . . la France devienne un vaste panthéon" [France must become a vast pantheon] (Huchard et al. 1990, 52).

Ultimately then, the ideal synthesis of writer, work, and monument was predicated not upon the presence of an actual, physical monument, but rather upon the broader idea, the metaphor of the monument. The armies of marble and bronze mobilized by statuemania were indeed only a symptom of the larger mentality behind them. One of the most illuminating accounts of this can be found, once again, in Sartre's *Les Mots*. Young Sartre's literary ambitions, we learn, involved building "des monuments véritables" [real monuments], that is, *textual* ones: "je n'aimais que les mots: je dresserais des cathédrales de paroles sous l'oeil bleu du mot ciel. Je bâtirais pour des millénaires. . . . et, plus tard, dans des bibliothèques en ruines [mes ouvrages] survivraient à l'homme" [I cared only for words: I would set up cathedrals of words beneath the blue eyes of the word sky. I would build for the ages. . . . and, later, in ruined libraries, [my works] would outlive man] (Sartre 1964a, 152; 1964c, 183). For this would-be "écrivain-martyr" [writer-martyr] (Sartre 1964a, 147; 1964c, 177) become "tout à fait posthume" [completely posthumous] (Sartre 1964a, 165; 1964c, 199) by age nine or ten, life itself is seen as only an intermediary phase on the way to literary immortality. More specifically, he explains, along with the discovery of his "vocation" as a writer,

je découvris que le Donateur, dans les Belles-Lettres, peut se transformer en son propre Don, c'est-à-dire en objet pur. Le hasard m'avait fait homme, la générosité me ferait livre; je pourrais couler ma babillarde, ma conscience, dans des caractères de bronze, remplacer les bruits de ma vie par des inscriptions ineffaçables, ma chair par un style, les molles spirales du temps par l'éternité, apparaître au Saint-Esprit comme un précipité du langage. . . . Je n'écrirais pas pour le plaisir d'écrire mais pour tailler ce corps de gloire dans les mots. (Sartre 1964a, 160–61)

[I discovered that in belles-lettres the Giver can be transformed into his own gift, that is, into a pure object. Chance had made me a man, generosity would make me a book. I could cast my missive, my mind, in letters of bronze; I could replace the rumblings of my life by irreplaceable inscriptions, my flesh by a style, the faint spirals of time by eternity, I could appear to the Holy Ghost as a precipitate of language. . . . I would not write for the pleasure of writing, but in order to carve that glorious body in words. (Sartre 1964c, 193–94)

The aspiring writer yearns to become a book; to accede to the permanence of bronze; to replace the ephemeral noise of his life with everlasting inscriptions, and the pliancy of time itself with the intransigence of eternity. More even than in the ideas expressed here, the ideal synthesis is inscribed in the very grain of Sartre's carefully wrought prose, and specifically in the multiple resonances of particular words: "couler" [to cast] applies to writing, thought, metallurgy, and typography; "corps" is at once the writer's body and his corpus. In a similar vein, remarked David d'Angers in 1837 (anticipating here, as elsewhere, the later evolution of statuemania), "La sculpture est le livre qui est chargé de transmettre aux époques les plus reculées non les notes sur la vie d'un homme, non une nomenclature de traits, mais le poème, l'apothéose d'une âme noble" [Sculpture is a book whose duty it is to transmit to the most distant of times not the details of the man's life, nor a record of his features, but a poem, a noble soul's apotheosis] (David d'Angers 1958, 1.399). Writer and sculptor thus use mirror images of the same metaphor to envision the great man's passage into eternity: Sartre construes the book as a monument; David d'Angers, the monument as a book.

Growing up during the early years of the twentieth century, Sartre had an understanding of literature as a heroic, monumental enterprise, an understanding informed by an "illusion rétrospective" [retrospective illusion] (Sartre 1964a, 166; 1964c, 199) that was not an idiosyncrasy of his, nor even of the grandfather who instilled it in him. Rather, it was characteristic of France in the first decades of the Third Republic: "ce mirage-là naît spontanément de la culture" [that mirage is born spontaneously of culture] (Sartre 1964a, 167; 1964c, 199). This ideal synthesis of writer, work, and monument was, from a Sartrean viewpoint, a collective neurosis.

The Manliness of Letters

Longtemps j'ai pris ma plume pour une épée: à présent je connais notre impuissance.
—Jean-Paul Sartre, *Les Mots* (1964a, 211)

[For a long time, I took my pen for a sword; I now know we're powerless]
—Jean-Paul Sartre, The Words (1964c, 253–54)

The nineteenth-century world of letters was a man's world, from which women were largely excluded. Accordingly, in the age of Balzac, Hugo, Flaubert, Zola, *and* Sand, both literature itself and the monument—in whose ideal image literature was cast—were seen as not only masculine, but also phallic.

As a microcosm of a deeply patriarchal society, the literary establishment was predominantly male as well, both in its makeup and outlook. For example, the *Société des gens de lettres*, the budding professional writers' organization (founded in 1838) was overwhelmingly male. The more venerable and exclusive *Académie française* was strictly male, and remained so until the induction of Marguerite Yourcenar in 1980 (although some progressive voices in the nineteenth century did argue for admitting women, particularly George Sand, even if she remained unenchanted by the idea; cf. below). The lopsidedly male membership in such organizations points to deep-rooted beliefs, attitudes, and prejudices that made French society balk at the idea of women as writers, and especially as great writers.

For one thing, literature was considered too public an occupation for women. The development of a vast literary marketplace, together with the period's broad veneration of writers,

and the spread of powerful new means for disseminating literary fame gave writers more public exposure than ever before. The public spotlight was an acceptable, indeed a desirable place for talented, ambitious men, but not for women. Respectable ladies belonged in the home, a theme amply illustrated by Daumier's lithograph series, *Les Bas-bleus* [The Bluestockings]. In these images, all manner of disasters—from adultery to shoe polish in the hot chocolate—befall households in which the woman neglects her conjugal and domestic duties to entertain literary aspirations. In an absolute sense, of course, a *femme publique* was a prostitute. By extension though, any public activity was suspect. It was often assumed that women who ventured outside the domestic sphere, as performers, creative artists, or writers, were of dubious morality: "La femme artiste ne peut être qu'une catin" [The woman artist can only be a slut] is how Flaubert's *Dictionary* formulates this particular received idea, one of several entries under the heading "Artistes" (Flaubert 1979, 489). Promiscuity (real or imagined) was thus censured in women writers, while tolerated, expected, even applauded in their male counterparts. It offered proof of exemplary virility and wide-ranging curiosity, qualities considered essential to the male literary imagination.

Despite such obstacles in their path, more women than ever before sought open, public recognition as writers. The development of the literary marketplace and rapid expansion of journalism did indeed create ample new opportunities, including ones for women. A work like Daumier's *Bas-bleus* attests both to women's emergence as authors and, in its virulence, to the anxiety this generated among men. Such a fuss was made about women writers because they posed a threat: ostensibly, to common sense, the French language, bourgeois values, or domestic tranquility. More profoundly and plausibly, women writers threatened male cultural hegemony. Thus Daumier, like so many of his artistic and literary peers, dismissed female counterparts as inferior for, while they could not prevent women from becoming writers, they could refuse to take their work seriously. With women of letters relegated to mediocrity, Parnassus could remain a men's club, much like what is represented in Nadar's *Panthéon*.

There were a number of important ways in which nineteenth-century France's male-dominated culture excluded women from the exalted category of literary greatness. A great writer was a genius, and genius itself considered inherently male. A female genius was therefore an impossible figure: a contradiction in terms; a freak of nature; at best, a man in disguise. Substantial literary production, while generally praised in men, was denigrated in women. A man who wrote prolifically might well—talent permitting—be constructing a monument, whereas a woman was just excreting pages: "La copie est une fonction chez madame Sand" [Writing, for Madame Sand, is a bodily function], remarked Gautier (Fermigier 1976, 9), for example. In addition, faced with the new uncertainties of the marketplace, the male literary world looked backward, emulating time-worn models of military-aristocratic heroism and distinction that were considered inappropriate for women. Men of letters alone were fit to do battle in the literary "arena" and, when successful, were rewarded with the ultimate heroic tribute—a traditionally male form—the monument.

Monuments had long been the province of men, not women, because they honored the virile glory of warriors and rulers. In her remarkable poem "Un arc de triomphe," Marceline Desbordes-Valmore both recognizes and subtly dismantles this heroic, male tradition of the monument (Desbordes-Valmore 1973). The use of the indefinite article in the title already relativizes the triumphancy of the arch and the military glory it celebrates. In the body of the poem, and particularly in the last two stanzas, Desbordes-Valmore goes much further:

La guerre est un cri de cigale
Pour l'oiseau qui monte chez Dieu;
Et le héros que rien n'égale
N'est vu qu'à peine en si haut lieu.

Voilà pourquoi les hirondelles,
À l'aise dans ce bâtiment,
Disent que c'est à cause d'elles
Que Dieu fit faire un monument.

(2.488)

[War is like a cricket's cry for the heavenbound bird;

And the incomparable hero
Can barely be seen from such a high spot.

That is why swallows feel at home in this building,
And say that it was for them
That God built this monument.]

Here the swallow, a recurrent figure of womanhood and maternity in Desbordes-Valmore's work, offers an alternative, feminine view of the monument. Seen from this perspective, the incomparable hero to whom the arch presumably pays tribute, shrinks into obscurity. By the end of the last stanza, moreover, the swallow's vision literally deconstructs the monument, transforming it from a man-made into a natural entity ("That God built"). Insofar as Desbordes-Valmore hands over the grandiose monument to a gentle mother bird, her vision remains a utopian one, in sharp contrast to the reality of a patriarchal culture bent on revering its great men. In another sense, Desbordes-Valmore's poem registers the historical decline in a certain warlike tradition of the monument. This decline was accompanied by a turn toward the commemoration of cultural heroes and the values they embodied, as Delacroix recognizes in an article on "Le Poussin," commenting on the recent plans for a monument to the seventeenth-century painter: "Le Poussin a attendu deux cent cinquante ans cette fameuse souscription à sa statue. . . . S'il eût brûlé seulement deux villages, il n'eût pas attendu aussi longtemps" [Poussin waited two hundred-fifty years for this notorious subscription for his statue . . . Had he burned but two villages, he would not have waited as long] (Delacroix 1923). Delacroix's remark exposes the long-standing historical link between monuments and military might, while also acknowledging that things had indeed changed over the past two centuries, to allow for the consecration of less bellicose *grands hommes*. Still, while monuments in nineteenth-century France increasingly honored not warriors, nor rulers, but cultural heroes like Poussin or Hugo, such figures did continue to be almost exclusively male, and were considered every bit as virile as their predecessors. In other words, on the real and imaginary pedestals of the French nation, great men of arms were supplanted by great male artists and writers, wielding paintbrushes and pens "mightier than swords." Great men of letters, in particular, were seen in downright phallic terms.

In nineteenth-century France, male literary greatness was associated closely—though covertly—with the phallus, that primordial embodiment of masculine power and prerogative. However, despite recent critical interest in gender issues and in the aesthetic and ideological implications of the body, this persistent identification of revered male writers with the phallus has attracted little critical attention. Perhaps such an oversight has occurred because the identification between writer and phallus was articulated across traditional boundaries between text and image, high and low art, canonical and marginal works, private and public realms. In addition, it was potentially obscene and thus not expressed openly. It was attenuated, indeed veiled, in various ways: by confidentiality in more private contexts; by indirectness of reference in more public ones; and, by mitigation through irony, innuendo, and humor. This elaborate game of hide and seek served, on the one hand, to maintain propriety, while on the other hand, as a sort of striptease of the signifier, it sustained the phallus's substantial symbolic value. Contemporary scholarship, however, thwarted perhaps by the nineteenth century's own veiling of the literary phallus, has largely overlooked this fruitful area of inquiry.

A broad range of evidence though—from notions about literary "paternity" and mighty pens, to caricatures of prominent male writers brandishing phallic attributes, to Flaubert's musings on overcoming writer's block through erection, to Rodin's prodigiously phallic Balzac monument—reveals a pervasive "phallic imaginary" underlying the period's conception of literary greatness. Superior men of letters were generally envisioned as virile figures. Likewise, inferior ones could be dismissed as impotent, even castrated, and women largely excluded from serious consideration as writers because, in the crudest sense, they just did not have it. Moreover, as Margaret Waller's work on fictions of impotence in the French romantic novel suggests, apparent exceptions to the ideal of the virile male writer actually confirm the prevailing orthodoxy (Waller 1993). "When," asks Waller rhetorically, "are men's claim to feminization and their complaints of impotence a ruse that helps maintain patriarchal power?" (3). Within the context of male dominance and of halting incursions therein by emergent women's movements toward the beginning and end of the century, swooning romantics and their decadent aesthete successors could affect impotence as a subterfuge, all the better to promote and profit from the reigning patriarchy. In this sense, flaunting impotence and flaunting virility are comparable, compensatory reactions to "anxiety about the devaluation of men's literary work and [the] crisis of male identity" (7).

Flaubert's frank correspondence with his nephew Ernest Feydeau provides the most explicit expression of such links between phallic and creative power, and of underlying tensions between weakness and strength, flaccidity and tumescence, oblivion and creation, that inform this phallic vision of male literary production. On December 19, 1858, for example, Flaubert described overcoming writer's block as a prolonged, masturbatory struggle to attain erection:

À chaque ligne, à chaque mot, la langue me manque et l'insuffisance du vocabulaire est telle, que je suis forcé à changer les détails très souvent. J'y crèverai, mon vieux, j'y crèverai.
N'importe, ça commence à m'amuser bougrement. Enfin l'érection est arrivée, monsieur, à force de me fouetter et de me manustirper. Espérons qu'il y aura fête. (Flaubert 1973)

[With each line, each word, language fails me and vocabulary is so inadequate that I must quite often change details. This'll kill me, old chum, it'll kill me. But it doesn't matter, this is starting to be damned amusing.
Finally, sir, by whipping myself up and manhandling myself, the erection has come. Let's hope a good time's in store.]

Similarly, on December 12, 1857, Flaubert wrote:

Pour me remonter le moral, je vais me livrer, dans le sein de la capitale, à des débauches monstrueuses, ma parole d'honneur! J'en ai envie. Peut-être qu'en me fourrant quelque chose dans le c . . . , ça me ferait b . . . le cerveau. J'hésite entre la colonne Vendôme et l'obélisque. Je ris, mais je ne suis pas gai. J'ai déjà, il est vrai, passé par des époques pareilles, et je ne m'en trouvais que plus vert ensuite. Mais ça dure trop! ça dure trop!

[To lift my spirits, I'm going right into the heart of the capital, to indulge in monstrous debauchery, take my word for it! I want to. Maybe by shoving something in my a[ss], that'll give my brain a h[ard-on]. I'm hesitating between the Vendôme column and the obelisk. I laugh, but my heart is heavy. It's true, I've gone through times like this before, and just felt renewed afterwards. But this has lasted too long! too long!]

In this homoerotic fantasy of grandiose proportions, Flaubert imagines himself penetrated by a giant column or obelisk, and absorbing the virility of the monument, to achieve the "mental erection" he needs to write—perhaps transposing, in a queer register, folk traditions in which women seek to cure infertility by visiting, touching, communing with megaliths. True, while playing the skeptical traveler in his *Voyage en Bretagne*, Flaubert had readily dismissed an "ithyphallic" interpretation of the prehistoric monuments at Carnac (Flaubert 1989, 133), and he would later poke fun at amateur archaeologists Bouvard and Pécuchet for overindulging in such a view: "pour Bouvard et Pécuchet tout devint phallus" [for Bouvard and Pécuchet, everything became a phallus] (Flaubert 1979, 180). Still, as a careful collector of commonplaces in his *Dictionnaire des idées reçues*, he could not help but note the provocative shape of the obelisk, and more generally of monuments like it, as well as the suggestive ambivalence of the word "erection" itself. In any case, in both letters, the erection is seen as the magic, vital principle that makes writing possible. The intimacy of personal correspondence and the self-deprecating irony of tone here allow Flaubert to posit the phallus as the very core of the writer's creative faculties.

In less private contexts, similar points of view were also expressed, but less explicitly. Numerous contemporary caricatures of Victor Hugo, for example, depicted him with phallic attributes: not only pens, but sceptres, swords, flagposts, lyres, even exclamation points (fig. 8) (cf. also Georgel 1985, 3, 93–94, 113, 117, 205, 209, 219, 224, 251, 392, 396) . While the frequency of these motifs was tempered by the relative indirectness of the reference and humor of the context, such works nonetheless manifested a phallic vision of Hugo, consonant with the period's general conception of literary greatness and, as we shall see, with Hugo's sense of his own exceptional virility, as well as with his visual imagination's predilection for phallic shapes.

Diverse biographical and textual evidence from the 1830s also shows Balzac, like Hugo, subscribing to—and envisioned through—a phallic view of literary greatness. In particular, Balzac's contemporaries were fascinated and delighted by his curious relationship to his legendary cane. In 1834, Balzac acquired an unfashionably large, elaborate, turquoise-encrusted walking stick, from which he promptly became inseparable: indeed, the cane became "cette partie intégrante de son être" [this integral part of his being], according to Balzac's publisher Werdet. In *La Canne de Balzac* [Balzac's Cane], Lucien Dällenbach observes that the cane came to be seen as both emblem and instrument of Balzac's literary prowess, not only by Balzac, but also by his contemporaries (1996). Among the period's many visual and verbal representations of Balzac's famous cane, three hold particular interest for our purposes here: Dantan Jeune's popular comic statuettes of the novelist, Grandville's sketch for a caricatural apotheosis of Balzac, and Delphine de Girardin's novel, *La Canne de M. de Balzac* [M. De Balzac's Cane]. The first of Dantan's 1835 statuettes (fig. 9) depicts Balzac sporting an exaggeratedly large, chest-high version of his cane. The second statuette, now lost but of which there remains a detailed engraving (fig. 10), took Balzac's identification with his cane to its logical extreme, depicting him simply as the cane, topped with his familiar long hair and tophat. As we shall see, this image prefigures Rodin's prodigiously phallic Balzac monument, both conceptually and iconographically—and it is worth noting, in this connection, that Dantan was apparently no stranger to erotic statuary, for a number of his contemporaries attest to the existence of his licentious "secret museum," which disappeared unfortunately after his death (Sorel 1989, 40). Along similar lines, Grandville's extraordinary sketch, (fig. 11), undated but clearly from after 1835 (we see the first Dantan statuette here), depicts a giant Balzac grasping a giant stick between his

Fig. 8. Charles Gilbert-Martin, *Le vieux Orphée (Old Orpheus).* © Photothèque des musées de la ville de Paris.

Fig. 9. Dantan jeune, *Balzac*. © Photothèque des musées de la ville de Paris.

Fig. 10. Théodore Maurisset, woodcut of Dantan jeune, *La canne de Balzac* (*Blazac's cane*).
© **Photothèque des musées de la ville de Paris.**

Fig. 11. J. J. Grandville, *Projet d'éventail (Project for a fan)* [with Balzac surrounded by characters from *The Human Comedy*]. © Photothèque des musées de la ville de Paris.

legs. Rays of creative brilliance extend outward from this staff, as does the crowd of Balzac's characters who, in turn, carry him along in a triumphal procession. Yet, unlike the statuette, which displays a real cane, the giant Balzac figure holds a *marotte*, or jester's stick, with bells on it and a head at top—a carnivalesque element, like the infant's scatalogical doodlings in the caricature of Hugo as sculptor, that benignly subverts the great man's literary glory, all the better to affirm it.

Delphine de Girardin's 1836 novel also stresses the creative power that the cane bestows upon Balzac for, when held in the left hand, it supposedly makes him invisible, giving him unrivaled powers of observation. In addition, Girardin comments suggestively on the cane itself, which the novel's protagonist Tancrède first notes at the opera:

> Sur le devant d'une loge d'avant-scène se pavanait une CANNE.—Était-ce bien une canne? Quelle énorme canne! à quel géant appartient cette grosse canne?

> Sans doute c'est la canne colossale d'une statue colossale de M.de Voltaire. Quel audacieux s'est arrogé le droit de la porter?

> Tancrède prit sa lorgnette et se mit à étudier cette *canne-monstre*....

> Quelle raison avait engagé M. de Balzac à se charger de cette massue? Pourquoi la porter toujours avec lui? Par élégance, par infirmité, par manie, par nécessité? Cachait-elle un parapluie, une épée, un poignard, une carabine, un lit de fer? (Girardin 1946, 87, 98)

[Along the edge of a front-box there paraded a CANE.—Was it indeed a cane? What an enormous cane! to what giant does this great cane belong?

No doubt it's the colossal cane from M. de Voltaire's colossal statue. What audacious fellow thinks he has the right to carry it?
Tancrède took up his opera glass and began to study this *monster-cane* ...
What had moved M. de Balzac to equip himself with this club? Why always carry it with him? Out of elegance, infirmity, obsession, necessity? Was it hiding an umbrella, a sword, a dagger, a rifle, an iron bed?]

Through a series of probing questions and comparisons with other phallic objects, Girardin stresses the cane's provocative shape and prodigious size and speculates on its provenance. Perhaps this is the "colossal" cane from a "colossal" statue of Voltaire, and "audacious" Balzac has "usurped" it. In one sense, this cane would simply be an emblem of literary distinction, conferring upon Balzac a status comparable to Voltaire's. In a profounder sense though, Girardin is venturing a provocative variation on standard promethean and oedipal themes, whereby Balzac would accede to literary greatness by stealing his exalted literary forefather's phallus. Significantly as well, at a time before statuemania per se, but when a figure like David d'Angers was already theorizing its later development, Girardin posits the cane as the magic, veiled phallus that gives power and prestige to the literary monument and to the writer it represents—articulating much the same connection between writer and phallus through statuary that would inform statuemania, culminating in Rodin's 1898 *Balzac*.

The larger framework of Girardin's narrative and her own situation as an author invite this sort of reading. First of all, in the broader context of the story, the cane acts as an instrument of sexual union, magically uniting the young protagonist Tancrède with his sweetheart Clarisse, when Balzac lends it to him. It also dissuades the talented young woman from pursuing a budding career as a writer. As the last lines of the novel inform us,

Tancrède emmena sa jeune femme à Blois, chez sa mère. Clarisse quitta Paris sans regrets; elle oublia les succès qu'elle y pouvait obtenir; ses voeux avaient été comblés au-delà de ses espérances. À Paris, elle n'était venue chercher que la gloire . . . elle y avait trouvé le bonheur.
Qu'est devenue la canne? dira-t-on.
VOUS ALLEZ LE SAVOIR:
Elle est retournée aux mains de M. de Balzac, et . . .
LES HÉRITIERS BOIROUGE
vont paraître!! (364–65)
[Tancrède brought his young wife to Blois, to his mother's. Clarisse left Paris with no regrets; she forgot about the success she might have had there; her wishes had been fulfilled, beyond her hopes. In Paris, she had only come to seek glory . . . she found happiness there.

What came of the cane? you might ask.
YOU SHALL KNOW.
It is back in M. de Balzac's hands, and . . .
THE BOIROUGE HEIRS
is going to be released!!]

The return of Balzac's cane marks a return to the reigning phallocracy of the nineteenth-century literary world. Clarisse leaves behind Paris, crucible of literary glory, for tranquil domesticity as a provincial wife, whereas the great male author, repossessed of his manly talisman, continues to produce his monumental *oeuvre*. This all resonates deeply with Delphine de Girardin's own predicament as a reasonably successful author in her own right, overshadowed however by illustrious male peers like Balzac, and her husband, the influential journalist, writer, and publisher Émile de Girardin. In her novel, before the last-minute retreat into orthodoxy, she indulges in a long fantasy of liberation from contemporary gender norms, imagining a literary *monde à l'envers* in which the great male author can be divested of his phallic cane, and a young woman can aspire freely to literary glory.

Thus, from evidence as varied as caricatures, novels, and correspondence there emerges a revealing pattern of associations in which the unsuccessful literary aspirant's putative impotence, even castration, contrasts sharply with the great writer's supposed virility as both creator and cultural hero. This is illustrated particularly well by Henri Demare's caricature "La fête de Victor Hugo, L'ordre et la marche de la fête, Engueulade par E. Zola" (1881) [Victor Hugo's birthday celebration. Order of the processional, Tirade by E. Zola] (fig. 12), which sets Zola's weakness against Hugo's power. The historical context here was upstart Zola's apparent dissent from the near-universal acclaim accorded Hugo at the time. While having admired Hugo during the Second Empire, Zola resented the poet's recent criticism of *L'Assommoir* [The Dram Shop] as too pessimistic, and accused him in turn of lapsing into "gâtisme humanitaire" [humanitarian senility] (Laster 1984, 175). In the composition, Hugophiles Auguste Vacquerie and Paul Meurice lead the procession in honor of Hugo's eightieth year, with the poet himself as a giant head, rising forcefully out of a tree planted in a ceremonial cart. On a discordant

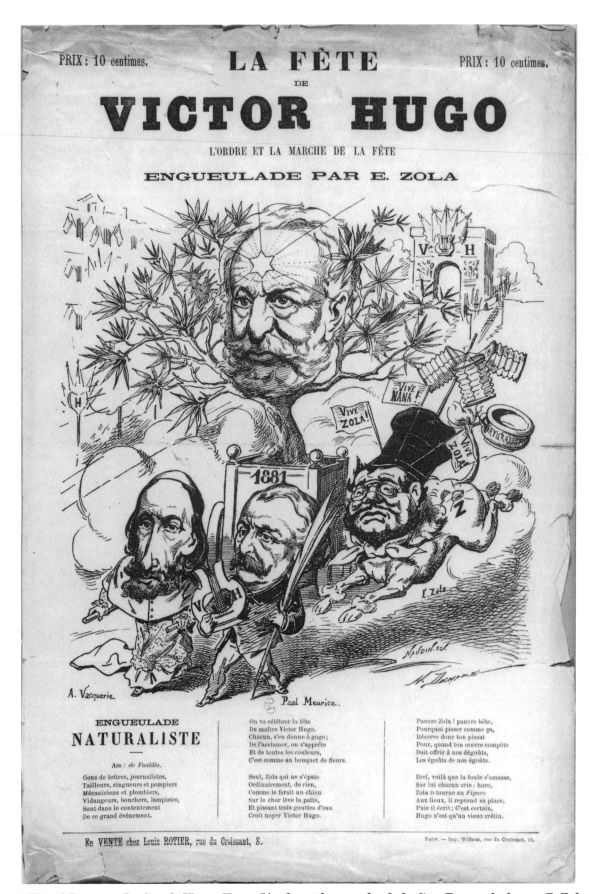

Fig. 12. Henri Demare, *La fête de Victor Hugo, L'ordre et la marche de la fête, Engueulade par E. Zola* (*Victor Hugo's celebration, Processional, An Earful from E. Zola*). © Photothèque des musées de la ville de Paris.

note Zola, depicted as a small dog, runs alongside, chamberpot tied to his tail, with little flags
announcing "Long live Zola!" and "Long live
Nana!" stuck in his hat. The "naturalist tirade"
below explains,

> Seul, Zola qui ne s'épate
> Ordinairement, de rien,
> Comme le ferait un chien
> Sur le char lève la patte,
> Et pissant trois gouttes d'eau
> Croit noyer Victor Hugo.

[Only Zola, who usually does not get worked up
over anything, lifts his leg on the cart as a dog
would and, pissing three drops of water, thinks he
can drown Victor Hugo.]

The text reduces the pursuit of literary glory
to a pissing contest, a crude display of manly
might in which Zola's efforts are hopelessly inadequate. Of course, in the image, we do not
actually see little dog Zola tinkling on big man
Hugo. Instead, the caricature suggests Zola's
impotence relative to Hugo in somewhat sub-
tler ways. Zola's myopia is exaggerated, his
body tilts downward, and the floppy bow beneath his chin, the fluffy tufts of fur round his
ankles and neck, together with the ample cur-
vature of his buttocks, combine to give him a
curiously feminine air. In contrast, Hugo's gaze
is powerfully penetrating and, with his vigorous "trunk" thrusting proudly upward toward
a bulging head, he looks remarkably like a
distended phallus. Hugo is also the principal
figure in the procession that forms the central, diagonal axis of the composition. Beyond
simply honoring Hugo, this parade aligns and
associates him with revealing emblems of the
great male writer: in the distance, the heroic
Arc de Triomphe, emblazoned for the occasion
with Hugo's initials; and, in the foreground, an
oversized pen, at once a conventional writerly
attribute (like the lyre Meurice carries in his
other hand) and, through its generous proportions and upright position, a suggestive phallic
proxy. While Hugo appears to be firmly "rooted"
and to move forward with unwavering deliberateness, Zola seems to float tentatively in mid
air, and does so at an odd angle, off to one
side of the image. Visually out of sync with the
procession, he is cut off from the celebration of

male literary greatness that it conveys. On the
most obvious level, the caricature simply acts
out the message already implied by the word-
ing and typography of the title above it, which
features "La Fête de Victor Hugo" in large, bold
characters, while relegating the "Engueulade
par E. Zola" to much smaller, less visible type.
Zola's efforts to disparage Hugo and promote
himself are made then to seem as fruitless as
they are ignoble, in light of the lavish public
tribute being paid Hugo here and of Zola's clear
marginalization from it. Just beneath the surface of the caricature, though, as the text of the
"tirade" confirms, there also lies a phallic vision
of Victor Hugo himself, and of literary greatness
in general.

This phallic vision of literary greatness entered its final, most grandiose phase from about
1870 to 1914, with "statuemania," as unprecedented numbers of public monuments were
raised to honor the nation's great men, particularly writers. Contributing to the phallic aura
of such works were the suggestive hardness
of their constituent materials and emphatic
verticality of their design, as well as the fact
that their raising was commonly designated
by the architecturally/anatomically ambivalent
term "érection." Indeed, in Flaubert's *Dictionnaire des idées reçues* [Dictionary of received
ideas], which he worked on in the 1870s, as
statuemania swung into high gear, the entry
for ÉRECTION reads,

> Ne se dit qu'en parlant des monuments
> "L'érection de l'Obélisque."
> "L'érection de l'Hercule Farnèse a eu lieu
>   hier aux Tuileries: beaucoup de dames y
>   assistaient"(Journal Officiel).
>   (Flaubert 1979, 513)

> [ERECTION
> Only said when speaking of monuments.
> "The erection of the Obelisk."
> "The erection of the Farnese Hercules took place
>   yesterday in the Tuileries: many ladies took
>   part in this."]

Here, Flaubert progressively, insidiously appro-
priates commonplaces, stock phrases, and inept
official prose to expose not only the physiological meaning of "erection," but also the broader
homology between monument and phallus that
the word implies—an identification between

monument and phallus deeply ingrained enough in the nineteenth-century imagination to figure among received ideas, yet covert enough to require Flaubert's linguistic excavation. The period's identification of writer and phallus was likewise deep-rooted and concealed. These identifications converged, moreover, in the phenomenon of literary statuemania. With the "erection" of great men of letters such a regular, public spectacle, and with so many literary monoliths filling public space, the writer, the monument, and the phallus became ever more closely associated—a development that would culminate in the extraordinary tumescence of Rodin's 1898 *Balzac*, yet was prefigured by the raising of the Obelisk of Luxor, six decades earlier.

Indeed, it is the Obelisk that recurs in Flaubert's musings on literary and monumental "erections." A gift from Egyptian Pasha Mehemet Ali, this ancient artifact was installed in the center of the *place de la Concorde* in 1836, where the guillotine once stood and Louis XVI was beheaded. Created not in modern France but in ancient Egypt (ca. 1250 B.C.), it commemorates no specific individual nor episode from French history and instead, complicit with the July Monarchy's attempts to ignore the past, obscures the founding event of postrevolutionary France, the regicide that broke definitively with the *Ancien régime*. Influential commentators from Hugo, Borel, Chateaubriand, and Michelet through Denis Hollier have therefore seen this monument as an anomaly, willfully irrelevant to the French experience and anticommemorative in nature: a relic from a distant time and land, strategically placed to conceal France's recent troubles, that ultimately stands for nothing. As Todd Porterfield argues, however, the obelisk plays a far more vital and complex role, bound up with France's national and imperial strivings at the time:

> Although many contemporary commentators want to have the obelisk stand for "nothing," the obelisk was inserted at this spot to negotiate the conflicting legacies of monarchal, revolutionary, and Napoleonic memories and monuments. It was placed there to conceal and suppress internal threats, to give France instead an urban, ideological, and national center to be read horizontally through space from the Arc de Triomphe, to Egypt,

to Algeria, and backward in time to the Roman emperors and pharaohs, circumventing the untidy political menaces hounding France since 1789. In short, the obelisk was enlisted to do what Tocqueville would recommend for France in 1840: it substituted France's "revolutionary passion" with a "national passion" founded on imperial expansion in the East. (Porterfield 1998, 15)

I would argue that the obelisk also offers a key iconographical and conceptual prototype for the latter nineteenth century's abundant monumental production, especially for early Third Republic statuemania. Diverse visual and verbal renderings of the obelisk—from prints to statuettes, from engineer Lebas' illustrated account of raising the monolith on to Flaubert's obscene references to its "erection"—reveal central features of later nineteenth-century monuments, namely: embodying the greater glory of the nation; figuring a heroic, male-dominated vision of French cultural superiority through a phallic form; and compensating rather than simply commemorating.

Engineer Jean-Baptiste-Apollinaire Lebas's 1839 account of raising the Obelisk in the *place de la Concorde* evidences the shift from a more overtly martial and political conception of the monument toward a seemingly more peaceful, ideologically oriented, "cultural" one. First, he notes, while the idea of bringing back an Egyptian obelisk was generally attributed to Napoleon, the great military man never executed this plan. When brought to France in the 1830s, the Obelisk was not a trophy of conquest, but rather a gift from Egyptian Pasha Mehemet Ali. To be sure, it might still recall the Egyptian campaign:

> Un événement dont l'influence a rejailli avec tant d'éclat sur les sciences et les arts, qui en a agrandi la carrière et étendu le domaine, méritait d'être symbolisé en quelque sorte par un monument élevé au sein de la capitale, en témoignage de reconnaissance pour les héros et surtout pour les savants qui y ont participé (Lebas 1839, 1)

> [An event that has so brilliantly revitalized the arts and sciences, that broadened their scope and expanded their dominion, deserved to be symbolized, as it were, by a monument raised in the heart of the capital, to bear grateful witness to the heroes, and above all to the scholars who took part in it.]

With hindsight, though, argues Lebas, this campaign appeared less a military operation than a boon to scholarship and the arts. As a reminder of the Egyptian campaign, the Obelisk celebrated contemporary France's cultural flowering—stimulated, in his view, by contact with the wonders of ancient Egypt.

This already suggests what the Obelisk "symbolized" for Lebas. A *Polytechnique* graduate and leading naval engineer when he tackled the Obelisk, since promoted to "Conservateur du musée naval" [Curator of the naval museum] and "Officier de la légion d'honneur" [Officer of the legion of honor] (Lebas 1839, title page; Sorel 1989, 169), Lebas was a faithful servant of the July Monarchy. His account presents an official view of the newly erected monument as embodying the greatness of the French nation and culture. Raising it was an extraordinary feat of French engineering, "une entreprise audacieuse, dont l'Europe moderne n'offre point d'exemple" [a daring enterprise, unknown to modern Europe] (Lebas 1839, 2). For Lebas, the skillful installation of the Obelisk, like its sheer presence in the capital, confirmed France's status as the contemporary equivalent of ancient Egypt. From the epigraph of his book ("Chaque peuple à son tour a brillé sur la terre, Par les lois, par les arts" [Each of the earth's peoples has had its turn to shine, / By virtue of its laws, its arts]) to its penultimate section on "l'art mécanique chez les anciens et les modernes" [ancient and modern mechanical arts] (187), he positions France as the latter-day avatar of ancient Egyptian civilization, with the Obelisk epitomizing this historical transfer of *grandeur*. The Obelisk thus heralds both Paris's primacy among modern European cities (with it, surpassing even the splendor of Rome) and France's superiority among modern nations.

Lebas' claims here are informed by that peculiarly French brand of synecdoche in which the capital stands for the whole nation and, more specifically, by an emerging notion of Paris as a gallery of national greatness—what June Hargrove (1990) calls "an open-air pantheon." Over the centuries, and particularly from the seventeenth onward, as the French court became fixed at Versailles, Paris grew substantially in size and influence. From Louis XIV on, and especially with Napoleon I, Paris became the center of just about everything in France. Napoleon the military conqueror and centralizing administrator also longed to consolidate French glory—to commemorate it here, on a large scale—though relatively little of this grandiose vision was realized during his reign. Such ambitions remained alive across the century however, particularly through the work and influence of David d'Angers, and ultimately were realized with the explosion of commemorative statuary under the Third Republic throughout France, but particularly in Paris.

As we have seen, what would become the *place de la Concorde* was conceived, in the mid eighteenth century at the tail end of the *Ancien Régime*, as the *place Louis XV*, displaying in its center Bouchardon's equestrian statue of its namesake in an ensemble that, despite some concessions to the emergent Enlightenment ideal of a more just and peaceable monarchy, remained an imposing celebration of royal power. Then, with the Revolution, this became the *place de la Révolution*, the central effigy of the monarch replaced with the guillotine, the instrument of regicide, removed in turn after the Terror, so that the site remained bare for four decades, even though numerous projects to fill the space were envisaged including, under Charles X, Pierre Cortot's plans for a *Monument Expiatoire* in honor of Louis XVI, "intended to recall the royalist account of Louis's martyrdom" (Porterfield 1998, 20). In 1795 (and again in 1830, following its Restoration rededication as *place Louis XV*), the square was rebaptized *place de la Concorde* and made a tribute to national unity ("concorde") and glory, flanked by statues representing France's greatest cities, with the Egyptian monolith placed in the strategic center as a finishing touch to the newly configured ensemble. "[L'Obélisque] s'élève maintenant sur la plus grande, la plus belle de nos places, où il rappelle de glorieux souvenirs" [(The Obelisk] rises now from our grandest, most beautiful square, where it recalls glorious memories], enthused Lebas, disingenuously (Lebas 1839, 12), burying the dubious legacy of the Terror beneath the "glorious memories" of the Egyptian campaign.

But it was not just by celebrating French greatness, and bolstering the current regime through a broadly ideological rather than an overtly political approach, that the Obelisk set a key precedent for Third Republic statuemania.

The well-attended and widely reported spectacle of a massive, public "erection" was also a preview of things to come.

Within a patriarchal, male-dominated society that saw physiological erection as the private, inner core of imagination, creativity, or genius, the phallic monument seemed to concretize and generalize such powers in a spectacular, public way. Within this cultural context, it is not surprising that, from the outset, the French saw the Obelisk as prodigiously phallic; indeed this was already the case when the monument, destined for the *place de la Concorde*, was just on its way from Egypt. Charles Philipon's 1832 lithograph, *Le Monument Expia-poire*, "proposing a diminutive and flaccid pear" for the center of the place, at once condemned the current regime (the "poire," slang for idiot, was reigning monarch Louis-Philippe), and looked back to Cortot's plans for a *Monument Expiatoire* as well as to the entire "succession of failed monuments and aborted regimes" associated with this site (Porterfield 1998, 22). It also looked ahead to the ancient Egyptian monolith, soon to be installed here, whose hard, angular verticality would offer a striking, deeply significant contrast to the soft, rounded form of the pear: "Inserted . . . at the Place de la Concorde, the obelisk reverses France's short-lived rejection of patriarchy during the Revolution. It also reverses France's sense of monumental impotence, which Philipon's limp pear statue had revealed, by introducing someone else's phallic authority" (37). Along similar lines, in 1833, still before the real Obelisk was raised and an anticipatory pasteboard model stood in its place, a print entitled "Obélisque de Luxe-nez" represented the monument as the gigantic, protuberant nose of Count d'Argout, governor of the Bank of France (fig. 13). The nineteenth-century imagination could already envision the Obelisk both as a monument to contemporary extravagance and as a hypertrophied part of the male anatomy. An 1836 *Mémoires de l'Obélisque de Louqsor, écrits par lui-même* [Memoirs of the Obelisk of Luxor; written by himself] presents a likewise anthropomorphized obelisk, whose "coeur de pierre" (1) has almost been burst by Paris's warm welcome, a detail suggesting not only that the monolith has feelings but also that when thus moved—stone constitution notwithstanding—he can become dangerously engorged with blood. Indeed, confesses this voluble Obelisk, he has been especially touched by the beauty of Parisian women:

ce qui m'enchante, moi, vieil amateur qui, à l'exception de Sémiramis et de Cléopâtre (grandes femmes qui aimaient le grand air), n'ai jamais vu que des odalisques voilées, c'est d'avoir à contempler chaque jour tant de beautés, de grâce et d'élégance; parole d'honneur, ce n'est pas pour vous flatter, excellens maris parisiens, mais vous avez des femmes que bien d'autres que moi trouvent charmantes. (11)

[this old lady's man, who only ever saw veiled odalisks—except for Semiramis and Cleopatra (great women who loved the great outdoors)—is delighted by such daily eyefuls of beauty, grace, and elegance; my word, esteemed Parisian husbands, without trying to flatter you, I must say that I am not the only one who finds your wives charming.]

Reading between the lines, one imagines vision engendering form, with the relentless contemplation of feminine charms inducing monumental priapism.

Dating from 1836 as well, Dantan jeune's caricatural statuette of Lebas depicts the engineer holding a pared-down version of the obelisk—his own, personal monolith (fig. 14)—much as the Balzac figures in this series wield (or even become) an equally phallic, over-sized cane. The legend to the published version of the Lebas caricature reads, "L'ingénieur Lebas nous apparaît dressant l'obélisque avec tant de facilité que son lourd fardeau ne l'empêche pas le moins du monde de danser sur une corde raide, et sans balancier" [Engineer Lebas is shown raising the Obelisk with such ease that his heavy load does not in the least prevent him from dancing upon a stiff cord, and without having to steady himself] (Menu 1987, 71). We have already noted Dantan's generally lewd turn of mind and, in particular, his predilection for phallic depictions of great men. In the case of the Lebas statuette, the raising of the Obelisk seems at once a technological exploit and a feat of individual, physical prowess. Moreover, the stiffness of the cord seems both an allusion to the actual raising of the monolith (at the last minute, the tow ropes were moistened so that, in drying, they would tighten, pulling the monument the needed few

Obélisque de Luxe-nez
Pyramide nasicale du juste milieu

Fig. 13. Fortuné Ferogio, *Obélisque de Luxe-nez, pyramide nasicale du juste milieu (Obelisk of Lux-nose, nasal pyramid of the* juste milieu). © Photothèque des musées de la ville de Paris.

Fig. 14. Dantan jeune, *Lebas.* © **Photothèque des musées de la ville de Paris.**

GUSTAVE EIFFEL (1855)

Fig. 15. Albert de Korsad, *Gustave Eiffel.* **Réunion des Musées Nationaux / Art Resource, NY.**

centimeters higher), and suggestive of erectile stiffness. In short, Dantan plays on much the same ambivalence as would Flaubert, appearing to pay tribute to the engineer for both erecting the monument, and having a monumental erection. Spectacular tumescence thus figures the ascendancy of modern French civilization.

As an outstanding feat of French engineering, the raising of the Obelisk also prefigured the yet more emphatically phallic and technologically advanced "erection" of the Eiffel Tower, in 1889, intended to display France's greatness to the world, on the occasion of both the Paris *Exposition Universelle* and centenary of the French Revolution. Albert de Korsad's 1889 caricature of Gustave Eiffel demonstrates moreover that a half century after Lebas's work with the Obelisk, ancient Egyptian structures were still invoked in such instances, and that the great man's accomplishments continued to be envisioned in phallic terms (fig. 15). Eiffel, with Notre-Dame suspended suggestively from his watch-fob at crotch level, flanked by the tower and a relatively smaller pyramid, flaunts his prodigious monument. "À la grandeur de l'oeuvre, on mesure la grandeur de l'homme" [The bigger the work, the bigger the man], reads an inscription on the pyramid: a fitting if equivocal motto as well for Dantan's *Lebas*, or Rodin's *Balzac*.

Hollier dismisses the Obelisk as a dysfunctional monument: "Monuments have commemoration as their function. This one was meant to induce forgetting" (Hollier 1989, 673). To be sure, monuments' ostensible function is commemoration. Yet they also have a substantial capacity for compensation. Indeed, in this sense, it is the Obelisk's ability to "induce forgetting" that helps make it a prototypical nineteenth-century monument. Rising impressively out of the site of the king's execution, it attempts not simply to conceal but to supplant the troubled *mémoire des lieux*, to displace a discordant past with a grandiose new vision of the nation—manifesting the broader compensatory

orientation of nineteenth-century monumental culture, that plays such a crucial role in the literary dream of stone in particular.

It is from this compensatory perspective that we need, ultimately, to understand Flaubert's quest for the writerly erection. Returning to his December 19, 1858 letter to Ernest Feydeau, we see that "érection," synonymous with literary creation, is preceded by a painful, prolonged, nearly aphasic state; is achieved only through great effort; and cannot be counted on to endure and prevail ("Let's hope a good time's in store."). For Flaubert, writing is at best an intermittent process, in which the author now and then "rises" to the occasion. His work emerges out of the abyss, out of an ever-present threat of inadequacy ("vocabulary is so inadequate"), impotence (i.e., inability to achieve the desired tumescence), silence ("language fails me"), even death ("This'll kill me, old chum, this'll kill me"). The writerly erection that enables him to create proceeds from a temporary filling of the void—a process acted out, explicitly, in his earlier letter to Feydeau, as the monumentally sodomized writer finally gets hard.

Paradoxically, while on the one hand Flaubert fancies himself writing books like the pyramids, on the other he remains terror-stricken before the blank page (the fact that his book-pyramid comparison occurs in a letter to the same correspondent as the passage above, and was written just over a year earlier, underlines the close juxtaposition of these views in his imagination). No doubt, Flaubert's legendary neuroses about writing can seem idiosyncratic when compared to the frank logorrhea of contemporaries like Balzac, Dumas, Hugo, Sand, or Zola. Yet Flaubert's underlying view of literary creation figures the broader compensatory pattern within nineteenth-century France's culture of monumentality. As we shall see in the next chapter, this is also the case for a writer like Balzac, who would seek to compensate for a dubious past with his textual monument.

2

Honoré de Balzac: Writing the Monument

Nous devons l'unité de cette oeuvre à une réflexion que M. de Balzac fit de bonne heure sur l'ensemble des oeuvres de Walter Scott. . . . "Il ne suffit pas d'être un homme, il faut être un système, disait-il. . . . Quoique grand, le barde écossais n'a fait qu'exposer un certain nombre de pierres habilement sculptées, où se voient d'admirables figures, où revit le génie de chaque époque, et dont presque toutes sont sublimes; mais où est le monument?

[I]l s'agit donc d'être . . . Walter Scott plus un architecte."

—Félix Davin, "Introduction aux *Études de moeurs au XIXe siècle*" (CH 1.1151–52)

[We owe the unity of this work to M. de Balzac's early reflection upon the whole of Walter Scott's works. . . . "It is not enough to be a man, you must be a system," he said. "While great, the Scottish bard only displayed a certain number of skillfully sculpted stones. Almost all are sublime, depicting admirable figures, and recapturing the genius of each period; but where is the monument?"

It is therefore a question of being Walter Scott plus an architect.]

—Félix Davin, Introduction to the *Studies of 19th-century Mores*

Aujourd'hui, Balzac est mort, et nous n'avons plus que son monument sous les yeux; il nous étonne par sa hauteur, nous restons pleins de respect devant un aussi prodigieux travail. Comment un ouvrier a-t-il pu tailler à lui seul un pareil monde?

—Émile Zola, "Balzac" (1906, 55)

[Today, Balzac is dead, and only his monument remains before our eyes; its height amazes us, such a prodigious work leaves us awestruck. How could one worker fashion such a world by himself?]

—Émile Zola, "Balzac"

"Balzac"

Balzac began to write his monument by fashioning his own identity, burying family ignominy and early personal failure beneath his prodigious literary production. As Proust's *Remembrance of Things Past* would spring from the teacup of involuntary memory, so *The Human Comedy* would proceed from its author's compensatory masquerade as "Balzac."

Characteristically, in his long, polemical introduction to *Le Lys dans la vallée* [The Lily in the Valley] (CH 9.917–66), the author defies his detractors: "Balzac," he insists, is his "nom patronymique" (928). This is and is not a lie. "Balzac" is not his patronymic in a conventional sense, that is, not the name of a long family line. His father, however, while born humble "Balssa," adopted the noble "Balzac" instead, and made a fine administrative career for himself, under the aegis of this impressive, albeit borrowed name.[1]

Like father, like son? Not exactly. For Bernard-François the bureaucrat, assuming an aristocratic name was little more than an *arriviste* ploy to capitalize on the period's rampant social flux. For son Honoré the writer, this move had deeper implications. In nineteenth-century France, with the development of both a faceless, mass public and a pervasive cult of the author, literary figures puzzled over who exactly they were supposed to be and how to frame the most appropriate, desirable, memorable, or just plain marketable image of themselves. From Chateaubriand's political jockeying and autobiographical myth-making; to Stendhal's one-man masked ball[2]; to Sand's gender-bending; to Hugo's successive incarnations as Romantic rebel, incorruptible exile, and benign grandfather of the Republic; to Flaubert's quasi-monastic seclusion; and on to Zola's early claims to scientific objectivity and later posturing in defense of Truth and Justice, nineteenth-century authors sought to define and redefine their identities in the public eye. As a rising star in a world that subjected its literary luminaries to increasing public scrutiny, Honoré de Balzac would be thrown back, again and again, on the question of his own identity and, in turn, on the larger paradoxes of becoming and being famous. More so than any of his siblings, Honoré de Balzac would embrace—and surpass—his father's imposture: the would-be Noble Author had the arms of the aristocratic Balzac d'Entragues family emblazoned not only on his book bindings (cf. above), but also on his carriage, and even on his dinnerplates. Being Balzac rather than Balssa became at once a paranoid obsession and a fount of creative energies. Indeed, the Balssa/Balzac dichotomy at the heart of his sense of self encapsulates a host of fundamental, broader issues within the period's nascent fame culture, juxtaposing past and future, private and public, provincial and parisian, commonness and greatness, obscurity and celebrity. But to understand the full resonance of Balssa/Balzac, we need to return

to the very beginnings of the author's literary vocation.

In 1819, as Bernard-François Balzac reached the end of a long career, his son embarked upon his own. Abandoning the law, Honoré de Balzac traded a safe but pedestrian future for the uncertain yet shimmering rewards of literature, moving into a *mansarde* on the rue Lesdiguières, where he devoted himself to the pursuit of literary glory. Less than two weeks later, though, his paternal uncle Louis Balssa was guillotined, perhaps wrongly, for strangling a pregnant farmhand he was suspected of seducing.[3] The *parvenu* Balzac family made no effort to save Louis, however, and their correspondence makes no mention whatsoever of this whole *ténébreuse affaire*. "Il y a une éloquence du silence," [This silence is eloquent,] notes André Maurois. "Le souci de la respectabilité l'emportait sur le devoir de solidarité, et même de justice. On était de bons bourgeois, mais sans excès de bonté" [Concern for respectability won out over their sense of solidarity, and even of justice. They were good bourgeois, but not exceedingly good] (Maurois 1965, 44).

Uncle Louis' disgrace was not all that the Balzac family wanted to hide in the summer of 1819. Their son's budding literary vocation was also a potential embarassment. "Songe à mon bonheur si j'illustrais le nom de *Balzac*. Quel avantage de vaincre l'oubli" [Think of my good fortune if I were to illustrate the name Balzac. What a great thing to vanquish oblivion], he wrote his favorite sister Laure on September 6, 1819 (Balzac 1960–69), well aware that, for the moment, such glory remained too hypothetical for comfort. While his parents were willing to bet on his eventual success—providing him with a surprisingly generous 1500 franc annual allowance for two years—they did not, however, want friends in Paris to perceive their son as a shiftless literary dabbler. To maintain appearances, they said that he was visiting with a cousin in Albi, the Balssa's hometown. Amid the family's overriding concern for propriety, there occurred in their minds this disturbing *rapprochement* between Bernard-François' youngest brother and his eldest son. Both represented potential liabilities to the family's hard-won honor. Fortunately, the condemned murderer was already out of sight in sleepy, distant Albi; likewise, the aspiring writer also needed to be relegated, if only temporarily and fictitiously, to that very same place from whence his father had escaped to seek a better life. Such are the precautions one takes, when so little separates success from failure, glory from disaster, Balzac from Balssa.

Ample echoes of all this in Balzac's later work confirm that the events of 1819 dramatized, indeed crystallized his predicament as an aspiring but utterly unknown writer, caught between peasant ignominy, bourgeois respectability, and aristocratic pretensions; shunning notoriety, but craving celebrity; haunted by both the shame of his family's real past and a dream of his own imagined future.[4] Occurring at such a critical juncture in his young life, this curious set of circumstances left a profound mark on his psyche, forever linking the rise of Balzac the writer with the fall of Balssa—as there lingered the threat of this suppressed past returning, to undo all that would have been accomplished.

For Balzac's father, "Balssa" had been undesirable as a socially disadvantageous name. For the son, "Balssa" came to represent a profounder impotence. Balzac's early work, notes Pierre Citron, displays a preoccupation with decapitation that, more than just a Romantic predilection, grew out of the "affaire Balssa":

Certes, . . . la montée du romantisme frénétique a amené chez bien d'autres écrivains l'évocation de la décapitation: en témoignent *Cinq-Mars*, *le Dernier Jour d'un condamné*, *l'Âne mort et la Femme guillotinée* de Janin, . . . *le Rouge et le Noir*. Mais chacun a abordé le thème une seule fois. Balzac seul l'a fait cinq fois au moins (on me dira qu'il écrivait cinq fois plus . . .): c'est sans doute que, sensibilisé dans ce domaine par l'affaire Balssa, il allait avec plus d'insistance que d'autres dans le sens de son époque pour exprimer ses propres obsessions. (Citron 1986, 69; cf. also Beizer 1986).

[To be sure, . . . the rise of frenetic romanticism moved many other writers to evoke decapitations: to wit, *Cinq-Mars*, *The Last Day of a Condemned Man*, Janin's *Dead Ass and the Guillotined Woman*, . . . *The Red and the Black*. But each dealt with the theme only once. Balzac alone did so at least five times (I realize he wrote five times as much . . .): no doubt, the Balssa affair had made him sensitive to this and, riding the trend harder than his contemporaries, he gave voice to his own obsessions.]

For Balzac, moreover, Uncle Louis' beheading seems to have associated "Balssa" with mutilation, with a symbolic castration, making the name antithetical not only to his social aspirations but, more importantly, to his ambitions as a writer—so bound up with a certain phallic imaginary of literary greatness. His dreams of literary glory, virility, nobility, and martial vigor joined together in an ideal of the mighty writer, wielding a pen more powerful than the swords of yore, building his literary edifice with his fertile imagination and, ultimately, becoming one with the formidable hardness of the monument upon passing into posterity. In this sense, *The Human Comedy*, like so many other nineteenth-century monuments, is a compensatory construct: through its elaboration, Balzac exorcises the original emasculation of "Balssa." In particular, like the phallic Obelisk of Luxor, Balzac's towering, textual monument was raised under the July Monarchy, to conceal and supplant the troubled memory of a notorious decapitation, displacing a shameful past with a grandiose vision of glorious possibilities.

In his reading of *Sarrasine*, Roland Barthes virtually ignores the powerful autobiographical implications of the central figure S/Z, just mentioning parenthetically that Z "est dans le nom de Balzac" [is in the name Balzac] (Barthes 1970, 113). Not only though is Z in Balzac, but S stands in its place in Balssa; indeed, the whole S/Z problematic is already contained in the juxtaposition of the writer's real and assumed family names, and echoes in the names of such fictional doubles as Balthazar Claës and Z. Marcas. While Barthes' reading identifies Z as "la lettre de la mutilation . . . la lettre de la déviance" [the letter of mutilation . . . the letter of deviance], it is in fact the letter S that distinguishes Balssa, and thus resonates with the memory of Louis' ignominious fate. As Barthes points out though, S and Z are but mirror images of each other:

S et Z sont dans un rapport d'inversion graphique: c'est la même lettre, vue de l'autre côté du miroir:

Sarrasine contemple en Zambinella sa propre castration. Aussi la barre (/) qui oppose le S de Sarra-Sine et le Z de Zambinella a-t-elle une fonction panique : c'est la barre de censure, la surface spéculaire, le mur de l'hallucination, le tranchant de l'antithèse, l'abstraction de la limite, l'oblicité du signifiant, l'index du paradigme, donc du sens.

[S and Z are related through graphic inversion: it is the same letter, seen from the other side of the mirror. In Zambinella, Sarrasine contemplates his own castration. Moreover, the slash (/) that sets the S in SarraSine against the Z in Zambinella instigates panic: it is the censor's mark, specular surface, hallucinatory wall, cutting edge of antithesis, abstraction of limits, obliqueness of the signifier, index of the paradigm, and therefore of meaning.]

In Balssa, Balzac contemplates the threat of his own "castration." He faces the disturbing possibility that his cherished, noble name could slip to the other side of the mirror—an ever-present menace to his identity made all the more urgent by the vagaries of nineteenth-century spelling: even at the great writer's death, his widow would still receive a bill for a plaster cast of his hand, addressed to "Madame *Balsaque*" (Maurois 1965, 597). For Barthes, the slash separating *S* from *Z* is the linchpin of meaning in the novella *Sarrasine*; in a broader historical and autobiographical context, though, it marks the founding fiction from which so many fictional identities would spring forth, the *roman des origines* at the origin of the Balzacian novel.

Forging Identities

Hier en rentrant chez moi, je vis un nombre incommensurable d'exemplaires de ma propre personne, tous pressés les uns contre les autres à l'instar des harengs au fond d'une tonne. Ils répercutaient dans un lointain magique ma propre figure, comme, lorsque deux glaces se répondent, la lueur d'une lampe placée au milieu d'un salon est répétée à l'infini dans l'espace sans bornes, contenu entre la surface du verre et son tain.
                —Honoré de Balzac, "Théorie du conte"
                        (Balzac 1955–63, 26.682)

[Upon returning home yesterday, I saw a boundless number of copies of myself, all crammed one against the other, like herrings in a barrel. They repeated my image magically on into the distance, just as, when two mirrors stand

opposite each other, the light of a lamp placed in the middle of a room is reproduced infinitely in the limitless space between the glass and its silvering.]
                —Honoré de Balzac, "Theory of the tale"

In the late 1830s, Balzac closed a letter to his friend Auguste de Belloy with:

Votre tout dévoué,
                        VIEUX
                        LOUP
            LE MAR   HEIN?
                        A BOUT
                        TYRE, etc. (Balzac,
1960–69, 3.503 [1838 or 1839])

[Your most devoted,
                        VELOUS
                        KETER
            THE MAR   INER
                        ABOU
                        TYR, etc.]

"Mar" was one of Balzac's nicknames, and root of his journalistic pseudonym "Mar O'C."[5] In this salutation, "Mar" serves as a powerful nominal matrix, with the "etc." after the last item on the list promising infinite metonymic inventions deriving from a single name. That the combination preceding the expansive "etc." is "martyre" is significant as well for, as we shall see at the end of this chapter, Balzac mined a rich martyrological vein, both in elaborating his fiction and in fashioning his own legend. While fanciful, the closing of this letter provides a telling glimpse into Balzac's creative imagination, a *mise-en-abyme* of *The Human Comedy* itself springing from the paradox of his pseudonymous signature—from his imposture as "Honoré de Balzac."

This sort of fictional chain reaction might best be understood as a process of "forging" identities, meaning at once creating and signing falsely—making things and making them up—a duality suggested by the abundance of both creators and forgers in Balzac's work, as well as by the word's Latin root *fabricare*, meaning "to fabricate" both in the sense of "to fashion" and "to lie," connoting at once creation and deception. Yet this process of "forging" actually began well before *The Human Comedy*, indeed from his debut as a writer, the vicissitudes of

Balzac's identity as author were a well-spring of fiction. To trace Balzac's early literary career, from his first scribblings through the beginnings of *The Human Comedy*, is to find intertwined, at every juncture, Balzac's ongoing efforts at self-fashioning, and his emerging plans for a monumental literary project.

At first, the aspiring author did not dare write under his "real" name. Loath to embarrass his family with his youthful "cochonneries littéraires" [literary rubbish] (Balzac, 1960–69, 1.158) he instead, in the 1820s, worked his way through a series of successively less fanciful pseudonymns: principally, "Lord R'Hoone," "Horace de Saint-Aubin," and "Victor Morillon."[6] During this initial pseudonymous period, Balzac already created increasingly elaborate, and increasingly plausible, fictional identities to accompany his pseudonyms—spinning what Pierre Barbéris (1985) has called "biographies mythiques." Concurrently, Balzac also showed his fascination with the monument and nascent interest in developing a monumental project of his own. In 1819, for example, he described the "classical" works of Homer, Virgil, Corneille, and Racine as monuments: "leurs oeuvres sont des monuments admirables dont on peut faire le tour sans pouvoir deviner les secrets de l'architecte" [their works are admirable monuments which you can tour without being able to guess the architect's secrets] (Balzac 1990, 1.594). "Without being able to guess" suggests that Balzac was indeed contemplating how such works were built and, as his correspondence reveals, at about this time he was already trying to create his own "premier monument" (Balzac 1960–69, 1.35–36). By 1823–24, Balzac was trumpeting the potential endurance of a work whose author aimed at literary immortality:

quant à tout ce que la terre pensera de lui, il s'en moquera comme du sable qui s'attache au Parthenon. Il tâche à être quelque chose et quand on veut élever un monument, on ne pense pas aux effrontés qui affichent le spectacle du jour sur la barricade. (1.233)

[as for what the world will think of him, he cares as much as the sand clinging to the Parthenon. He is trying to be something, and when you want to raise a monument, you do not think about those who shamelessly put up posters, on the barricades, for today's show.]

The serious writer strives to frame a monument, comparable to the Parthenon, paragon of enduring beauty and value, inured to the passing "sands" of time and contemporary whim. Conversely, uninspired scribblers can only muster a temporary posting (*affiche,* an emblematically debased, mechanically reproduced, modern form) on a temporary structure (*barricade,* with all its revolutionary associations). Both the medium and its means of support exemplify inconsequentiality, instability, and impermanence. With the bad faith that characterizes much of Balzac's writing on the world of letters, he claims to think only of posterity. But, as so frequently elsewhere, Balzac did think and worry about his literary competitors. Paradoxically, his yearning toward posterity proceeded largely from his concern with the present: his drive to distinguish himself from his contemporaries spurred him to "raise a monument," guiding him toward the eventual design of *The Human Comedy* as a sprawling, textual monument to his own everlasting glory.

In 1826, Balzac turned his back on publishing and tried instead to make his mark as a printer. He lacked business sense, however, and, as Roger Pierrot notes, 1828 would be "l'année du désastre commercial et du retour à la littérature" [the year of commercial failture and of a return to literature] (CH 1.87). In a strange coincidence that one can imagine resonating in Balzac's psyche, the final liquidation of his printing establishment would occur on August 16, the ninth anniversary of his uncle Louis Balssa's execution, thus conflating commercial failure and family ignominy, a double dishonor for which literary success once again promised the only antidote. In April, as he took the first step toward relinquishing his brief career as a printer, abandoning the type foundry he had launched the preceding year, Balzac moved into and furnished an apartment on rue Cassini, hiding under the name of his brother-in-law Surville, in order to rededicate himself to the pursuit of literary glory—recalling the concurrent secrecy and ambition of the aspiring writer's move to the *mansarde* on rue

Lesdiguières, nearly a decade early. Emblematically, in his study on rue Cassini, Balzac placed a statuette of Napoleon, a mini-monument with a message: "Sur le fourreau de l'épée" [On the sword's scabbard,] notes André Maurois, "un bout de papier portait cette phrase: *Ce qu'il n'a pas achevé par l'épée, je l'accomplirai par la plume.* **HONORÉ DE BALZAC**" [was a piece of paper bearing this sentence: *What he did not finish with the sword, I shall accomplish with the pen.* **HONORÉ DE BALZAC**] (Maurois 1965, 130). The bold prediction is underwritten, in capital letters, by the signature that would make it possible: like the pen, synecdoche of the author, the famous name—or rather the name destined for fame—contains in embryonic form the grand works that will bring their author glory. Names for Balzac are a privileged repository: just as characters' names in *The Human Comedy* condense and "store" the narratives we associate with them, the author's name might "contain" his entire novelistic production, a whole world of fictional identities emerging out of his own.

Standing watch over his study, Balzac's plaster Napoleon would presumably have witnessed the selection of this revealing epigraph to the "Avertissement du Gars" (a preface for what would become *The Last Chouan*): "nous avons vu passer tant de grands hommes oubliés qu'il faut entreprendre aujourd'hui quelque chose de monumental pour vivre dans la mémoire des hommes" [we have seen so many forgotten great men pass by that today something monumental must be undertaken, to live on in the minds of men] (CH 8.1668). While attributed to Rivarol, this text may well have been composed by Balzac (8.1668, n. 2). Emerging from the abyss of his early literary and commercial failures, haunted by the towering example of Napoleon, and on the brink of both producing the first text to figure later in *The Human Comedy* and of signing it with his "real" name, Balzac already links his future renown explicitly with the conception of a monumental project.

In 1829, Balzac turned his back on his early literary pseudonyms, signing *The Last Chouan or Brittany in 1800* as "Honoré Balzac"; during the following year, he would integrate the nobiliary particle.[7]

In the 1830 preface to *The Wild Ass's Skin*, he definitively consecrated "Honoré de Balzac" as his authorial signature, by acknowledging authorship of *The Physiology of marriage* after the fact—and would vaunt his literary heroism for so doing, because "il y a péril à l[a] signer" [there is danger in signing it] (CH 10.49),[8] thus further indulging his phantasms about the mighty pen-wielding writer.[9] From this point on, Balzac would continue to sign all literary works with his "real" fake name (even if he still used outright pseudonyms in journalistic writing, as was largely the practice at the time). Significantly, these developments coincided with the writing and publication of his *Scenes of Private Life*, the first global conception for the material that would become *The Human Comedy*. Further evidence of an overarching design for his ambitious project, and the technique of recurring characters, which would enable its elaboration, appeared progressively over the next few years.

The Human Comedy was thus born with its author's public identity as "Honoré de Balzac"— an identity that, in some sense, was rehearsed by his earlier, pseudonymous "biographies mythiques," yet also, in some sense, was a departure from them. Paradoxically, Balzac's attempts to assert the authenticity and legitimacy of his signature invariably conjure up the specter of the pseudonym.[10] Indeed, the name "Honoré de Balzac" functions as the keystone of its author's textual monument by partaking at once of the signature *and* the pseudonym.[11] Etymologically, a pseudonym is a lying name, from the Greek verb *pseudein*, "to lie," pointing up the rich confluence here of authorial deception and literary creation. The name "Honoré de Balzac" at once conceals the biographical truth of the author's ancestry and early literary dabbling, constituting the prototypical "Balzacian" fiction that enables the invention of a vast, populous, and verisimilar fictional world. Balzac's "lying" signature is the sort of fiction that strains to pass itself off as real, much like the entire realist project it engenders, which seeks to blur boundaries between the world within *The Human Comedy* and the world outside. The primordial importance of Balzac's identity in the elaboration of *The Human Comedy* thus proceeds not only from his belief in the quasi-magical power of the name and of the author's signature in particular,[12] but also from the highly ambiguous ontological status of the appellation "Honoré de Balzac," which straddles the real and the fictive—lying, in both senses of the word, at the origin of Balzacian realism.

In the mid 1830s, at a time when Balzac had largely established the framework for his novelistic project and embarked upon writing it, his continued obsession with his assumed name attests to its central importance in his creative enterprise. We discern echoes of Balzac's own situation in his character Lucien Chardon/de Rubempré. In the first part of *Lost Illusions*, for example, published in 1837, Lucien's paramour and promoter Mme de Bargeton justifies the young writer's ascendance before the local *angoumois* nobility:

> elle dit que si les gentilshommes ne pouvaient être ni Molière, ni Racine, ni Rousseau, ni Voltaire, ni Massillon, ni Beaumarchais, ni Diderot, il fallait bien accepter les tapissiers, les horlogers, les couteliers dont les enfants devenaient des grands hommes. . . . le génie était toujours gentilhomme (CH 5.171)

> [she said that if gentlemen could be neither Molière, nor Racine, nor Rousseau, nor Voltaire, nor Massillon, nor Beaumarchais, nor Diderot, then the children of upholsterers, clockmakers, and knifemakers must be accepted as great men. . . . Genius was always gentlemanly]

Literary genius is inherently noble. Still, it helps to have a noble name, so that the public will not underestimate one's true worth, and like his creator, Lucien Chardon adopts a glorious, old name (Rubempré), embellished by the nobiliary particle. The corollary to a true aristocrat (like Vigny) illustrating his venerable name through personal merit is the commoner, like Balzac or his character Lucien, adorning naked talent with the nobility of an assumed name.

A pair of lesser known texts from 1836 reflect back, yet more explicitly, on the vicissitudes of the author's identity: his early experimentation with pseudonyms, the underlying shame of "Balssa," the potential glory but also the precariousness of "Balzac." *Vie et malheurs d'Horace de Saint-Aubin* [The Life and Misfortunes of Horace de Saint-Aubin] offers a definitive farewell to his early pseudonyms; the "Historique du

procès du *Lys dans la vallée*" [Account of the *Lily in the Valley* trial], the most emphatic defense and illustration of his assumed name. Together, they set into play the full range of contradictory possibilities that inform Balzac's efforts to define and refine his identity as a writer, and emerge as the illustrious author of a great work: glory and obscurity, heroism and ignominy, personal merit and family lineage, originality and venerability, legitimacy and illegitimacy, towering monumentality and castration.

The largely forgotten but revealing *Life and Misfortunes of Horace de Saint-Aubin*, written by Balzac but signed by Jules Sandeau,[13] is a short "biography," published as an introduction to the Souverain edition of Saint-Aubin's "oeuvres complètes" (Sandeau 1948). On one level, the edition was simply a marketing ploy to capitalize on Balzac's earlier pseudonymous production, without jeopardizing his growing reputation as author of the *Scenes of Private Life* and *Studies of 19th-century Mores*, the forerunners of *The Human Comedy*. On another level, this publication "killed off" Horace de Saint-Aubin, manifesting Balzac's own evolving conception of the complete works as the author's tomb, and of biography as "life and death writing" (cf. below).

Life and Misfortunes is proffered not just as Horace de Saint-Aubin's last incarnation, but also as the culmination of all Balzac's early "biographies mythiques," for it combines three of his pseudonyms to explain Horace's heritage as the son of "François de Villerglé, comte de Rhoon, seigneur de Saint-Aubin" (34). The Revolution ruins Horace's family and his widowed mother decides that her son should not know of his origins, in order to "préserver sa jeunesse du souffle des ambitions" [protect his youth from ambition's spark] (37). His biography thus recounts his discovery of his noble birth and resultant awakening of his literary aspirations, clearly echoing the intertwining of Balzac's own "discovery" (i.e., invention) of noble origins and pursuit of literary glory. Balzac's phantasms about legitimating his identity loom large here, particularly through insistence on the specular relation between the author and his pseudonymous alter-ego. During Saint-Aubin's parting visit to young Balzac, Honoré receives Horace "comme un frère," and reads him his *Scènes de la vie privée*. Moved, Horace bids farewell to literature: "Je brise ma plume et je rentre dans l'ombre d'où je n'aurais jamais dû sortir" [I do break my pen and return to the shadows from which I should never have emerged] (99). This declaration is all the more significant in light of how the *Notice* construes literary creation:

> Par cette fatalité littéraire qui nous dispute toujours notre paternité réelle pour nous mettre sur le dos les enfants que nous n'avons point faits, on a prétendu que les oeuvres d'Horace de Saint-Aubin étaient sorties d'une plume illustre aujourd'hui . . .

> [Inevitably, our true literary paternity is questioned, while we are given charge of children we never spawned; thus was it claimed that the works of Horace de Saint-Aubin came from a now-famous pen.]

Through this equation of "children" and "works," the phallic pen procreates. In abandoning literature, Horace breaks it, symbolically castrating himself. Demoted from writer to nonwriter, fallen from Olympian heights into the void, Horace returns to a sort of zero degree of glory, that original, castrated state from which Balzac himself escaped to become a writer.

With the threat of castration looming, Balssa cannot be far behind, nor can the desire to compensate with a monumental construction:

> On montre encore . . . les tourelles ruinées d'un château que le comte de Rhoon tenait de ses ancêtres, et que ses ancêtres avaient reçu, dit-on, de la munificence de saint Louis. . . . [Il] l'habitait encore lorsqu'il partit pour aller prendre part au soulèvement de la Vendée. Une heure avant son départ, le comte avait mis de ses propres mains le feu au castel de ses aïeux, . . . La flamme dévora tout et ne laissa sur la colline que quatre tourelles noircies qui portent aujourd'hui le nom du château de *Salbar*. (34–35)

> [One still can see the ruined turrets of a castle that count Rhoon got from his ancestors, and that his ancestors were said to have received from saint Louis' munificence. . . . (He) still lived in it when he left to take part in the Vendée uprising. One hour before his departure, with his own hands, the count set fire to his ancestors' castle. . . . The flames consumed all, leaving upon the hill only four blackened turrets that now are called the castle of *Salbar*.]

The text's use of italics calls attention to this near-anagram of Balssa. Beyond such an obvious connection with the author's real family name and resemblance to his pseudonymous sosie's name (*Saint-Aubin*), Salbar also evokes a whole network of associations with Bernard-François Balzac's abandonment of the name Balssa and pursuit of worldly ambitions.[14] Like Saint-Aubin's father, Bernard-François Balzac had tried to destroy "his ancestors' castle," that is, an edifice named "Balssa." Once again, Louis Balssa lurks beneath the surface, and not only through the anagram, for the castle Rhoon received from his ancestors, who received it from theirs, was originally a gift from the great king *Louis* the Pious. This saintly primogenitor, who established the aristocratic glory of *Salbar*, contrasts with the murdering uncle who confirmed Balssa's essential ignominy. According to the antithetical logic that links Balzac's socioliterary ambitions and denial of his true ancestry, the Louis who degrades hides behind the Louis who ennobles. For Saint-Aubin's family, the razed castle of Salbar is the emblem of suppressed noble origins, just as conversely, for Balzac, Balssa embodies repressed peasant origins, over which he would erect the monument of *The Human Comedy*. In light of this elaborate play on the presence or absence of both noble origins and their royal sanction, it is significant that Rhoon participates in the counterrevolutionary Vendée uprising, and that "R," conventional cipher of *rex*, or king, is the letter that has been slipped into Balssa to form Salbar (a name that also provides a near-palindrome of fellow *Tourangeau* Rabelais, paradigm of French literary glory, and probably Balzac's most cherished literary precursor, whom he emulated especially in his *Droll stories*).

It is revealing as well to see what escapes from the fire set by count Rhoon. The old servant Georges, faithful to the family after their downfall,

> avait sauvé de l'incendie du *Salbar* un *Traité du Blason* et l'avait précieusement conservé; aussi ne sauriez-vous imaginer la douleur du pauvre Georges lorsqu'un jour il ne trouva plus que la reliure de ce livre. Horace avait bourré son fusil avec les feuillets. (38)

> [had saved from the *Salbar* blaze a *Treatise on Heraldry* and had carefully conserved it; you could

thus not imagine poor George's distress when one day he found only the book's binding left. Horace had stuffed his rifle with the pages.]

Genealogical knowledge survives, despite destruction of the ancestral edifice. Even when Horace witlessly destroys the precious treatise, the story of his true heritage is passed on by a local aristocrat. It is as if Horace were haunted, even pursued by his ancestry—figuring Balzac's own anxieties about his family origins. In another sense, the stubborn persistence of genealogical knowledge here figures the importance of genealogy within Balzac's ongoing effort to forge identities, from the early "biographies mythiques," to the legitimation of his borrowed name, to the creation of his fictional characters. Indeed, the young rustic's ignorant recklessness does not affect the book's binding—an object so often fetishized in the nineteenth century and, in particular, a privileged site for Balzac's genealogical fictions (where, as we have seen, he displayed the arms of the Balzac d'Entragues). Similarly, in addition to the countless genealogical explanations in *The Human Comedy*, Balzac had coats of arms made for the principal aristocratic families peopling it and, though these were ready by 1839, he did not integrate them until 1842 when launching the first edition of his work under the collective title *The Human Comedy* (Lotte 1963). His strategies for legitimating his identity thus spill over into the treatment of his fictional characters' identities and, in the broadest sense, genealogical fiction plays a pivotal role in the overall elaboration of *The Human Comedy*. Embedded in Balzac's own signature, the fiction of his noble origins had underwritten his project from its inception.

In the "Account of the *Lily in the Valley* trial," Balzac's version of his recent court battle with his publisher Buloz, he once again pursues the process of self-invention and self-fashioning that began with the "biographies mythiques." More specifically, he seeks to rectify the "false" image that the press had painted of him during the trial by listing his "true" qualities including, above all, the legitimacy and venerability of "Balzac":

mon nom est sur mon extrait de naissance comme celui de M. de Fitz-James est sur le sien; . . .

s'il est d'une vieille famille gauloise, ce n'est pas ma faute . . . mon nom de Balzac est mon nom patronymique, avantage que n'ont pas beaucoup de familles aristocratiques . . . Il n'est pas de gentilhomme qui n'ait quelque nom primitif, son nom de soldat franc. . . . Je ne suis point gentilhomme dans l'acception historique et nobiliaire du mot, si profondément significatif pour les familles de la race conquérante. Je le dis, en opposant orgueil contre orgueil; car mon père se glorifiait d'être de la race conquise, d'une famille qui avait résisté en Auvergne à l'invasion. . . . (CH 9.928)

[my name is on my birth certificate like M. de Fitz-James' is upon his; . . . if it is that of an old gallic family, this is not my fault . . . Balzac is my patronymic, a privilege not shared by many aristocratic families . . . There is not a single gentleman without an original, frankish soldier's name. . . . I am not a gentleman in the noble, historic sense of the word, so deeply meaningful for the families of the conquering race. I say this, setting pride against pride; my father gloried in being of the conquered race, from a family in Auvergne that had resisted the invasion.]

Balzac begins by invoking the authority of the modern *état civil*, for the birth certificate or *acte de naissance*, which records a person's entry into the institution, must substantiate contemporary claims of onomastic legitimacy (ironically, undermined by the use of "Fitz-James" as an example, "fitz" meaning the illegitimate son, in this case of James II). He soon shifts to a longer historical perspective, using Henri de Boulainvilliers' theories on conquering versus conquered races (popularized by Balzac's contemporary Augustin Thierry) to glorify his name, by postulating an original gallic race that would predate the aristocracy descended from the germanic conquerors. If he admits then that he is not a gentleman in the conventional sense, it is only in order to claim this superior status.

While the title of this defunct branch "ne saurait [lui] appartenir" [would not belong to him], he would instead be descended from a collateral branch of the same family, "une famille . . . d'où sont sortis les d'Entragues" [a family . . . from which the d'Entragues descended] (9.929). However, in the far less public context of a letter to Alcide de Beauchesne, Balzac is clearly not fooled by his fictional genealogy:

Mon père prétendait être de la souche de la maison Balzac d'où venaient collatéralement les d'Entraigues, à eux la couronne [de marquis], mais ils sont éteints. Moi je m'en moque. La noblesse aujourd'hui c'est 500 000 francs de rentes ou une illustration personnelle. (Balzac 1960–69, 2.710)

[My father claimed to be from the branch of the Balzac family from which the d'Entragues descended—let them have the (marquis') crown—but their line is extinct. I could not care less. These days, nobility is a 500 000 annual income or individual renown.]

Balzac returns to this last point in the "Account"; since the Revolution, "il n'y a plus dans un vieux nom que l'obligation de se faire un mérite personnel, afin de reconstruire une aristocratie avec les éléments de la noblesse" [there is nothing left in an old name besides the duty to achieve personal merit, in order to reconstruct an aristocracy with elements of the nobility] (CH 9.928). In the paradoxical new "meritocracy" of postrevolutionary France, those with illustrious names are obliged to illustrate them. Examples are given of those who have shown how to "refaire l'édifice abbatu" [rebuild the demolished structure], the expression recalling the ruined castle of "Salbar." These examples moreover—"M. de Chateaubriand et M. de Lamartine dans les lettres; M. de Talleyrand dans les congrès; beaucoup de généraux et de colonels de vieille roche sur les champs de bataille" [M. de Chateaubriand and M. de Lamartine in literature; M. de Talleyrand in diplomacy; many old guard generals and colonels on the battlefield] (928–29)—liken literary achievement to the virile glory of the political and military arenas, and underscore the importance of genealogy, linking it to the landed aristocracy's possession of "old rocks" [vieille roche]. Those whose families own such relics, this implies, would be better able to rebuild and build great things, from the "edifice" of Ancien Régime France, to new literary "monuments." Being noble Balzac, rather than lowly Balssa, pre-qualifies him as a monument-maker. Moreover, Balzac experimented with literary pseudonyms, settled on his definitive signature, and began work on what would become *The Human Comedy* at a time of nascent interest in the "restoration" of historical monuments, and during the period of the Bourbon Restora-

tion. In the broadest sense, reactionary, legitimist Balzac's use of verbs like "reconstruct" and "rebuild" betrays the larger compensatory ideal of *restauration*—at once archaeological and political—underlying his monumental literary aspirations.

The apology of the name Balzac in the "Account" concludes with some particularly revealing assertions:

Pour rassurer les commentateurs, j'ajouterai que mon homonyme littéraire, l'illustre Balzac, l'auteur des *Lettres*, s'appelait GUERS, et prit son second nom d'une petite terre située près d'Angoulême, comme M. Arouet s'appela M. de Voltaire. J'irai plus loin: je dirai que, si je m'appelais Manchot ou Mangot, que mon nom me déplut, ou ne fût pas sonore et facile à prononcer comme l'ont été tous les noms illustrés, je suivrais l'exemple de Guers, de Voltaire, de Molière, et d'une foule de gens d'esprit. Quand Arouet s'est appelé Voltaire, il songeait à dominer son siècle, et voilà une prescience qui légitime toutes les audaces. (930)

[To reassure critics, I shall add that my literary homonym, the great Balzac, author of the *Letters*, was named GUERS, and took his second name from a small property located near Angoulême, just as M. Arouet called himself M. de Voltaire. I shall go even further: I would say that if I were named Onehand or Unhand, if my name displeased me or were not melodious and easy to pronounce like all illustrious names, I would follow the example of Guers, Voltaire, Molière, and so many other clever people. When Arouet took on the name Voltaire, he was thinking about dominating his century.]

Balzac argues here for the legitimacy of adopting a name adequate to one's talent and, concurrently, seeks to legitimate the "audacity" of his name, through a slippery series of equivalencies:

Honoré de Balzac
= l'illustre Balzac = [Guez =] GUERS [= guerre]
= Voltaire = Molière
but: ≠ Manchot, ≠ Mangot, [≠ Balssa]

He begins by retreating behind his "homonyme littéraire" [literary homonym], a flattering substitution that confers a well-established literary value upon his name. Then, instead of spelling the initial name of his name-sake "Guez," he opts for a less common form, "GUERS." The use of capital letters calls attention to a choice which, through the homophone "Guerre" [war], stresses the martial aspect of the name. Including the famed "author of the *Letters*" among the "clever people" who have changed their names, he does not, however, use the borrowed title (de Balzac), but rather the original name, "Guers." In this way, both consonance (Guers, Voltaire, Molière) and parallel construction (of X, of Y, of Z) provide a sense of cohesiveness among disparate elements, linking "l'illustre Balzac" (and, by association, his homonym Honoré de Balzac) with the most famed names in French literature—or rather, quite appropriately, with its most glorious pseudonyms. Conversely, a vulgar-sounding, unflattering name like "Manchot" or "Mangot" ["Onehand" or "Unhand"] is clearly unsuitable for an aspiring writer and, by definition, an "armless" or "handless" name cannot write.[15] Connoting a lack of class and marketability, as well as denoting physical mutilation, "Manchot" is a symbolically castrated, impotent name, on several levels at once. The hypothetical statement "If I were named Onehand" belies the real disgrace of being a Balssa, especially after the execution of Uncle Louis. Indeed, the entire apology of the name Balzac in the *Account* is haunted by the specter of Louis Balssa: we sense it not only in the name "Manchot," but also in the anecdote about a printer condemned to death, as well as in the urgency with which Balzac declares, "je n'ai pas, Dieu merci, taché mon nom" [thank God I have not sullied my name] (929).

Balzac was likewise preoccupied with the aptness of his characters' names (as we have already seen *à propos* Lucien in *Lost Illusions*, and as exemplified by the elaborate reading of the eponymous hero's name in the novella *Z. Marcas*). In 1835, just a year before defending his own name in the *Account*, Balzac published *Father Goriot*, starring his most successful *climber*, Rastignac, whose name—like that of "Massiac," which it replaced in the manuscript—possesses the same "hard," final "c" of success that distinguishes Balzac from the truncated, castrated name Balssa. Just as importantly, making the struggling student of *Father Goriot* the same character as the worldly Rastignac of the earlier *Wild Ass's Skin* marked

the true beginning of recurring characters, the technique that would pull the disparate parts of *The Human Comedy* together into a massive, cohesive, and realistic whole (Pugh 1974, 79–80). Recurrence would, in short, take Balzac's design for a literary monument to another level, expanding the process of forging identities from the creator to the characters peopling his vast fictional world. In 1832, Balzac had indeed framed a premonitory vision of all this, in his *Theory of the tale*, imagining the emergence of "a boundless number of copies of myself." Recurrence did not just proceed however from the idiosyncrasies of Balzac's fertile imagination. Blossoming within the cultural climate of early nineteenth-century France—marked by increased efforts at official control of individual identity and by the rise of a pervasive new "marketplace of fame"—the technique of recurring characters, and the overarching novelistic design which it enabled, resemble such emergent forms and institutions as the *état civil*, the biographical dictionary, modern advertising, even the modern cemetery. Looking more closely at these affinities shall help us to understand better how Balzac's textual monument is constructed.

The Archival Rival

Revolutionary and postrevolutionary France witnessed an explosion of archival activity: police archives, the museum, the library, the catalog, the *Bottin* (a directory of names and addresses), the guidebook, the dictionary, and the *état civil*. In the 1842 foreword or *Avant-propos* to *The Human Comedy*, Balzac proposes to "faire concurrence à l'*état civil*" [rival the *état civil*] (CH 1.10) suggesting his project's affinity with this particular archival institution and, more generally, with the burgeoning nineteenth-century archives. What exactly might it mean, though, for a novelist to rival the *état civil* archive? The most obvious answer would be that Balzac is, as elsewhere, proclaiming his mimetic ambitions—declaring himself the secretary of society. This reading proves inadequate, however, for it proceeds from an insufficient understanding of the *état civil*, an institution with a very particular history, shaped by the specific epistemological and ideological shifts that accompany the development of "disciplinary" bureaucracy.

Emerging as an increasingly powerful institution in the wake of the French Revolution, the *état civil* participates in the rise of what Michel Foucault (1975) calls discipline. Disciplinary power, the subtle control of the individual through diverse means, is bound up inextricably with official regulation of individual identity. The *état civil* records each major event affecting a person's name or civil status: birth, marriage, death, divorce, disownment, and so on. It monitors identity in much the same spirit as police archives or the practice of registering prostitutes, both of which also emerged during this period. The *état civil* thus constitutes a coherent system for generating and conserving essential archival material about the lives of individual citizens. While the modern *état civil* began to emerge only with Revolutionary and Napoleonic legal reforms, it was anticipated in many respects by Roman legislation and by more than a thousand years of subsequent evolution.[16] Throughout the course of this prehistory, we can discern a broad, historical movement toward more widespread, uniform, and permanent documentation. Finally, secularization of parish record-keeping during the revolutionary period paved the way for transformation of the *état civil* into a coherent institution under Napoleon, particularly with the implementation of the 1803–04 *Code civil*.

The *état civil* that modern France has inherited from the Napoleonic era is thus a rigorously codified institution with a strong normative bent, designed to assure the uniqueness and stability of individual identity. Its guiding principle is that of total inclusion: each major event in a person's life must be recorded. Likewise, all persons in society, however marginal, must be registered. In this way, the *état civil* offers an ambitious, if ultimately unattainable, vision of complete control and comprehensiveness. Nothing would be allowed to stand outside this monumental archival construct, this rendering of an entire society in paper, this demographic *oeuvres complètes*.

As we have seen, Balzac was in search of a monumental literary design from the outset of his career as a writer. He also had reason to be particularly receptive to the archival model offered by the *état civil*. He not only belonged to the first generation to grow up under the new regime of the modern, secular *état civil*, but also, as a child, saw its workings from a privileged vantage point. His father was appointed an *état civil* officer by Napoleon and served for nearly five years, between 1803 and 1808. Later, Balzac's formal law training and apprenticeship as a clerk would acquaint him intimately with the Napoleonic Code (Lichtenthäler 1988). Not surprisingly, his treatment of legal technicalities, in such texts as *Cousin Bette* or *The Vendetta*, reveals precise knowledge of articles pertaining to the *état civil*. Yet the Balzacian novel's affinity with disciplinary bureaucracy in general, and the *état civil* in particular, goes beyond the thematic and into the representational realm, entering into the very fabric of Balzac's literary project. In *The Novel and the Police*, D. A. Miller argues persuasively that in the nineteenth century, the exercising of disciplinary, policing power permeated "the very practice of novelistic representation" (Miller 1988, 20). Seen through this Foucaldian lens, Balzac's designation of the *état civil* as an explicit model exposes crucial connections between the disciplinary power of the archive and representational strategies in *The Human Comedy*.

The first connection involves the representation of the individual: like the *état civil*, *The Human Comedy* is a vast, textual machine for fabricating individual existence. The institution's rise to power indeed enables it to "give birth" for, no longer a natural, inherent part of a person's being, individual identity emerges from the documents that would prove one's existence. As a powerful "realist" tool for making characters seem to exist, the technique of recurring characters functions much like the *état civil*. While the *état civil* constitutes a person's existence by documenting his or her identity periodically, Balzac's technique makes a fictional character "exist" by repeating its name regularly, in different works, until the name no longer seems part of an individual text, but of a larger system—in fact that of *The Human Comedy*, yet which we begin to confuse with the world outside. In both cases, it is periodic identification within a vast textual system that "guarantees" a person's existence outside the written document. By simply entering the system, an individual begins an implied trajectory through it. Even if this itinerary is never realized, the sense that it could be bestows upon the individual a "glow" of ontological plenitude. It is thus not repetition per se, but the potential for repetition within a textual system, that underwrites individual existence, be the system that of the *état civil* or of *The Human Comedy*.

Nineteenth-century writers on the *état civil* recognized the institution's ability to engender and, pursuing this thinking to its logical conclusion, held that without his or her *état civil* a person, in a sense, does not exist.[17] In the nineteenth century, this new linking of documentation and individual existence provoked great anxiety over the possibility that the bond could be broken. On the one hand, an unscrupulous person (e.g., Balzac's Jacques Collin, a.k.a. Vautrin) could assume a false identity.[18] On the other hand, there arises the equally troubling possibility that individuals could be denied their *état civil* and rendered officially nonexistent—precisely the premise of *Colonel Chabert*, as we shall see.[19] Either way, through assumption or denial, identity reveals its underlying precariousness: it is a construct to be made and unmade.

The second important connection between the *état civil* and Balzacian representation involves narrative for, while Balzac's panoptic narration constantly "polices" individual identity, names in *The Human Comedy* also act as repositories, or "files," that contain the story of the individual's life in radically condensed form. First of all, the penchant for monitoring identity often provides the narrative "motor" propelling the Balzacian novel from brief sequences of suspense, uncertainty, and recognition, to the grand quests to claim or renounce names, find them or find out what they mean, that structure entire novels. This is particularly evident amid the intense policing and counter-policing of the Vautrin Cycle (*Father Goriot, Lost Illusions, Harlot High and Low*) but also true in much less obvious contexts. In *The Wild Ass's Skin*, for example, the protagonist's identity is withheld suspensefully at first but, when revealed, the name "Raphael de Valentin"—like the skin itself—prefigures the young man's fate through the narrative models of desire, passion, and youthful martyrdom offered by namesakes Raphael Sanzio, Saint Valentin, and even the less well-known Valentin in Goethe's *Faust*.[20]

In this sense, the entire plot of *The Wild Ass's Skin* manifests Raphael's realization of a destiny inscribed at once in the prophetic talisman and in his own name.

While the drive to control and understand names generates narrative, names in *The Human Comedy* also compress and "store" narrative. Indeed, it is difficult to talk about recurring characters without conjuring up their stories, for a recurring name accumulates the narrative baggage of the character's involvement in other texts.[21] Recurrence compresses narrative within the character's name.[22] Similarly, a name recorded by the *état civil* bears the legacy of the person's individual and family history. In Balzac's *The Vendetta*, when Luigi Porta and Ginevra Piombo marry, the story of the hatred between their families is inscribed on the *état civil* register, along with their names:

La haine des Porta et des Piombo, de terribles passions furent inscrites sur une page de l'*État civil*, comme sur la pierre d'un tombeau sont gravées en quelques lignes les annales d'un peuple, et souvent même en un mot: Robespierre ou Napoléon. (CH 1.1088)

[The hatred between Portas and Piombos, such terrible passions, were inscribed upon a page of the *État civil* just as, upon a tombstone, the annals of an entire people are carved in just several lines, and often in only one word: Robespierre or Napoleon.]

Balzac's choice of metaphor says a great deal about his narrative project, both its intertwining of individual and collective history, and its emulation of the *état civil* archive and the funerary monument as models of extreme compression, as repositories for narrative, indeed as *lieux de mémoire* [realms of memory]. This passage provides telling *mises-en-abîme* both of Balzac's general philosophy of art ("une oeuvre d'art . . . est, dans un petit espace, l'effrayante accumulation d'un monde entier de pensées, c'est une sorte de résumé" [a work of art . . . is the fearsome accumulation of a whole world of thoughts in a small space, it's a sort of summary] (Mozet 1990, 25) and, more specifically, of his evolving socio-aesthetic enterprise, in which "scenes of private life" and contemporary French history fuse in a novelistic design that partakes at once of the archive and the monument, that not only records and preserves worthwhile stories, but also provides a vehicle for their transmission into the future.

In the broadest sense, *The Human Comedy* forms an archive of its own, a civil register of the fictional society it depicts. This archive has been replicated and condensed by the many "indexes" and "biographical dictionaries" for the text. These, in turn, crowd the shelves, card catalogs, and now computerized catalogs of burgeoning scholarly archives. Significantly, Balzac himself composed a biographical dictionary entry for Rastignac in the preface to *A Daughter of Eve*, anticipating at least the first step in an archival house of mirrors that Vincent Descombes characterizes as irresistible:

> L'idée d'un répertoire des personnages de *La comédie humaine* appartient à la fiction balzacienne plutôt qu'à l'érudition critique. Entreprendre de composer ce répertoire, c'est entrer dans le jeu de Balzac. Consulter de tels répertoires, c'est se prendre au jeu. (Descombes 1983, 251)

> [The idea of an index of characters in *The Human Comedy* belongs more to Balzacian fiction than to literary scholarship. To make an index like this is to play Balzac's game. To look things up in such indexes is to be drawn into the game.]

While Descombes is right to insist on the intensely fictional and ludic nature of *The Human Comedy*-as-archive, he neglects its powerful sociohistorical dimension. *The Human Comedy* is indeed so profoundly marked by the disciplinary spirit of the archives that it has inspired many a commentator, starting with its author, to spin off further archival material about itself. To put this another way, *The Human Comedy* "rivals" the *état civil* not only by incorporating the institution's particular logic into its representational strategies, but also through a remarkable ability to generate further archival renderings of itself, through its tremendous capacity for self-perpetuation. Significantly, these renderings often take the form of biographical dictionaries—a genre, as we shall see, so bound up with nineteenth-century fame culture in general, and with Balzac's designs on posterity in particular.

While most any part of *The Human Comedy* could illustrate these arguments about Balzac's

work as archival rival, *Le Colonel Chabert* has the advantage of condensing, within a short space, an overriding preoccupation with identification, a strong linking of individual existence with documentation, a trenchant critique of this new ontological order and, above all, powerful echoes of the author's troubled relation to his own identity.

The old man who appears in the solicitor Derville's office claiming to be "le colonel Chabert" poses a dilemma. Is this "déterré" [dug-up cadaver] (CH 3.316) the famous Napoleonic colonel, killed at the battle of Eylau? Is he human or not?[23] Is he even still alive?[24] At the heart of the problem is *la comtesse Ferraud*, Chabert's remarried "widow" who conspires to deny him his identity: "elle voulait l'anéantir socialement" [she wanted to annihilate him socially] (362).

The description of Derville's office launches us into a world of legal documents, overflowing with files and folders, impregnated with "le parfum particulier aux bureaux et aux paperasses" [the smell characteristic of offices and paperwork] (313). This is the bureaucratic realm in which the drama of Chabert's existence, or nonexistence, will be played out.[25] According to the old man's version of the story, he was not killed at Eylau, just seriously injured and buried alive, not in a distinctly marked, individual grave—as in the *Père-Lachaise*, analogue, as we shall see, of the biographical dictionary— but rather in an anonymous, communal one. He survives this ordeal, "remembers" who he is, and has documents drawn up "dans les formes juridiques, voulues par le droit du pays . . . en vue d'établir [s]on identité" [in the legal manner required by the country's laws, in the hope of establishing his identity] (326). However, his "death" has been recorded, both by the *état civil* and by history books (324). Literally, after Eylau, Chabert *is* history. Meanwhile, his wife remarries and has children. When he returns to France, penniless, people do not believe his claims; in his words:

> quand je propose, moi, mendiant, de plaider contre un comte et une comtesse; quand je m'élève, moi, mort, contre un acte de décès, un acte de mariage et des actes de naissance, ils m'éconduisent . . . J'ai été enterré sous des morts, mais maintenant je suis enterré sous des vivants, sous des actes,

sous des faits, sous la société tout entière, qui veut me faire rentrer sous terre! (328)

[When a beggar like me pleads against a count and countess; when a deadman like me protests against a death certificate, a marriage license, and birth certificates, they show me the door . . . I was buried beneath the dead, but now I am buried beneath the living, beneath documents, facts, society as a whole, all wishing me below ground again!]

This passage equates papers with people, implying that the count, countess, and their children *are* "a marriage license and birth certificates"; "the living" the same as "documents." The flesh-and-blood Chabert cannot prove who he is, nor that he even exists, without the right paperwork. The novella thus dramatizes the emergent ontological order in which documentation constitutes a person's existence. In this postsacred world of disciplinary bureaucracy, human identity loses its divine sanction. No longer a given, it must instead be fabricated; it becomes a social fiction. Chabert is an emblematic figure in this respect, for as a foundling, he begins life in a "natural" state, bereft of family or community ties[26]—on some level at least an appealing prospect for Louis Balssa's ambitious nephew. A foundling represents a sort of *tabula rasa*, upon which such a grandiose identity as "le Colonel Chabert, *comte de l'Empire*" can be inscribed.

At the battle of Eylau, however, this identity is taken away, and Chabert's story comes full circle. The crucible of the communal grave strips the living person of an identity that remains, instead, in the textual record of his life. The old man describes tellingly his emergence from the anonymous burial ground: "j'étais sorti du ventre de la fosse aussi nu que de celui de ma mère" [I had emerged just as naked from the belly of the earth as from my mother's] (326). He becomes an "enfant trouvé" [foundling] again—naked, helpless, dependent on strangers. Unable to reclaim his identity, he is condemned to a second childhood, at the Bicêtre asylum ("Avec toute la naïveté d'un gamin" [With all the naïveté of a kid] he appears "tomb[é] en enfance" [reverted to childhood] (372). When Derville greets him here as "Chabert," he replies, "Pas Chabert! pas Chabert! je me nomme Hyacinthe. . . . Je ne suis plus un homme, je suis le numéro 164,

septième salle" [Not Chabert! Not Chabert! I'm named Hyacinthe. . . . I am no longer a man, I am number 164, seventh room]. Marginalization as "Hyacinthe" (an appropriately natural, floral name), and marginalization as "164" are conflated, exposing an underlying oblivion from which he emerges, and to which he returns. As readers, we never really doubt that the old man is Chabert, the eponymous hero of the story—a typical identification between title and protagonist in *The Human Comedy* (e.g., *César Birotteau, Ursule Mirouët, Louis Lambert, Cousin Bette*, and so on). Likewise, from the outset, we are guided by Balzac's own leanings and moved toward sympathy for this stoic figure, exemplar of old-fashioned virtue and honor, in his vain struggle against the legalistic perfidy of modern bourgeois society (cf. Pierre Barbéris's "Introduction," 3.293–309). As readers, we do not participate in but rather witness the interpretive problem of the old man's identity, filtered through the novella's affinity with the literature of the fantastic. While not a *conte fantastique* per se, *Colonel Chabert* was written when the fantastic was in vogue, and—probably in large part for marketability—Balzac uses many of the genre's familiar elements: ghosts (Chabert, remarks Barbéris, is a *revenant* [297]),[27] the macabre (Chabert digs himself out from under a pile of cadavers, using a gigantic, detached arm [325]) and, most importantly, insanity. Derville's first reaction, when the old man identifies himself as "le Colonel Chabert," is to think, "C'est un fou!" [He's a madman!] (322). This view is corroborated by the nature of his injury, a deep head wound which, as he explains, leaves him for six months in a state of "catalepsie . . . entre la vie et la mort, ne parlant pas, ou déraisonnant quand je parlais" [catalepsy . . . between life and death, not speaking, or talking nonsense when I did speak] (326). Even years later, the scar that remains is read automatically as the mark of his mental incapacity.[28] When he comes back to his senses ("en recouvrant ma raison" [regaining reason]), the old man's claims to be Chabert make others think him insane: he is locked up "comme fou à Stuttgart" [as a madman in Stuttgart] (327), for example. On his way to France, moreover, he has an apparent relapse: "j'eus un accès de névralgie à la tête, et restai six semaines sur la paille dans une auberge!" [I had an attack of neuralgia in my head, and spent six weeks, penniless, at an inn!] (331–32). Back in France, the possibility of detention in the Charenton asylum is a constant threat (333, 343, 350, 358, 366). As a consequence of his head wound, Chabert loses not only his mental faculties and his identity, but his rights as a husband as well. More than just incapacitating, the wound is an emasculating one; the scar remains as the tangible mark of Chabert's symbolic castration.

There are within the text, as so often in the literature of the fantastic, competing versions of the same story: one obeys the laws of nature and reason; the other moves beyond them, into the supernatural realm of dreams, and insanity (Todorov). The narrative seems to lend equal credence to these divergent possibilities by refering to the protagonist variously as "l'inconnu," "le vieillard," "le colonel Chabert," "Chabert," "le faux Chabert," or "le prétendu colonel Chabert" [the stranger, the old man, colonel Chabert, Chabert, the false Chabert, or the supposed colonel Chabert].[29] The most ambivalent element in the text is the set of documents supposed to prove the old man's identity definitively. Indeed, the story sets up a sort of "administrative uncanny" that in many ways anticipates Gogol, or even Kafka, by setting up a bureaucratic labyrinth. After the old man has spoken to Derville about these papers, the solicitor sends away for them. When an envelope arrives months later, bearing Prussian, Austrian, Bavarian and French stamps, the contents are unreadable: Derville "prit la lettre et l'ouvrit, mais il n'y put rien lire, elle était écrite en allemand" [took the letter and opened it, but he could read nothing, it was written in German] (335). Translated, this turns out to be a preliminary letter from a "notaire de Berlin" [Berlin notary], in which it is claimed that the documents requested will arrive within days, and be completely in order ("parfaitement en règle, et revêtues des légalisations nécessaires pour faire foi en justice" [perfectly in order, and bearing the authentications needed to carry weight legally] (351). Nothing more is said about these elusive papers until Derville consults with countess Ferraud to tell her that Chabert actually exists: "Je ne vous parlerai pas de l'incontestable authenticité des pièces" [I shall not speak of the unimpeachable authenticity of the documents], he asserts, "ni de la

certitude des preuves qui attestent l'existence du comte Chabert" [nor of the certainty of proofs that attest to the existence of count Chabert] (351–52). Derville mentions the documents only to say that he will not talk about them. Have they been received, indeed do they even exist? The only other reference to the documents comes a few pages later, when countess Ferraud sends her secretary to "demander chez Derville communication des actes qui concernaient le colonel Chabert, de les copier et de venir aussitôt" [ask Derville's office to produce the documents concerning colonel Chabert, to copy them, and to come straight away] (362). The countess has apparently assumed that the documents exist, based upon Derville's elliptical statement. In this way, the only "hard" evidence about the documents is the letter predicting their arrival, although even this is mediated by translation, a typical strategy for heightening ambivalence in the literature of the fantastic.[30] Furthermore, the seemingly illusory nature of these documents is enhanced by the letter's point of origin: Berlin, a town Balzac associates with E. T. A. Hoffmann, father of the fantastic.[31]

Finally, even if we could prove the documents' existence, could these prove Chabert's? Not without help. But what kind? The old man prefaces the story of his rebirth with this disclaimer:

Laissez-moi vous établir les faits, vous expliquer plutôt comme ils ont dû se passer, que comme ils sont arrivés. Certaines circonstances, qui ne doivent être connues que du Père éternel, m'obligent à en présenter plusieurs comme des hypothèses. [326]

[Let me establish the facts for you, and explain how they must have occurred, rather than how they happened. Certain circumstances, that must be known only to God Almighty, require me to present them as hypotheses.

His papers, even if they were to materialize, would remain inconclusive, for they are based on such hypotheses, not on objective facts. Ultimately, only God can know the old man's identity. Here, as so often in *The Human Comedy*, we glimpse Balzac's nostalgia for a divinely governed, natural order—tempered however by his keen awareness of irrevocable change. The novelist can indulge his nostalgia by playing God, by pretending to be the guarantor of identity: we should believe that the old man is Chabert because Balzac has so willed it. Yet, within the modern, bureaucratic world represented in *The Human Comedy*, God almighty, the ultimate guarantor, remains disconcertingly silent, offering no guidance, and leaving man to his own devices in establishing human identity.

While much in *Le Colonel Chabert* works to thwart human efforts to identify the old man definitively, there is nonetheless a revealing "moment of truth." When he appears suddenly during a meeting between Derville and Mme Ferraud, she pretends not to recognize him. "[V]oulez-vous des preuves?" he cries, " Je vous ai prise au Palais-Royal. . . . Vous étiez chez la" [Do you want proof? I had you at the Palais-Royal. . . . You were at Madame] (357–58). The countess turns pale, protests, flees. Derville is now certain of his identity as Chabert. What has happened? To be sure, to convince a discerning legal mind like Derville's, the revelation has not been of a divine, but rather of a juristic nature. Chabert's dilemma has been that society, epitomized by his treacherous wife, has, in denying his identity, relegated him to complete marginality. Now, however, he returns the favor, marginalizing the person who had marginalized him, exposing her as a former, and not very high-class prostitute, a category of person subjected to particularly keen bureaucratic and police scrutiny in the nineteenth century.[32] He uses disciplinary, policing tactics against his wife as leverage in making his own case; by relying upon the sort of legalistic evidence— names, addresses, "proof"—that has until now been used against him, he can in turn establish his identity to the satisfaction of a skeptical, but honest person like Derville. While the scene in Derville's office thus confirms Chabert's identity, this has no bearing though on his status in society. The countess's continued disdain prompts him to renounce his claims and return to the administrative limbo from whence he had come. Indeed, as Derville suggests upon seeing the old man at Bicêtre, Chabert's defamation of the countess only hardened her resolve to deny him his identity: "S'il est dans cet hospice au lieu d'habiter un hôtel, c'est uniquement pour avoir rappelé à la jolie comtesse Ferraud qu'il l'avait prise, comme un fiacre, sur la place" [If he is in this home instead of in a mansion, it is solely for having reminded pretty countess Ferraud that he had gotten her on the street, like a fiacre] (371). While Chabert's positive identification rules out the possibility of his insanity, the even more frightening and paradoxical state of his official nonexistence remains. Ironically, by exposing the countess's identity as a social fiction, he underscores the fragility of his own identity as "Chabert," for he too was born, not to greatness, but to ignominy.

On one level, Chabert's story dramatizes the general precariousness of human existence in the modern world of archives and birth certificates. Under the new reign of secular existence, embodied most saliently by the Napoleonic *état civil*, individual identity is conceived as fundamentally man-made, emerging out of specific bureaucratic conventions and practices. In this new ontological order, each citizen's identity is necessarily a fiction that can be fabricated but also lost, revoked, destroyed. Chabert thus would play the modern Everyman, perched perilously above the existential abyss.

Yet the vicissitudes of Chabert's life are so extraordinary. "Quelle destinée!" exclaims Derville at the end of the text, "Sorti de l'hospice des Enfants trouvés, il revient à l'hospice de la *Vieillesse,* après avoir, dans l'intervalle, aidé Napoléon à conquérir l'Egypte et l'Europe" [What a destiny! Coming from the foundling's home, he returns to the Old Age home after having, in the interim, helped Napoleon conquer Egypt and Europe] (373). Chabert's life is not only linked to, but patterned on Napoleon's— on the master narrative of success and failure for nineteenth-century France.[33] In between oblivion and further oblivion, Chabert becomes a great conqueror; significantly, on the manuscript, Derville's pronouncement reads, 'après avoir conquis l'Europe" [after having conquered Europe], making Chabert and Napoleon appear synonymous. Indeed, in its own way, Chabert's story acts out the full Napoleonic saga, from initial ascendance, to grand conquest, to exile, to momentary return, and on to permanent exile.[34] Ultimately, the more sensational the fiction of identity—a foundling becoming a famous colonel, a whore a countess, a Corsican outsider the emperor of France, or an unknown scribbler of dubious ancestry a great writer—the more spectacular might be its unraveling. On another level then, Chabert embodies Balzac's own, deepest concerns about his identity: for he who rises from obscurity to monumental accomplishment within his lifetime, there necessarily looms the correspondent possibility of as dramatic a fall.

Life and Death Writing

Les *Biographies* à venir seront le Panthéon, le Tartare et l'Élysée des Nations athées. C'est là ce qu'on appelle le progrès.
—Charles Nodier ("Avant-propos,"
in *Biographie contemporaine* 1837, 2)

[Biographies shall be the Pantheon, Tartar, and Elysium of godless nations. That is what we call progress.]
—Charles Nodier ("Foreword," *Contemporary Biography*)

While Chabert is said to sink into obscurity at the end of the text, the novella itself and the larger novelistic cycle to which it belongs survive, and continue to tell his story. *The Human Comedy* functions as a proving ground for its ambitious characters and provides an enduring record of their travails and accomplishments. Memorializing them, it also memorializes in turn the author who has sung their lives. This is a conception closely akin to both the biographical dictionary and the modern cemetery.

Through the latter part of the eighteenth century, into the nineteenth, and on to the present, Western civilization has been immersed in an ever-rising flood of biography that shows no signs of relenting.[35] Beneath this seeming continuity though, substantial changes have occurred. Posterity is not what it used to be, nor is biography. Our conception of fame has become remarkably present-minded. Contemporary celebrities blaze brilliantly, then fade into everlasting oblivion. Best-selling biographies of such figures cash in on a person's momentary renown while it lasts, usually while he or she is still alive. Within literary studies moreover there has been a recent vogue for understanding biography as "life-writing," a notion that privileges the here and now of a person's lifetime over whatever might lie beyond.[36] Unfortunately, these tendencies—both popular and scholarly—have obscured the powerful connections that once linked biography and death.

In nineteenth-century France though, posthumous glory was considered the highest form of renown and biography, like editions of complete works, or public monuments, generally consecrated the accomplishments of the dead, not the living. In particular, this mortuary dimension was central to the biographical dictionary, a genre that flourished at the time, with the period's penchant for biography channeled into its paradigmatic reference format for, much as the eighteenth century was the age of encyclopedias, the nineteenth was instead that of dictionaries, works which, as Nicole Savy argues, could have significant monumental pretentions.[37] In his "Discours préliminaire" [Preliminary discourse] to Michaud's *Biographie universelle*, the period's leading biographical dictionary, Nodier hailed the project's extraordinary goal of encompassing,

dans une espèce de *suprême jugement* toutes les époques, tous les pays, toutes les opinions, toutes les gloires, toutes les célébrités, tous les crimes enfin et toutes les vertus qui ont marqué le passage des races et des temps écoulés [v, my emphasis]

[in a sort of supreme judgement all the periods, countries, opinions, glories, celebrities, crimes and virtues that have marked the passage of peoples and of time]

This idea of the biographical dictionary as last judgment recalls the preliminary sketch for Nadar's *Panthéon*, in which the names of living writers destined for immortality are recorded, by a figure of Death, into a giant, leather-bound, dictionary-like volume (cf. above). As this might suggest, nineteenth-century biography was at once life and death writing that recounted the significant events of great lives in order to negotiate between the here and now and the hereafter, to articulate the famous person's passage into the posterity of the culture's collective memory, with death marking the boundary between contemporary celebrity and fame everlasting. In this respect, the affinities between the *Biographie Universelle*, nineteenth-century France's premier biographical dictionary, and the *Père-Lachaise*, its greatest cemetery, are particularly instructive.

Historically, the rise of the biographical dictionary closely paralleled that of the modern cemetery in France. Both flourished in the wake of the French Revolution, with important early developments dating from the First Empire. In a broader sense, they both took part in the emergence of a pervasive fame culture and tried to fill the void created by a general decline of the belief in a Christian afterlife.

Significant new legislation on burials enabled the founding of the *Père-Lachaise* cemetery in 1804. For several decades before this, concerns about hygiene and the increasing secularization of society had turned public opinion against the tradition of churchyard burial, and fostered a lively reflection on alternatives. It was, however, the *Décret du 23 prairial an XII* [*Decree of June 12, 1804*] that definitively set up the modern French cemetery as a distinct space outside of or at least separate from the city. This was a significant milestone within the larger historical evolution that Philippe Ariès (1977) calls "l'exil des morts" [the exile of the dead]. The enormous project of establishing the *Cimetière de l'est* or *Père-Lachaise* as an external cemetery for the city of Paris was taken on with great zeal by Nicolas Frochot, then Prefect of the Seine—the Haussmann of the *Père-Lachaise*. Despite the administration's best efforts, the public was hesitant at first to use the new cemetery. The burial there in the mid-teens of several Napoleonic heroes, plus the transfer of the tombs of Héloise and Abélard, Molière, and La Fontaine at about the same time, succeeded finally in attracting the public, and by the beginning of the Restoration it had become fashionable as a place both to be buried and to stroll. As young Balzac wrote to his sister Laure in 1819, "Je sors rarement, mais lorsque je *divague*, je vais m'égayer au Père-Lachaise. . . . Et tout en cherchant des morts, je ne vois que des vivants" [Rarely do I go out, but when I *ramble*, I go cheer myself up at the *Père-Lachaise* . . . And while looking for the dead, I only see the living] (Balzac 1960–69, 1.35–36). Significantly, the promoters of the *Père-Lachaise* had chosen to commemorate the same authors—Molière and La Fontaine—that Balzac would, a scant decade later, single out for the analogous honor of complete works editions and accompanying biographical sketches.

The first edition of the *Biographie Universelle*, begun in 1810 and published between 1811 and 1862, was the brainchild of the brothers Joseph-François and Louis-Gabriel Michaud (1767–1839 and 1773–1858, respectively). It set an example for all others to criticize, imitate, and attempt to surpass, so much so that competitors inevitably chose similar names.[38] The *Biographie Universelle* itself consisted originally of 52 volumes in alphabetical order, though with supplements it ran to 85.

As Charles Nodier's comments in the preface suggest, the *Biographie Universelle* differed from earlier reference works, and in much the same way as the *Père-Lachaise* differed from the older churchyard cemeteries. Specifically, Nodier lamented "cette *Encyclopédie* si vantée, que l'absence de méthode et de système a fait nommer *'la Babel des connaissances humaines'*" [that much-vaunted *Encyclopedia*, whose lack of method and system earned it the name, *"the Babel of human knowledge"*] (v), with "Babel" here not so much a metaphor for monumental striving, as for extreme chaos. Like the *Père-Lachaise*, the *Biographie Universelle* was a significant departure from such an undifferentiated piling-up of remains from the past: both were much more clearly organized and thus could readily be explored without getting lost. The resulting popularity of the *Biographie Universelle* engendered many imitators, as well as its own second edition, published between 1854 and 1865, in 45 somewhat thicker volumes. Like the *Père-Lachaise*, the *Biographie Universelle* became a "place" to go, to marvel at and perhaps be inspired in turn by the spectacle of greatness. It was a *Père-Lachaise* for the armchair stroller.

Over time, the biographical dictionary and the cemetery became victims of their own success. Through the nineteenth century, the *Père-Lachaise* grew, and more and more cemeteries like it were established, both around Paris and in the provinces. Within these cemeteries, permanent plots or *concessions à perpétuité*, at first the exception, gradually became the rule, and available to an ever-broader, and less distinguished range of the social spectrum. Much the same development occurred among biographical dictionaries. As the preface of the 1852 *Nouvelle biographie universelle* observes, "Depuis la publication de la *Biographie Universelle*, . . . une foule d'éloges, de notices, de renseignements en tout genre ont paru,. . . . Chaque ville, chaque village a voulu compter au nombre de ses concitoyens, sinon des grands hommes, du moins des hommes remarquables"[39] [Since the publication of the *Biographie Universelle*, a plethora of eulogies, notices, and various information has appeared. Each town, each village wanted to count among its citizens, if not great men, at least remarkable ones]. As they evolved and flourished amid the general postrevolutionary democratization of fame, cemetery and dictionary alike honored ever-greater numbers but, in so doing, would end up diluting the very distinction they sought to confer. "L'immense appétit que nous avons pour les biographies," remarked Baudelaire, "naît d'un sentiment profond de l'égalité" [Our tremendous appetite for biographies comes from a profound feeling of equality] (1975–76, 2.28).

From an aesthetic point of view, the modern French cemetery and the biographical dictionary share specific stylistic features such as indexing and the concise encapsulation of life stories: for the cemetery, these take the form, respectively, of abundant maps, tables, and guides for the mourner or stroller; and of funerary inscriptions that at least give birth and death dates, and in some cases include further biographical information. In much the same way as plots and tombs would vary in size according to the wealth and importance of the deceased, articles in the *Biographie Universelle* vary in length according to the person's relative place in history. They range from a brief paragraph for, say, an obscure sixteenth-century hungarian nobleman, up to the 160 pages alloted Napoleon Bonaparte. As Michaud junior explains in the opening lines of the Napoleon article, Bonaparte was "le plus grand personnage des temps modernes, ou du moins celui qui tient dans leur histoire la place la plus étendue" [the greatest figure of modern times, or at least the one that takes up the most space in the historical record]. Along similar lines, the preface to one of the Michauds' principal competitors, the *Nouvelle biographie universelle*, announces that it will allot "célébrités réelles" [real celebrities] the room their stature commands, and promises to avoid incongruity "*en proportionnant, aussi exactement que possible, la longueur des articles à l'importance des personnages*" [by making the length of the articles as precisely proportionate as possible to the figures' importance] (i, their emphasis). For an age that so valued monumentality, the space someone occupied—in the city, or on the page—indexed his greatness. We shall see this again later on, in examining Victor Hugo's progressive "conquest" of literary glory.

In the broadest sense, the biographical dictionary and the modern French cemetery are similarly commemorative and monumental, their impressive forms striving to match the greatness contained within. The *Biographie Universelle* consists of dozens of massive, leatherbound volumes. Not surprisingly, the metaphor of the monument occurs repeatedly in contemporary discussion of the work. According to Nodier's preface, the dictionary's contributors have worked to "tailler et sculpter la pierre que chacun apportait à l'édifice de tous" [cut and sculpt the stone that each brings to the edifice that all are building] (vi); this "edifice" is also called "ce beau monument historique" [this fine historical monument] (vi) or, better yet, "cette nécropole des illustrations politiques, guerrières, scientifiques et littéraires de l'univers" [this necropolis of the universe's political, military, scientific, and literary greats] (vii). Similarly, in his "Avant-propos" [Preface] to the *Biographie contemporaine*, Nodier compares the biographical dictionary to cyclopean masonry and to the monumental ideal of Babel: "l'histoire offre l'aspect de ces constructions cyclopéennes qui se bâtisssaient par le seul artifice de la juxtà-position, et qui n'avaient point de ciment. Les notices biographiques, ce sont les pierres de l'édifice. Finira Babel qui pourra" [history offers the example of those cyclopean constructions built only through juxtaposition, and without cement . . . The biographical entries are the stones of the edifice. May he who can finish Babel] (1). The medium of fame is in large measure its message, and in the nineteenth century, the figures included in a "monumental" work like the *Biographie Universelle* were necessarily already dead, whereas biographical articles about living celebrities of the day appeared in journalistic contexts whose ephemeral nature matched the tenuousness of the renown they evoked. It is in this sense that Michaud's dictionary was construed as a necropolis; a city of the dead; in short, a cemetery.

As vehicles for fame, these new cities of the dead, whether of paper or stone, shared a common desire to confer posthumous distinction. Thick biographical dictionaries and burgeoning agglomerations of funerary marble were seen as analogous monuments to great men and their accomplishments. This is very much like the prevailing vision at the time of authors' complete works. Balzac's decision, as an aspiring publisher in the mid 1820s, to publish complete works of Molière and La Fontaine and to preface these with brief lives of the authors reminiscent of *Biographie Universelle* entries, may have been influenced by the elevation of the same two authors, a decade earlier, to prominent positions in the *Père-Lachaise*, a tribute that apparently caught his imagination, for he makes a point of detailing it in the biographical notice to his *Oeuvres complètes de La Fontaine* (Balzac 1955–63, 26.21). In addition, Balzac asserts,

Aussi avons-nous cru élever le seul monument digne de La Fontaine en publiant ses oeuvres complètes, ornées de tout le luxe de la typographie, contenues dans un volume facile à transporter, et d'un prix qui les rend accessibles à toutes les fortunes, malgré la beauté des vignettes et du papier. Là est l'éloge, parce que le poëte y est tout entier; là est sa vie, parce que là sont toutes ses pensées. [26.20]

[We also believe that we are raising the only monument worthy of La Fontaine by publishing his complete works, decorated with all the luxury typography can offer, contained in a conveniently portable format, at a price affordable for all pocketbooks, despite the beauty of the vignettes and the paper. There is the tribute, because the whole poet is there, there is his life, because all his thoughts are there.]

At once luxurious yet affordable, monumental yet portable, this *oeuvres complètes* is emblematic of modern, democratic fame. Not just a monument to La Fontaine, Balzac's edition purports to actually "contain" the poet: anticipating the later nineteenth century's ideal synthesis, Balzac already endorses a vision of literary glory in which the writer, his work, and the monument are as one.

Nineteenth-century cemeteries and biographical dictionaries also participated actively in the creation of renown. Cemeteries like the *Père-Lachaise* provided a vital space in which sculptors (Pradier, Préault, Rude, Bartholdi, and so many others) proved their talents, orators displayed their eloquence (e.g., Hugo eulogizing Balzac), and climbers of all sorts (e.g., young Balzac, or his alter-ego Rastignac) gathered to galvanize their fervent ambitions in the shadow of exemplary lives (emblematically, at the end of *Le Père Goriot*, Rastignac hurls his challenge at Paris—"À nous deux maintenant!" [It's between us now!]—from the heights of the *Père-Lachaise*). The most successful would, in turn, be buried here and likewise revered, perpetuating the fame-making cycle. In much the same way, Michaud's dictionary functions as a textual fame machine. Lamenting the death of many early contributors, Nodier writes,

Hélas! depuis longtemps un grand nombre de ces hommes célèbres ne vivent plus que dans leurs écrits.... après avoir consacré leur génie et leurs veilles à ce grand ouvrage, [ils] sont venus réclamer leur place dans cette nécropole des illustrations politiques, guerrières, scientifiques et littéraires de l'univers. [vii]

[Alas! For a long while many of these famous men have dedicated their genius and their sleepless nights to this great work, (they) have come to claim their place in this necropolis of the universe's political, military, scientific and literary greats.]

As the old guard die out and become part of the dictionary, new talents ("des noms nouveaux, des esprits jeunes" [new names, young minds]) emerge to sing the lives of their predecessors, guarantee the continued fame of the dictionary ("féconder sa gloire" [fructify its glory]) and, above all, prepare for their own, imminent apotheosis in Michaud's biographical necropolis (vii). Nodier himself was eventually enshrined in the work, as was, among many other contributors, Mme de Staël. As the article on her remarks, *"La Biographie Universelle doit s'enorgueillir d'avoir compté madame de Staël parmi ses collaborateurs: elle voulut bien l'enrichir des articles ASPASIE, CAMOENS ET CLEOPATRE"* [The Universal Biography ought to be proud to count Mme de Staël among its contributors: she enriched it with articles on ASPASIA, CAMOENS, and CLEOPATRA] (it is a sign, however, of the limitations on women's literary glory at the time that France's greatest living woman writer would be assigned these particular, relatively marginal subjects— all foreign, and mainly female). Understood at the time as more than just repositories of the famous dead, cemetery and dictionary alike were thought to generate renown for the living,

preparing their entry into posterity. In this respect, these analagous forms resemble Balzac's
conception of *The Human Comedy* as an *oeuvres
complètes*, that he frames in life, to perpetuate
his renown after death.

Criticism has dealt abundantly with the vital
links between autobiography and much modern fiction, from Romanticism on, yet less attention has been paid to equally compelling
connections between biography and fiction. As
Nicole Mozet observes though, "Au XIXe siècle
le biographique sous toutes ses formes a en-
vahi les fictions" [In the nineteenth century,
the biographical, in all its forms, invaded fic-
tion] (Mozet 1990, 174). Balzac's involvement
with biography, while less extensive than, say,
Dumas',[40] is nonetheless central to his fiction,
and to the development of his monumentalizing
conception for *The Human Comedy*. Already,
in the early 1820s, Balzac mingled biography,
fiction, and self-promotion, inventing "biographies mythiques" (Barbéris 1985, 21) for his
various literary pseudonyms. As a publisher
in the mid 1820s, Balzac hoped to make his
fortune producing complete works of great authors (Molière, La Fontaine) for which he wrote
introductory "notices biographiques." While unsuccessful commercially, this enterprise already
associated both the writing of biography and
Balzac's own pursuit of success with the idea
of consecrating an author through an *oeuvres
complètes*.

In 1829, with his literary collaborator
L'Héritier de l'Ain, Balzac wrote a *Mémoires
de Sanson* [*Memoirs of Sanson*], a life of the executioner Charles-Henri Sanson that has generally been dismissed as a hasty *ouvrage de
librairie*, significant only for containing what
would later be called "Un Épisode sous la Terreur" [An Episode under the Terror], the brief
Scene of political life. "Entreprise alimentaire,"
esteems Pierre Citron, "le texte est décousu, de
peu d'intérêt, et les exécutions elles-mêmes n'y
occupent pas une très grande place" [A money-
making enterprise, the text is discombobulated,
of little interest, and even the executions themselves do not figure substantially in it] (Citron
1986, 68). At the time, however, Balzac was
already in search of a broader unifying principle, a larger system to link the diverse parts

of the novelistic project he was, for the moment, calling *Scenes of private life*. Sanson's
example may, in fact, have helped guide Balzac
toward the overall design he would eventually
choose. A prototypical recurring character, Sanson reappears in such distinct though related
episodes of French history as the execution of
Louis XVI, and that of Robespierre. His substantial public reputation derives from his pivotal role in French history, rather than from
any particular personal merit. This suggestive
example of a larger system propelling an otherwise ordinary figure to extraordinary renown
prefigures the way in which the vast textual
machinery of *The Human Comedy* fabricates
fame for even its most seemingly unremarkable
characters.

At one memorable point in the *Mémoires*,
Sanson trades preserved heads and victims' life
stories with the phrenologist Gall, who excels
at recounting "la biographie de chaque personnage, en manière d'épitaphe, c'est-à-dire très la-
coniquement" [each character's biography, like
an epitaph, in other words laconically] (Balzac
1955–63, 26.171). Equating head with head-
stone, decapitation with recapitulation, this extraordinary scene, rich in metonymic possibilities, both resonates with the memory of Louis
Balssa and provides a compelling, early model
of the narrative condensation so central to the
technique of recurring characters that would
enable the overall construction of *The Human
Comedy*. It is not surprising, of course, for the
man who cuts heads off and lives short to be
depicted as fancying both phrenology and biography. The fact that Balzac does too, however,
points to the author's broader identification
with Sanson, part of a complex process of self-
definition accompanying the progressive formulation of his ambitious novelistic project. As
royalist regicide, Sanson regretted being what
Balzac was straining to become: the "author" of
post-*ancien régime* France, his *oeuvre* as revolutionary as his avowed politics were retrograde.
Identifying with an executioner figure, Balzac
would also seem once more to be exorcising the
infamy of Uncle Louis Balssa's execution for
murder, so antithetical to his own aspirations
as Noble Author.

In 1833, Balzac published an enthusiastic review of "La Partie mythologique de la *Biogra-*

phie universelle" [The Mythological Section of the *Universal Biography*]:

> Ce livre est à la *Biographie Universelle* à laquelle il sert d'appendice, ce que les idées sont aux hommes. Les trente mille noms qui surnagent au-dessus des générations ont pris cinquante-deux volumes. Les dieux et les idées ont eu quatre volumes. Dans l'état actuel de nos connaissances, cette oeuvre est certes celle où s'est condensée, sous le plus petit espace, la plus vaste des sciences: la métaphysique. . . . [c'est] le répertoire de toutes les idées-mères. . . . Aucun livre n'est plus fécond! [Balzac 1955–63, 27.258–59]

> [This book is to the *Universal Biography*, for which it serves as an appendix, what ideas are to men. The thirty thousand names that have stood the test of time took fifty-two volumes. Gods and ideas had four volumes. In the current state of our knowledge, this work is certainly the one that condenses, in the smallest space, the vastest of the sciences: metaphysics. . . . (It) is the index of all our Ur-ideas. . . . No book is more fertile!]

This is high praise from the self-proclaimed "plus fécond de nos romanciers" [most fertile of our novelists]. Beyond his fascination with extreme condensation, he seems particularly intrigued by the concept of a vast study of human endeavor crowned by a potent distillation of its underlying ideas. By the following year, Balzac would settle on much the same structure for his own project, adding the *Études philosophiques* [Philosophical studies] and *Études analytiques* [Analytical studies], to reveal the "causes" and the "principes" behind the "effets sociaux" described in his *Études de moeurs au XIXe siècle* [Studies of 19th-century mores] (CH 1.11).

The period 1834–35 has generally been considered a turning point in Balzac's quest for a larger design, not only because he established this tripartite structure, but also because he began using the recurrence of characters systematically. Even so, he still lacked the global title for his project and, with it, the crucial idea of *The Human Comedy* as his own *Oeuvres complètes*. Here, once again, Balzac's work with biography, and with the *Biographie Universelle* in particular, helped guide him. His 1835 article on Brillat-Savarin, in the *Biographie universelle*, opens with an enthusiastic account of

how Brillat-Savarin owed his fame entirely to the publication of one masterful work:

> ses contemporains eux-mêmes l'ignoreraient aujourd'hui, sans la publication d'un livre, la *Physiologie du goût*, qui, sur la fin de ses jours, lui donna tout à coup une réputation incontestée. Les événements de sa vie ont acquis par cela seul toute l'importance que peut avoir la biographie des hommes célèbres. [Balzac 1955–63, 27.262]

> [Even his contemporaries would not know of him today, without the publication of one book, the *Physiology of Taste*, which, at the end of his days, suddenly gave him an undisputed reputation. Through this alone the events of his life acquired all the importance that the biography of a great man can have.]

As the choppy, syntactical packing of the first sentence suggests, Balzac is forcing Brillat-Savarin's story in line with his own aspirations, collapsing the publication of a great singular *oeuvre*, the death of its author, and the acclaim lavished upon him, in a virtually instant, almost magical apotheosis. Balzac does mention elsewhere, in passing, the four other books Brillat-Savarin published before the *Physiologie*, but he does so in as few words as possible at the very end of the article (268–69). This seeming afterthought is part of a larger strategy; privileging some writings over others, it seeks to make Brillat-Savarin synonymous with the *Physiologie*, prefiguring Balzac's efforts to become synonymous with *The Human Comedy*. Through Brillat-Savarin, Balzac rehearses his campaign to marginalize or disavow everything he wrote besides *The Human Comedy*, and thereby consolidate his reputation as the author of a distinctly selective complete works.

Elsewhere in the article, Balzac asserts that, as Brillat-Savarin "a toujours laissé beaucoup de lui dans son livre . . . on serait tenté d'inscrire sur la reliure de *la Physiologie du Goût*: 'Ci-gît l'âme de feu Brillat-Savarin'" [always left much of himself in his book, . . . one would be tempted to inscribe upon the binding of the *Physiology of Taste*, "Here lies the soul of the late Brillat-Savarin"] (268). To begin with, this provides further evidence of Balzac's obsession with book binding. Moreover, the biographical dictionary entry, the epitaph, and the ideal of an *oeuvres complètes* as the author's final resting place meet here in a tribute to Brillat-Savarin that once again betrays Balzac's own ambitions, aspirations toward posthumous distinction implicit in the very act of contributing to the *Biographie Universelle*. In fairness, Balzac's contribution to the dictionary was certainly motivated in part by practical considerations, as it enabled him to acquire a complete edition of this costly, long-coveted work, an eminently useful reference tool for a would-be "secretary of society." Yet even his 1833 review of the "Mythological section" already points to the broader, underlying motivation here, the quest for fame, by casting the *Biographie Universelle* as a repository for renown, a work in which only the most famous of names prevail ("surnagent au-dessus des générations" [survive the test of time]). Moreover, as Nodier contends in his preface, an article in Michaud's *Biographie universelle* proclaims the renown of the person it eulogizes, while also promising fame for the eulogizer; in this respect, it resembles that influential fixture of French literary culture, the *discours* or acceptance speech at the *Académie Française*, in which one pays tribute to a great predecessor as the necessary first step toward one's own "immortalization." Balzac's 1835 contribution to the *Biographie Universelle* also proceeds, in large measure, from a desire to one day be consecrated in the dictionary himself, like so many of the contributors before him.[41]

As this suggests, his article also marks an important intermediary stage in his evolving plans to live on through a monumental *oeuvre* of his own invention. At a point in his career when Balzac was already channeling his ambitions into setting up his larger textual system, while still unsure of its ultimate design, Michaud's dictionary provided a ready-made and instructive model—so much so that he would soon imitate it in the 1839 preface to *A Daughter of Eve*. In this important further reflection on his emerging "plan général" [general framework] (CH 2.262), Balzac envisions a biographical dictionary, not for flesh-and-blood notables, but rather for his fictional characters:

Aussi l'éditeur de ce livre disait-il assez spirituellement que, plus tard, on ferait aux *Études de moeurs* une table de matières biographiques, où l'on aiderait le lecteur à se retrouver dans cet immense labyrinthe au moyen d'articles . . . [265]

[Moreover, the publisher of this book remarked wittily that, later on, there would be a biographical index, to help the reader find his way through this immense labyrinth, by means of articles . . .]

After a long entry for Rastignac, written in the present tense and detailing the events of his life (and which, like the list of works on Carrier-Belleuse's monument to Dumas, ends with an expansive "etc."), Balzac concludes:

Nous ne continuerons pas cette plaisanterie destinée à faire ressortir les inconvénients que l'auteur a la bonne foi de signaler lui-même, et qui peut-être paraîtront de profondes combinaisons quand cette *Histoire des moeurs* aura des commentateurs, si toutefois elle peut trouver des lecteurs à l'époque difficile à prévoir où le français d'aujourd'hui aura besoin d'être commenté [265–66]

[We shall not continue this joke, designed to demonstrate the drawbacks that the author himself has pointed out in good faith, and that shall perhaps seem like profound conjunctions when this *History of mores* shall have commentators, if it even shall still have readers in that faraway time, when modern French would require commentary.]

Balzac presents his project as an "immense labyrinthe," a monumental construction in which the visitor needs guidance, like that offered by the maps, tables, and guides for strollers in the *Père-Lachaise*, or by the indexes, notes, bibliographies, and alphabetical ordering that orient the readers of dictionaries. Here this takes the form of an imagined *Tableau des matières biographiques* [Biographical table of contents], whose purpose would, as Descombes observes, be to "accompagner la lecture à la façon dont on s'accompagne d'un guide pendant la visite d'un monument, lequel est chargé de signaler en cours de route les curiosités inapparentes et les relations cachées entre ce qu'on a sous les yeux et le reste" [accompany our reading as would a guide, whose job it is, while we visit a monument, to point out along the way curiosities not apparent to the untrained eye, and hidden connections between whatever we are seeing at the moment, and the rest] (254). Furthermore, invoking a topos that we find as well in Zola's essay on Balzac in *Les Romanciers naturalistes* [Naturalist novelists], and in the dedication to Nadar's *Panthéon*, Balzac projects the reception of his work into an almost unforseeably distant future ("that faraway time, when . . ."). While concerned about his contemporary readership, Balzac is also writing with posterity in mind. His repeated disclaimers belie the seriousness of what he is doing and its centrality to his literary undertaking. Asserting that he will not continue "this joke" here, he acknowledges that it could be continued: his entire *oeuvre* could, and later would, repeatedly, be recast as an ersatz biographical dictionary. Through his seemingly off-hand homage to Michaud and company, he points as well to the affinities between his evolving narrative project and the biographical dictionary and, more broadly, to the central importance of biography in the conception and realization of his entire aesthetic enterprise. By the late 1830s, when Balzac wrote the preface to *A Daughter of Eve*, his work with biography had not so much been abandoned, as transformed. No longer the biographer of real-world eminences, nor the biographer of already canonical authors and publisher of their *oeuvres complètes*, nor even the compiler and biographical prefacer of his erstwhile pseudonym's works, Balzac was instead writing the lives of his own fictional celebrities. Soon, he would declare himself author of a complete works-in-progress called *The Human Comedy*, a kind of fictional *Biographie Universelle*, with himself as sole biographer of record, poised to bask in the reflected glory of so many noteworthy lives.

Balzac's Fame Machine

Balzac, qui a tant cherché l'absolu dans un certain nombre de découvertes, avait presque trouvé, dans son oeuvre même, la solution d'un problème inconnu avant lui, la réalité complète dans la complète fiction.
—George Sand, *Autour de ma table*
(Paris: Michel Lévy, 1876), 200

[Balzac, who searched so ardently for the Absolute in various discoveries, almost found in his own work the solution to a problem unknown before him: complete reality within complete fiction.]
—George Sand, *Around my table*

l'Esprit du siècle, ne l'oublions pas, est aux machines.
—Villiers de L'Isle-Adam, "La Machine à gloire"
(1986, 592)

[Let us not forget that the spirit of the times belongs to machines.]
—Villiers de L'Isle-Adam, "The Fame machine"

In his day, Balzac tried to manipulate his public image to best advantage by peddling his own wares in the fashionable salons and literary reviews of his day. Yet with his quirky, impetuous manner and general inelegance, he succeeded less at this than many more polished, but now largely forgotten contemporaries. Instead, he mainly owes his fame, and especially his posthumous fame, to his monumental *Human Comedy*. One might imagine that such a monument, as a literary mausoleum, a metaphorical mass of stone, would be static, inert. Yet *The Human Comedy* is not just an end but a means for securing renown, an extraordinarily dynamic vehicle, a complex piece of textual machinery—indeed, with all due respect to Villiers de l'Isle-Adam's skepticism, a truly effective fame machine.

We have already considered in some detail its workings: how the technique of recurring characters provides its key organizing principle; how recurrence engenders realism; how, in particular, like the *état civil*, it fabricates so many individual identities and, out of this, a larger social fabric; how Balzac's overarching project for *The Human Comedy* evolves out of his engagement with the "life and death writing" of biography; how the biographical dictionary, itself analogous to the modern cemetery, provides Balzac with a model for a textual "necropolis" that, more than just a repository of renown, is also an active fame generator, reflecting renown back on the biographer, memorializing the memorializer over time. At this point it will be useful to explore as well how the technique of recurring characters intersects fruitfully with the "marketplace of fame," especially as Balzac's work moves forward in history.

In his piece on recurring characters, Michel Butor argues that

la relation de ce qu'on dit d'un personnage fictif dans un roman avec ce qu'on en dit dans les autres, est exactement la même que celle de ce qui est dit d'un personnage réel dans la *Comédie humaine* avec ce qu'on en dit ailleurs. [Butor 1959, 268]

[the relationship between what is said of a fictional character in one novel and what is said in the others, is exactly the same as that between what is said of a real person inside *The Human Comedy*, and what is said outside.]

Real-world celebrities gain renown by figuring repeatedly in "toute une littérature, une presse, une conversation" [a literature, press, and conversation unto themselves]: essentially Braudy's "marketplace of fame." Repetition is the key to reputation, much as in modern advertising with, as noted in *César Birotteau*, "l'effet de piston produit sur le public par un article réitéré" [the piston-like effect upon the public of a repeated advertisement] (CH 6.204). The technique of recurring characters promotes Balzac's fictional celebrities as the marketplace does real ones, yet with a twist. Balzac's fictional literary celebrity Canalis, for example, does not end up standing in for this or that real poet but rather, as Butor contends, represents a potential poet, one who does not exist but should ("qui n'existe pas dans la réalité et qui devrait y exister" [who does not exist in reality but should]). Canalis thus strikes the reader as "bien plus clair . . . bien plus révélateur" [much clearer . . . much more revealing] (Butor 1959, 274–75) than his real-world counterparts. His perceived ontological plenitude is characteristic of modern fame culture for, as Braudy argues, the fragmented modern individual locates an idealized wholeness in celebrities: "the essential lure of the famous is that they are somehow more real than we and that our insubstantial physical reality needs that immortal substance for support" (Braudy 1986, 6). A colorful invention, Canalis mirrors yet also surpasses, even supplants pale reality. He is a compelling simulacrum, a synecdoche of the entire, seductively believable fictional world of *The Human Comedy*.

Celebrities are thus, as Butor argues, a particularly noteworthy phenomenon within Balzacian fiction, emblematic of the way Balzac's characters seem even more striking, more memorable than their contemporary, real-world "models." This ability to rival, and in some ways surpass the renown of real historical figures,

suggests that Balzac's characters are implicated in a fictional marketplace of fame—distinct, yet not entirely separate from the real one. Through recurrence, Balzac extends the marketplace of fame right into *The Human Comedy* and, to some extent, *The Human Comedy* into the marketplace of fame. Such extension, indeed interpenetration, is facilitated by the nature of this marketplace which, like the *état civil*, is a largely textual system ("toute une *littérature*, une *presse*," to use Butor's terms). Extension implies continuity, with a resultant blurring of boundaries between reality and fiction: particularly ambivalent, the fictional celebrity acts as a sort of shifter between realms. Extension does not, however, mean simple replication. Instead, there is an *intensification* of the marketplace within *The Human Comedy*, as even seemingly less significant members of the work's invented society are elevated to some sort of celebrity or notoriety: most notably through recurrence across texts, but also through starring roles in individual texts, and, through Balzac's broad preoccupation with fame, so deeply embedded in the fabric of the work that, for example, a successful hat-maker is billed as "le Nucingen des casquettes" [the Nucingen of hats] (CH 6.377)

Butor's comments suggest that, much as *The Human Comedy* is designed to "rival" the *état civil*, the fame of its fictional characters rivals, and can even surpass, that of real-world figures. Of course, an imagined literary celebrity like Canalis will never replace Lamartine in the *Classiques Larousse* nor supplant Victor Hugo in the *Panthéon*. Yet can we be so sure that lesser figures from *The Human Comedy* will not take, indeed have not taken precedence over their real-world equivalents? Butor reminds us that in the *Introduction to the Study of 19th-century Mores* Balzac, through his spokesman Félix Davin, speculates,

En voyant reparaître dans *Le Père Goriot* quelques-uns des personnages déjà créés, le public a compris l'une des plus hardies intentions de l'auteur, celle de donner la vie et le mouvement à tout un monde fictif, dont les personnages subsisteront peut-être encore, alors que la plus grande partie des modèles seront morts et oubliés. [CH 1.1160]

[When they saw some earlier characters reappear in *Father Goriot*, the public understood one of the author's boldest intentions, to give life and movement to a whole fictional world, whose characters shall perhaps live on, when most of their models shall already be dead and forgotten.]

Real people will be forgotten, while Balzac's fictional analogues of them will be remembered, as recurrence continues, over time, to promote both these characters and the larger fictional world they inhabit.

Such "bold intentions" recall a persistent legend about Balzac's life. On his deathbed, the novelist supposedly mustered the strength to make one final request of his old friend Dr. Nacquart: "Allez chercher Bianchon" [Go look for Bianchon] (Lotte 1947, *En marge* 7). With his last breaths, the creator would thus summon again one of his most frequently recurring characters. Abandoning his real doctor for his invented one, he supplants a historical personnage with a fictional character and, by extension, forsakes the real world for that of his fiction. This story's appeal derives from linking the physical death of the author and the survival of his fiction. On the verge of death, Balzac opens a magical door onto another realm: might Bianchon save Balzac, we wonder, not for life in our world, but for an afterlife in *The Human Comedy*? The author might live on not just *through* but actually *in* his works (cf. Roland Chollet, Ci-gît Balzac, in *Groupe International de Recherches Balzaciennes* 1993, 283–98). This account of Balzac's last minutes, like so many other deathbed stories, may be apocryphal, the product of posthumous mythmaking. Indeed, like some of Hugo's supposed last words, "C'est ici le combat du jour et de la nuit" [This here is the battle between day and night] or "Je vois de la lumière noire" [I see black light] (Robb 1998, 522–23), offering an Hugolian aesthetics in a nutshell, Balzac's appeal to Nacquart sounds too true to be true. Whether the story is true or not, Balzac's underlying phantasm about the reality of the world within *The Human Comedy* has been influential, promulgated over time by the work's ongoing, internal marketplace of fame.

As the *Introduction to the Studies of 19th-century Mores* suggests, Balzac hoped to impose such a view upon his readers, yet it was perhaps too much to ask of his *contemporary* readers. The *Introduction* claims only that the latter "understand" the author's intentions, not that they have fallen under the spell of their realization. The readers of the 1830s and 1840s knew the prominent figures of the first half of the nineteenth century and would not have confused them with their fictional doubles. Yet how many of us today could, for example, name three well-known journalists of the period? For readers of Balzac, though, Émile Blondet, Étienne Lousteau, and Raoul Nathan spring to mind. This is because we live in a future that Balzac envisioned, in which the characters of *The Human Comedy* live on while their real-world counterparts are long since dead and, but for a privileged, supremely famous few, forgotten. As time passes, the real-world marketplace of fame changes: only transcendantly famous names (Napoléon, Victor Hugo, and so on) remain in circulation; lesser eminences fade from view. Meanwhile, *The Human Comedy* survives. Its internal marketplace of fame continues to promote and perpetuate its characters, its own reputation, and that of its creator. Balzac serves moreover as the ultimate repository for narrative: underwriting each individual text, the signature "Honoré de Balzac" is the most widely recurring name in *The Human Comedy*. As the names of Balzac's myriad characters recur within his textual fame machine, they come to seem not only "real," but also more meaningful, more compelling, more famous, and this aura reflects back, a thousandfold, upon their creator—a process well-illustrated by the Grandville drawing (fig. 11) in which a giant, enthroned Balzac is carried along the path to glory by the multitude of his grateful characters.

The ideal reader that Balzac postulates in the *Introduction to the Studies of 19th-century Mores*, the reader of the future, is thus born not of a collective memory, but of a collective *amnesia*—Balzac's textual monument would in this sense, like the Obelisk, possess a curiously productive ability to "induce forgetting" (Hollier 1989, 673; cf. above). Like Stendhal, Balzac locates his ideal audience in the future. There is an important difference, however: Stendhal's future reader is distinguished by greater intelligence and finer sensibility; Balzac's, by his gullibility, or rather by a lost cultural competence that results in perceiving not only the characters, but the entire society represented within *The Human Comedy* as real. Today, as the actual nineteenth century slips further into the past and out of our memories, we continue to read Balzac's fictional representation of it. For the modern reader, Balzac's version has in many ways become the real thing. Indeed, by century's end, Oscar Wilde could already assert that "The nineteenth century, as we know it, is largely an invention of Balzac" (1909, 41). To cast this provocative idea in contemporary terms, we might think of *The Human Comedy* as an early exercise in virtual reality, a monumental simulacrum, a pioneering theme park called "Nineteeth-Century Land," or perhaps simply "Balzacland."

Canonization

vous, ô Honoré de Balzac, vous le plus héroïque, le plus singulier, le plus romantique et le plus poétique parmi tous les personnages que vous avez tirés de votre sein!
—Charles Baudelaire, *Salon de 1846* (1975–76, 2.496)

[you, o Honoré de Balzac, the most heroic, most peculiar, most romantic and most poetic of all the characters you have wrenched from your bosom!]
—Charles Baudelaire, Salon of 1846

–Et pourquoi vous livrer à la souffrance? Ce qui nous coûte notre vie, le sujet qui, durant des nuits studieuses, a ravagé notre cerveau; toutes ces courses à travers les champs de la pensée, notre monument construit avec notre sang devient pour les éditeurs une affaire bonne ou mauvaise.
—Honoré de Balzac, *Illusions perdues* (CH 5.371)

[–And why let yourself suffer? For publishers, what costs us our life, the subject that, during long nights of study ravaged our brain; all these journeys through realms of ideas, our monument made of our blood, becomes a good or bad deal.]
—Honoré de Balzac, *Lost Illusions*

Balzac's posthumous apotheosis has sprung as well from models of "canonization" already inscribed in his text that derive in turn from kindred religious traditions: consecrating a body of writing as scripture, and consecrating a person as a saint. An author's canonization is generally understood more narrowly today, as the process whereby an author becomes an esteemed, established part of the canon, figuring on reading lists, published in complete works editions, and so forth. Yet Balzac's case demonstrates that

"canonization" can be a richer, more polyvalent concept. In particular, we shall see how divergent but related forms of canonization are woven into *The Human Comedy*; how these are bound up with the monumental vision of literary greatness in nineteenth-century France; how, over time, these have sparked a double mythologizing of his life and work; and, finally, how late portraits of Balzac have helped foster much of the same myth-making process.

The one religious tradition of canonization defines which sacred texts are genuine or authoritative and thus belong officially to church scripture. Such an understanding of the concept has fostered its use, within literary criticism, as a metaphor for the institutional privileging of selected texts. But seeing canonization as just a synonym for institutionalization neglects its original, devotional premise: that this holy writ emanated from a divine presence. In the Romantic imagination, however, amid quasi-religious veneration for literary creators and their creations—Bénichou's "sacre de l'écrivain"—the writer became that divine presence, and his work, the holy writ. The author's sacredness made the work sacred.

This vision of canonization informed the trajectory of Balzac's literary career. As we have seen, through the 1820s, he struggled to define himself, to establish his identity as Honoré de Balzac, noble author, a worthy figure ready to produce great works. In the 1830s, Balzac turned his energies from defining himself to defining his *oeuvre*. As he evolved his overarching novelistic project, he experimented with such global titles as "Scenes of private life" and "Studies of mores" before, by 1840, settling on "The Human Comedy." He then began searching for a publisher and, on October 2, 1841, signed a contract for the publication of *The Human Comedy* as his "Oeuvres complètes." The actual publication would begin in 1842, run to eighteen volumes, and take more than a dozen years, from the final ones of his life to the first few after his death. Balzac's designation of *The Human Comedy* as his *oeuvres complètes* was a radically "Napoleonic" gesture of self-apotheosis, or rather of self-canonization. As we have seen, a complete works, analogue of the monument, was an honor normally reserved for a dead author and, while supposedly "complete," Balzac's "works" were really a selection that, by excluding less impressive or central elements like theater, juvenalia, and journalism, aimed to consolidate the grandeur of his legacy. Balzac thus substituted himself for posterity, as the arbiter of his own greatness.

The other religious tradition of canonization, the sanctifying of a worthy person, has been neglected as well by contemporary criticism, yet also ran deep in the Romantic imagination—specifically, in a Romantic mythology of the author that remains crucial to our understanding of Balzac as a literary figure. This is the tradition in the Roman Catholic Church "of declaring a dead person a saint. . . . preceded by beatification and by an examination into the life and miracles of the person" (*Webster's New Twentieth-Century Dictionary* 2nd ed.) The deceased ascends to sainthood through the exemplarity of the life he has lived and of the "miracles" he has performed, but also, above all, through martyrdom, which hurls his prerequisite good works into sharper focus. Likewise, the great writer would accede to literary posterity through the excellence of his *oeuvre*, with a heroic but untimely death dramatizing this ascenscion.

The Human Comedy abounds with tales of martyred characters, from Raphaël de Valentin to Cousin Pons, drawing heavily on the powerful tradition of Christian martyrology for narrative paradigms of inevitable death. For example, Pierrette Lorrain's prolonged agony and eventual demise at the hands of the Rogron siblings is characterized repeatedly as martyrdom; baroness Hulot is described as "une martyre" by the baron's former mistress Josépha who, with a distinctly devotional gesture, "baisa respectueusement la robe de la baronne" [respectfully kissed the baroness' dress] (CH 7.385); Z. Marcas' name rings with the sound of martyrdom, as the narration is only too willing to point out ("Ne vous semble-t-il pas que l'homme qui le porte doive être martyrisé?" [Does it not seem to you that a man so named should be a martyr?; 8.829]); and César Birotteau, we are told in the closing line of the novel, is "un martyr de la probité commerciale à décorer de la palme éternelle" [a martyr to commercial integrity, who should be eternally honored] (6.312). In particular, Balzac relishes recounting the plight of doomed, obsessive seekers and creators like Frenhofer or Balthazar Claës, in

so many ways analogues of their maker. Accounts of such gloriously catastrophic destinies seem, moreover, to presage the martyrdom of an author who ruined his health in a vain struggle to complete his monumental literary project. Indeed, from Hugo's funerary oration onward, there has prevailed a largely hagiographic treatment of Balzac, culminating in André Maurois's *Prométhée, ou la vie de Balzac* [Prometheus, or the life of Balzac] (1965), which casts the author of *The Human Comedy* as a modern Prometheus, a martyr of creation. "La vie de Balzac," asserts Maurois, likening the writer's fate to that of his characters, "s'achevait comme un roman de *La Comédie humaine*. . . . Il mourait brûlé par ses désirs, épuisé par les actes imaginaires de ses créatures, victime de son oeuvre" [Balzac's life ended like a novel in *The Human Comedy*. . . . He died scorched by his own desires, exhausted by the imaginary acts of his characters, the victim of his own work] (597). Perhaps the "victim" of his work in this life, Balzac has been its beneficiary in the hereafter, his posthumous legend greatly enhanced by the prestige of such martyrdom. In these ways, the posthumous success of Balzac and his *Human Comedy* draw upon both religious traditions of canonization at once: not only the scriptural tradition, with the work sanctified by its author, but also the martyrological tradition, with the author sanctified by his work—a sort of reciprocal monumentalization that exemplifies the "ideal synthesis" of writer, work, and monument that prevailed, in later nineteenth-century France, in the decades following Balzac's death.

Images tell much the same story, of Balzac setting in motion a double apotheosis of his life and work, by trying to establish a definitive visual imprint of himself. Like his will to fix a definitive textual version of *The Human Comedy*, this proceeds from and in turn helps promote much the same heroic vision of him as an author. The year 1842 thus saw not only the launching of the first three volumes in Balzac's self-proclaimed complete works, but also his analogous effort to position and preserve his physical appearance for posterity, through two effigies in particular: a daguerreotype and a bust. It is as if, having found the right form to carry his words into the future, he now sought to do the same with his image, to frame a portrait

Fig. 16. Anonymous, after Louis-Auguste Bisson, *Honoré de Balzac*. © Photothèque des musées de la ville de Paris.

for his textual mausoleum, a frontispiece of the author, a premonitory vision of Saint Balzac's apotheosis.

On June 2, 1842, Balzac posed for the only known daguerreotype of him (fig. 16), by Louis-Auguste Bisson (Chotard 1990, 18–23). He overcame his supposed wariness about photography to do so (Nadar 1979, 2.978), suggesting just how keen he was to explore the fledgling medium's potential to memorialize its subject. Balzac, it seems, wanted not only to be photographed, but to be photographed in a particular way. In the resulting plate, he eschews the formality typical of early daguerreotypes, with no overcoat or tophat to signal his place in the contemporary social order. Instead, he wears a plain, loosely draping work shirt, open wide at the neck: comfortable garb for staying home and writing, but also reminiscent of the classical dress David d'Angers recommended to lend an air of timelessness to great men's effigies and thus suggestive both of current travails and future glory. His pose draws attention to his right—his writing—hand, alluding as well to his work as a writer. The hand is placed, moreover, upon his heart, at once the supposed seat of the emotions and most vital of the organs. Is he just getting in touch with his inner self? Or, is he having a premonitory heart tremor, foreseeing the end of his life and of the creative activity it supports? If so, this would dramatize his impending mortality, together with the literary immortality it promises—a juxtaposition rendered all the more poignant here by photography's collapsing of presence and absence, life and death. This carefully posed image, we gather, as the hand gesture urges on such questions, is a portrait of the writer as both sensitive, creative being, and literary martyr-to-be. The gesture also invokes a broader, Napoleonic paradigm of the nineteenth-century great man, for it recalls Bonaparte's trademark hand-on-stomach pose. This is true as well of the Napoleonic "man of destiny" gaze he strikes that appears to pierce beyond the here and now to the hereafter, yet is also intensely self-absorbed, immersed in the subject's creative fervor. Balzac's garb and stance thus construct essentially the same vision of himself as he was weaving into *The Human Comedy* at the time: that of a writer firmly rooted in the world of his cre-

ation, all the better to carry him forward into posterity.

In November of the same year, Balzac again demonstrated his will to be immortalized visually when, during a dinner at Victor Hugo's house, he agreed to David d'Angers' offer to make his bust (Sarment 1980, 47). David, in so many ways the precursor of later nineteenth-century statuemania, was a self-styled recorder of posterity, and unlike the medallions that he had made of so many contemporary figures, a bust was a more prestigious form, more closely associated with enduring renown. When the work was delivered in 1845, it had in fact become a "colossal" bust—in other words, as monumental a form as could be accorded a living celebrity at the time, for full-length statues were reserved for deceased glories. Victor Hugo, himself obsessed with posterity and in some sense the godfather of this vehicle for immortalization that originated under his roof, integrated it prominently in the account of his deathbed visit to Balzac. This took place during the final throes of the novelist's long illness, for "M. de Balzac était atteint depuis dix-huit mois d'une hypertrophie du coeur" [M. De Balzac had for eighteen months been suffering from a hypertrophied heart] (Hugo 1972, 3.190). In the account, Hugo first observes "le buste colossal en marbre de Balzac par David, . . . [qui] se dressait vaguement dans cette ombre comme le spectre de l'homme qui allait mourir" [the colossal marble bust of Balzac by David . . . (that) stood in the shadows, seeming distant, like the specter of a man about to die] (191). Then, as he approaches the deathbed, the signs of physical decay overwhelm: "la gangrène y est. . . . la peau et la chair étaient comme du lard. . . . une odeur de cadavre emplissait la maison. . . . une odeur insupportable s'exhalait du lit" [gangrene has taken hold . . . his skin and flesh are like lard. . . . A cadaverous stench fills the house . . . an unbearable stench rose from the bed] (191–92) Finally, he compares the dying writer's countenance with his marble effigy:

Il avait la face violette, presque noire, inclinée à droite; la barbe non faite; les cheveux gris et coupés court, l'oeil ouvert et fixe. Je le voyais de profil, et il ressemblait ainsi à l'Empéreur. . . . Je redescendis, emportant dans ma pensée cette figure livide; en traversant le salon, je retrouvai le buste immobile, altier et rayonnant vaguement, et je comparai la mort à l'immortalité. [192–93]

[He had a purple, almost black face, tilted to the right; unshaven; with short grey hair, his eyes open and steady. I saw him in profile, which made him look like the Emperor.... I came back down, thinking of that ghastly face; as I crossed the drawing room, I saw again the steadfast bust, haughty and faintly shimmering, and I compared death with immortality.]

Balzac's face is a study in purple and black, portending imminent putrefaction. This contrasts with the noble, stony radiance of the bust and the mortality of the flesh with the immortality embodied by statuary. Hugo also likens moribund Balzac's profile to Napoleon's, a seemingly implausible association, for it is hard to imagine that the corpulent, agonizing novelist truly resembled the emperor. The comparison works in other ways though. In one sense, this is Hugo's own Napoleon complex— his life-long quest for literary glory through emulation of the Napoleonic model—projected onto dying Balzac, whose supposed resemblance to Napoleon would thus signify his greatness as a writer. In another sense, the entire deathbed vignette seems a reminiscence of the 1842 daguerreotype and of the vision Balzac fashioned of himself there, from the soon-to-be fatal heart disease that seems retrospectively to confirm the foreboding in that earlier hand-on-heart gesture, to the mix here, as in the photo, of Napoleonic emulation, impending mortality, and projected immortality.

Displaying his usual egocentrism, Hugo saw dying Balzac as he would have liked to be seen, with the great writer's passage into posterity cloaked in an air of heroic martyrdom and portentous monumentality. Several days later, in his funerary oration for Balzac, Hugo would elaborate further upon these same themes:

> Tous ses livres ne forment qu'un livre, livre vivant, lumineux, profond, où l'on voit . . . Toute notre civilisation contemporaine. . . .
> Voilà ce qu'il a fait parmi nous. Voilà l'oeuvre qu'il nous laisse, oeuvre haute et solide, robuste entassement d'assises de granit, monument! oeuvre du haut de laquelle resplendira désormais sa renommée. Les grands hommes font leur propre piédestal; l'avenir se charge de la statue . . . Hélas!

Ce travailleur puissant et jamais fatigué . . . sort des contestations et des haines. Il entre, le même jour, dans la gloire et dans le tombeau. Il va briller, désormais, au-dessus de toutes ces nuées, qui sont sur nos têtes, parmi les étoiles de la patrie (Hugo 1968b, 7.316–18)

[All his books make up one deep, vibrant, luminous book, in which we see all of our contemporary civilization.
This is what he did among us. This is the work he leaves us, solid and tall, a robust heap of granite courses, a monument! a work from whose heights his renown shall radiate outward from now on. Great men make their own pedestal; the future takes care of the statue. Alas! this mighty, indefatigable fighter leaves behind hatred and conflict. On the same day he enters into his tomb and into glory. He shall shine, from now on, above the clouds, above our heads, among the stars of our nation.]

To an adept of the "dream of stone" like Hugo, Balzac's premature end is exemplary for its evocative compression of the author's life and literary afterlife, with a singular—and singularly monumental—*oeuvre* propelling him to this apotheosis. Hugo's final homage to Balzac, like the narrative of his last visit to the novelist, is moving but far from disinterested. As witness to the agony and death of a rival like Balzac, Hugo already contemplated his own literary posterity. In his treatment of these events Hugo rehearsed the themes that would guide his own efforts at self-apotheosis through the latter part of his life, as we shall see in detail later on: the Napoleonic model, the monumental measure, the prefiguring of eternal glory through contemporary opposition ("des contestations et des haines"), the ultimate triumph of genius's resplendent "light," and the great writer's invaluable contribution to the greater glory of the nation.

A quarter century after Balzac's passing, George Sand died in great pain, though in a manner less amenable to heroic treatment, of a blocked intestine. Unlike Flaubert, Hugo did not attend the funeral, but his devoted friend Paul Meurice read the master's eulogy, asserting, "George Sand a dans notre temps une place unique. D'autres sont les grands hommes, elle est la grande femme" [George Sand occupies a singular place in our time. Others are great men, she is the great woman] (Hugo 1904–52, 3.242). This seems high praise, yet Hugo was in the habit of spinning such commemorative rhetoric, and his physical absence perhaps speaks louder than words of his true enthusiasm for Sand. There is moreover no reference whatsoever in the address to monuments, unlike Hugo's earlier oration for Balzac, dominated by the monumental metaphor, even though delivered at a time when the dream of stone was not yet as pervasive as it had become by the 1870s. Could the great woman writer also be seen in such monumental terms?

3

George Sand: Visions of the Great Woman Writer

[Cette question des] bizarres disparates qui existent entre
le talent d'un écrivain et sa physionomie. . . . intéresse les
femmes-poètes encore plus que l'auteur lui-même.
—Honoré de Balzac "Préface," *La Peau de chagrin*
(CH 10.51)

[(This question of the) bizarre mismatches that exist between
a writer's talent and his appearance is of even greater interest
to poetesses than to the author himself.]
—Honoré de Balzac, "Preface," *The Wild Ass's Skin*

An Image Problem

On avait à Paris une caricature sur [Madame Récamier];
elle entra un jour dans un magasin de gravures, et on la lui
offrit sans la connaître. . . . Elle fut surprise d'abord; mais
elle regarda cette gravure de sang-froid. "Sans doute, dit-
elle au marchand, cette personne a mauvaise réputation.
—Point du tout, répondit-il sur-le-champ; c'est une dame
dont la réputation est sans tache." Et il continua de lui
prodiguer des éloges qui, n'étant pas suspects, la con-
solèrent de l'intention qu'on avait pu avoir en traçant la
caricature qu'elle avait entre les mains.
—Charles Monselet, *Statues et statuettes
contemporaines* (1852, 75)

[In Paris there was a caricature of (Madame Récamier);
one day she entered a print shop, and it was offered to
her without knowing who she was. . . . She was surprised
at first; but she looked at it without losing her composure.
"There can be no doubt," she said to the merchant, "that
this person has a bad reputation." "—Not at all," he said
straight off. "She's a lady whose reputation is unsullied."
And he continued to lavish praise that, because it was beyond suspicion, made her feel better about the intentions
behind the drawing she had in her hands.]
—Charles Monselet, *Contemporary statues
and statuettes*

Je leur montrai l'argile originale du buste de ma jolie
cousine, Mme Récamier, par Chinard, et son portrait en
miniature par Augustin; ils en furent si ravis, que le docteur, avec ses grosses lèvres, baisa le portrait, et que le
capitaine se permit sur le buste une licence pour laquelle je le battis, car si tous les admirateurs de l'original
venaient en faire autant, ce sein si voluptueusement con-
tourné serait bientôt dans le même état que l'orteil de

saint Pierre de Rome, que les pèlerins ont raccourci à
force de le baiser.
—Jean-Anthelme Brillat-Savarin, *La Physiologie
du goût* (1982, 177)

[I showed them the original clay bust of my pretty cousin,
Mme Récamier, by Chinard, and her miniature portrait
by Augustin; they were so delighted that the doctor kissed
the portrait with his fat lips, and the captain took such
liberties with the bust that I hit him for it, because if
all the original's admirers did the same, its voluptuosly
rounded bosom would soon be in the same state as Saint
Peter's big toe, which pilgrims to Rome have shortened by
kissing it so much.]
—Jean-Anthelme Brillat-Savarin, *The Physiology
of Taste*

Achieving unparalleled renown as a woman of
letters, George Sand challenged contemporaries
to think of her as a great writer in the monumental mode usually reserved for men. On the
whole, nineteenth-century women writers suffered from an "image problem," at once general
prejudice against them and specific lack of rele-
vant iconographical precedent through which
their greatness could be envisioned. Sand's
uniqueness can best be understood against the
backdrop of her less successful female peers
and, in particular, by examining a substantial
yet neglected body of iconographical evidence,
for many in nineteenth-century France envisioned the possibilities and limitations of female
literary greatness in the image, indeed largely
through images, of George Sand.

112

Je n'aime pas que les femmes écrivent.
—Napoléon Bonaparte[1]

[I don't like women to write.]
—Napoleon Bonaparte

To be sure, women had written and published in previous centuries, yet in nineteenth-century France, unprecedented numbers sought open, public recognition as authors. As Béatrice Slama observes, "Tout au long du siècle . . . de plus en plus nombreuses sont les femmes qui écrivent et publient. . . . [et] revendique[nt] le statut de 'femme auteur,' d'"auteure'" [All across the century . . . there are more and more women who write and publish. . . . (and) claim the status of "woman author," of "authoress"] (Slama 1980, 214–16). With the number of women authors growing, names for them abounded. "[A]uteures, autrices, auteuses et autoresses" were among the designations brandished proudly by women, or wielded derisively by their male critics, notes Christine Planté in La petite soeur de Balzac [Balzac's little sister], the best general study to date of the nineteenth-century woman author's predicament (1989, 25). This proliferation of women as authors was conditioned, moreover, by the broader hierarchization of the literary world, with women disproportionately represented at the lower end of the scale. While feminine declensions of auteur [author] filled discussions of literary women, the more exalted term écrivain [writer] rarely was used. This discrepancy, as Planté notes, manifested the broader view that an auteur simply wrote, whereas an écrivain created works of artistic merit:

la femme auteur, ce n'est pas un écrivain. "Auteur, selon Littré, est plus général qu'écrivain" et se dit pour "toute composition scientifique ou littéraire, en prose ou en vers . . . Mais écrivain ne se dit que de ceux qui a écrit en prose des ouvrages de belles-lettres ou d'histoire; ou du moins, si on le dit des autres, c'est qu'alors on a la pensée fixée sur leur style . . ." A travers ce mot, il s'agit en somme davantage d'une pratique, d'un métier, de la littérature comme institution sociale, que de l'écriture comme création artistique et devenir d'un sujet dans le langage. On reconnaît des femmes auteurs avant de parler de femmes écrivains: c'est qu'il est plus facile (encore que ce soit de mauvais gré) de leur concéder le droit d'accès à un nouveau gagne-pain, et à une pratique sociale, qu'elles ont de toute façon déjà obtenu dans les faits, que de leur reconnaître la dignité d'artistes et de sujets à part entière. (26–27)

[the woman author is not a writer. "Author," according to Littré, "is more general than writer" and is said for "all scientific or literary compositions, in verse or prose . . . But writer is only used to speak of those who have written literary or historical works in prose; or at least, if it is used to speak of others, it is because of an overriding preoccupation with style . . ." As this suggests, it is more a matter of writing as a practice, a trade, and of literature as a social institution, than of artistic creation or of a subject emerging through language. Society recognizes women authors before speaking of women writers, because it is easier to allow them (however reluctantly) the right to a new sort of livelihood, and to a social practice, which in any case they had already obtained, than to recognize their dignity as artists and as full-fledged subjects.]

Women were thus, however reluctantly, admitted into the category of auteur, the degré zéro of authorship. For the most part, though, they were denied entry into the more esteemed category of écrivain. Oddly, Planté's otherwise discerning analysis neglects an important and far more restrictive third category: that of the great writer, or grand écrivain, who was thought to create exceptional works of lasting literary worth and, in so doing, to attain resplendent, enduring, posthumous fame. Although the smallest of the three categories, this rarefied realm is crucial because it represents the monumental ideal—the "dream of stone"—toward which the literary world aspired. Women were all but excluded from this category, however. The hierarchy of value in the nineteenth-century world of letters can perhaps best be envisioned as a series of increasingly exclusive, concentric circles, with most of the growing number of women authors only in the outermost zone of auteurs; a much smaller number could reach the middle range of écrivains; and, only Mme de Staël and Sand might accede to the inner sanctum of grands écrivains.

Germaine de Staël (1766–1817), was the leading femme de lettres of the generation preceding Sand's. For many of Sand's contemporaries, comparison with Staël seemed inevitable. In 1870, for example, one commentator noted, "aucun [des hommes illustres de ce siècle],

Victor Hugo excepté, ne saurait, je crois, laisser derrière son nom la traînée lumineuse dont resplendira dans l'avenir le souvenir de deux femmes, Mme de Staël et George Sand" [none (of this century's illustrious men), except for Victor Hugo, could, I believe, leave behind such a luminous trail as that with which the names of two women, Mme de Staël and George Sand shall shine in future] (BHVP Dossier, Notices biographiques [signed "Auguste Luchet"]). There is evidence as well that Sand saw Staël as her rival: the novel *Consuelo* can in many ways be considered her response to Staël's *Corinne*[2]; in a January 20, 1852, letter to Louis-Napoléon requesting clemency for friends, Sand compared herself to Staël (Sand 1964–91); and her choice of a pseudonym may even have, however unconsciously, been informed by a desire to recall her famous predecessor through identical initials. While singling out Staël as Sand's main female rival, contemporaries also tended to see Sand prevailing. Characteristically, Jules Janin's biographical sketch of Sand in the 1836 *Biographie des femmes auteurs contemporaines* [Biography of contemporary women authors] casts her literary début as an eclipse of Staël, speculating that, "[son] apparition eût fait mourir de chagrin et de douleur, elle-même madame de Staël, si madame de Staël eût été sa contemporaine" [(her) emergence would even have made madame de Staël die of pain and chagrin, if madame de Staël had been her contemporary] (444). Indeed, while in retrospect Staël could be said to rival Sand in the critical esteem accorded her writing, she never achieved Sand's broader, public renown, for literary fame itself was transformed radically in the years separating their careers (Staël died in 1817, Sand in 1876).

In a general way, writers became the object of much greater publicity under the July Monarchy than they had been earlier on. More specifically, as Sand was making her career during the 1830s and 1840s, the rapid expansion of the press, proliferation of such inexpensive publications about celebrities as biographical sketches or lithographic galleries, and particularly keen interest in the figure of the *femme auteur* propelled her to unprecedented notoriety as a woman of letters. When Germaine de Staël died, moreover, the monumental vision of literary greatness was only just starting to take shape, with the literary work beginning to be seen as a monument. In contrast, the half century surrounding Sand's death in 1876 would witness the culmination of the literary "dream of stone." From about 1850, writers were seen increasingly as monuments and, from around the time of Sand's death through the turn of the century, there triumphed an ideal synthesis of writer, work, and monument, manifested most emphatically by the phenomenon of statuemania. Singled out as the leading woman writer of her day, Sand could embody the female challenge to this fundamentally male vision of literary glory, the possibility that a woman be considered a truly great writer and monumentalized accordingly. Moreover, for better or worse, Staël's broader public appeal seems to have suffered and Sand's to have benefited from perceptions of their physical appearances. Characteristically, while the entry for Staël in an 1843 *Galerie des dames françaises distinguées dans les lettres et les arts* [Gallery of French ladies distinguished in arts and letters] begins glowingly with, "C'est un des premiers écrivains du siècle" [She is one of the top writers of her century], it ends with lukewarm commentary on her looks: "Madame de Staël n'était pas jolie; sa figure était forte, ses yeux pourtant étaient d'une grande beauté" [Madame de Staël was not pretty; her face was heavyset, though her eyes were very beautiful]. The article allows Staël only beautiful eyes (a feature often emphasized in representing female intellectuals, as we shall see), and suggests that the allure of the "beau portrait" [handsome portrait] reproduced here derives not from her otherwise nonexistent physical charms, but rather from the talent of the artist, Gérard, who created it. In a similar vein, remarks Stendhal in his correspondence, "Mme de Staël a perdu entièrement la grâce en montrant sa supériorité" [Mme de Staël completely lost all her grace as she showed her superiority] (Stendhal 1962–68, 1.315). Likewise, Charles Monselet's biographical sketch of Mme Récamier recounts "Cette aventure d'un homme qui se trouvant placé entre madame de Staël et madame Récamier, eut la maladresse de dire:—Me voilà entre l'esprit et la beauté!—Sans posséder ni l'une ni l'autre, répondit madame de Staël" [This story of a man who, finding himself placed between madame de Staël and madame Récamier, was so inept as to say:—Here I am between brain and beauty!—Without possessing either one, responded madame de Staël] (Monselet1852, 71). In contrast, a sonnet accompanying a print of the Charpentier Sand portrait praises her as "Reine de poésie et reine de beauté!" [Queen of poetry and queen of beauty] (BHVP Dossier). Within a cultural context in which the growing number of women writers was capturing the public imagination, and visual depictions were playing an ever-greater role in shaping literary fame, yet iconographical traditions for representing female greatness remained predicated upon an ideal of feminine beauty, Staël's plainness was thought at odds with her literary talents and sparkling wit, and ultimately proved detrimental to her reputation, whereas Sand's beauty was perceived as complementing her literary talent and enhanced her reputation. For such reasons, despite the esteem in which Staël and her work were held, Sand was the one that her contemporaries tried more frequently and enthusiastically to "envision"—at once to depict and to conceive of—as a great writer, indeed as *the* great woman writer.

As Planté's analysis of names for the *femme auteur* suggests, scholarship has until now approached the "problem" of the nineteenth-century woman author largely through words, not images. In particular, recent commentators like Planté, Slama, Nicole Mozet, or Michelle Perrot have probed the various ways in which nineteenth-century literary and broader societal discourse would exclude, marginalize, puzzle over, and (sometimes) even promote women authors. What though of nineteenth-century France's unprecedentedly abundant images of its women authors? From satirical prints of stereotypical bluestockings or *bas-bleus*, to more reverential portraits of individual *femmes de lettres*, and on to pioneering sculptural tributes, images played a significant part in a massive, ongoing reflection on the *femme auteur*. Literary and historical research on the nineteenth-century woman author has, for the most part, by focusing almost solely on verbal commentary, neglected this substantial, highly suggestive body of visual evidence. Because of Sand's extraordinary stature, however, there has been a history of efforts, from Viscount Spoelberch de Lovenjoul through Georges Lubin, including exhibitions at the *Bibliothèque*

historique de la ville de Paris in 1954 and *Bibliothèque nationale* in 1954 and 1977, to identify, authenticate, date, and catalogue images of George Sand. Guided though by what Lubin, in his preface to the Pléiade *Album Sand,* calls "le . . . souci d'authenticité" [the concern for authenticity] (1973, 8), these studies have been long on erudition yet short on broader critical perspective, and excluded many of the abundant, popular representations of Sand which, while perhaps of dubious documentary or even artistic merit, prove revealing in other ways (of the 480 images of Sand, her work, circle, and milieu in Lubin's *Album,* only 85 are actually of Sand). While not really addressing the rich interplay of iconography and ideology, and thus telling us little about how the period envisioned the *femme auteur* in general and Sand in particular, such scholarship does at least provide a solid point of departure for inquiry along these lines.

Recent art historical research has paid a great deal of attention to nineteenth-century images of women yet, as Janis Bergman-Carton observes, it has focused on "victimized women" like courtesans and prostitutes, rather than intellectual women (1). In *The Woman of Ideas in French Art, 1830–1848*, Bergman-Carton attempts to rectify this imbalance, by resurrecting the "woman of ideas," a figure "prevalent in nineteenth-century art and life yet ignored in twentieth-century critical literature" (1995, 1). The term "woman of ideas" is defined further as "a figure principally identified by her nineteenth-century contemporaries (satirically or not) as an intellectual being who recognizes and uses the power of words to influence public opinion" and it designates exclusively "women operating in the fields of literature and politics—two highly visible, valued, and interactive aspects of French public life" (2). While Bergman-Carton's study does provide many useful insights into the visual representation of nineteenth-century intellectual women, including George Sand, its overall orientation diminishes its specific relevance to our inquiry. In one sense, its focus is too broad for our purposes: ranging from female revolutionaries of 1830 and Saint-Simonians, to *bas-bleus*, to *femmes liseuses*, on to female embodiments of the Republic, its contribution to an understanding of women writers in particular is necessarily

limited. By considering such a variety of intellectual women together, as all "women of ideas,"
it also largely sidesteps the issue of their divi-
sion according to the period's hierarchies of
value. In another sense, its focus is too narrow for our purposes: ending in 1848, it misses
the culmination of the "dream of stone" in the
second half of the century, and the concurrent
resistance in French culture toward integrating
women writers, even George Sand, into such a
fundamentally male vision of literature. Recently, Luce Czyba (1995) and Bertrand Tillier
(1993) have also devoted brief studies to caricatures of Sand. While useful in some respects,
their studies do not address what is most unique
about Sand, what distinguishes her absolutely
from other women authors of the period. Focusing on caricature, with its satirical, leveling tendencies, they neglect the revealing incursions
that the later Sand iconography would make
into the reverential, transcendant realm of the
monument. Czyba and Tillier, like Bergman-
Carton, thus concentrate on images that situate
Sand comfortably among (if invariably at the
head of) her female peers, while not considering
other evidence, of a monumental bent, that instead singles her out as a potential great writer
and rival of her most revered male counterparts. At very least, though, their research already establishes that the case of George Sand,
like that of the nineteenth-century woman author generally, has a visual as well as a verbal
dimension: that it is also, fundamentally, an
"image problem."

I argue, throughout this book, that in nineteenth-century France authors were largely understood through images, and this is especially
striking in the case of the period's women of
letters. Images of literary women are the site of
particularly rich aesthetic and ideological ferment, fueled not only by the rapid evolution of
visual media, and concurrent transformation of
fame in general and literary fame in particular,
but also by the emergence of so many women authors and the public's broad preoccupation with
them. The emergent mass-media's *machine à
gloire* sought to satisfy the public's growing appetite for information about and images of its
leading writers—in other words, to satisfy what
George Sand, regarding her own appearance,
called "la curiosité . . . un peu niaise du lecteur"
[the reader's somewhat dim-witted curiosity]

(Sand 1970, 1.467). Paul Jacob's 1843 *Galerie
des femmes de George Sand* [Gallery of George
Sand's women] provides an extreme example
of this burgeoning celebrity voyeurism, offering
up fictional characters in place of their author.
It is as if images of the author alone could not
suffice to meet the public's raging demand. Indeed, the *Galerie* is organized as an extended
visual metaphor, with an initial frontispiece of
Sand followed by a string of lithographs of her
novelistic characters who take turns standing
in for their creator.

Images of nineteenth-century women of letters fall into three general categories that corre-
late with what the period saw as the three principal levels of literary prestige: those of the *auteur*, the *écrivain*, and the *grand écrivain*. Each
category of images is marked by a set of predom-
inant characteristics, contradictions, and tensions, such as relative rareness or commoness,
reverence or irreverence, and presumed permanence or impermanence, that speak as well
to the period's overall vision of female literary
activity.

The most common images of literary women
were those of generally anonymous, broadly satirized, and stereotypical *femmes auteurs*. In one
sense, this profusion simply reflects the sociohistorical phenomenon of women breaking into
the literary and journalistic marketplace. The
same rapidly expanding popular press that,
from about 1830 onward, provided women authors with extensive new venues for their work,
also registered their proliferation with abundant articles and illustrations devoted to them.
In another sense, women were most commonly
depicted as *auteurs* because this was an effective way of dismissing them, of relegating
them to mediocrity at best. Thus, images of
the *femme auteur* delight in satirizing their
subjects' aspirations, morals, appearance, and
behavior, and defuse through ridicule their ostensible threats to male cultural, political, and
sexual hegemony. Characteristically, when the
femme auteur is depicted writing, this is shown
in a negative light. In a more subtle way, by
casting women as types, these images deny
them individuation. To be sure, the abundant
contemporary representations of *plumitifs*, or
undistinguished men of letters, treat their subjects in a similarly stereotypical and dismissive
manner. Yet images that represent *la femme*

auteur rather than any particular *femme au-teur* also continue earlier typological traditions depicting women as virgin, mother, muse, or abstract principle (e.g., Melancholy, Bounty, the Republic, and so on; cf. Warner 1985), though not as worthy of public distinction on their own, individual merit. Even at the very upper reaches of the *auteur* ranks, approaching the realm of the *femme écrivain*, while there can be nonsatirical depictions of individual women, individual identity nonetheless remains largely subordinated to broader categories, and nonin-tellectual ones at that (e.g., the classical beauty, or the contemporary beauty, as we shall see in the 1836 *Biography of contemporary women authors*).

Portraits of *femmes écrivains* were much less common than the myriad images of *femmes au-teurs* in the popular press. The relative rareness of such images was at once symptom and cause, both reflecting and reinforcing women's exclu-sion from the realm of the *écrivain*. Nonethe-less, while modest in number, the *femme écri-vain* portraits actually produced appear re-freshingly respectful, even reverential, rather than satirical. While not generally showing their subjects writing, they instead convey in-tellectual intensity and creative force through such iconographical conventions as large, pen-etrating, dark eyes and a prominent *front de penseur* or thinker's brow (as in the 1839 Char-pentier portrait of Sand), as well as active, expressive hands that gesture, hold books, or touch the woman's head thoughtfully. To be sure, conventional marks of intellectual and artistic distinction like these tend to give *femme écrivain* portraits a general family resemblance. At the same time, though, these portraits also depict clearly identified, recognizable figures like George Sand, Delphine de Girardin, or Marie d'Agoult, rather than anonymous, stereo-typical *femmes auteurs*. Women illustrious enough to be considered *écrivains* are nec-essarily individuated, in portraiture, through distinctive features or attributes, as well as through captions, titles, or other explanatory verbiage. They also would generally appear in more prestigious media, from prints in better periodicals through statue busts and bas-relief medallions—thus occupying the middle range within nineteenth-century fame iconography, between disposable newspaper caricature and

the enduring public monument, between pass-ing celebrity and lasting fame.

The more prestigious the medium then, the less frequently nineteenth-century women of letters were represented in it, hence the notable lack of women in the most prestigious form, the free-standing, posthumous, public monu-ment. The rareness of such sculptural trib-utes to women is all the more noteworthy in comparison with the concurrent proliferation of statufied *grands hommes*. According to June Hargrove,

> The paucity of commemorations to women can easily be written off as inevitable in the male-dominated society of the last century. Neither the position of women in society nor the attitudes of men toward them favored such monuments. But the archival evidence suggests that the causes for the lacuna are more complex; at least, the failed projects for celebrations of women collapsed for reasons comparable to any of the other aborted plans. (1990, 160)

The fact remains, however, that far fewer women than men were considered candidates for commemorative statuary in the first place, a discrepancy that needs to be understood as an exclusion of women from the realm of great-ness, and from the enduring renown thought to accompany it. Running against the grain, monumental tributes to women—in those rare instances when they were realized—prove rife with contradictions, a tendency already evident in Titon du Tillet's Parnasse françois, that key eighteenth-century predecessor of nineteenth-century great men monuments. As Judith Col-ton notes, Titon's sculptures of Madame de la Suze, Madame Deshoulières, and Mademoiselle de Scudéry, in the guise of the Three Graces, are "in all probability the first . . . statues of women intellectuals we know of in modern times" (Colton 1979, 21). Yet, unlike their male counterparts, these women are executed on a somewhat smaller scale, segregated as a group on a small ridge in the middle of the composi-tion, and not individuated through attributes of their creative activity, but rather distinguished simply as exemplars of female beauty.

In iconographical terms, the very idea of rep-resenting an outstanding woman writer through sculpture conflicted with the traditions for statuary depiction of women available to the nineteenth-century artist. For one thing, there was a tradition of sensual or erotic statuary, of which Pradier's work provides a prime nineteenth-century example (De Caso 1988, 49–50). This tendency de-monumentalized women, making their bodies appear pliable, yielding, or ganic. It sought to turn stone to flesh, not flesh to stone, as in contemporary statues of great men. Emblematically, Pradier's 1832 *Satyre et Bacchante*, which caused a sensation at the time, offers up the sinuous body of its model, actress Juliette Drouet, then his mistress, but soon to become Victor Hugo's. The obvious prurient bent of Pradier's marble contrasts with the heroic treatment given, in life and beyond, to Drouet's great love, the great man of letters, underscoring the period's divergent horizons of possibility for representing male and female subjects through sculpture. There was as well a venerable religious tradition of representing women as goddesses, saints, or virgins, prolonged in the nineteenth century by the proliferation of monumental madonnas (cf. Anne Pingeot, Les Vierges colossales du Second Empire [Colossal virgins of the Second Empire] in Pingeot 1986, 208–13). While statues like these embodied female excellence and enduring value of a particular sort, they did so by celebrating the subject's holiness and virtue, not her creative achievements. There was as well a long tradition of representing women in statuary as allegorical figures, given new currency since the Revolution by innumerable female embodiments of the Republic. Insofar as this typological orientation generalized its subjects, it conflicted with celebrity portraiture's need to individuate. For example, this tension informs Clésinger's seated statue of Sand for the *Théâtre Français*, originally entitled "Littérature" rather than "George Sand" (Lubin 1973, 162): while clearly a likeness of the sculptor's illustrious mother-in-law, it is presented as the embodiment of an abstract idea, rather than a tribute to her individual renown. Moreover, the fact that Joan of Arc was by far the French woman most often honored in nineteenth-century monuments can be explained by the convergence in her not only of powerful cultural cross-currents (e.g., catholicism and secular republicanism, mysticism and pragmatism, nationalism and individualism, medievalism and *revanchisme*) but also of dis-

tinct iconographical possibilities, for she lent herself to both the religious and allegorical traditions (i.e., depicting her as saint and national icon), and to an overwhelmingly male tradition of the statufied military hero. Joan was an exception in so many ways, and not in the least because she could be represented in male garb and as a warrior. For the most part, however, the phallic nature of the great man statue made it an inappropriate medium for the representation of great women. True, within the "monde à l'envers"—upside-down world—of caricature and popular prints, as Janis Bergman-Carton has demonstrated (passim), "women of ideas" were often shown menacing, even usurping the phallus, yet these are carnivalesque gestures that pretend to overthrow the nineteenth-century literary world's reigning phallocracy, all the better to reaffirm it. The ostensible threat of female intellectual ascension could thus be neutralized through satire. But the realm of the monument offered no such reassuringly reversible *monde à l'envers*. Public statuary was an earnest, reverential, idealizing medium that instead represented things as the male-dominated culture wanted them to be, and this did not include granting a woman the phallic embodiment of the monument.

The predicament of the nineteenth-century woman author is thus not only a word but an image problem. It is also a word and image problem, with the collective vision of literary women emanating both from words or images in isolation, and from the rich interactions between them (e.g., between the illustrations and accompanying texts in newspapers like *L'Illustration*), as well as from words used, ekphrastically, to conjure up images. No doubt, even images of remarkable George Sand, particularly the endless renditions of the influential Delacroix and Charpentier paintings or the later Nadar photographs, can seem unremarkable in themselves at first glance. Yet they take on much fuller meaning when studied as part of the wide range of cultural productions that struggled to make sense of the period's most celebrated woman writer, including writings on Sand and her work, other images of Sand, and images of other women of letters.

The following section, "La 'grande femme,'" looks more closely at how, from the beginning of her career, depictions of Sand constantly distinguished her from the crowd of contemporary women authors, while remaining much more ambivalent about the question of her fame living on. Next, "Sand's Metamorphoses" explores how Sand's image would evolve from the beginning to the end of her career, and beyond, with an early tendency toward expansiveness seeming to promise monumentality, although this was followed by an apparent later retreat from such a possibility. Finally the last section, "A Monument of her own?" examines to what extent Sand would indeed be monumentalized, in her later years and after her death.

La "grande femme"

Cette femme célèbre entre toutes les femmes célèbres . . .
—Jules Janin, George Sand, in *Biographie des femmes auteurs contemporaines* (1836, 444)

[This most famous of famous women . . .]
—Jules Janin, George Sand, in *Biography of Contemporary Women Writers*

Pauvre chère grande femme! . . . Il fallait la connaître comme je l'ai connue pour savoir tout ce qu'il y avait de féminin dans ce grand homme, l'immensité de tendresse qui se trouvait dans ce génie. . . . Elle restera une des illustrations de la France et une gloire unique.
—Gustave Flaubert, 25 June 1876 letter to Turgeniev (Flaubert 1973)

[Poor, dear great woman! You would have needed to know her as I did to know just how much of the feminine there was in this great man, how much tenderness in this genius . . . Unique in her glory, she shall remain one of France's all-time greats.]

Sand was a unique woman writer, yet how exactly was she seen vis-à-vis her literary sisters on the one hand, and male peers on the other?

Ideologically charged views about *femmes auteurs* were projected wholesale onto George Sand. Women authors were evaluated at once on their writing, morals, and physical beauty (as if such divergent criteria should, even could be considered on the same plane). Sand, too, was judged in this fashion, but hyperbolically so, through extreme, often mutually contradictory positions worthy of Bouvard and Pécuchet: celebrated as an incomparable literary talent, extraordinarily loving mother, and ravishing beauty, Sand was also dismissed as a worthless scribbler, wanton adulteress, and repulsive hag. Where women authors on the whole called

the period's rigid gender distinctions into question, Sand seemed to wreak havoc on them: she relished such conventionally feminine, domestic activities as making jam and knitting, yet also cultivated a "masculine" image, using a male pseudonym, smoking cigars, wearing men's clothes in public. Women authors as a category interested and troubled their contemporaries; Sand fascinated and positively baffled them. Assessments of Sand vacillated wildly—between adulation and condemnation, praise and censure, exhibition and suppression—venting general perplexity over women authors.

Even as an emblematic figure of the *femme auteur* then, Sand stood out emphatically among her female peers, and did so from the very beginning of her literary career in the early 1830s. From the mid 1830s onward, moreover, images clearly signified Sand's preeminence among women authors. Within caricature, for example, only Sand was likely to be treated as a distinct individual, given celebrity status through representation of her familiar face, or reference to her familiar name. During the 1830s and 1840s, women of letters were, as a rule, depicted in caricature as types rather than individuals, and either remained anonymous or were given such stock *bas-bleu* names as "Ophélia," "Arsinoé," or "Eudoxie" (examples from Daumier 1974). In contrast, Sand's likeness received exaggerated individuation through the *charge*, a celebrity form otherwise reserved for such notorious male contemporaries as Balzac, Hugo, or Dumas. As Bergman-Carton notes, Sand alone "was given the exposure of caricatural treatment" (1995, 60), although Charles Monselet's anecdote about a caricature of Mme Récamier (cf. epigraph above) suggests at least some exceptions to this rule. Sand's name would also appear, independent even of her likeness, providing an exemplar of female literary success, as in Daumier's lithograph of quarreling *bas-bleus*, captioned, "Ah vous trouvez que mon dernier roman n'est pas tout-à-fait à la hauteur de ceux de Georges [sic] Sand . . . ! Adélaïde, je ne vous reverrai de la vie!" [Ah, you think that my last novel is not quite on the level of Georges (sic) Sand's . . . ! Adélaïde, I never want to see you again!] (Daumier 1974, 13).

Sand's preeminence became particularly apparent in images grouped, in individual compositions or larger collections, with ones of other

Fig. 17. Gérard-Fontallard, *Congrès masculino-foemino littéraire* **(***Masculino-femino literary conference***).
Photo by M. Garval.**

contemporary women of letters. Luce Czyba observes, for example, that in Gérard-Fontallard's "Congrès masculino-foemino littéraire" [Masculine-feminine literary meeting], which places Sand among Virginie Ancelot, Eugénie Foa, Sophie Gay, and Delphine de Girardin, "une place de choix est réservée à la figure de G. Sand, debout, dominant tous les autres *bas-bleus* assis" [a choice spot is reserved for the figure of G. Sand, standing, dominating all the other, seated bluestockings] (Czyba 1995, 14) (fig. 17). We shall observe the same pattern, later on, in both the 1844 engraving from *L'Illustration*, entitled "Les Femmes de lettres françaises contemporaines" ["Contemporary French women of letters"] and in Nadar's 1854 *Panthéon*. For now, though, it will be useful to look more closely at the 1836 illustrated volume, which Bergman-Carton treats only summarily in her study. This volume is important not only because it is emblematic of Sand's distinction vis-à-vis her female peers, but also because of the ambivalence it displays about her potential posterity.

The *Biography of Contemporary Women Authors* is an anthology of biographical sketches, accompanied by portraits of the authors in question, brief samples of their work, and facsimiles of their handwriting. Nodier's introduction already acknowledges a disparity in the stature of the women included here—"toutes les renommées n'y sont pas égales, et . . . tous les auteurs . . . n'ont pas les mêmes droits aux succès" [all renowns are not created equal, and . . . all authors . . . do not have the same rights to success] (*Biographie des femmes auteurs contemporaines* 1836, 14)—and, later on, Jules Janin's biographical sketch of Sand repeatedly stresses her superiority over female peers. Likewise, the corresponding lithographic portrait of Sand, based on a Jules Boilly drawing, is strikingly different from those of the other women authors in the collection (fig. 18). All the other portraits fall neatly within one of two categories: classical beauties in classical dress; and, contemporary beauties in contemporary dress, with abundant ruffles, collars, lace, jewels, braids, tresses, bonnets, and so on. Mme Guizot provides an example of the first type (fig. 19); Anaïs Ségalas, of the second (fig. 20). Sand alone fits in neither. Her attire is contemporary, but very simple; her hair unadorned; and her jewelry limited to the same cross that would later figure in the famed Charpentier painting. On the whole, her portrait seems to provide an accurate likeness; however, the head seems slightly too large for the body, and the features just a touch exaggerated. There is thus an emphasis not only on Sand's head, but also, more specifically, on her ovoid face, prominent forehead, and dark eyes framed by dark, arching eyebrows, all of which Bergman-Carton identifies as conventional marks of the woman of ideas. In contrast, the portraits of all the other women seek simply to idealize their subjects' beauty, through the delicacy and regularity

Fig. 18. Jules Boilly, *George Sand.* **Cliché Bibliothèque nationale de France.**

of their features. In short, while Sand's portrait signifies brains, the others merely display beauty.

The classical and contemporary beauties in this anthology also all share a curious disability: their hands are either not visible, or held at rest—folded, gloved, or holding gloves, and never held above midriff. In contrast, Sand's right hand, her writing hand, is held high against her chin in a contemplative attitude. Her fingers are joined together, index to thumb, as if holding an invisible pen. The significance of this gesture becomes clearer still when we compare Sand's portrait not only to those of her manually deficient peers in the anthology, but also to the Boilly drawing from which the portrait derives (cf. Lubin 1974, 73). In a general way, the composition is cropped in the print, concentrating our attention on both the sitter's head and her right arm. In the drawing, Sand holds up her somewhat shadowy left hand, while in the lithograph, the image is reversed,

Fig. 19. Jules Boilly, *Mme Guizot*. Cliché Bibliothèque nationale de France.

Fig. 20. Jules Boilly, *Anaïs Ségalas*. Cliché Bibliothèque nationale de France.

and Sand's writing hand, now bathed in light, becomes the focal point of the composition. This transposition takes on its full meaning when related to the broader, cultural significance the period accorded the writing hand. As the inclusion of handwriting facsimiles in this volume or Clésinger's later cast of Sand's arm remind us (cf. Lubin 1974, 126), within the nineteenth-century cult of the writer, the writing hand was a favorite fetish, and popular synecdoche of the writer, so much so that, as Luce Czyba notes of Alcide Lorentz's lithograph "De la femme faite homme et culottée par la pipe" [Of woman become man, and panting on a pipe (this only approximates the word play on "culotter," to season a pipe, and "culotte," pants)] (fig. 28), the work of a right-handed author like Sand could conveniently be disparaged by depicting her scribbling with her left hand.[3] In this 1836 anthology, then, through Sand's overall appearance and, above all, through the foregrounding of her prolific hand, she is distinguished

from her female peers. Amid such lovely literary wallflowers, Sand alone stands out as the true embodiment of the contemporary woman writer. Among *femmes auteurs*, she is the only one taken seriously as an *écrivain*.

In the *Biography of Contemporary Women Authors*, both text and image consecrate Sand's status as a unique contemporary woman writer. While the portrait of her goes no further than this, the accompanying article does speculate—ambivalently though—upon the potential durability of her renown. In addition to characterizing Sand repeatedly as a "grand écrivain" (442, 451, and 454), it affirms that she has few rivals among contemporary men of letters, and none among women, "soit dans le passé, soit dans le présent, soit dans l'avenir" [either in the past, in the present, or in the future] (447). The very next paragraph expostulates, though, on the fickleness of fame in general and the suddenness of Sand's celebrity in particular: "George Sand. . . . fut la grande énigme, la grande occupation, la grande autorité de huit jours" [George Sand. . . . Was the great enigma, the great pre-occupation, the great authority for all of eight days] (448). The article ends, moreover, addressing women by asserting that Sand is "reine chez les hommes, roi chez vous!" [queen among men, king for you!] (455). While prevailing over all female peers, she nonetheless ranks next best among great men: but is that good enough to attain literary immortality? In this way, although the question of Sand's posthumous reputation is raised here, it clearly remains open. The *Biography of Contemporary Women Authors* thus sets an important precedent for the ambivalence of later images, that would speculate on Sand's posterity by experimenting with the ultimate consecration of the monument.

Sand's Metamorphoses

de tous les drames attachés au nom de George Sand, le plus beau, le plus attrayant par un intérêt invincible, c'est . . . l'histoire des métempsychoses de l'écrivain et du romancier.
　　　　—Paul Jacob, *Galerie des femmes de George Sand*
　　　　　　　　　　　　　　　　　　(1843, ii)

[of all the dramas associated with George Sand, the finest, the most irresistibly attractive, is . . . the story of the writer and novelist's reincarnations.]
　　　　—Paul Jacob, *Gallery of George Sand's Women*

Sand's public image changed significantly in the middle of her career, around 1850. In the preface to his 1843 *Galerie des femmes de George Sand*, Paul Jacob anticipated key elements of this shift, considering what he saw as changes to the title character in Sand's 1838 revision of *Lélia*:

> La preuve que Lélia pouvait être considérée comme le portrait idéal de George Sand, c'est que l'auteur l'a changé quand la méditation et les enseignements de la douleur ont imprimé à sa physionomie un nouveau caractère. . . . Voyant que son image n'était plus la même, George Sand a refait son ancien portrait, comme on change les ajustements d'une peinture à la mode passée. Elle a mis une guimpe blanche sur cette belle poitrine, autrefois éclatante de diamants; elle a éteint le feu du regard, l'ironie de la bouche et l'orgueil du front. La statue grecque est presque transformée en madone. La princesse superbe finit au couvent. [viii–ix.]

[The fact that the author changed Lélia when reflection and painful lessons had transformed her physiognomy proves that this character can be considered George Sand's ideal portrait. Seeing that her image was no longer the same, George Sand redid her old portrait, just as one might retouch an old-fashioned painting. She put on a high-necked blouse over that lovely bosom, that used to sparkle with diamonds; she subdued the fire in her gaze, the irony in her smile, and the pride upon her brow. The greek statue was nearly transformed into a madonna. The stunning princess ended up in a convent.]

Jacob exaggerates such changes for the purposes of his larger argument about the relationship between Sand and her characters. This passage, like the entire *Galerie*, is predicated upon the widespread phantasm of the nineteenth-century author and character's interchangeability.[4] Lélia, however, is the one Jacob singles out as Sand's true alter-ego, her "ideal portrait." Through Lélia, he imagines Sand evolving from the passionate abandon of youth to a more staid and prudent maturity. Sand's earlier transformative ability (she can "change" or "remake" her image at will) gives way as she settles into an ultimate, stable incarnation—this sense of finality being conveyed, in particular, by the verbs *éteindre* [extinguish or subdue] and *finir* [finish or end up]. Significantly, Jacob also casts Sand's metamorphosis largely in visual terms (i.e., *portrait*, *image*, *peinture*, *statue*, and so on). The metaphor of Sand's transformation as a statue is prescient in another way as well, for neither the pagan goddess nor the Christian virgin provides an appropriate representation of the illustrious writer, pointing toward later difficulties in finding a sculptural embodiment of Sand's glory. While the actual shift in the public's vision of Sand would occur later than either her revision of *Lélia* or Jacob's assessment of it, his comments do nonetheless set out the broad lines that this shift would follow: a move from scandal to virtue, and from volatility to stability; the importance of the visual in all this; and the dilemma of how to honor the great woman writer with a monument.

When we examine the abundant visual and verbal representations of George Sand, two distinct visions of her emerge successively: first, an elusive, protean Sand haunts the imagination of the French public from the dramatic beginnings of her career in the early 1830s through her involvement in the socialist political agitation of 1848; then, the stolid, benevolent, "bonne dame de Nohant" arises between 1848 and her death in 1876, becoming crystallized in certain Nadar photographs of the 1860s and predominating by the turn of the century. In a general way, these phases correspond, historically, with the nineteenth century's two most intense periods of ferment over the "woman question." As Planté explains,

[Ces] deux temps forts . . . voient une intensification du débat sur les femmes, leur place dans la société, et leur accès aux activités intellectuelles et artistiques: les années 1830, temps d'une mise en cause des valeurs provoquée par les bouleversements politiques et sociaux des cinquante années précédentes où apparaissent à la fois de grandes figures de femmes écrivains, comme George Sand, et l'ébauche d'un premier mouvement collectif d'émancipation; et la fin du siècle, où la multiplication des débats sur les femmes culmine dans l'idée de "guerre des sexes" et dans un violent déchaînement antiféministe et misogyne. Ces deux moments se ressemblent par l'intensité du désarroi qu'ils révèlent, mais s'opposent aussi en ce que le premier paraît malgré tout riche de possibles et d'espoirs, alors que le second voit, en même temps que les premières victoires des mouvements féministes, un durcissement et une intolérance qui font singulièrement hésiter à penser l'histoire des rapports de sexes sous la catégorie du progrès, et une brutalité dont les excès suscitent encore aujourd'hui le malaise. (Planté 1989, 17–18)

[At these two highpoints . . . the debate over women, their place in society, and their access to intellectual and artistic activities intensified. The 1830s were a time in which the political and social upheavals of the preceding fifty years brought about a questioning of established values, and there appeared both the first women writers to be seen as significant public figures, like George Sand, and the beginnings of a first, unified liberation movement. At the end of the century, raging debates over women culminated in the idea of a "war of the sexes," and in a violently antifeminist, misognynous backlash. These two periods are characterized by similarly intense ferment, yet differ in that the first nevertheless seems rich in hopes and possibilities, while the second, despite the feminist movements' first victories, saw a hardening and intolerance that give pause to anyone wanting to see the history of gender relations in terms of progress, as well as a level of brutality that still makes us shudder today.]

As the cause of women in France moved from a wealth of possibilities and hopes in the 1830s to a certain hardening and intolerance toward the *fin-de-siècle*, images of its most famous woman writer evolved likewise from an earlier, feverish vision of newness, multiplicity, and flux toward a later reductive, reactionary one which, in large measure, erased its radical predecessor and helped plunge Sand into depths of critical disfavor from which she has only recently reemerged.[5] Yet, amid such a historical backlash, as Planté's analysis suggests, some unprecedented "victories" could still occur: in Sand's case, this included the raising of monuments to her after her death.

GEORGE SAND
(M dudevant)

Fig. 21. Anonymous, *George Sand*. Photo M. Garval.

Fig. 22. A^te. Legrand, *George Sand*. Photo M. Garval.

Fig. 23. Nargeot, *George Sand* (after Charpentier). Photo M. Garval.

A sampling of Sand portraits from the 1830s and 1840s displays their great variety (figs. 21–28). While these images, and the many others like them, are all recognizable as the same person (celebrity *oblige*), they do depict Sand in an impressively wide range of guises: from dowdy to glamorous; classicizing to contemporary; exotically hispanizing to anglophilic Parisian stylish; and, variously gendered. To be sure, several factors can help account, in part, for this variability. Before the advent of photography "fixed" celebrity likenesses in the public eye, portraits of the famous were necessarily more open to imaginative interpretation. Sand's efforts to reinvent herself seem, moreover, to have heightened artists' creative impulses, inspiring them to continue reinventing her. In any case, through its variety, the early Sand iconography fostered an initial vision of her as infinitely changeable, as preeminently polymorphous.

While individual portraits of Sand can each present only one image of her, a single text can more easily convey the multiplicity suggested by the sum of the early portraits. For example, Jules Janin's biographical sketch of Sand

in *Biography of Contemporary Women Authors* begins:

Qui est-il ou qui est-elle? Homme ou femme, ange ou démon, paradoxe ou vérité? Quoi qu'il soit, c'est un des plus grands écrivains de notre temps. D'où vient-elle? Comment nous est-il arrivé? Comment tout d'un coup a-t-elle ainsi trouvé ce merveilleux style aux mille formes, et dites-moi pourquoi il s'est mis ainsi à couvrir de ses dédains, de son ironie et de ses cruels mépris la société entière? Quelle énigme cet homme, quel phénomène cette femme! quel intéressant objet de nos sympathies et de nos terreurs, cet être aux milles passions diverses, cette femme, ou plutôt cet homme et cette femme! (*Biographie des femmes auteurs contemporaines* 1836, 439)

[Who is he or who is she? Man or woman, angel or demon, paradox or truth? In any case, one of the great writers of our time. From where has she come? How did he get here? How, so suddenly, did she find this wonderful style with its thousand variations, and tell me why he has taken

Fig. 24. Eugène Delacroix, *George Sand*. Photo M. Garval.

to showering all of society with his disdain, his irony, and his deep contempt? This man is such an enigma, this woman such a phenomen! What an interesting object of our sympathy and our fear, this creature of a thousand different passions, this woman, or rather this man and this woman!]

Here, Janin employs a host of rhetorical strategies—a barrage of questions and exclamations, constant fluctuation between masculine and feminine, expressions of multiplicity like "this creature of a thousand different passions" or "this wonderful style with its thousand variations"—to conjure up this bafflingly elusive, multifaceted figure. Along similar lines, later in the article, Janin muses that Sand is "tour à tour un capricieux jeune homme de dix-huit ans, et une très-jolie femme de vingt-cinq à trente ans. . . . deux êtres aux milles noms divers, aux milles passions contraires, aux milles caprices imprévues!" [by turns a capricious young man of eighteen, and a quite lovely woman of twenty-five to thirty . . . two beings of a thousand different names, a thousand contrary passions, a thousand unforeseen caprices!] (448).

GEORGES SAND

Fig. 25. Julien, *Georges* [sic] *Sand*. Photo M. Garval.

Adolphe Pictet's *Une course à Chamounix* [On the road to Chamounix] (1839), with illustrations by Tony Johannot, is probably the most elaborate evocation of younger Sand's supposed multifariousness. This suggestive yet largely forgotten work is based upon its author's experiences traveling in Switzerland with Sand, Franz Liszt, and Marie d'Agoult, and even includes a humorous drawing of Liszt, d'Agoult, and Pictet that Sand made during the trip. Written not as a memoir but as an ironic and amiably self-deprecating *conte fantastique*, it is narrated by the "ami le plus intime" [most intimate friend] (195) of a largely autobiographical, somewhat thick-headed, and pedantic figure, called simply "le major" (on the title page, Pictet himself is identified as "Major Fédéral d'artillerie"). At the beginning of the story, Pictet's alter-ego *le major* is invited to join "Franz" (Liszt), his companion "Arabella" (Marie d'Agoult), and their friend "George" on a

Fig. 26. Julien, *George Sand*. Photo M. Garval.

Fig. 27. Alcide Lorentz, *Miroir drolatique* (*Comical mirror*). Photo M. Garval.

trip to Chamounix. Throughout the text, George is the wellspring of the fantastic, with mystery, disorientation, troubled dreams, and seemingly supernatural occurrences all flowing from the "énigme" (9) of her identity. Indeed, from the outset, *le major* puzzles over the wildly contradictory accounts of George that he has heard:

> Les faits et gestes de George ont eu le privilège d'occuper singulièrement l'imagination du public. . . . C'est un homme fort dangereux, habile à prendre toutes sortes de masques. On assure même qu'il se déguise quelquefois en femme pour mieux ourdir les trames perfides dont les fils lui sont confiés. . . .
>
> [En regardant George,] le major comprit qu'il avait sous les yeux un de ces miroirs à mille faces dans lesquels l'âme semble se jouer en pleine liberté. [2, 5, 14.]

> [George's movements preoccupied the public imagination. . . . He is a most dangerous fellow, able to assume all sorts of disguises. It is even

claimed that he sometimes dresses as a woman, all the better to carry out the perfidious plots entrusted to him. . . .

(Looking at George,) the major understood that he had before his eyes one of those thousand-faceted mirrors, in which the soul seems to enjoy complete liberty.]

For *le major*, as for the public generally, George proves "un sphinx redoutable" [a formidable sphinx] (50). As in the Janin piece, generic ambiguity reigns here, with the major thinking that this woman who dresses as a man is a man who dresses as a woman. Her nationality and station in life are no less fraught with confusion, nor is it clear whether the two children with whom she travels are real. Is George Italian, French, or Dutch (4)? Is she "un célèbre romancier" [a famous novelist], "une manière de paysan" [a sort of peasant] traveling in Switzerland for Parisian herbalists (4),

DE LA FEMME FAITE HOMME,

ET CULOTTÉE PAR LA PIPE.

—

Fig. 28. Alcide Lorentz, *De la femme faite homme, et culottée par la pipe* (*Of woman become man, and panting on a pipe*). Cliché Bibliothèque nationale de France.

"un émissaire du grand comité révolutionnaire européen" [an emissary from the great European revolutionary committee] (5), "une femme charmante . . . qui écrit des romans délicieux" [a charming woman . . . who writes delightful novels] (6), "un bel esprit" [a fine mind], "un gros rustre de paysan" [a big peasant clod], "un sombre conspirateur" [a shady conspirator], "un écolier malin" [a clever schoolboy], "une belle dame en costume de voyage" [a lovely lady in travel garb] (8), or simply—as this seemingly unlimited ability to metamorphose would suggest—"le diable" [the devil] (7)? Indeed, in typical *conte fantastique* fashion, there are repeated intimations of George's diabolical connections. When, for example, *le major* thinks he has discovered that her children are made not of flesh and blood but of cardboard, he exclaims, "Dieu me garde de me mettre en route avec ce nécromancien qui voyage accompagné de deux enfants de carton, pour faire croire qu'il est

femme et mère. Je ne sais si c'est un homme ou une femme, mais à coup sûr c'est un diable" [God preserve me on the road with this sorcerer who travels accompanied by two cardboard children, to make people believe that he is a woman and mother. I do not know if this is a man or a woman, but surely it's a devil] (25). Meanwhile, such formulations as "able to assume all sorts of disguises" and "one of those thousand-faceted mirrors, in which the soul seems to enjoy complete liberty" underscore the character's protean nature, while also suggesting divergent explanations for it. Pictet's "George"—and, by implication, her namesake the novelist—is a master of disguise, who assumes different selves at will; or, a bewildering funhouse mirror, reflecting back observers' gazes. These parallel possibilities pose a fundamental question: as relations between author and public were renegotiated within nineteenth-century French literary culture, to what extent did authors cultivate their own image, or did society construct it for them? Just how thoroughly these tendencies are interwoven in the development of nineteenth-century writers' reputations is suggested by a text like the preface to *The Wild Ass's Skin*, in which Balzac tries to promote a positive image of himself while lamenting that the public also conjures up its own often inaccurate and unflattering images of authors.

The closer Pictet's narrator comes to George, the more elusive and disorienting she becomes. In the latter part of the text, this already unsettling figure is transformed further by the distorting lens of the fantastic, with help from some strong punch and opium-laced cigars, to produce hallucinatory visions of rare intensity. Soaring omnipotently through the cosmos atop a lotus leaf, metamorphosing into a peacock feather, Medusa head, or burst of fireworks, and haunting the author's nightmares astride a giant, black cat (fig. 29), George becomes the very embodiment—better yet, the disembodiment—of the fantastic. In short, through "George," Sand is seen here as what *le major*, a Sanskrit scholar like Pictet himself, calls "kamaroupî," meaning "celle qui se transforme à volonté" [she who can transform herself at will] (108). The translation is apparently an accurate one and, as Pictet would no doubt have known, the first part of the word, *kama*, also means "love" or "desire," as in *Kama Sutra*.[6] This points to

Fig. 29. Tony Johannot, *Un cauchemar* (*A nightmare*). **Cliché Bibliothèque nationale de France.**

an erotic subtext, not only in this work but in so many representations of Sand, particularly through 1848.

This vision of Sand as polymorph persisted throughout the early part of her career. In an 1844 biographical sketch, for example, Sosthènes de la Rochefoucauld would still describe her in much the same terms: "C'est un Caméléon, c'est un prisme aux mille couleurs que cette personne dont le caractère, aussi remarquable que le talent, offre un composé de tous les contrastes" [This person is a Chameleon, a thousand-colored prism, whose character is as remarkable as her talent, offering an amalgam of every imagineable contrast" (Cate 1975, epigraph). The events of 1848 and Sand's active involvement in them marked the culmination of this highly visible protean phase, as the revolutionary woman writer came, in turn, to embody the revolution, with all it implied of promise and salvation, turbulence and instability. Advocating publicly the cause of republican socialism, most notably in a series of published *Bulletins*, Sand was indeed portrayed widely in the press as muse, mother, *and* whore of the Revolution. Accordingly, as Luce Czyba and Janis Bergman-Carton have demonstrated, contemporary caricatures were not only critical of Sand's political activism, but also rife with innuendo about the nature of her relations with such figures as Pierre Leroux or Ledru-Rollin (Bergman-Carton 1995, 47 and 52; Czyba 1995, 16–17).

The transformative ability ascribed to Sand from the early 1830s through 1848 implies not only a general expansiveness on her part, but also a level of creative power and independence otherwise associated with the period's male literary figures. She seemed, that is, to have what the male narrator of Balzac's "Facino Cane" describes in himself as the gift of "seconde vue" [second sight], the ability to "Quitter ses habitudes, devenir un autre que soi par l'ivresse des facultés morales, et jouer ce jeu à volonté" [leave behind one's habits, to become someone other than oneself through an exaltation of the moral faculties, and to play this game at will"] (CH 6.1020). Significantly, in Pictet's *On the Road to Chamounix*, this ability derives from a phallic, stone "talisman," a large crystal lodged in the head of Sand's double "George."[7] This is an extraordinarily literal illustration of her ability to

"think like a man," akin to the period's fetishization of the "front de penseur" or thinker's brow, and more general fascination with phrenology. As George explains to the bewildered *major*, "j'ai la bosse merveilleuse qui donne tout pouvoir sur le monde phénoménal" [I have the wondrous lobe that lends total power over the physical world] (7). Opening up her head, she takes out the talisman, "une pierre plus brillante cent fois que le plus beau diamant" [a stone a hundred times more brilliant than the most beautiful diamond], and explains that "toute ma puissance en dépend" [all my power comes from it] (7). Intrigued, *le major* steals George's invaluable talisman as she sleeps and, now possessed of it himself, dreams of vast power and creative energy:

son être se trouvait tout-à-coup doublé en puissance et en étendues. . . . Il se sentait un pouvoir immense de production, et . . . il en vint à rêver qu'il était assis sur une haute montagne, le front couronné d'étoiles, une harpe d'or entre les mains, et qu'il improvisait une épopée cosmologique auprès de laquelle l'Iliade et le Mahâbhârata n'étaient que de mauvaises chansons à boire (122–23)

[suddenly he found his power and range doubled. . . . He felt within himself tremendous creative energy, and . . . ended up dreaming that he was seated atop a high mountain, his brow crowned with stars, a golden harp in his hands, as he improvised a cosmological epic that made the Iliad and Mahâbhârata seem like vulgar drinking songs.]

The talisman also, it seems, makes *le major* "invulnérable," as if protected by "une armure enchantée" [enchanted armor] (133). Despite George's pleas, he does not return it, for "une voix intérieure" [an inner voice] tells him that "d'inestimables avantages se trouvaient attachés à sa possession" [possessing it brings inestimable advantages] (135). Indeed, whenever *le major* falters in an "improvisation philosophico-poétique" (143) with his fellow travelers, he reaches instinctively for the "pierre mystérieuse" [mysterious stone] in his pocket, and his eloquence springs forth anew. Later, when George and *le major* are riding a mule together, George feels "comme un corps pesant et dur qui lui battait la jambe" [like a hard, weighty member that was beating against her leg] (159). "Qu'est-ce donc que cela, major?" exclaims George. "[C]'est votre poche qui se montre si outrageusement aggressive. Que diable y avez-vous mis?" [Now what is that, major? It seems to be your pocket that is so outrageously aggressive. What the devil have you put there?" Before *le major* can stop her, "George glissa la main dans la poche fatale et en tira . . . la pierre lumineuse!" [George slipped her hand in the fateful pocket and pulled out . . . the luminous stone!] (159; the author's ellipsis here hints at what other sort of hard, "outrageously aggressive" thing an attractive young woman might expect to find inside a man's pocket while riding together astride a swaying mule.) George puts the crystal back in her head immediately and regains her powers: "de ses yeux jaillit de nouveau ce regard limpide et profond qui n'appartient qu'au génie" [from her eyes there shone again that deep and limpid gaze that belongs only to genius] (160). She then condemns *le major* for his theft, "pour dérober le feu sacré qu'il n'appartient qu'à Dieu seul d'allumer dans le sein des mortels" [for stealing the sacred fire that God alone may light in mortals' hands] (160). The crystal then, like the cane in Delphine de Girardin's *M. de Balzac's Cane*, would be the quintessence of literary genius, the irreducible core of the writer's creative faculties. Obviously phallic as well, like the cane, it embodies what was seen as the fundamentally male capacity to create literary works.

What, however, aside from curiosity, had motivated *le major* to commit his theft in the first place? He had apparently been tormented by a nightmare in which George, straddling a giant black cat, inflicts a sort of intellectual castration, tearing books containing his ideas from their orderly place on his shelves, and hurling them at him (118). The accompanying Johannot illustration of this scene (fig. 29) adds a telling visual pun: the female author appears joined with the cat's erect tail, thus possessed of *une queue*, at once tail and penis (much the same visual pun as in a Bertall caricature of Manet's *Olympia*, as T. J. Clark observes [1984, 144]). When *le major* awakens from his emasculatory nightmare, he declares, "C'est intolérable! il faut en finir!" [It's intolerable! Enough is enough!] (Pictet 1838, 119) and proceeds to

wrest George of her phallic talisman. His theft is therefore a retaliatory act, a stealing-back of the stolen phallus. The premise of Pictet's text—a man taking the writerly phallus from a woman—thus transposes what would, from a nineteenth-century male perspective, have been the real outrage: a contemporary woman writer usurping the male prerogative of literary creation.

Pictet's *On the Road to Chamounix*, like Girardin's *M. de Balzac's Cane*, is an example of an emergent genre, a curious hybrid that might best be called "celebrity fiction." This was a blend of popular biography and short narrative fiction, at the crossroads of a burgeoning paraliterature of fame, and of the period's rapidly evolving fictional field. It used elements of a contemporary celebrity's life (Sand actually traveled to Chamonix; Balzac actually owned an elaborate cane) both as a marketing ploy and point of departure for interweaving a fanciful, even fantastic plot, with social, aesthetic, and cultural commentary. Through the fictional adventures of "George," Pictet would seem then to be taking aim at Sand herself and at the unique challenge she posed to the period's male-dominated literary establishment. The benign presence in the text of Marie d'Agoult's double "Arabella" reminds us, moreover, that unlike Sand, her female peers were systematically excluded from the highly phallic realm of literary glory.

Sand's extraordinary celebrity faded somewhat after her participation in the political failure of 1848. There are multiple explanations for this relative decline, including: a generally cooler reception of her "idealist" literary work, amid the triumph of realism, as Naomi Schor has argued; Sand's own withdrawal from both the national political arena and the Parisian literary scene, as she largely retreated to her country home at Nohant; the quiet stability of her long-term involvement with the pleasantly mediocre Alexandre Manceau, in contrast to her highly publicized, tempestuous relations, earlier on, with such luminaries as Musset and Chopin; and the general societal prejudice whereby men are thought to gain and women to lose value as they age. In this respect, a comparison with Victor Hugo is instructive: whereas Sand's star languished during the Second Empire, Hugo, though in exile, managed to shore up his reputation and emerge from the period as France's preeminent cultural hero.

During the last quarter century of Sand's life, there arose a distinctly tamer, sanitized vision of her. Naomi Schor describes it in this way:

> Sand's most enduringly successful fictional creation . . . [was] her truly astonishing transformation of herself from an object of scandal into the supreme figure of propriety, the good mother par excellence, the popular public persona and cultural artifact that came to be known as the "Bonne Dame de Nohant" (Schor 1993, 179)

In Schor's view, this was the culmination of a deliberate, "slow, indeed lifelong elaboration," involving the pursuit of idealism in general and, in particular, the creation of an ideal mother that can be traced through both Sand's fiction and her autobiography. While "impossible to date . . . with any precision," this transformation "seems to have been completed in the mid-1850s." Schor concludes that "for Sand idealism . . . became a way of life, indeed of afterlife," through "the self-fashioned image of the benevolent chatelaine and doting grandmother"—even if this vision, "congenial to Third Republic morality," has more recently been replaced by an equally idealized, "cigarette-smoking, cross-dressed liberated woman for our times" (183).

Schor is right to characterize Sand's transformation into the "bonne dame de Nohant" as an "astonishing" one and, more specifically, as a shift from scandal to motherly propriety (contemporary evidence does not, however, support her capitalization of the epithet). While she is right as well to concede the impossibility of dating this precisely and to see it as the result of a gradual evolution, the idea that the transformation was somehow "completed" by the mid-1850s is, as we will see, a more dubious proposition. Equally questionable are Schor's emphasis on Sand's control over her own transformation and on the generally positive aspect of her incarnation as the "bonne dame." First of all, while this vision of Sand began to take hold around mid century, it did not culminate until the *fin-de-siècle*. It is true that Sand played an important role in forming this part of her legend, holding court at Nohant to a constant succession of Parisian visitors and winning over through her kindness and generosity a local populace alienated, earlier

on, by her reputation for libertinism and leftist politics. Yet the press, and popular culture in general, also played a significant role in framing this vision of Sand as the "bonne dame de Nohant"—and, especially, in elaborating its less flattering aspects. In contrast to France's concurrent monumentalization of great men, the transformation of Sand into an exemplar of provincial, motherly virtue appears trivializing and reductive. Finally, while Schor sees the figure of the "bonne dame" emerging out of the realist/idealist dichotomy in nineteenth-century French fiction, it was also conditioned by the broader Paris/provinces dichotomy in French culture, with Sand devalued, in the public eye, through her provincialization.

The vision of Sand as the "bonne dame de Nohant" became associated not only with the epithet itself, but also with an influential Nadar likeness of her. In the mid 1860s, Nadar photographed Sand in various types of dress (including with a curly Louis XIV wig), yet one guise in particular captured the public's imagination: that in which Sand wears a loose-fitting, striped dress and distinctive tridentate earrings (fig. 30). In the early part of her career no single image, not even the famed Charpentier portrait, dominated the Sand iconography the way this depiction would later on. Certainly, the rise of photography, with its documentary bent, helps to explain the general shift from a profusion of dissimilar images to a handful of similar ones. It does not, however, explain the overwhelming privileging of one particular effigy. This phenomenon seems rather to betray a new reductiveness, in contrast to the expansiveness that characterized the earlier, protean vision of Sand.

While Nadar's Sand certainly appears more tranquil and composed than, say, Pictet's "George," there is nothing in the likeness itself, in its creation, or in its initial reception to suggest the trivializing view of her that would become associated with it. Nadar was a great admirer of Sand, and Sand herself seems to have been pleased with the results of her sittings with him. When an engraving of her in this guise was first showcased in *L'Illustration* in 1864 (fig. 31), it was described in flattering terms:

> Nous donnons le portrait de Mme Sand d'après la récente photographie de Nadar. Ce portrait rend

Fig. 30. Nadar, *George Sand*. Photo M. Garval.

rend congé de sa famille, de ses amis, se re-
on cabinet, et écrit jusqu'à quatre heures du
e lui faut pas plus de cinq heures de som-
f heures, elle est éveillée, et la journée qui
ressemble à celle qui a précédé. On ne re-
s en Mme Sand, pendant le jour, que la femme
toute entière à ses amis, toute dévouée à leurs
cet abandon, si aimable chez une femme or-
arait bien plus aimable encore chez cette
génie.

Nous donnons le portrait de Mme Sand d'après la récente photographie de Nadar. Ce portrait rend admirablement le caractère de la belle tête de Mme Sand, de
ce visage énergique où la beauté se mêle à la majesté.
Les yeux si beaux et si doux, la bouche grande, mais
superbe, l'oreille mince et fine, le contour si pur des
lignes, tout est vrai. Sous l'écrivain de génie, on retrouve la petite-fille de Maurice de Saxe ; il y a de la
grande dame dans ce grand homme !

EDMOND TEXIER.

ÉRUPTION DU VOLCAN DE L'ILE DE LA RÉUNION.

AU DIRECTEUR.

Salazie, île de la Réunion, 6 février 1864.

Depuis les derniers jours du mois de décembre, le volcan de la Réunion est en éruption, et présente un des
plus beaux spectacles que la nature puisse offrir. Un

GEORGE SAND — D'après une photographie de Nadar.

Fig. 31. *George Sand* **(after Nadar). Photo M. Garval.**

admirablement le caractère de la belle tête de Mme Sand, de ce visage énergique où la beauté se mêle à la majesté. Les yeux si beaux et si doux, la bouche grande, mais superbe, l'oreille mince et fine, le contour si pur des lignes, tout est vrai. Sous l'écrivain de génie, on retrouve la petite-fille de Maurice de Saxe; il y a de la grande dame dans ce grand homme. (Texier 1864, 203)

[Here is the portrait of Mme Sand, after the recent Nadar photograph. This portrait captures admirably Mme Sand's beautiful head, her energetic face with its mix of beauty and majesty. All is true: her beautiful, soft eyes, her large but superb mouth, her delicate ears, the harmonious lines of her countenance. Beneath this brilliant writer we find Maurice de Saxe's grandaughter; there is a great lady inside this great man.]

Nadar's effigy of Sand is thus thought to figure not goodliness and simplicity but rather innate nobility, majestic beauty, and literary genius. In short, despite Schor's dating of a "complete" transformation ten years earlier, Sand is not yet seen here as the "bonne dame," but rather as a cross between a noble *grande dame* and an accomplished *grand homme*.

Less than a decade after the Nadar portrait's very favorable first appearance in *L'Illustration*, though, Touchatout's 1873 *Trombinoscope* would appropriate this same likeness, but to very different effect (fig. 32). Here, Sand's features are grossly caricatured and, in the accompanying text, both her literary talent and physical appearance are described ambivalently:

Mme George Sand fut pendant longtemps un véritable réflecteur de tous les hommes de talent qu'elle côtoyait; ses oeuvres s'imprégnaient immédiatement des dernières sensations qui lui avaient été communiquées. . . .

Au physique, Mme Georges [sic] Sand est une femme au regard doux et profond; le front est élevé, la bouche expressive. Tout dans ce visage harmonieux de lignes, dénote l'esprit et la bonté.

[For a long while, Mme George Sand was a sort of reflector of all the talented men she frequented; her works were immediately impregnated with the latest sensations that had been communicated to her.

Physically, Mme Georges (sic) Sand is a woman with a gentle and profound gaze, a prominent brow, and an expressive mouth. All in this harmoniously-drawn face denotes wit and goodness]

When read alone and even more so when read together with the image, this text is full of troubling contradictions. It demotes Sand from the gender-neutral "écrivain de génie" of the 1864 *L'Illustration* piece, but still calls her a "femme de génie."[8] It locates the source of this genius though in the great men she has known, and makes obvious insinuations about their relations (we infer that more than just Sand's works have been "impregnated" by the latest "sensations" "communicated" to her by the male luminaries she frequents). Sand's gaze is described as both "gentle" and "profound"—already an apparent contradiction—whereas the drawing depicts her staring out blankly into the void: she is gentle here, perhaps, but certainly not profound! Similarly, the text highlights Sand's prominent forehead, while in the drawing this celebrated *front de penseur* practically disappears, giving Sand a distinctly more Neanderthal look. Touchatout affirms, moreover, that Sand's entire face signifies "wit" and "goodness." This is equivocal praise, for sheep are good too—and indeed, in the drawing, the author of popular pastorals is associated with sheep through proximity (she stands next to them), through vocation (as shepherdess), and through resemblance (the ovine rendering of her hair contrasts with its treatment in other versions of the same portrait). True, Touchatout's insinuations about Sand's promiscuity do hark back to one particular aspect of the earlier vision of her as protean firebrand. On the whole, however, the *Trombinoscope* piece, with its intimations of bleating obtuseness, bucolic benevolence, and simplicity bordering on simple-mindedness, constitutes a significant step toward an evolving, trivializing vision of Sand as the "bonne dame de Nohant."

In the *Trombinoscope*, moreover, the shepherd's crook that Sand holds doubles as a pen. This conjunction of writing instrument and rustic implement heralds a concurrent reduction of her vast literary production to the pastoral novels and, eventually, to anthologized excerpts from them. By 1882, we see this tendency firmly entrenched, with a cover of *Le Papillon* (June 4, 1882) (fig. 33). Sand appears in the now familiar guise with the tridentate earrings, flanked by scenes from her novels interwoven with scrolls bearing the titles. The works foregrounded are none other than *La Mare au diable* [The Devil's Pond] and *François le Champi*. Their titles,

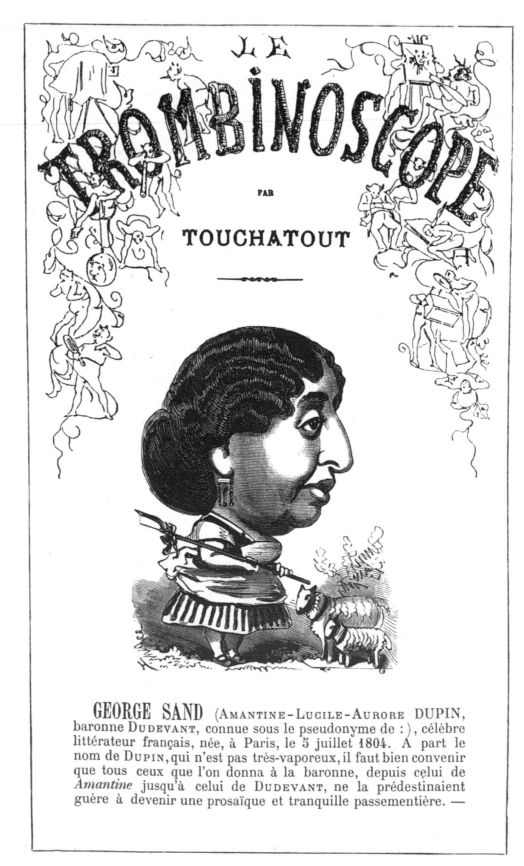

GEORGE SAND (Amantine-Lucile-Aurore DUPIN, baronne DUDEVANT, connue sous le pseudonyme de :), célèbre littérateur français, née, à Paris, le 5 juillet 1804. A part le nom de DUPIN, qui n'est pas très-vaporeux, il faut bien convenir que tous ceux que l'on donna à la baronne, depuis celui de *Amantine* jusqu'à celui de DUDEVANT, ne la prédestinaient guère à devenir une prosaïque et tranquille passementière. —

Fig. 32. Touchatout, *Le Trombinoscope: George Sand*. Photo M. Garval.

Fig. 33. Edmond Morin, *George Sand*. Photo M. Garval.

displayed beneath Sand's portrait instead of her name, now define her identity. Sand is thus reduced as a writer through identification with only a part—the most provincial part—of her *oeuvre*. This contrasts sharply with the period's totalizing, synthetic concept of *l'homme et l'oeuvre*, in which the great man is thought synonymous with the whole of his monumental work. Unlike Balzac living on through, in, and as *The Human Comedy*, Sand is denied any such aggrandizing posthumous myth.

By the turn of the century, this view of Sand as little more than a modest, benevolent, provincial grandmother predominated. In 1904, for the centenary of her birth, *L'Illustration* published a tribute, featuring an article by Maurice Kahn entitled "George Sand à Nohant. L'Art d'être grand'mère" [George Sand at Nohant. The Art of being a grandmother]. The first part of the title clearly situates Sand at her provincial home. The second evokes her grandmotherly benevolence—with a memorable if condescending turn of phrase that, nearly a half century later, André Maurois would reuse as the concluding chapter title of his Sand biography. The article is accompanied moreover by one of the familiar Nadar photographs of Sand in the striped dress.[9] While this portrait of Sand is almost identical to the one featured forty years earlier in the same publication and praised as the embodiment of energy, majesty, and genius, here it simply is captioned "George Sand grand'mère."

The last paragraphs of the 1904 *L'Illustration* article encapsulate its vision of Sand:

Telle elle vécut les dernières années de sa vie, telle, près de trente ans après sa mort, elle vit encore dans le souvenir de ses petites filles, dans la mémoire des paysans qui l'ont connue. A Nohant, à La Châtre, à Angibault, les aventures de sa jeunesse, l'histoire compliquée de son existence fiévreuse, qu'elle-même avait à la fin presque oubliée, apparaissent comme des légendes incertaines et un peu calomnieuses, venues de Paris, bonnes à satisfaire les méchants. . . .

L'image qu'y évoque son nom, en cette année de centenaire, est bien celle de la bonne aïeule aux bandeaux gris, qui, malgré son grand âge et les rigueurs de l'hiver, faisait des lieux en cabriolet pour soigner un paysan malade: c'est la grand'mère penchée vers un petit lit; c'est la tendresse ingénieuse et la bonté simple; c'est la

«bonne dame de Nohant»,—la *boune mé* . . . [Kahn 1904, 6–7]

[Just as she lived for the last years of her life, so, nearly thirty years after her death, she lives on in the memory of her grandaughters, and of the peasants that knew her. In Nohant, in La Châtre, in Angibault, her youthful escapades, and the complicated story of her frenzied existence, which toward the end she had nearly forgotten herself, seem like dubious and a bit slanderous tales, spun in Paris for the benefit of wicked gossips.

Indeed, in this centenary year, her name evokes the image of a goodly grandmother with her gray hair pulled back in a bun, who despite her advanced age and the harsh winter weather, would travel for miles in her cabriolet to care for a sick peasant. A grandmother leaning over a small bed, she embodied ingenious tenderness and simple goodness; she was the "bonne dame de Nohant,"— the *boune mé* . . .]

Here, the anticlimactic, final phase of Sand's life determines the tenor of her posthumous reputation. She does not live on gloriously, in the memory of the nation, but rather quietly, in the fond remembrance of her grandaughters and local peasants. *Berrichon* place names ring here with the persistent presence of village belfries, while Paris seems as far from what Sand has become as it is in the minds of mistrustful locals who have never been near the big city. A calm, deliberate life of good works has apparently supplanted Sand's earlier, "frenzied" existence. While admirable, her goodness is not grandiose nor heroic, but "simple" and modest: emblematically, she leans toward the smallness of "a small bed." Already demoted from "writer of genius" to "woman of genius" in earlier articles, she now exemplifies no more than "ingenious tenderness," further circumscribing her talents. Similarly, the woman who once dared rename herself as masculinized, anglo-sophisticated "George Sand," yet has already been rebaptized as the proper, provincial "bonne dame de Nohant," is now further provincialized, through *berrichon* patois, as "la *boune mé*," or "good ol' granny."

The expression "The Art of being a grandmother" in Kahn's title refers not only to Sand but also to Victor Hugo and his 1877 collection of poems, *L'Art d'être grand-père* [The Art of being a grandfather], a text which in many ways crystallized the late nineteenth-century myth of Hugo. This allusion would have been partic- ularly obvious in 1904, just two years after the triumphant celebration of the poet's centenary, and during a period when excerpts from this collection figured prominently in public school readers. The comparison here with Hugo is in- structive once again for, at the same time he was converted into a monumental ancestor, a grandfather figure for the entire Third Repub- lic, Sand's transformation into a virtuous grand- mother radically reduced her standing within French culture.

In these various ways, Kahn's article moves well beyond the reductiveness of the *Trom- binoscope*. It seeks to erase Sand's turbulent, Parisian past and recast her as small-town sim- plicity and gray-haired goodliness incarnate. Coinciding historically with both the wholesale aggrandizement of great men like Hugo and the apotheosis of Paris as *haut-lieu* of the *avant- garde* (Shattuck 1958), this identification with virtuous but sleepy provinciality necessarily di- minished Sand's public stature and minimized her perceived significance as a national cultural figure.

A Monument of Her Own?

Expliquer par quel enchaînement de circonstances s'est accomplie l'incarnation masculine d'une je- une fille, comment Félicité des Touches s'est faite homme et auteur; pourquoi, plus heureuse que Mme de Staël, elle est restée libre et se trouve ainsi plus excusable de sa célébrité, ne sera-ce pas satisfaire beaucoup de curiosités et justifier l'une de ces monstruosités qui s'élèvent dans l'humanité comme des monuments, et dont la gloire est fa- vorisée par la rareté ? car, en vingt siècles, à peine compte-t-on vingt grandes femmes.
— Honoré de Balzac, *Béatrix* (CH 2.688)

[To explain what set of circumstances brought about this young girl's transformation; how, that is, Félicité des Touches turned herself into a man and an author; and why, more fortunate than Mme de Staël, she remained freer, and thus freer to enjoy her celebrity; would this not satisfy a great deal of curiosity and explain one of these monstrous things that rise up in human history like monuments, and whose rareness enhances its glory? For twenty centuries yield barely twenty great women.]
— Honoré de Balzac, *Béatrix*

It is a sign of both Sand's uniqueness and the pervasiveness of the dream of stone itself that her literary stature would even be considered in monumental terms, both during her life- time and beyond. Remarkably indeed, despite widespread misogyny, the perceived maleness of both literature and the monument and, above all, the trivialization of Sand herself as the "bonne dame de Nohant," the later Sand iconog- raphy would nonetheless, in taking stock of her extraordinary life and work, have recourse to the monument.

In commentary on male writers that dates from the second half of the nineteenth cen- tury, the metaphor of the monument abounds. It is conspicuously absent, though, from com- parable discussion of female writers—even il- lustrious Sand, with her voluminous *oeuvre*. In contrast, a number of contemporary images of Sand engage, in one way or another, with the monument; perhaps the rapid evolution of visual media at the time enabled them to be more imaginative in this respect. This section will look at three particularly revealing images, produced from the mid 1840s through the mid 1860s, that all invoke the prestige of the monu- ment in representing Sand's greatness, yet each in different ways, and with different sorts of hesitation. After Sand's death, two public mon- uments to her were raised, and the final part of this section will look briefly at these real monuments, and their significance, in light of the earlier efforts to envision her fame in mon- umental terms.

The first image, "Contemporary French women of letters" by Gustave Staal, was pub- lished in *L'Illustration* in 1844 (fig. 34), ac- companied by an article dealing with women writers, and particularly with the seven de- picted in the engraving (Femmes de lettres françaises contemporaines, 1844). The article abounds with reservations and contradictions that make us wonder why most of these seem- ingly lackluster literary figures should be hon- ored at all. The anonymous author stresses Girardin's beauty and ambition over her writ- ing; laments Desbordes-Valmore's "peinture des passions dangereuses" [painting of dangerous passions] (266); praises Voïart for decency and lack of pretension, while deploring her gram- mar, spelling, and punctuation; appreciates

Fig. 34. Gustave Staal, *Femmes de lettres françaises contemporaines (Contemporary french women of letters)*. Photo M. Garval.

Tastu and Ancelot above all for their chasteness and purity, not their literary merits; and, though he speaks highly of Reybaud's *oeuvre*, says little of substance about it, for he claims, with eroticized condescension, that he does not want to "déflorer, par une sèche dissection des oeuvres de cette artiste, les poétiques parfums qu'elles exhalent" [deflower the poetic fragrances of this artist's works, by coldly dissecting them] (267).

Sand, as usual, provides the exception. The section on her comes first and is much longer and more frankly laudatory than the others: more than just "à la tête des femmes de lettres contemporaines" [at the head of contemporary women writers], she is "tout simplement . . . un des plus beaux génies littéraires qui aient lui sur le monde" [quite simply one of the finest literary geniuses ever to have shone upon this earth] (266). Like the text, the image clearly privileges Sand over her female peers (as in the earlier *Biographie des femmes auteurs contemporaines*), while remaining ambivalent about the quality and potential staying power of female literary glory in general. The engraving surrounds a portrait medallion of Sand with six smaller medallions of other contemporary women writers. While Sand's prevalence is immediately clear, the durability of the fame implied by the portraits here is not. On the one hand, their grouping together seems to form a larger, public monument, the kind the period used to convey posterity; on the other, individual medallions like these, commonly used at the time to depict celebrities of the day, might be assumed to figure contemporary more so than enduring renown.[10] Upon closer examination, the engraving turns out to partake of both these modes. In her reading of this image, Janis Bergman-Carton maintains that "Sand's enlarged . . . and centered portrait floats encircled by the others, like the pistil to its petals or like Saturn to its moons" (1995, 199). She is right about the size and centrality of Sand's image, which figures the superior scope of her contemporary fame, yet mistaken about whose portrait "floats." Sand's portrait does not; it is in fact the only one grounded *as a sculpture*. Its firm placement upon a pedestal figures the greater solidity of her renown as well. Conversely, it is the medallions of the other, lesser women writers that "float," suggesting

their less solid, less permanent renown. True, these medallions do appear connected and, ostensibly, supported by a network of vines and branches. Yet, even if this tenuous organic support were adequate for now, it cannot last, for it is mortal; it must necessarily perish as the monument carries its memorializing mission into the future. If not sooner, then certainly later, when vines and branches give way, the medallions themselves must topple and shatter, or perhaps simply roll away out of view, leaving only Sand standing proudly, on her pedestal, as the paragon of female literary glory. In short, the lesser women writers are subject to the vagaries of the inorganic, condemned to mortality. Sand alone accedes to the stony durability of the inorganic and, it would seem, to literary immortality.

Thus, at mid-century Sand could, it seems, be consecrated through the monument, at least when she is with other women. What if she were depicted among great men, as in Nadar's 1854 *Panthéon*, or in a "photobiographie" series from a decade later? Like the 1844 "Contemporary French women of letters," both of these works use monumental elements to depict Sand's greatness, yet in significantly different ways. As we shall see, Nadar's *Panthéon* falters in its hommage to Sand by transforming her into a monument prematurely, while the "photobiographie" deftly sidesteps the question of a real monument, evoking instead the broader monumentality of Sand's accomplishments, and of her status as a literary figure.

In the *Panthéon Nadar*, (fig. 3), a serpentine procession of caricatured male celebrities, arranged roughly in order of relative prominence, moves forward toward the lower left-hand corner of the composition. Here, at the head of the procession, stands a small group of statue busts and bas-relief medallions consisting—aside from George Sand—of deceased male celebrities: Balzac, Chateaubriand, Frédéric Soulié, Paul-Louis Courier, and Charles Nodier. Nadar's *Panthéon* thus acts out the opposition between passing and permanent fame, momentary celebrity and enduring, posthumous glory. While the living men in the *Panthéon* are represented as caricatures, dead men have turned to stone, transformed into monuments to their own supposed immortality (a prognosis that has proven less true for Soulié, Courier, and even

Nodier, alas, than for Balzac or Chateaubriand). Nadar's lithograph therefore depicts both a procession and a process: a procession in which contemporary celebrities march toward fame everlasting, but also, in a larger sense, the process by which they attain transcendant, posthumous renown.

At first glance, George Sand's depiction in the *Panthéon* seems only to signify her unparalleled renown. Her bust stands firmly upon a fluted pedestal, in the extreme foreground. She seems placed, therefore, at the very head of the procession, the point to which all her contemporaries aspire. Bathed in light, she is the visual focus of the composition; and, she is number one in the lithograph's numerical key.

In addition, as in earlier images, Sand is clearly singled out as the period's leading woman writer. She seems at first to have little in common with the other women in the composition, clustered in the third row. These less illustrious women of letters, *Mesdames* "Ch. Reybaud, Tastu, Adèle Esquiros, Desbordes-Valmore, Comtesse d'Agoult, Clémence Robert, Anaïs Ségalas, Delphine de Girardin, and Louise Collet-Révoil," are depicted as small statue busts, perched upon a plank balanced precariously upon the head of womens' advocate Ernest Legouvé.[11] This implied association with the nascent feminist cause underscores their undifferentiated womanhood, rather than the individual literary merit that presumably has earned them a place in the pantheon. They stand in contradistinction to Sand, whose disdain for the fledgling women's movement belied her own views on the need for equality, and whose prominence in this composition clearly figures her literary preeminence. Relegated instead to the background, the lesser female celebrities are further devalued by the way in which they are displayed—precisely how cheap plaster statuettes were sold then by ambulant vendors, as a contemporary print shows (fig. 35). The intimation here is that these *femmes de lettres* are like *femmes publiques* whose bodies were also peddled in the street. In this view, female literary activity in general is analogous to prostitution, and publication in particular implies not only the public dissemination of a woman's *oeuvre*, but also a morally reproachable public offering of her self (cf. Bergman-Carton 1995, 183).

In one sense, the *Panthéon Nadar* seems to disparage only these lesser women of letters, while revering Sand unconditionally. In other ways, it treats all women in the same, peculiar manner, dismissing them as preposthumous statues. Unlike the men, who are caricatured while alive but statufied when dead, all the women here, Sand included, were still alive, yet represented as busts. To be sure, even by mid century, depicting living literary celebrities as statues was already an iconographical convention, generally used to signify the writers' anticipated immortality. In this case, though, premature statufication takes on a different meaning because women are represented this way, while their male counterparts are not (unlike, say, Marcelin's 1853 caricature "Illustrated novels," which features a statufied Sand alongside busts of Sue, Hugo, and Balzac, the only one of the group no longer alive; cf. introduction). Previous scholarship offers little help in understanding this, for the very limited attention to this aspect of the *Panthéon* has focused on why Sand and the other women were not caricatured, rather than on why they were statufied. The catalog for *Nadar, les années créatrices* (published in English as simply *Nadar*) argues unconvincingly that Sand could simply not be caricatured because she had refused to pose for a preliminary photograph (Hambourg, Heilbrun, and Néagu 1994, 317). Bertrand Tillier ventures that the decision not to caricature Sand could be "un témoignage de l'admiration de Nadar" [an expression of Nadar's admiration], and that depicting all women this way demonstrates that "le crayon de Nadar semble peiner à s'attaquer aux traits féminins, alors qu'il n'épargne pas ceux des hommes de lettres" [Nadar's pencil seems reluctant to attack womens' faces, while not sparing those of male writers] (Tillier 1984, 28). There are several problems with this analysis. While Nadar did admire Sand, the *Panthéon* shows this through her privileged placement in the composition, not through her statufication. Likewise, being caricatured in the *Panthéon*, far from perceived as an "attack," was seen by contemporaries as an honor—so much so, for example, that for the Goncourt brothers, a desire to figure in the popular lithograph won out over their feelings of solidarity for cousin Charles de Villedeuil in a row with Nadar at the time (Chotard 1990,

Personne n'en veut plus pour deux sous.

Fig. 35. A. D., *Personne n'en veut plus pour deux sous (Nobody wants them for two sous).* © Photothèque des musées de la ville de Paris.

73–74). Within the representational logic of the *Panthéon*, moreover, being caricatured amounts to a necessary prequisite for the great writer's later immortalization in stone. Thus, while Nadar's premature statufication of women authors might seem to venerate them, it in fact excludes them doubly from the literary men's club in his lithograph. They are excluded from the procession, for they cannot march toward posterity without legs. They are also excluded from the all-important process of becoming "immortal" in which the men participate—an exclusion confirmed by the absence of noteworthy female predecessors (e.g., Germaine de Staël), this absence made all the more flagrant by the prominent presence of their male counterparts (Balzac, Chateaubriand, et al.). From an archetypal perspective, moreover, there may be a certain moral censure implied here, for the fate of these women, turned to stone before their time, recalls that of Lot's wife, similarly punished for what could be construed as similar offenses (i.e., overreaching, violating patriarchal interdictions to see or be seen). In these ways, the women in Nadar's *Panthéon*, even George Sand, can achieve only the dubious consecration of contemporary notoriety, and not posterity, not a lasting place in the memory of the nation. Such monumental, posthumous glory was apparently reserved for great men like Balzac or Hugo.

In particular, a comparison between Hugo and Sand is unavoidable here, for they are juxtaposed prominently in Nadar's composition. This is telling. While Sand may be first in the lithograph's numerical key, she appears hopelessly paralyzed, petrified, frozen in time: a figure of abortive promise. In contrast, Hugo occupies the crucial first place in the lithograph's procession. Though already in exile at the time, he stands poised at the head of his illustrious male peers, leaning forward under the weight of his massive, brilliantly lit forehead, ready to take that next, inevitable step into immortality.

The "photobiographie" of George Sand (fig. 36), from 1865–66, uses the same format as the other compositions in this series: a recent photograph of a celebrity is surrounded by drawings of the person's life and work. The photographs in the series are by various artists, in this case Nadar, with drawings by Carlo Gripp; the over-

all compositions were produced by the photographic studio of Pierre Durat. While neatly delineated margins and the caption "GEORGE SAND, née à Paris" [GEORGE SAND, born in Paris] make the Sand photo look, at first, like a tiny "carte de visite," the composition as a whole works instead to magnify this image. Sand's effigy looms against a background of thumbnail vignettes, and shading alongside her portrait places it on a distinct, elevated plane, making it seem affixed to some massive wall. This architectonic illusion is doubly reinforced: first, the "wall" of the portrait plane blends seamlessly into the wall displaying Sand's 1848 Republican bulletins; second, the central columns in the final vignette line up with the bottom of the photo, as if supporting a structure overhead. Of the nine marginal vignettes, five deal with Sand's literary achievements. In the first, the author exhibits a gigantic copy of the novel *Indiana*, which launched her career as George Sand. Overhead float the words "Génie littéraire," emanating rays of brilliance. Behind stands a writing table with discarded paper underneath, suggesting that a manuscript composed of just such ordinary-sized sheets has somehow been transformed into the colossal tome depicted here. This mirrors the equally magical transfiguration that occurs from the preceding vignette ("Baronne DUDEVANT") to this one ("GEORGE SAND!"), from the slouchingly seated and passive (though actively bored) Baroness to the statuesque "literary genius" displaying her monumental work. While male writers routinely fill reams of paper in contemporaneous illustrations, this depiction of Sand's creative activity, and the foregrounding of the monumental work to which it leads, is exceptional, a rare nineteenth-century image of "*la femme* et l'oeuvre." Similarly, the next two vignettes, "Premiers romans" and "Oeuvres dramatiques" also feature giant copies of Sand's works. In the following one, "Les écrivains modernes à côté de George Sand" [Modern writers beside George Sand], she towers over predominantly male peers. Finally, in "Sur les fauteuils de l'Académie Française" [Upon the seats of the French Academy], oversized copies of Sand's works stage a kind of "sit-in" at the French Academy, as the displaced academicians look on with surprise and, in some cases at least, doff their hats deferentially.

Fig. 36. Pierre Durat and Carlo Gripp, *Photobiographie des contemporains: George Sand*. Photo M. Garval.

The Sand "photobiographie" comes into sharper focus when compared with two others in the same series: Victor Hugo, paragon of male literary fame (fig. 37); and popular singer Thérésa, the only other woman featured (fig. 38). In all three compositions, the vignettes begin chronologically, on top, with the earliest events or scenes, proceed down both sides simultaneously, and conclude at bottom center. As already noted, it is significant that oversized books are used to evoke Sand's literary production, even if they are not as massive or abundant as those in the Hugo composition. While such monumentalizing of the literary work was commonplace in contemporary caricatures of male writers, it was rarely used with their female counterparts. Thérésa's writings, for example—her "Chansons" and "Mémoires" [Songs and Memoirs]—are perfectly ordinary in size, as their placement next to small objects (glasses, cups, bottles) makes immediately clear. It is revealing as well that the "photobiographie" of Hugo presents only his public identity as writer and orator, while those of the two women blend the public and the private. This suggests the extent to which nineteenth-century women, even when famous, are more readily associated with private, domestic space. There is moreover a curious paradox at work here. A celebrity is by definition a public figure and, it would seem, a tribute to him would necessarily revolve around his public life. Yet, depicting a woman as strictly public risks casting aspersions on her virtue—as in the term "femme publique"—and could thus undermine the intended tribute.

In each of the three "photobiographies," the vignette at bottom center projects into the future. For Thérésa, banal *chanteuse*, this means a modest vision of imminent wealth: not posterity, just prosperity (represented by a treasure chest marked "caisse d'une ✡," the six-pointed star signifying *étoile*, not *juive*—star, not jewess —in this context). In the case of Victor Hugo, incomparably illustrious man of letters, this final vignette is commensurately grander. In the initial vignette of the Hugo composition, young Hugo leads the Romantic invasion, which knocks over statue busts of the great French classical authors Racine and Boileau. The final vignette provides the logical conclusion to this displacement. Entitled "Plus tard" [Later], this

scene clearly takes place after Hugo's death. His statue, hoisted onto a pedestal bearing his name, takes its place in a line of great male poets, likewise memorialized, which recedes into the horizon, and into the past: Hugo, Shakespeare, Dante, and so on. Hugo thus becomes a monument to his own everlasting glory, like the statufied male authors in Nadar's *Panthéon*. As the juxtaposition with the chairs above the final vignette suggests—one is labeled "Pairie" [Peerage], the other, "Académie Française"—Hugo's place in French culture will be assured in death as it was in life.

What of George Sand? What cultural space might the great woman of letters occupy during her life and beyond? Not a seat in the *Académie Française*, as no woman would be so honored until 1980. Nonetheless, when the "photobiographie" of Sand was made in the mid 1860s, there had just been a flurry of debate on the question of women, particularly George Sand, in the Academy. This included Sand's own contribution, "Pourquoi les femmes à l'Académie?" [Why women in the Academy?] (1981), which argues that it would not do women any good to be part of such a retrograde institution. On an obvious level, the vignette "Upon the seats of the French Academy" seems simply to weigh in on this debate. It appears to favor Sand's nomination, by making her books stand, or rather sit in for her, an identification reinforced by the structural similarity between the rectangular books and rectangular photo above them. On a less obvious level, the vignette surpasses the here and now of partisan squabbles over admission into the Academy, projecting beyond Sand's life and into her afterlife as a cultural figure—into the realm of the monument. This scene is, after all, the equivalent of the vignette "Plus tard" in the Hugo composition, representing the poet's posthumous memorialization. More than just a proxy for excluded Sand, the giant books also form a monument of sorts to her. The parallel lines of propped-up books resemble rows of tombstones, with the titles of Sand's works as epitaphs to the memory of their author. This would moreover be a characteristic tribute for the period. As we have seen, nineteenth-century France witnessed the dramatic rise of the modern cemetery, together with an unprecedented profusion of funerary monuments, as the 1995 exhibition *Mémoire*

Fig. 37. Pierre Durat and Carlo Gripp, *Photobiographie des contemporains: Victor Hugo.* **Photo M. Garval.**

Fig. 38. Pierre Durat and Carlo Gripp, *Photobiographie des contemporains: Thérésa.* **Photo M. Garval.**

de marbre [Memory of marble], at the *Bibliothèque historique de la ville de Paris*, so amply demonstrated (Le Normand-Romain 1995). This image of Sand's complete works as a graveyard is informed as well by the contemporary notion of an ideal synthesis of writer, work, and monument, otherwise associated with her male counterparts. Sand's fame would thus live on resplendently through her monumental *oeuvre*, the image suggests, in contrast to the questionable "immortalization" offered by membership in the eminently forgettable ranks of the Academy. Finally, on yet another level, Sand's photo depicts a kind of monument. As we saw earlier, the overall composition already gives the photo structural mass. In addition, the columns that appear to support this mass are also those that hold up the familiar dome of the *Académie Française*—whose shape Sand's head and torso approximate. The great woman writer would thus stand in for the venerable edifice, becoming not *la bonne dame de Nohant* but *la dame du quai Conti*. In this way, George Sand would be transformed into the famed cupola of the *Académie Française*, overarching, perhaps even transcending the so-called "immortals" below. Moreover, in contrast to the increasing provincialization of her public image at the time, a paradigmatically Parisian monument is appropriated here in her honor.

As vehicles for representing Sand's fame, each of these three images has its limitations. The earliest one depicts Sand's fame living on through the monument, but only when she is among other women—and women, specifically, that the accompanying article describes as mediocre. The latter two images set a higher standard, attempting to see her fame in relation to that of great men as well. The first of these images pays singular homage to Sand but short-circuits her access to lasting fame by statufying her too soon; the second evokes Sand's monumentality ingeniously, but without trying to envision an actual monument to her. In different ways then, all three images betray the period's broader difficulty in monumentalizing the great woman writer.

It perhaps requires a shift in perspective to look at images like these and see a positive evolution in society's view of women writers. In recent years, with the flourishing of feminist criticism, much attention has been paid to the general refusal, in nineteenth-century France, to take women seriously as literary figures. Little has been said about attempts, however incomplete, halting, or flawed, to imagine the previously unimaginable, to frame a vision of the great woman writer. Yet, denying and imagining literary greatness need to be understood as reactions to the same sociohistorical phenomenon—to women's widespread emergence as authors and, in particular, to Sand's challenge to the virtual male monopoly on literary glory. Despite their hesitations and flaws, images like these helped prepare George Sand's eventual, posthumous consecration in stone. More broadly, such images, and the actual monuments that followed them, helped French culture imagine the very category of the great woman writer.

Within the three decades following Sand's death, she was honored by two significant, free-standing, public monuments. The first, by renowned sculptor Aimé Millet (1819–91), was placed in the center of La Châtre, in Sand's beloved Berry, in 1884, less than a decade after her death (fig. 39); the second, by the less illustrious François Sicard (1862–1934), was placed in the Luxembourg Gardens, in Paris, in 1904, for the centenary of her birth (fig. 40). These are monuments, no doubt, commissioned and executed at the height of statuemania, inaugurated with ceremonial fanfare and substantial press coverage at the time and still in place today. In both, however, Sand is passive, pensive; seated, not standing; and not particularly large either. These are atypically unassuming and unheroic monuments, still marked by much the same hesitation as in earlier efforts to imagine Sand's eventual monumentalization. In part, the limited scope of the Sand monuments just reflects the period's standards for appropriateness, indeed for propriety, in paying public tribute to a woman. The prevailing view held that, for women, private, domestic space was the realm of virtue; public space, of promiscuity, indecency, shame. Accordingly, a more ambitious, public commemoration of a woman could run a greater risk of defaming her. Thus, much as public scenes are tempered by private ones in the female *photobiographies*, these monuments to Sand avoid an appearance of "immodesty" by remaining modest in conception. In a broader sense, these two monuments figure

LE MONDE ILLUSTRÉ

JOURNAL HEBDOMADAIRE

ABONNEMENTS POUR PARIS ET LES DÉPARTEMENTS
Un an, 24 fr.; — Six mois, 13 fr.; — Trois mois, 7 fr.; — Un numéro, 50 c.
Le volume semestriel, 12 fr. broché. — 17 fr., relié et doré sur tranche.
LA COLLECTION DES 27 ANNÉES FORME 54 VOLUMES
Secrétaire de la Rédaction : M. ÉDOUARD HUBERT

BUREAUX
13, QUAI VOLTAIRE
28ᵉ Année, Nᵒ 1429. — 16 Août 1884

DIRECTION ET ADMINISTRATION, 13, QUAI VOLTAIRE
Toute demande d'abonnement non accompagnée d'un bon sur Paris ou
sur la poste, toute demande de numéro à laquelle ne sera pas joint le
montant en timbres-poste, seront considérées comme non avenues. —
On ne répond pas des manuscrits envoyés.
Directeur : M. PAUL DALLOZ

LA STATUE DE GEORGE SAND, inaugurée à La Châtre (Indre), le 10 août. — (M. AIMÉ MILLET, statuaire. — Dessin de MM. DUPONT et LEPÈRE.)

Fig. 39. Dupont and Lepère, *La Statue de George Sand*. Photo M. Garval.

COURRIER DE PARIS

On célébrera dans quelques jours le centenaire de George Sand. La Comédie-Française jouera *François le Champi,* l'Odéon donnera aussi une de ses pièces. Le gouvernement inaugurera, dans le jardin du Luxembourg, une statue qui est l'œuvre du sculpteur Sicard. J'espère que nos étudiants rêveront souvent devant ce monument. L'artiste ne nous a pas représenté la bonne dame de Nohant, mais une femme jeune, jolie, romantique. C'est ainsi que devait être George Sand quand elle vint, en 1831, à Paris.

Statue de George Sand, par Sicard, qui doit être placée dans le jardin du Luxembourg.

Elle fuyait son mari et, quelques années après, elle obtenait sa liberté. Mais ses premiers romans expriment les souffrances qu'elle ressentit dans sa vie conjugale. Elle a flétri l'égoïsme et la maladresse de certains maris. Elle a créé ce type de la femme incomprise, dont la littérature devait si singulièrement abuser jusqu'à ce que Flaubert en eût fait justice dans *Madame Bovary.* Mais les

admirent l'étonnement enfantin des griffons, l'indolence souple et mélancolique des lévriers, l'agitation vaine et joyeuse des fox-terriers, la méfiance attristée des dogues, la brutalité paisible des danois, la méditation des bassets.

Concours des poils ras ! Concours des poils longs ! Concours de trompes aussi. Aboiements et cors ! Le jury, insensible aux rumeurs du dehors et aux inutiles recommandations, semble sourd aux bruits du dedans. Il examine, il distribue sagement les prix et les mentions. Ce n'est point sans émotion qu'on voit les propriétaires présenter à leurs juges les concurrents intimidés.

Tel chien, chargé de couronnes et de médailles, vaut quelques dizaines de mille francs. Mais ce ne sont pas des avantages matériels que les exposants recherchent : c'est la gloire. La vogue semble aller, cette année, vers le chow-chow, vers le chien chinois.

C'est évidemment un aimable animal. Il a surtout le mérite d'être assez rare. Il bénéficie encore de la curiosité qu'excitent les événements d'Extrême-Orient. Le chow-chow est la grande attraction de l'exposition canine. Vers sa grâce bizarre se penchent les femmes aux robes harmonieuses, les hommes aux redingotes impeccables. Les chiens d'Europe considèrent sans défiance cet Asiatique et redoutent vaguement le péril jaune.

ANDRÉ FAGEL.

LA VENTE DE LA PRINCESSE MATHILDE

Toiles de maîtres, objets d'art, bibelots précieux, joyaux dont quelques-uns étaient historiques, on disperse en ce moment les collections de Mᵐᵉ la princesse Mathilde.

Vous pensez bien que tout le « public habituel des grandes ventes » est là présent, mélange de mondains désœuvrés et curieux, d'amateurs prêts à tous les sacrifices, si l'on sait bien s'y prendre, — et tel commissaire-priseur s'y entend à merveille, — de marchands de Vienne, de Londres et de Berlin, sans compter tous ceux de Paris.

Les enchères vont rondement. Et tant de choses jolies ou belles choses, amassées dans l'hôtel de la rue de Berry, s'en retournent maintenant aux quatre vents, comme elles en étaient venues.

L'une des œuvres les plus intéressantes de la collection va pourtant rester chez nous. C'est un portrait ovale, que le catalogue, — modestie d'expert incertain ou suprême rouerie, — désignait ainsi : « École française, dix-huitième siècle : *Portrait d'un gentilhomme* ». Pas de nom d'auteur, alors que tant de collectionneurs sont

Fig. 40. François Sicard, *Statue de George Sand*. Photo M. Garval.

the continued reticence, in nineteenth-century French society, about honoring a great woman writer as whole-heartedly and unreservedly as it would her male counterparts.

Of the two, however, the Millet monument in La Châtre is the more imposing. Somewhat larger than life, it rests squarely upon a substantial pedestal, engraved with titles of Sand's works.[12] Sand is represented in middle age, thus not in either of the guises that otherwise dominate her iconography, but would lend themselves poorly to commemorative statuary. She is no longer the elusive, protean figure of her earlier years, but not yet the simple, goodly "bonne dame" of later on. Instead, she appears in a rare incarnation, particularly well-suited to a monumental tribute: a mature woman, at the apogee of her literary renown. As one contemporary article noted, "Le sculpteur l'a représentée à l'âge de sa plus grande gloire, c'est-à-dire à quarante ans environ" [The sculptor depicted her at the peak of her glory, in other words at about forty years of age] (La Statue de George Sand 1884, 87); this formulation does infer though that Sand's star had since faded. The sculptor, a disciple of David d'Angers, was a leading academic artist at the time who received commissions for monuments to such great men as Vercingétorix (Alise-Sainte-Reine 1864), Chateaubriand (Saint-Malo 1875), Edgar Quinet (Bourg 1883) and Louis Joseph Gay-Lussac (Limoges 1890). While Millet's renown certainly lent prestige to the Sand monument, its placement in a quiet square in sleepy La Châtre lessened the appeal and potential impact of this tribute to her, as was the case as well with the 1896 monument to Marceline Desbordes-Valmore, in Douai, "a town whose geographic marginality reflected the place of women writers in the French literary canon" (McCall 1999, 48). Revealingly moreover, while Millet made two maquettes, "une debout, l'autre assise" [one standing, the other seated], the subscription committee adopted the less grandiose, seated one (Dumesnil 1891, 44).

Unlike the larger Millet, the Sicard monument in Paris is only life-sized and placed practically at ground level. There is no mention of Sand's works. She appears very young and delicate, even sylphid: an idealized beauty, much like those in the 1836 anthology; a Romantic muse at best (cf. Bouteron 1934). In short, there is nothing to indicate that this is a homage to a successful writer and not just another embellishment to one of Paris's loveliest public parks. The earlier, provincial monument thus seems to take Sand a good deal more seriously than this later, Parisian one. Moreover, while placement in a major Parisian park could confer greater prestige than placement in a small provincial one, Sicard's name offered somewhat less luster than Millet's.[13]

What of these monuments' contemporary reception? The Millet comes closest in grandeur and sense of purpose to monuments honoring the period's great men of letters, yet depicting Sand as a mature and successful writer did not sit well with contemporary observers. Revealingly, whereas conventional depictions of great man monuments place us at a vantage point below, so that the statue looms expansively above (fig. 43), in the Monde illustré cover featuring the La Châtre monument (fig. 39), this perspective is reversed. Here we are asked to gaze down upon a figure reined in by a vignette surrounded, in turn, by delicately ornamental woodland scenes. Thus attenuated—appearing smaller than it is, and associated with the transitory beauty of the natural world, and inconsequentiality of the decorative arts, rather than with the grandeur and stony durability of commemorative statuary—this tribute to Sand is trivialized, even demonumentalized. Similarly, in the juxtaposed E. A. Tilly engravings of the new Diderot and Sand monuments, published in L'Illustration on August 9, 1884 (fig. 41), whereas Diderot brandishes his quill pen frankly, the Sand statue has been rotated so that her pen remains hidden and only her book appears, thus transforming her from a woman writer into a more conventional, less threatening femme liseuse (cf. Bergman-Carton, passim, on the abundant representations of the femme liseuse). One critic wrote, moreover, upon seeing Millet's statue at the 1884 Salon, that he would have liked Sand to appear younger and prettier: "J'aurais souhaité peut-être une George Sand moins mûre. Dans les arts plastiques, surtout quand il s'agit d'une femme, ne faut-il pas toujours autant que possible chercher à se rapprocher d'un idéal de beauté?" [I might have wished for a less mature George Sand. In the plastic arts, particularly when dealing with a woman, is it not best, in so far as possible,

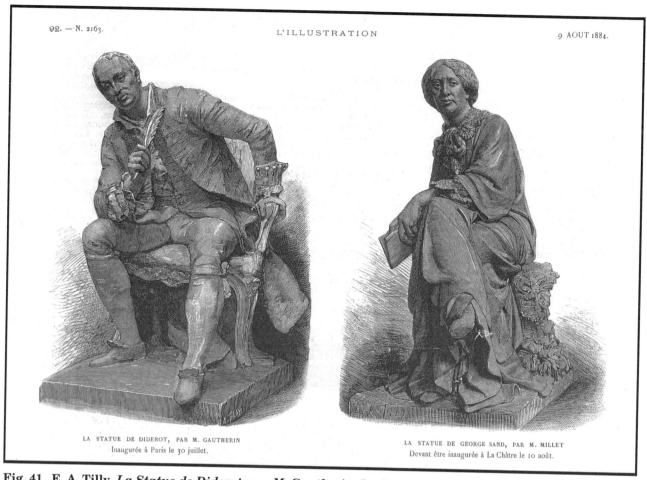

LA STATUE DE DIDEROT, PAR M. GAUTHERIN
Inaugurée à Paris le 30 juillet.

LA STATUE DE GEORGE SAND, PAR M. MILLET
Devant être inaugurée à La Châtre le 10 août.

Fig. 41. E. A. Tilly, *La Statue de Diderot, par M. Gautherin; La Statue de George Sand, par M. Millet.* **Photo M. Garval.**

to always strive toward an ideal of beauty?" (BHVP Dossier). Typically for the period, in the absence of a viable tradition for representing great women writers, this commentator invokes instead the long-established iconographical tradition of idealized feminine beauty. In particular, he prefers the ephemeral and, as such, antimonumental beauty of youth, suggesting again an underlying uneasiness with Millet's Sand appearing not only too old, but too monumental. His wishes for a callower, comelier monument came true, it seems, in the later work by Sicard. Here we find neither the mature, successful writer of the Millet monument, nor the figure of the literary has-been "bonne dame de Nohant" that prevailed at this time, nor even, perhaps, the young, protean Sand that this later vision had supplanted. So young and delicately feminine is Sicard's Sand that it seems to depict

her before the start of her literary career. This is how André Fagel, writing in the "Courrier de Paris" rubric in *L'Illustration*, chose to see it: "L'artiste ne nous a pas représenté la bonne dame de Nohant, mais une femme jeune, jolie, romantique. C'est ainsi que devait être George Sand quand elle vint, en 1831, à Paris" [The artist did not depict the good lady of Nohant, but rather a young, pretty, romantic woman. This is how George Sand must have been, in 1831, when she came to Paris] (Fagel et. al 1904, 354). The use here of the verb "devoir" is especially significant, articulating at once the author's attempt to recreate the historical moment of Sand's arrival in Paris and a desire to relegate Sand to that pivotal moment. In this way, Fagel's commentary is reminiscent of Maurice Kahn's "The Art of being a grandmother," also published in *L'Illustration*, only five weeks

Fig. 42. Anonymous, *Inauguration du monument de George Sand dans le jardin du Luxembourg: Mme Séverine dépose des fleurs devant la statue (Inauguration of George Sand's monument in the Luxembourg Garden: Mme Séverine places flowers before the statue).* **Photo M. Garval.**

later. The prevailing *fin-de-siècle* vision of Sand as the "bonne dame de Nohant," while reductive, generally recalled in some way at least her earlier literary successes; in these instances, however, Sand the writer is plunged virtually into oblivion. As we have seen, Kahn's article seeks to erase all memory of her Parisian past (unlike the earlier *Photobiographie*, which foregrounds the Parisian roots of "GEORGE SAND, née à Paris"), and ends by transforming her into a berrichonne "boune mé," such a homespun, rustic figure that we wonder if she would even know how to write. Similarly, Fagel's interpretation of Sicard's monument strips her of her literary career, the ostensible reason for the monument. In this view, Sicard's Sand— in limbo, having left her provincial home, yet not having settled down in the city to make her way as a writer—is denied entry into the nineteenth-century master narrative of young provincial talent conquering fame and fortune in Paris. In a telling contrast, the 1884 review in *L'Illustration* of the La Châtre statue points

out that Millet's Sand is dressed as she would have been while visiting Nohant (La Statue de George Sand 1884, 87): in her provincial monument, she therefore appears as a successful Parisian returning to her country home, while in her Parisian monument she plays the hopeful provincial eternally arriving in the capital.

Sicard's Sand, far more decorative than commemorative, blends quietly in among the flowers and trees, enhancing the aesthetic and spiritual appeal of the park, haven for harried city dwellers in need of tranquil, restorative meditation. "J'espère que nos étudiants rêveront souvent devant ce monument" [I hope that our students shall often dream before this monument], remarked Fagel (1884, 354). Similarly, the subsequent coverage in *L'Illustration* of the inauguration noted that Sand was "assise sur un rocher, en une attitude méditative" [sitting upon a rock, in a meditative posture], and that the monument was "placé au bord d'une pelouse du jardin du Luxembourg, non loin de la grille faisant face au Panthéon" [located at the edge of a lawn in the Luxembourg garden, not far from the gate opposite the Pantheon] (Le Centenaire de George Sand 1904, 20). The Sicard monument thus provided a place not of lasting memory for the nation, but of momentary, bucolic "reverie" for passing students. Its placement in the Luxembourg, at the edge of a lawn, behind the formidable "grille" opposite the *Panthéon*, figures Sand's marginalization vis-à-vis the grandiose manifestations of male glory (much as the original review of Sicard's statue was relegated to the catch-all "Courrier de Paris" section of *L'Illustration*, followed by items about the dog show at the Tuileries—"l'exposition canine attire le public le plus élégant" [the dog show draws a most elegant crowd]—and the auction of Princess Mathilde's "toiles de maîtres, objets d'art, bibelots précieux, joyaux" [old master paintings, art objects, precious ornaments, jewels]). The grateful *patrie* honored its great—and even not-so-great—men triumphantly, both within its official temple of renown and throughout what June Hargrove calls the "open-air Pantheon" of Paris (The Statues of Paris: An Open-air Pantheon). In contrast, the sole Parisian monument to the nineteenth century's most illustrious woman writer relegated her to a modest patch of lawn, a well-traveled part of a prestigious Parisian park no doubt, but also a verdant setting reflecting her provincialized public image at the time (and also oddly fulfilling the command "Laissez verdure" [Leave greenery], which Sand pronounced without further explanation on the eve of her death). Along similar lines, in its coverage of the 1904 inauguration ceremony, *L'Illustration* featured two photographs of prominent contemporary women of letters paying tribute to their predecessor: Séverine places flowers (fig. 42), and Mme Worms-Barretta reads poetry before the monument. In both there seems, for the period, to be an unusually high percentage of women participating in the official ceremony. It is tempting, in retrospect, to see here inspiring examples of early twentieth-century "women of ideas" paying homage to their great foremother. Yet these scenes have too much the look of a lady's auxiliary meeting or, at best, a suffragette tea party. Why, one wonders, was more of male officialdom not in attendance and why, if Sand were truly so valued as a literary figure,

would there not have been an address by a more illustrious male writer like Anatole France, already a member of the Académie Française at the time? Such "feminization" of the inauguration ceremony also figures the period's broader marginalization of Sand the writer. The fact that the Sicard statue garnered a medal of honor at the Salon of 1905 (Hargrove 1990, 217) seems to confirm, moreover, that it was perceived as unobjectionable yet unremarkable, an embodiment of pleasing mediocrity.

From our modern perspective, it is easy to be disappointed by the Sand monuments and their reception, to underestimate the novelty and cultural significance of such monuments being raised, viewed, and discussed openly and earnestly. That public monuments to a woman writer were raised at all, at this time, was in itself an extraordinary development. If we adopt a longer historical view, such efforts take their place in a broader process of cultural formation, leading to less ambivalent public acclaim for such twentieth-century women writers as Colette, Simone de Beauvoir, Marguerite Yourcenar, or Marguerite Duras. This has not meant bigger and better monuments for these women, however; indeed, there have been few monuments at all for men or women. In the interim, the monumental vision of literary greatness has declined, and today a grand public statue to a celebrated contemporary man of letters is no more imaginable than one to a female counterpart. What then is the legacy of nineteenth-century France's attempts to think of Sand in monumental terms, from earlier iconographical experiments like Nadar's *Panthéon*, or the *photobiographie*, through the two monuments actually raised? It is, simply put, the idea that a woman can be taken seriously as a great writer: if no longer through real or imagined statufication, then through such tributes as Yourcenar's groundbreaking induction into the *Académie Française* or Duras's appearance on the televised literary talk show "Apostrophes."

Nadar's *Panthéon* and the *photobiographie* series already provide useful juxtapositions of Victor Hugo and George Sand, nineteenth-century France's most acclaimed man and woman of letters. Such works could only try to anticipate the writers' posterity. By the centenaries of their birth, however, the now deceased writers had entered the afterlife of the

78. PARIS — Monument de Victor Hugo   C. M.

Fig. 43. Ernest Barrias, *Monument de Victor Hugo*. Photo M. Garval.

nation's collective memory, and revealingly different monuments to them were raised, in Paris, within two years of each other. In the 1902 Barrias monument Hugo sits heroically atop a colossal "Rocher des proscrits," dominating the square that bears his name (fig. 43). This paradigmatic great man monument appears all the more ambitious and imposing when compared with Sicard's 1904 Sand, seated fetchingly upon a low rock, seeming little more than a fashion accessory for the beautiful *jardin du Luxembourg*. The comparison here between the grandiose incarnation of male literary fame and its understated female counterpart is striking indeed, yet somewhat misleadingly so. As we have seen with Millet's monument, it was possible, in nineteenth-century France, for the period's most celebrated woman writer to be honored more grandly. In addition, there is much more to the question of Hugo's monumentality than is apparent through an initial glance at the 1902 tribute. Upon closer

examination, Barrias's monument appears less impressive than excessive, even bombastic. An uneasy hodgepodge of Hugo's literary and political identities that caused controversy at the time, it was torn down only 39 years later, with little public regret. When it was erected, moreover, at the apparent peak of statuemania, French culture was already awash in mass-produced Hugo memorabilia that was heralding the arrival of new, nonmonumental modes of renown. The Barrias monument, and the cultural context surrounding it, are emblematic of deep, rich contradictions within Hugo's unparalleled literary glory: of grotesqueness amid the grandeur; of renown at once monolithic and multiple, solemn and farcical; and, of inevitable cultural change despite a persistent dream of permanence. In the next chapter then we will see that, much as Sand's case tests the limits of female monumentality, Hugo's case tests the limits of male monumentality.

4

Victor Hugo: The Writer as Monument

"Victor"

In a burst of enthusiasm he would later regret (cf. below), Balzac dedicated *Lost Illusions* to Victor Hugo, the well-named "Victor" of the period's battles for literary fame and fortune:

Vous qui, par le privilège des Raphaël et des Pitt, étiez déjà grand poète à l'âge où les hommes sont encore si petits, vous avez, comme Chateaubriand, comme tous les vrais talents, lutté contre les envieux embusqués derrière les colonnes, ou tapis dans les souterrains du Journal. Aussi désiré-je que votre nom victorieux aide à la victoire de cette oeuvre que je vous dédie, et qui, selon certaines personnes, serait un acte de courage autant qu'une histoire pleine de vérité. [CH 5.123]

[Privileged like Raphael or Pitt, you were already a great poet at an age when other men are still small; like Chateaubriand, like all true talents you struggled against the envious souls hidden behind columns, or lurking in the subterranean depths of the Press. This is why I wish for your victorious name to help carry this work toward victory—this work that I hereby dedicate to you and which, as some have told me, is as courageous as it is truthful.]

Balzac wrote dedications to dozens of works, but this was a particularly important one for him. Published in 1843, *Lost Illusions* was to be the keystone of *The Human Comedy*, "l'oeuvre capitale dans l'oeuvre" [the main work within the work] (Balzac 1967–71, 2.172). The perilous pursuit of literary glory is one of its principal themes, a fictional reverberation of the perceived stakes for Balzac, who considered this novel's success crucial to his own. Dedicating it to Victor Hugo, he appealed to the power and prestige of the writer who, by this time, had dominated the French literary world for more than a dozen years. To be sure, Balzac's play

on the name "Victor" reflects his obsession with the cratylistic, even talismanic power of names and, in particular, of his own name as the vital, primordial force driving his entire literary project (cf. chapter 2). But, in a larger sense, Balzac's comments also manifest a widespread, and in many ways ambivalent sense of Hugo as a literary conqueror.

As Baudelaire remarked, "Les nations n'ont de grands hommes que malgré elles.... Et ainsi, le grand homme a besoin, pour exister, de posséder une force d'attaque plus grande que la force de résistance développée par des millions d'individus" [Nations only have great men in spite of themselves...And thus in order to exist, the great man must be more powerful, more aggressive, more resistant than millions of other individuals] (Baudelaire 1975–76, 1.654). Victor Hugo was just such a great man, who came to be seen as a uniquely monumental figure through his unparalleled conquest of literary glory. Taking his nation by storm, Hugo achieved what Claude Roy (1958) calls "La conquête d'un siècle en quatre-vingts livres" [The conquest of a century in eighty books] (preface). Hugo's "vanquished" contemporaries viewed his conquering zeal with a mix of admiration, envy, resentment, exhilaration, and fatigue. André Gide articulated his beleaguered countrymens' sense of exasperation most memorably with his famous 1902 retort to the question "Quel est votre poète?": "Hugo—hélas!" [Who is your poet? Hugo—alas!] (reply to a survey in *L'Ermitage,* February 1902; Robb 1998, 619). Gide made his pronouncement after Hugo's death, yet much the same sentiment was already expressed from early on in Hugo's career. An exchange in Balzac's *Wild Ass's Skin* even anticipates Gide's formulation of a weary response to an inevitable question: when, during a discussion of contemporary writers, one character asks, "—Et Victor Hugo?" another replies, "—C'est un grand homme, n'en parlons plus." [—And Victor Hugo?—A great man, let's not talk about him any more] (CH 5.102 [var. i]).[1] Hugo's contemporaries did in fact talk on and on about him; indeed, no other nineteenth-century writer inspired so much commentary or such an extensive iconography. Yet one can also understand the impulse to stop talking: why bother when, as we shall see, Hugo was such a voluble advocate on his own behalf?

The sheer scope of Hugo's renown is best conveyed by Pierre Georgel's 810-page catalogue, *La Gloire de Victor Hugo*, published in 1985 to accompany the *Grand Palais* exhibition honoring the centenary of the writer's death. The fruit of intense collaboration among nearly three dozen contributors—Maurice Agulhon, Arnaud Laster, Ségolène Le Men, Chantal Martinet, Guy Rosa, Jacques Seebacher, and Anne Ubersfeld, to name but a few—it remains a model of interdisciplinary scholarship. In his introduction, Georgel thus characterizes its purpose and orientation:

Le présent ouvrage, inventaire, commentaire et prolongement de l'exposition, dont il épouse la formule et le plan, réunit une somme d'informations et de réflexions, en grande partie inédites. Il indique—il voudrait indiquer—dans quelle direction "interdisciplinaire" peut se renouveler l'approche du XIXe siècle, rejoignant ainsi d'autres entreprises animées par le même projet, comme la revue *Romantisme*, le recueil collectif *Les lieux de mémoire* . . . et le futur Musée d'Orsay. (26)

[A commentary on, as well as inventory and continuation of the exhibition, this work follows its format and organization, gathering together a substantial quantity of unpublished information and analysis. It would hope to suggest the "interdisciplinary" direction that our approach to the century can take, along the lines of such like-minded enterprises as the journal *Romantisme*, the collective volume *Realms of Memory*, and the soon-to-be opened Musée d'Orsay.]

Marking a significant departure from so much earlier, partisan commentary, stuck in well-worn paths of hugophilia and hugophobia, Georgel's catalogue aspires to be "*Sur* la gloire et non *à* la gloire de Victor Hugo" [*About* Victor Hugo's glory, and not *to* his glory] (23). With evident fascination for the many curiosities and excesses of Hugo's glory, yet with careful critical detachment, Georgel and his team consider the phenomenon within its rich social, cultural, political, and intellectual contexts, through a series of brief essays, interspersed with ample illustrations. The first and longest of the catalogue's four sections, *La "figure" de Victor Hugo* [Victor Hugo's public image], of greatest interest for our purposes, is divided in turn into four subsections—"Les images," "La presse et les biographies," "Hugo dans le débat politique et social," and "Les hommages publiques" [Images, Press and biographies, Hugo's place in politics and society, and Public homages]—containing essays on such diverse topics as "Images 'populaires,'" "Hugo 'quarante-huitard'?", and "Un dieu chasse l'autre: la 'Ford' sur le piédestal de Victor Hugo" [Popular images, Hugo '48'er, and One god replaces another: the "Ford" on Victor Hugo's pedestal].

La Gloire de Victor Hugo takes a buckshot approach to its bewilderingly large subject, tackling anything from Hugo commemorative plates, to Louise Bertin's 1836 opera *Esméralda*, to newspaper reporting of Hugo's funeral, to Émile Gallé's *art nouveau* glass tributes, to film versions of Hugo's works, and statistical evidence on their dissemination in print. As a result, the catalogue's overall contribution to our understanding of Hugo's glory, while substantial, remains somewhat diffuse. This chapter, while conceived in much the same spirit of interdisciplinary inquiry as the catalogue and deeply indebted to its wealth of groundbreaking scholarship, is more narrowly focused. Like the catalogue, it is not written *to* the glory of Hugo, yet it is also not *about* his glory in the same wide-ranging way, necessarily leaving aside such matters as book illustration, film adaptations, or theatrical productions, fascinating in themselves, yet only tangential to our emphasis on the rise and fall of nineteenth-century France's literary dream of stone. This chapter thus follows Victor Hugo's progressive conquest of glory over the course of his long career and beyond, tracing the evolution of his fame vis-à-vis the historical evolution of fame itself.

Tout ce qui est grand a une horreur sacrée. . . . On éprouve ce sentiment bizarre, l'aversion du grand. On voit les abîmes, on ne voit pas les sublimités; on voit le monstre, on ne voit pas le prodige.

[All that is great inspires holy terror. We feel this bizarre aversion to greatness. We see the abyss, not the soaring heights; we see the monster, not the genius.]
—Victor Hugo, chapter on La Convention in *Quatrevingt-treize* (1965, 150)

Balzac's dedication to *Lost Illusions* suggests that while no doubt entitled to extraordinary renown ("le privilège des . . . vrais talents" [privileged like all true talents]), Hugo also cultivated it vigorously ("vous avez . . . lutté" [you struggled]). Through constant, one might say shameless self-promotion, he determined in large measure how his contemporaries understood his glory, defining the terms—if not necessarily the tenor—of the extensive mythology that evolved around him. Balzac's homage touches as well upon several other themes in this mythology. Hugo appeared destined for glory from an early age. Born with and spanning his century (cf. "Ce siècle avait deux ans" [This century was two years old]; Hugo 1964–67, 1.717–19), he somehow had the privilege, or just the presumption, to speak for his nation and time. A "grand poète" surrounded by "hommes . . . petits," Hugo enjoyed absolute preeminence among contemporary writers. His true peers were therefore to be found, instead, in a distinguished lineage of great geniuses. The true, lasting worth of these glorious precursors had been confirmed, moreover, in posterity's eyes, by the narrow-minded opposition of their age. So, too, would it be for contemporary greats. "Comme tous les hommes supérieurs," contends Hugo in his 1824 obituary of Byron, "il a certainement été en proie à la calomnie" [Like all superior men, he was doubtless the target of slander] (Hugo 1968b, 2.463). Indeed, throughout Hugo's long public career, this romantic view on the prestige of adversity would help recuperate his momentary difficulties— from bad reviews, to the loss of loved ones, to his long exile—as mounting evidence of his greatness.

Above all, and in every possible way, Hugo cultivated a monumental image of himself. He had many extraordinary qualities; modesty was not one, however. He strove to appear larger than life in his sorrows and misfortunes (cf. e.g., "Tristesse d'Olympio" [Olympio's sadness]; Hugo 1968b, 1.1093–98), and positively colossal in his triumphs ("Colosse de bronze ou

d'albâtre, / Salué d'un peuple idolâtre" [Colossus of bronze or alabaster, Hailed by an idolatrous populace; 1.734] reads a song of himself woven into an 1828 tribute to the sculptor David d'Angers). Hugo's public also saw him, for better or worse, as a monumental figure. Pierre Georgel puts it this way:

L'attribut le plus constamment prêté à Hugo, à tout propos et de toutes parts, c'est la démesure. Depuis ses premières interventions publiques, toutes les métaphores de l'immensité, de l'énormité, de l'altitude, toutes les figures appropriées de la fable et de l'Histoire, ont été utilisées et ressassées pour rendre compte à la fois de sa personnalité, de la nature de son oeuvre et de sa place dans le siècle. "Un *grand* homme": jamais, peut-être, la formule n'a été à ce point pris à la lettre. Et cette grandeur s'impose d'abord en termes matériels, quantitatifs, comme si l'expérience première—élémentaire et prépondérante—que les contemporains eurent de Victor Hugo était un fantastique encombrement, une présence physique et morale sans commune mesure avec celle des simples mortels ou même avec des autres grands hommes. (Georgel 1985, 88)

[Excess is the characteristic most often attributed to Hugo, by everyone, and for every occasion. From when he first entered into the limelight, every metaphor of hugeness, enormity, and height, every resource that History and fiction could offer to account for the nature of his work, his personality, and place in his time, was used and abused. Never, perhaps, was the expression "A *great* man" taken so literally. And this greatness was expressed first in material, quantitative terms. It was as if contemporaries' primary, basic, and overriding impression of Victor Hugo was that of an incredible burden, a physical and moral presence on a completely different scale from that of mere mortals, or even of other great men.]

As Georgel's comments suggest, Hugo's public took its cue from his self-aggrandizing gestures and elaborated endless variations on the theme of Hugo the "sur-homme" [superman]. In nineteenth-century France, while Balzac's *Human Comedy* best exemplified the monumental literary work, Victor Hugo best exemplified the monumental writer; indeed, his towering example largely defined the period's evolving vision of the writer as a monument. Along similar lines, while Sand embodied the possibilities and limitations for female monumentality,

Hugo embodied those for male—for the greatest possible—monumentality. Hugo's colossal persona tested the public's capacity for admiration and devotion, but also for patience, indulgence, and credulity. His gigantism did make an easy target. Detractors could readily cast it in a negative light, as egotism, excess, even monstrosity. Alternately, as we shall see a bit later on, they could try to shrink the great man down to a more manageable size by accusing him of pettiness.

As a public figure then, Hugo realized the full potential of the French words "monument" and "monumental" as expressions of both praise and blame. According to the *Trésor de la langue française* (1971–94), "monument" can mean "objet ou personne énorme" [enormous object or person] and "Personne que ses qualités placent hors du commun" [Person whose qualities place him beyond the ordinary] yet, in a familiar and pejorative sense, the expression "un monument de" [a monument of] followed by a substantive signifies "Une chose révélatrice d'une qualité poussée à son plus haut point" [a thing marked by a quality pushed to its extreme], as in "un monument d'ignorance" [a monument of ignorance] or "un monument d'horreur" [a monument of horror]. Similarly, while "monumental" usually means large or imposing in a positive sense (i.e., grand, noteworthy, memorable, and so on), it also can connote excess ("Qui étonne par son caractère démesuré. Synon. *énorme, monstre. Orgueil monumental; bêtise, erreur, ignorance monumentale*" [Which astonishes through its excessive character. Synon. *enormous, monstrous. Monumental pride; monumental stupidity, error, ignorance*]). It can be used as well "Pour souligner le caractère choquant d'une chose, d'une situation" [To underscore the shocking nature of a thing, of a situation], as in the expression, "C'est monumental!" [It's monumental!]; and, applied to a person, it can signify "Exceptionnel par ses défauts" [Exceptional in his shortcomings], as in Jules Renard's *Journal*: "Rosny . . . traite Hugo de crétin de génie, de monumental imbécile" [Rosny says Hugo is a brilliant cretin, a monumental imbecile] (1965, 1228).

Perceptions of Hugo's monumentality ran the gamut of such connotations, from uncommon qualities to exceptional flaws, grandeur to monstrosity. In particular, such perceptions were filtered through the aesthetic debate, framed in the first half of the century, between classics and romantics, proponents of harmony and measure versus advocates of evocative excess. Seeing Hugo's monumentality in a negative or a positive light depended largely upon where one stood in this debate. Yet even among those of a romantic bent, who considered excess an aesthetic virtue, assessments of Hugo's monumentality could ring ambivalent. Baudelaire, for example, characterized Victor Hugo as "grand, terrible, immense comme une création mythique, cyclopéen pour ainsi dire" [great, terrible, huge as a mythic creation, cyclopean as it were] (Baudelaire 1975–76, 1.117), echoing Sainte-Beuve's earlier use of "cyclopéen" to describe his illustrious peer (Maurois 1964, 186, 300–303). While "grand" and "immense" seem unambiguously laudatory, at least from Baudelaire's point of view, "terrible" already introduces a darker, more troubling note. "Cyclopéen," while it can mean simply enormous or gigantic, is also an architectural term for a primitive type of masonry, made of massive, uneven stones. It thus suggests roughness, irregularity, crudeness, and primitiveness, characteristics harder to see as expressions of unmitigated praise. Following moreover on the heels of "mythique," "cyclopéen" also conjures up the one-eyed giants of Greek mythology, who supposedly had assembled the rugged walls of ancient Mycenae, and the most famous of whom, Polyphemus, ate six of Ulysses' men before the hero tricked and blinded him to escape. Likening Hugo to the Cyclops casts him as the source of a powerful but monolithic vision; the lumbering creator of a rough-hewn literary monument; a dangerous, barbaric figure; and, ultimately, a sort of tragic dupe. This latter view of Hugo as, in Renard's phrase, a "monumental imbécile," is a recurrent theme in Hugo criticism, both during his lifetime and beyond. According to a March 4, 1860, entry in the Goncourt brothers' journal, "Ce qui . . . frappe surtout dans Hugo, qui a l'ambition de passer pour un penseur, c'est l'absence de pensée" [What is most striking about Hugo, who wishes to be seen as a thinker, is his absence of thought] (Goncourt 1989). Other influential commentators, from Désiré Nisard to Gustave Lanson, also saw Hugo as a prodigious generator of melodious phrases and striking images, somehow mentally deficient though in his extreme facility: a gifted yet simple-minded windbag, a kind of literary *idiot savant*.[2] Along the same lines, in the last years of his life, as the Third Republic's preeminent cultural hero, Hugo repeatedly made long-winded, platitudinous pronouncements on liberty, reason, peace, democracy, science, and progress, reminiscent of similarly flatulent tirades by the pharmacist Homais in Flaubert's *Madame Bovary*. As Léon Daudet notes, "Bien que Flaubert admirât et adorât Hugo, il a tracé, dans Homais, sans le vouloir, un portrait assez réussi des ultimes réflexions du maître, touchant les choses du catholicisme et de la foi. Il est très exact de dire qu'en ce domaine Hugo était devenu 'bête comme l'Himalaya'" [Although Flaubert admired and adored Hugo, in Homais he drew, unintentionally, a quite successful portrait of the master's late reflections upon matters of catholicism and faith. It is quite right to say that in this respect Hugo had become "as stupid as the Himalayas"] (Daudet 1922, 43). Hugo could seem as monumental in his stupidity as in his talent.

After the publication of Hugo's *Notre-Dame de Paris* in 1831, the public soon came to see the cathedral as the epitome of Hugo's monumentality. Numerous contemporary caricatures of Hugo astride, enthroned upon, even joined with the cathedral, reveal the period's contradictory view of him as a monumental figure (Georgel 1985, 88–89). The earliest of these is an 1833 drawing by "MD" that appeared in *La Charge* in its "Galerie des fous contemporains" [Gallery of contemporary fools]. It depicts a strange, hybrid creature, "Hugoth," whose head, dominated by a hyperbolically prominent *front de penseur* or thinker's forehead, appears to spring organically from a fragment of Gothic masonry (fig. 5). Pétrus Borel, who wrote the accompanying verses, was a great admirer of Hugo, and the drawing is clearly intended as a tribute; however, there are also some discordant elements at work. Beneath the drawing, in Hugolian-sounding alexandrains, Borel exclaims, "Epoque tant étroite / Où Victor Hugo seul porte la tête droite / Et crève le plafond de son crâne géant" [This oh so narrow age / When Victor Hugo alone carries his head high / And smashes the ceiling with his giant skull] (Écalle and Lumbroso 1964, 111). In one sense,

the drawing plays on Hugo's reputation as a champion of Gothic architecture, the author of several articles and a popular novel that take up this cause. In another, it represents Hugo as truly one with the monument. The punning title "Hugoth" also conjoins the writer and the Gothic edifice, though its truncated ending recalls as well the destructive, barbarian people whose name (however mistakenly) was given to the architectural style. In the rhymed caption, Hugo alone among his peers holds his head up proudly yet, in breaking through the narrow confines of his age, his gigantic skull shatters the ceiling. His irrepressible expansion is impressive, but also menacing. In short, "Hugoth" depicts a figure of innovation and domination, but with troubling overtones of recklessness, immoderation, danger, monstrosity, even barbarism. Hugo the conqueror, like Napoleon—his model in so many ways—inspired both adulation and dread.

In Grandville's 1839 "Grande course au clocher académique" [Great academic steeplechase] (fig. 44), instead of Hugo's head growing out of Notre-Dame, the cathedral appears to grow out of his head, a motif found as well in a roughly contemporary, caricature bust (fig. 45). Before the doors of the French Academy, Hugo literally rises above his peers (Vigny, Dumas, Balzac, et al.), standing upon column-like piles of his works. Sporting a long robe, a giant pen in one hand, and the miniature Notre-Dame atop his head, he is surrounded by such admirers as Paul Foucher, Pétrus Borel, and Arsène Houssaye. The key below reads, "**Victor Hugo**. Pape littéraire coiffé de Notre-Dame de Paris et entouré de ses enfants de choeur" [**Victor Hugo**. Literary pope wearing Notre-Dame de Paris on his head, and surrounded by his choir boys] (Georgel 1985, 38). On one level, as in Borel's "Hugoth," the juncture here of forehead and cathedral underscores the prevailing vision of Hugo's forehead as the physiological embodiment of his monumentality. As Pierre Georgel explains, though Hugo was of average size, his large forehead did resonate deeply in the popular imagination: "Siège traditionnel de la pensée et symbole du pouvoir (*Caput*, le "chef"), dôme et couronne, le front bombé, largement découvert, est à lui seul un monument et signifie une totale rupture d'échelle entre le surhomme et le commun des mortels" [A high, rounded forehead is the traditional seat of thought and

Fig. 44. Grandville, *Grande course au clocher académique* (*Great academic steeplechase*). © Photothèque des musées de la ville de Paris.

symbol of power (Caput, the "chief"), a dome and a crown, indeed, in itself a monument that embodies a total break between the superman and mere mortals] (89). While in Grandville's drawing, the miniature cathedral serves, ostensibly, as a papal crown, emblem of power and prestige, it also partakes of the jester's cap (recalling Dantan's *marotte*-wielding Balzac of 1836, cf. above) and the dunce cap.[3] Indeed, if Grandville's Hugo does not exactly glow with intelligence, the similarly crowned, anonymous caricature bust seems downright dim-witted: like young Charles Bovary, an imbecile with monumental headgear (fig. 45).

In an 1841 Benjamin Roubaud caricature for the *Panthéon Charivarique*, a giant Hugo sits upon the thick volumes of the 1832–42 Renduel-Delloye edition of his complete works as his lilliputian countrymen line up to dump

sacks of money in a huge chest at his feet, labeled "Rentes" [Income] (fig. 46). His colossal body sprawls out possessively over significant edifices in the French capital: as the catalogue for the exhibition *Benjamin Roubaud et le Panthéon Charivarique* notes, "Victor Hugo domine la vie culturelle parisienne au travers des monuments de la capitale" [Victor Hugo dominates parisian cultural life through the capital's monument] (Guillaume and Le Men 1988, 29). Specifically, as Hugo leans against the familiar facade of "his" cathedral, one foot rests on the *Académie Française*, to which he had just been elected; the other, on the *Théâtre Français* (where not only *Hernani* but also *Le Roi s'amuse* and *Lucrèce Borgia* premiered) and near the *Théâtre de la Porte-Saint-Martin* (where *Marion Delorme* premiered). Suggestively, in the space between Hugo's legs, stands

Fig. 45. Anonymous, *Buste-charge de Victor Hugo* (*Caricature bust of Victor Hugo*). © Photothèque des musées de la ville de Paris.

the phallic *Colonne Vendôme*, whose Napoleonic glory Hugo had sung in both *Odes et Ballades* and *Chants du crépuscule*, and which appeared similarly juxtaposed with the poet's midsection in Louis Boulanger's frontispiece for *Odes et Ballades* (Georgel 1898, 192). In the sky, to the right of Hugo's head, swirls a kind of nightmare vision of small, grotesque creatures, reminiscent of a scene from Bosch. Beneath the image, in much the same "fantastique" spirit, we find a pastiche of Hugo's 1829 poem, "Les Djinns" [The Genies], but with Hugo's glory as its subject. In Benjamin's caricature as well,

as in so many other images of Hugo, there is an accumulation of iconographical detail (important buildings and monuments, giant leatherbound volumes, oversized pens always at the ready), attesting to the writer's colossal stature in the literary world, and to his gargantuan literary production. Yet neither the image nor the text here offers an unambiguous celebration of Hugo's greatness. For one thing, Hugo's trancelike concentration seems directed at nothing loftier than the swelling treasure chest at his feet. Hugo's avarice, as this suggests, was a popular target for those who sought to debunk the great man as petty—so familiar, in fact, that it figures in Flaubert's *Dictionnaire des idées reçues*.[4] While Hugo's physical presence here is monumental, his posture is not. As Montaigne's adage affirms, sitting is antimonumental—"Et au plus eslevé throne du monde si ne sommes assis que sus nostre cul" [And on the world's highest throne, we only sit upon our ass][5]—and Hugo's slouching attitude here makes him all the less dignified. Furthermore, while Guillaume and Le Men are right to point out the thematic connection between "Les Djinns" and the "monde fantastique" floating beside Hugo's head, this vision calls to mind as well Goya's "Sleep of Reason Engenders Monsters," in which a slumping, slumbering figure at left also gives rise to a flight of ghoulish creatures at right. Recalling this famous, cautionary image, Benjamin's drawing calls into question the fruits of Hugo's unbridled, Romantic imagination. Along similar lines, the accompanying parody of "Les Djinns" mocks both Hugo's Romantic aesthetic ("Il condense / Mort et danse, / Rire et pleurs / Il mélange / L'homme et l'ange, / Et la fange / Et les fleurs" [He condenses / Death and dance, / Laughter and tears / He mixes / Man and angel / And mud / And flowers]) and his grandiose public image ("Hugo!!! . . . Sa puissance / Est immense . . . Il est grand, il est grand . . . Son vaste front rayonne et verse la pensée / Sur la foule," etc. [Hugo!!! . . . His power / Is immense . . . He is great, he is great . . . His vast brow shines and showers thought / upon the crowd]) Ultimately though, it is the intertext of "Les Djinns" itself that is most damning. This tale of a city assailed by supernatural forces casts an ominous shadow over the analogous scene depicted in the caricature, namely Hugo's "fantastique

SPECIMEN DU DESSIN CONSACRÉ CHAQUE VENDREDI

AUX PORTRAITS ET CHARGES

Des Notabilités politiques, financières, littéraires, dramatiques, musicales, artistiques, industrielles, &c.

PANTHÉON CHARIVARIQUE.

Hugo !!!
Cet homme
In-folio
Dégomme
Rimeurs
De Rome;
Auteurs
Qu'on nomme
Ailleurs.

Sa puissance
Est immense;
Il condense
Mort et danse.
Rire et pleurs,
Il mélange
L'homme et l'ange,
Et la fange
Et les fleurs.

Il est grand, il est grand, mes frères,
Il a sous ses pieds les palais,
A ses genoux les ministères,
Sous sa main les sociétaires
De ce bon Théâtre Français.
Son vaste front rayonne et verse la pensée
Sur la foule qui boit attentive et pressée,
La manne de son verbe et le bruit de sa voix.
Car lui, c'est l'Empereur! — Les autres sont des Rois,

Des ducs, des princes,
Comtes, barons;
Ils ont provinces,
Ils ont fleurons;
Mais, qui qu'en grogne,
Aux plus lurons
Lui, sans vergogne,
Prend, taille et rogne
Leurs écussons.

Grand, petit
Tout finit;
Loi suprême !
Hugo même
La subit.
Vivace
Hier
Il passe
Pair.

Fig. 46. Benjamin Roubaud, *Panthéon Charivarique.* © Photothèque des musées de la ville de Paris.

encombrement" [incredible burdening] (Georgel 1985, 88) of the Parisian cultural landscape. Implicitly, like the genies he conjures up in his poem, the author too is a malevolent power besieging the city.

As principal author of his own monumental myth, Hugo was emblematic of his age. In the nineteenth century, with the general democratization of fame and, more specifically, with the rise of the literary marketplace, modern advertising, and new visual media, there emerged a new breed of self-styled, self-aggrandizing celebrities, from Lord Byron to Walt Whitman, Napoleon to P. T. Barnum (Braudy 1986, 498–506). In France, writers like Balzac and Sand positioned their work and manipulated their public personas through polemical articles and prefaces, and such self-fashioning practices as dandyism, cross-dressing, and identification with iconic, individuating attributes (e.g., Balzac's cane or Sand's cigars). Among nineteenth-century French writers, though, Victor Hugo was the unrivaled master of self-promotion.[6] According to Léon Daudet,

> Convaincu que la postérité s'intéressait passionnément à ses faits et gestes, Hugo cultivait sa gloire naissante, puis montante, puis zénithale, littéraire, politique, philanthropique, jusque dans ses plus minimes effigies, ayant grand soin d'écheniller, de cacher, d'enterrer, de taire tout ce qui aurait pu apporter une ombre, ou une altération légère, à l'image olympienne qu'il désirait transmettre aux siècles futurs. (Daudet 1922, 25)

> [Convinced that posterity was passionately interested in his every move, Hugo cultivated his glory as it emerged, grew, and reached its apex, becoming literary, political, philanthropic. No depiction of him was too humble to escape his vigilance, indeed he took great care to minimize, hide, bury, silence anything that could have cast a shadow, or brought a slight change to the olympian image he wished to transmit to future generations.]

Daudet's reactionary politics and divorce from Hugo's grandaughter Jeanne explain the nastiness of his tone, yet the substance of his assessment holds true. He encapsulates key elements in Hugo's relation to fame, including: Hugo's keen sense of his own greatness, ardent pursuit and rapid attainment of renown, extraordinarily broad appeal, vigilant management of present appearances with an eye steadfastly on posterity, and skillful orchestration of his life in the service of his everlasting renown. As a more recent, more dispassionate biographer like Graham Robb observes, Hugo's life was "the work on which he lavished the greatest amount of love and ingenuity" (Robb 1998, xv). Yet more than just his *chef d'oeuvre*, Hugo's life is perhaps, as Daudet's comments suggest, a sort of *oeuvres complètes* in progress, a monumental and seemingly totalizing vessel for braving posterity—from which, however, as with Balzac's *Human Comedy*, the author excluded anything that might not contribute to his everlasting glory.

Daudet's opposing of "ses plus minimes effigies" [his humblest depictions] and "l'image olympienne" [olympian image] underscores as well a fundamental paradox in Hugo's prodigious self-promotion: his obsessive attention to the smallest details of his public persona could, in its pettiness, undermine the very grandeur it strained to establish. Pettiness was indeed a kind of Achilles' heel for Hugo, and detractors like Daudet sought to deflate his stature by dwelling upon examples of all sorts, from vanity, to avarice, to sexual peccadilloes. In Hugo's case, contends Daudet, "c'est en prenant le contre-pied minutieux de sa légende qu'on obtiendrait sa plus juste biographie" [you arrive at the most accurate biography by turning his legend completely on its head] (Daudet 1922, 35). "Minutieux" here means not only detailed but small, "minute": in effect, he is proposing that we scrutinize Hugo with a kind of reverse telescopic vision, to transform the giant into a midget. Even commentators more sympathetic to Hugo's literary merits than Daudet could not help criticizing the great public figure's personal pettiness. Ironically, for example, after Hugo accepted the flattering dedication to *Lost Illusions* (Balzac 1960–69, 4.507), which trumpets the great man's triumph over "les envieux embusqués derrière les colonnes, ou tapis dans les souterrains du Journal" [the envious souls hidden behind columns, or lurking in the subterranean depths of the Press], Balzac learned that Hugo had let one of his protégés, Édouard Thierry, attack the novel in a newspaper article. Furious, Balzac wrote Mme Hanska, quoting a line from *Un grand homme de province à Paris*

[A great man from the provinces in Paris]: "Ce n'est pas d'un grand poète. On est grand poète et petit homme. C'est surtout de lui qu'on peut dire: *C'est un grand écrivain et un petit farceur*" [This is not worthy of a great poet. One can be a great poet and a little man. *He's a great writer and a little joker.* The expression fits him to a tee] (Balzac 1967–71, 2.114–15). This perceived disjunction between public (published) and private selves, which Balzac also explored incisively in his 1844 novel *Modeste Mignon*, is a leitmotif in nineteenth-century discourse on celebrity, and figures prominently in contemporary assessments of Hugo.

Daudet's use of terms like "effigie" and "image" also points to the highly visual nature, not only of Hugo's work, but of his glory. To begin with, Hugo had a profoundly visual imagination. Richly evocative images pervade his writing and, while many nineteenth-century writers sketched and painted extensively (cf. *Dessins d'écrivains du XIXe siècle* catalogue), Hugo's graphic production was among the most substantial, both in quality and quantity (Van Tieghem 1985, 254). Hugo's visual imagination also meshed fruitfully with the period's blossoming visual culture, and particularly with emergent fame-making media such as lithography and photography. He had a talent, that is, for choosing striking, memorable, eminently reproducible images of himself and his work: staging the rag-tag *Battle of Hernani*, defending Gothic architecture as embodied in the cathedral of Notre-Dame, gazing back defiantly at his homeland from Jersey's *Rocher des Proscrits* or *Outlaw's rock*, growing his grandfatherly white beard, even insisting on a pauper's hearse (*le corbillard des pauvres*) which, amid the pomp of his official funeral, provided a dramatic contrast—"la dernière antithèse" [the last antithesis] according to Romain Rolland (1952, 25–26). While Daudet suggests that Hugo exerted absolute control over his public image, this is certainly an overstatement: rather, Hugo gave a substantial, initial impetus to the broader, public myth-making machinery.

Hugo did, however, long to control images and, more broadly, as a "conqueror," to control space. In this respect, he emulated a Napoleonic model of territorial conquest, of *rayonnement*, understanding Paris as the center from which French glory radiated outward. To be sure,

a well-orchestrated island exile could add poignancy to the great man's renown—i.e., Napoleon on Elba then Saint-Helena, and Hugo on Jersey then Guernsey—but only insofar as this offered a striking contrast to Paris and to what had already been achieved there. As Hugo would write of Paris, in 1867, from the vantage-point of exile, "C'est à Paris qu'est l'enclume des renommées. Paris est le point de départ des succès. Qui n'a pas dansé, chanté, prêché, parlé devant Paris n'a pas dansé, chanté, prêché et parlé" [The anvil of renown is in Paris. Paris is the starting point for success. Whoever has not danced, sung, preached, spoken before Paris has not danced, sung, preached, and spoken] (1964, 658). Paris was the "anvil" where fame was forged. Like so many of his contemporaries, Hugo considered Paris primordial and indispensable for fame, and he strove to make it his own through his words, to rewrite the symbolically charged space of the French capital in his name. Throughout his career, he wrote often and memorably about Paris, particularly about its great monuments, as André Maurois recalls—overenthusiastically, perhaps—in the conclusion to his biography:

Au-dessus de l'océan d'oubli qui a englouti tant d'oeuvres du XIXe siècle, l'archipel Hugo dresse fièrement ses hautes cimes couronnées de riches images. Les monuments qui sont les symboles des plus grands souvenirs de la France demeurent liés, indissolublement, à tel ou tel vers de lui. Des tours de Notre-Dame, *qui sont l'H de son nom*, au dôme des Invalides, sous lequel frissonnent encore les drapeaux qu'agita son souffle, de l'Arc de Triomphe à la Colonne Vendôme, Paris tout entier nous apparaît comme une ode à Victor Hugo, poème de pierre, dont les hauts lieux de notre histoire seraient les strophes. (Maurois 1954, 566–67)

[Surmounting the ocean of oblivion that has engulfed so many works from the 19th century, Hugo is like an island chain, its high peaks rising up proudly, topped with fine images. The monuments that symbolize France's greatness remain linked, indissociably, with one or the other of his verses. From the towers of Notre-Dame, that are the H in his name, to the dome of the Invalides beneath which flags still waver to the sound of his voice, from the Arc de Triomphe to the Vendôme Column, all Paris appears to us as an ode to Victor Hugo, a poem in stone, with the great bastions of our history as its stanzas.]

Maurois seems to have in mind poems like those to the Vendôme Column (Hugo 1964–67, 1.395, 825) and *Arc de Triomphe* (1.359, 936), or bird's eye views of Paris from the heights of Notre-Dame, yet Hugo dealt extensively too with the social and structural underbelly of Paris, its crypts, prisons, slums, and sewers, in such works as *Notre-Dame de Paris*, *Les Misérables*, or *Le Dernier jour d'un condamné*. In one sense, Maurois overstates his case, for it is far-fetched to think that we still see Paris as Hugo's property; indeed, the idea of Notre-Dame as the "H" in Hugo now seems more laughable than inspiring. In another, Maurois understates things, for Hugo's literary assault on Paris aimed wider even than his biographer suggests, encompassing high and low, light and dark, rich and poor, strong and weak, as he attempted to make his conquest of the French nation's glorious heart all the more complete.

> La vraie naissance, c'est la virilité.
> [Manhood is our true birth.]
> —Victor Hugo, "Paris" (1964, 656)

Hugo's capturing of literary glory also had a significant sexual dimension, as the lexical possibilities of the word "conquest" already suggest. There are libidinal undercurrents in the broader public vision of Hugo, and in his vision of himself. Numerous contemporary caricatures of Hugo depicted him with phallic attributes: oversized pens in particular, but also scepters, swords, flagposts, lyres, or exclamation points (cf. above). While the frequency of these motifs was tempered by the relative indirectness of the reference, and by the humor of the context, such works nonetheless manifested a distinctly phallic vision of Hugo. This was consonant not only with the period's general conception of literary greatness, but with Hugo's sense of his own exceptional virility as well, confirmed by his numerous liaisons, with Juliette Drouet, Léonie d'Aunet, Judith Gautier (daughter of his old friend Théophile), Sarah Bernhardt (who starred in several of his plays), Madame Baà (the black woman who brought his disturbed, runaway daugher Adèle back from the Antilles), various servant girls, including Juliette Drouet's chambermaid Blanche Lanvin, and many others. The terms through which Hugo envisioned his sexual prowess even overlapped

with the phallic representations of him in the popular press: the penis, he told Blanche when she touched it, is a lyre only poets know how to play (Hugo 1972, 4:journal entry, 15 August 1873; cf. fig. 9 above). His journals indicate moreover that he remained sexually active until just weeks before his death at 83.[7] Hugo's abundant sketches and watercolors also reveal a visual imagination haunted by the phallic shape of lone trees, towers, ships' masts, and curious figures with only a large head rising up from their legs (cf. e.g., Petit, Pierrot and Prévost 1985, 37, 66, 80–81, 87, 89, 203, 241).

What is most interesting in all this is the way in which sexual, territorial, and literary conquest intertwined, both in Hugo's mind and in representations of him. In this respect, the story of his own creation provided a sort of master narrative. In a letter that informed twenty-year-old Victor Hugo of his conception high atop a mountain, his father Léopold Hugo speculated on the lasting effects of such a lofty beginning: "Créé, non sur le Pinde, mais sur un des pics les plus élevés des Vosges, lors d'un voyage de Lunéville à Besançon, tu sembles te ressentir de cette origine presque aérienne" [You were created, not upon the Pindus, but atop one of the highest peaks of the Vosges, during a trip from Lunéville to Besançon, and you seem to feel the effects of this almost celestial beginning] (qtd. in Decaux 1984, 52). Here, Léopold Hugo compares the site of his son's conception to the haunt of Apollo and the Muses ("the Pindus") and alludes to the young man's nascent vocation as a poet (you seem to feel the effects of this almost celestial beginning), implying links between procreation, a privileged location, and poetic creation. Victor Hugo's extraordinary conception in an extraordinary place would be the point of origin for extraordinary works yet to come. As this passage suggests, Léopold Hugo himself had a hearty sexual appetite; he enjoyed an illustrious career as a Revolutionary and Napoleonic war hero, always, as here, dashing across France and across Europe, from one glorious conquest to another; and, he had some literary ambitions of his own. In sum, his enterprising son Victor was a great deal like him, and probably one of the main purposes of the father's bizarre message was to persuade his son of how much he had inherited from him, despite their long estrangement. Moreover, Léopold Hugo's account already conjugated sexual adventur-ousness, territorial ascendancy, and the pursuit of literary glory, elements that would become central to Victor Hugo's personal mythology and public image, interwoven throughout his career, and even beyond. Examples include: his numer-ous poems about delightful voyages of geograph-ical and sensual discovery, in the company of an obliging female companion, all sung in the service of his literary posterity; and, in a more intimate, less exhibitionistic vein, a remarkable *carte de visite* composed for Léonie d'Aunet. Key dates in their illicit affair are inscribed within the giant letters of the word "SOUVENIR," writ-ten above a hazy Parisian skyline in which only the Vendôme Column, Notre-Dame, the *Arc de Triomphe* and the *Panthéon*—monuments cru-cial to Hugo's *oeuvre*, his glory, and pursuit of glory in general—are drawn distinctly in the foreground (fig. 47). Notre-Dame especially, symbol of Hugo's literary preeminence, stands just right of center. The overall composition dis-plays Hugo's desire for the kind of ascendancy over the Parisian cityscape ascribed to his per-son in Benjamin's caricature, and to his work by Maurois. "Souvenir" thus commingles the most private and public of conquests, commem-orating simultaneously Hugo's sexual prowess, literary greatness, and, in the largest sense, Rastignacian triumph over Paris itself, capital of passion and glory.

The visual-verbal fantasy of Hugo's "Sou-venir" anticipates similarly grandiose and symbolically charged *cartes de visite* composed during his exile (cf. below). Eerily, it also an-ticipates Hugo's funerary procession forty years later. The word "Souvenir" cuts across Paris, from the *Arc de Triomphe* to the *Panthéon*, pre-cisely the route of Hugo's posthumous immor-talization. Even more strangely perhaps, the libidinal subtext of "Souvenir" prefigures the lasciviousness that certain observers ascribed to Hugo's 1885 funeral. Romain Rolland, for one, recounting the first phase of the event, in which Hugo's body lay in state beneath the *Arc de Triomphe*, evokes a curious mix of Napoleonic glory and dionysian revelry:

Place de la Concorde, les villes de France étaient en deuil . . . Mais à l'Étoile, autour de l'Arc, où le dieu dormait vainqueur sur le champ de gloire arraché au grand rival, Napoléon—pas question de pleurs ou de prosternations . . . Une Kermesse de Jordaens . . . (Rolland 1952, 25–26)

[On the place de la Concorde, the cities of France mourned . . . But at (the place de) l'Étoile, all around the arch, where this god slumbered vic-toriously upon a battlefield taken from his great rival Napoleon, there was no time for tears or hand-wringing . . . It was a festival painted by Jordaens . . .]

Several contemporaries made explicit what Rol-land only suggests, namely a wave of sensuality radiating out from Hugo's wake beneath the Arch. Edmond de Goncourt's *Journal* entry for June 2 reads,

la nuit qui a précédé l'enterrement de Hugo, cette nuit de veille désolée d'un peuple, a été célébrée par une copulation énorme, par une priapéee de toutes les femmes de bordel en congé coïtant avec les *quelconques* sur les pelouses des Champs-Élysées—mariages républicains que la bonne po-lice a respectés. (Goncourt 1989, 2.1162)

[the night before Hugo's burial, the nation's sad vigil, was celebrated by prodigious copulation, by a priapic orgy, as all the city's whores, on leave for the night, coupled with any poor slob on the lawns of the Champs-Élysées—and the police respected these good republican unions.]

Elaborating further on the "funérailles *fouta-toires* du grand homme" [great man's *fucknifi-cent* funeral] Goncourt claims that, "Depuis huit jours, toutes les Fantines des gros numéros fonctionnent, les parties naturelles entourées d'une écharpe de crêpe—*le con en deuil*" [For the past eight days, all the big whorehouses' little Fantines have been working with a black veil draped over their private parts—*their cunts in mourning*]. Escholier notes, however, that Goncourt was probably "victime d'une mystifi-cation" [the victim of a hoax] on the part of Maupassant and Zola (Escholier 1953, 636; cf. also Fosca 1941, 405). In the chapter of *Les Déracinés* entitled "La vertu sociale d'un ca-davre" [The social virtue of a cadaver], Mau-rice Barrès describes Hugo's grandiose funeral, its triumphant progression through Paris, its profound effect upon the populace and, in par-ticular, the orgy that the event seems to have provoked on the night of May 31:

Fig. 47. Victor Hugo, *Souvenir*. © Photothèque des musées de la ville de Paris.

Comme tous les cultes de la mort, ces funérailles exaltaient le sentiment de la vie. La grande idée que cette foule se faisait de ce cadavre, et qui disposait chacun à se trouver plus petit, charriait dans les veines une étrange ardeur. C'était beau comme les quais des grand ports, violent comme la marée trop odorante qui relève nos forces, nous remplit de désirs. Les bancs des Champs-Élysées, les ombres de ses bosquets furent jusqu'à l'aube une immense débauche. Paris fit sa nuit en plein air. . . . Combien de femmes se donnèrent alors à des amants, à des étrangers, avec une vraie furie d'être mères d'un immortel! Les enfants de Paris qui naquirent en février 1886, neuf mois après cette folie dont ils reçurent le dépôt, doivent être surveillés. (Barrès 1988, 465–66)

[Like all cults of the dead, this funeral exalted the feeling of life. The crowd's grandiose ideas about this cadaver made everyone feel smaller, and stirred a strange ardor in their veins. It was like walking along a busy port, as the heady scent of the tide awakens our senses, and fills us with desire. Until dawn, the benches and shady groves along the Champs-Élysées were the scene of vast debauchery. Paris slept outside that night. . . . How many women gave themselves then to lovers, to strangers, burning to give birth to an immortal! The children born in Paris in February 1886, nine months after being infused with this madness, should be watched carefully.]

In much the same spirit as in the *carte de visite* for Léonie d'Aunet, Barrès's Hugo manages here, even from the beyond, to both besiege the city of Paris, and ravish its women. It is not just that the orgy surrounding his cadaver is inspired by him; rather, in an apparent mass delusion ("cette folie"), the women of Paris believe they are coupling with him. Perhaps, urges Barrès, this is not a delusion; perhaps, amid the furor of this extraordinary night, through a kind of seminal transmigration, these women are actually impregnated by Hugo. The progeny of such not quite immaculate conceptions, while potential "immortel[s]" themselves, will also need to be watched carefully ("doivent être surveillés"). They will be true, that is, to the contradictory legacy of their famous progenitor, a phenomenal talent, destined for glory from the outset, yet also disconcerting, even menacing in his expansive greatness.

In Barrès's version of the funeral, Hugo's conquest of space, his final, physical possession of Paris, and of its female inhabitants, leads directly into his conquest of time, with the posthumous survival of his genius, his spirit and, in the largest sense, his glory. This is a pivotal transition for, ultimately, achieving transcendant fame means vanquishing time itself: projecting beyond the here and now, into the collective, cultural memory. In this chapter, we shall indeed see how Hugo, in his ingenuity and determination to shape his fame, preferred not to leave his posterity to chance, seeking instead to conquer time during his life. From his initial conquest of the present—his *siècle*—in the 1820s, 1830s, and 1840s, he expanded outward toward the future by positioning himself as prophet during his Second Empire exile, and finally took on the past as well by posing as ancestor during his Third Republic apotheosis.

The transition acted out in Barrès's account of the funeral points toward the profound interrelatedness of space and time, both within nineteenth-century France's monumental vision of literary greatness in general, and within the specific, emblematic case of Victor Hugo's monumental renown. Throughout Hugo's career, the monument and, in a broader sense, monumentality, embodied the idea of his extraordinary fame in two principal ways. The massiveness of the monument figured Hugo's present-day prominence, and its durability figured his enduring renown. In other words, Hugo's monumentality provided a powerful, plastic metaphor, both of his contemporary celebrity and of his posthumous glory, his presumed cultural permanence. It is in this latter sense as well that Victor Hugo, nineteenth-century France's paradigmatically monumental writer, needs to be understood as what Pierre Nora (1997) calls a "lieu de mémoire" or realm of memory, as Georgel suggests in his opening remarks to *La Gloire de Victor Hugo* (1985, 23–26).

This first section has set out the main thematic elements in Hugo's progressive conquest of glory: his precocious sense of destiny and energetic self-promotion; his emulation of Napoleon in particular, and strategic invoking of other distinguished precursors; his ability to capitalize on adversity and misfortune; and, above all, his monumental renown, its interrelated visual, spatial, temporal, and sexual dimensions, and both the positive and negative light in which this monumentality was

viewed by the public. The following sections shall therefore proceed historically. The next, "Growing pains," begins with the origins and early development of Hugo's quest for fame, from his childhood through his departure into exile at mid-century. After this, "Glorious Exile" examines how Hugo's renown continued to expand during the Second Empire, despite his long absence from France. "Pre-posthumous apotheosis" looks at his triumphant renown during the early Third Republic, while he was still alive, but his death and presumed passage into posterity were eagerly anticipated. Finally, "From monumentality toward ubiquity" considers developments from Hugo's death to the turn of the century when, amid massive adoration, though few actual monuments to him were raised, Hugo memorabilia abounded—both indicating his vast, transliterary appeal at the time, and prefiguring a broader shift from the period's heroic, monolithic conception of literary glory, to the beginnings of a modern mass-media, mass-market brand of celebrity. Throughout all this, we shall seek to understand Hugo's conquest of glory in relation to the emergence of the monumental vision of literary greatness in nineteenth-century France, the broader evolution of French literary culture, and the history of modern literary fame in general.

Growing Pains

How can we begin to explain Hugo's expansive sense of himself, where it started, and how it evolved? Charles Baudouin's *Psychanalyse de Victor Hugo*, first published in 1943 and dated in some ways, still offers useful insights. The first chapter, "Caïn: le motif des frères ennemis," evokes the fiercely competitive atmosphere of Victor Hugo's formative years. Extremely frail as a child, he was also the youngest of three brothers. These factors colored his relations with his siblings from the outset: "une débilité inquiétante, . . . s'ajoute à sa situation de cadet pour développer en lui, lorsqu'il se compare à ses frères, le sentiment d'une infériorité douloureuse et jalouse" [in addition to being the youngest brother, he was also alarmingly weak which, when he compared himself to his brothers, gave him a growing sense of painful, envious inferiority] (Baudouin 1972, 26). He compensated for his weak body, it seems, with a powerful head:

> La "grosse tête," le "grand front"—dont Hugo garda toujours une fierté que les caricaturistes exploitèrent,—la supériorité intellectuelle enfin, dont ce "grand front" était le signe, cela fut le point d'appui sur lequel le "petit Victor" construisit très vite son système compensateur. (27)

> [Very quickly, "little Victor" built up his compensatory system around his "big head," his "big brow." Caricaturists made the most of this pride in his big forehead which, ultimately, was a sign of his intellectual superiority.]

Examples from Hugo's work, and from his wife's account of him in *Victor Hugo raconté par un témoin de sa vie* [Victor Hugo told by a witness to his life], reveal a full-blown *"complexe du front"* [forehead complex] in which, for him, the forehead was "le symbole même du désir de supériorité" [the very symbol of his desire for superiority] (28). Later on, as we have seen, his forehead would indeed figure prominently in representations of his greatness. Here, as in so many other instances, Hugo's self-styling set the broader, public *machine à gloire* moving in a particular direction.

In his relations with Eugène, sixteen months his senior, Victor's desire for dominance played out tragically in their rivalry for the affections of childhood friend Adèle Foucher. She married Victor. Eugène suffered a mental breakdown during the wedding reception, slipped into insanity soon thereafter, and died in 1837, without having recovered. As a young man Victor also vied with both Eugène and eldest brother Abel (born 1798) for literary honors; he soon triumphed in this rivalry as well. True to his name, he emerged from such youthful antagonisms as a "victor," though not without residual guilt, as the fratricidal "Cain" to brothers Eugène and (appropriately named) Abel. By the early 1820s Victor Hugo was ready for grander, more public conquests. Instinctively, he switched from competing with his brothers to jockeying for position among the emerging young writers and artists of his day. He would soon prevail in this arena as well.

What more inspiring example might a budding conqueror follow than Napoleon's, particularly if such emulation could be divorced from the morass of Napoleon's politics? As Braudy observes,

> although national imperialisms spread out across the world in the nineteenth century, Napoleon had a greater personal influence on artists than on politicians, who invoked his name if at all as a kind of individualist megalomania unfit for either republics or monarchies to imitate. But his career had sanctioned and symbolized a personal freedom to aspire to whatever heights one chose. (Braudy 1986, 416)

Hugo's generation of writers and artists, and he even more so than his peers, were guided by the "gleaming possibility" (437) that Napoleon's example embodied. While Hugo's views on Napoleon the political and historical figure evolved a great deal over the years, his emulation of Napoleonic glory remained constant.

From the outset, Hugo wrote under the long shadow of Napoleon. The very first verses that he is reported to have crafted, while not yet showing great poetic promise, are nonetheless marked by his fascination with Napoleonic military might: "Le grand Napoléon / Combat comme un lion" [Great Napoleon / Fights like a lion] (Van Tieghem 157). As Hugo's abilities and ambitions blossomed, he pursued what can best be described as a "Napoleonic" conquest of literary territory. Hugo's literary *furia francese* ranged boldly over genres and subjects, never flinching at dauntingly huge ones, from *Notre-Dame de Paris* to *Dieu*. While others (Dumas, Balzac, Sand, Sue, Zola, and many, more minor figures like Féval or Ponson du Terrail) also wrote ambitiously and voluminously, no one else's production could compare with Hugo's in combining such exceptional quality, quantity, breadth, and depth, not to mention longevity.

True to the Napoleonic model, Hugo came to dominate the contemporary world of letters not only through his extraordinary achievements, but also through his commanding personality. During the 1820s, he led a series of "cénacles," small groups of like-minded, aspiring writers and artists. The last, most coherent, and influential of these, which united conservative and liberal romantics, including Vigny, Sainte-Beuve, Baron Taylor, Balzac, Mérimée, Dumas, and Nerval, met from 1827 through 1830 in Hugo's apartment on *rue* Notre-Dame-des-Champs. The defining moment for Hugo's leadership of the French romantic movement came in 1830, with the so-called *Bataille d'Hernani*, the uproar over his new play. For forty-five representations at the *Comédie-Française*, romantics and classics in the audience traded cheers and jeers over each couplet. The furor surrounding *Hernani* had been anticipated and, while daring to forego the traditional *claque* of paid applauders, Hugo nonetheless planned a vigorous defense of the play: "Attaquée comme elle le serait, elle avait besoin d'être énergiquement défendue" [Because it would be attacked, it needed to be vigorously defended] (1964, 1621). For the premier, Hugo organized his supporters into "tribus" and "bataillons" [tribes and battalions] whose "chefs" [leaders] were charged with executing "leur plan stratégique . . . leur ordre de bataille" [their strategic plan . . . their battle formation] (1623). The romantic "janissaires" [janissaries] were perceived by their classical adversaries as "une bande d'êtres farouches et bizarres, barbus, chevelus, habillés de toutes les façons, excepté à la mode" [a band of fierce, weird, bearded, hairy creatures, dressed in every possible way, save in fashion] or, better yet, as "ces hordes de barbares" [these barbarian hordes] invading the "asile" [sanctuary] of classicism, reeking fertilely of garlic sausage and urine (1626). To give his troops courage, Hugo distributed to the leaders small squares of red paper upon which he had scrawled "Hierro." This meant "combat" in Hugo's special code (Barrère 1984, 93), and iron in Spanish, a language linked at once with violence and lust, both from a broader romantic perspective and, personally, for Hugo, who also used it to record amorous dalliances in his journal. Once again, literary, territorial, and sexual conquest intertwined in Hugo's imagination.

Amid the extended martial metaphor of the *Bataille d'Hernani*, the aging actor Joanny, who played don Ruy Gomez, was a living link to the Napoleonic past. A former soldier, he had lost two fingers fighting under general Hugo's command: "Il montrait à l'auteur sa main mutilée et lui disait avec une certain emphase qui lui était naturelle:—Ma gloire sera d'avoir servi jeune sous le père et vieux sous le fils" [He would show the author his disfigured hand and say, with a certain grandiloquence that came

naturally:—My glory shall be to have served under the father when young, and under the son when old] (Hugo 1964, 1620). Perhaps, during the *Bataille*, Victor Hugo could be mistaken for his father the Napoleonic war hero; more likely though, he could be mistaken for Napoleon himself. During the feverish preparations for the opening night, at a time when Sainte-Beuve was falling in love with Adèle Hugo and out of friendship with her husband, he wrote the busy playwright, his admiration mixed with bitterness: "à voir ce qui arrive depuis quelque temps, . . . je ne puis que m'affliger, regretter le passé, vous saluer du geste et m'aller cacher je ne sais où; Bonaparte consul m'était bien plus sympathique que Napoléon empereur" [seeing what has been going on for a while, . . . I can only feel pained, regret the past, greet you perfunctorily, and go hide wherever I can; I liked consul Bonaparte a great deal more than Emperor Napoleon" (Maurois 1954, 179). With the *Bataille*, Hugo acceded to absolute dominion in the world of letters, though not, as Sainte-Beuve's letter suggests, without alienating some of the friends made along the way. In any case, the *Bataille* soon spread beyond its elite, Parisian origins, to become a popular, national phenomenon:

La querelle s'étendit dans les départements. A Toulouse, un jeune homme, nommé Batlam, eut un duel pour *Hernani*, et fut tué. A Vannes, un caporal de dragons mourut, laissant ce testament: 'Je désire qu'on mette sur ma tombe: *Ci-gît qui crut à Victor Hugo*.' (Hugo 1964, 1626–27)

[The dispute spread to the provinces. In Toulouse, a young man named Batlam fought a duel over *Hernani*, and was killed. In Vannes, a corporal in the dragoons died, leaving this testament: "I wish there to be written on my tombstone, *Here lies he who believed in Victor Hugo*."]

Again, the Napoleonic overtones ring loud and clear, with young men throughout France prepared to sacrifice in the great man's name. The 1830s, moreover, like the 1880s, were a period of tremendous liberalization and expansion of the press in France. The *Bataille d'Hernani*, with Hugo at the center of the fray, was a defining media event of the 1830s, anticipating in many ways the unprecedented coverage of

Hugo's agony, death, and state funeral a half-century later.

No doubt, Napoleon's triumphs—his self-coronation at Notre-Dame or stunning victories like those at Austerlitz and Jena—inspired Hugo in his conquest of the contemporary literary world. But grand successes alone could not fulfill Hugo's dreams of Napoleonic glory, for Napoleon's legend had a darker, tragic side as well. Though Napoleon himself was perhaps not entirely aware of it, this would prove the most important element in his lasting fame:

> he never quite realized the extent to which his political and military defeat was the necessary step to making him an overwhelming success in the psychic life of western Europe. Like Byron's lameness and his melancholy, Napoleon's failure at Waterloo may have reconfirmed his audience's ability to identify with him. (Braudy 1986, 416)

Without defeat and rejection, Napoleon would only have been a latter-day Caesar or Alexander, not the brooding, romantic figure with such broad appeal in the popular imagination. More conscious of these paradoxes than Napoleon may have been, Hugo cultivated his own aura of darkness to temper the brilliance of his successes for, without the darkness, his fame might be mistaken for the blithe, superficial celebrity of an Eugène Sue, Frédéric Soulié, or Alexandre Dumas, *père*. In other words, Hugo also looked toward Elba, Waterloo, and Saint-Helena for inspiration, to lend a deeper, darker, more poetic, more poignant dimension to his glory. A master of antithesis, Hugo contrasted success with failure, triumph with disaster, acclaim with condemnation, exultation with mourning, to give his glory its greatest possible magnitude. Following Napoleon's example, he crossed a traditional military and aristocratic model of triumphant grandeur with a more modern, romantic paradigm of prestige through adversity and misfortune that celebrated the solitary hero and creator, at odds with society, neglected, spurned, banished. "Le sublime est en bas. Le grand choix, / C'est de choisir l'affront" [The sublime lies down below. The great choice, / Is choosing to be insulted] wrote Hugo, in a poem with the emblematic title "Les Malheureux" [The Unhappy] (Hugo 1964–67, 2.716). From early on, even while embarking on grand literary conquests, Hugo also played the role of the anointed outcast. Hugo's greatest opportunity for such posturing would come during the Second Empire when, though scoring phenomenal popular successes with such works as *Les Châtiments*, *Les Contemplations*, and *Les Misérables*, he wallowed self-consciously in the anguish of his exile.

Yet already in 1818, with Napoleon on Saint-Helena, a sixteen-year-old Hugo speculated about what *he* would do on a deserted island ("Ce que je ferais dans une île déserte" [What I would do on a desert isle]; cf. below). Similarly, in 1827, at twenty-five, and in a mode reminiscent of his predecessor Rousseau, Hugo would claim that he, as the author of a polemical literary manifesto, the *Préface de Cromwell*, "s'offre donc aux regards, seul, pauvre et nu" [offers himself to the public eye, poor, naked, and alone] (Hugo 1968a, 61); that he "n'a jamais pris grand souci de la fortune de ses ouvrages, et . . . s'effraye peu du *qu'en dira-t-on* littéraire" [never cared much about what happened to his works, and . . . worries little about what the literary world might say]; and, that his was "la voix d'un solitaire *apprentif* de nature et de vérité, qui s'est de bonne heure retiré du monde littéraire" [the voice of a lone student of nature and truth, who early on retreated from the world of letters] (62). This was a stunning example of bad faith, for Hugo offered himself up to the public gaze, not simply naked, poor, and alone, but rather in the most heroic guise possible; he always worried about the fate of his works; from the beginning, he hurled himself headlong into the world of letters; and so forth. Yet, just to adopt Daudet's position that systematic counterpoint reveals Hugo's biographical truth ("C'est en prenant le contre-pied minutieux de sa légende qu'on obtiendrait sa plus juste biographie") would be missing the point. In the *Préface*, as so often throughout his career, Hugo embraced what Braudy calls "the posture of reticence and the sanction of neglect" (1986, 390–449; cf. chapter 1). As Hugo writes in his essay on Paris, the greater the true worth of "les talents, les esprits, les génies" [talents, great minds, geniuses], the more disputed is their fame during their lifetime; however, "À la mort, les incontestés décroissent et les contestés grandissent. La postérité veut toujours retravailler à une gloire" [In death, the unopposed shrink and the opposed grow. Posterity always ends up revising glory] (1964, 658).

While Napoleon's influence was preponderant, Hugo also defined himself and his glory by invoking other literary, intellectual, and spiritual precursors. Through such diverse means as letters, articles, prefaces, references in his works, even inscriptions in the woodwork of his house on Guernsey, Hugo created a flattering chain of substitutions, a self-glorifying metonymy, a genealogy of his own greatness. In a strictly literary sense, Hugo's strategic use of precursors exemplified Jorge Luis Borges' assertion that authors create their own: "The fact is that each writer creates his precursors. His work modifies our conception of the past, as it will modify the future" (Borges 1999, 365). In a political sense, it would help Hugo justify his odyssey from monarchist to Republican, and through various partisan stripes inbetween. Finally, in a larger historical sense, Hugo's practice had its roots in a Christian tradition of prophets as precursors that culminated in Renaissance neo-platonism (exemplified by the depiction of Old Testament prophets in the Sistine Ceiling), before developing further, along secular lines, into the Enlightenment glorification of genius, then into the nineteenth-century cult of great men as cultural heroes. Drawing freely upon different facets of this evolution, he invoked precursors from Moses, to John of Patmos, to Leonardo da Vinci, to Voltaire, to Chateaubriand, lending the broadest possible historical resonance to his glory, making the march of western civilization culminate in Victor Hugo.

Hugo chose Chateaubriand as his first major precursor. In 1816, at fourteen, he supposedly wrote in his journal, "Je veux être Chateaubriand ou rien" [I want to be Chateaubriand or nothing] (Decaux 1984, 163; Maurois 1954, 60). In 1819, when he and his brothers founded a literary review, they named it *le Conservateur littéraire*, an obvious homage to Chateaubriand's political review, *le Conservateur*. When Chateaubriand read Hugo's "Ode sur la mort du duc de Berry" [Ode on the death of the duc de Berry] in the *Conservateur littéraire* of March 1820, he is reported to have called the young poet an "enfant sublime"[sublime child] (Decaux, 194–95).

This memorable phrase may be apocryphal; indeed Chateaubriand later denied saying it. However, his high opinion of Hugo at the time is borne out by the fact that when he was named ambassador to Berlin later that year, he urged the young man to accompany him as an attaché. In any case, the burgeoning French press noticed the older writer's encouragement of the young aspirant, and the phrase "enfant sublime" was widely circulated, marking the beginning of Hugo's true celebrity, as noted in *Victor Hugo raconté par un témoin de sa vie*: "M. Agier fit, dans *le Drapeau blanc*, un article sur l'ode et cita le mot de M. de Chateaubriand. Cette parole du grand écrivain fut répétée partout, et Victor entra dans la vraie célébrité" [M. Agier wrote an article in *le Drapeau blanc*, and quoted M. de Chateaubriand's phrase. The great writer's words were repeated all round, and Victor enjoyed true celebrity for the first time] (1964, 1590) The image that the phrase conjured up was irresistible, with the great literary figure of one generation seeming to pass on the torch to his chosen successor.

Hugo's early enthusiasm for Chateaubriand was significant in various ways. In the most obvious sense, it demonstrated his ambition to take over from Chateaubriand as the great French author of his day. Yet Chateaubriand was more than just a glorious writer for the budding second generation of romantics, under the Restoration; he was the contemporary paragon of glory itself having, in large measure, filled a vacuum created by Napoleon's decline and death. Through the early and mid 1820s Hugo looked not only toward the memory of Napoleon, but toward the living example of Chateaubriand as well, to sanction his own ambitions. Incoherent as this position might seem politically—conservative, royalist Chateaubriand had been Napoleon's sworn enemy—it made sense for the pursuit of fame. Hugo began his quest for glory, that is, by emulating the most shining models at hand, even if their politics were irreconcilable.

This points as well to a larger tendency, cutting across Hugo's career: his extraordinary political flexibility. As Hugo noted already in the early 1850s,

voici les phases successives que ma conscience a traversées en s'avançant sans cesse et sans reculer un jour,—je me rends cette justice, vers la lumière:

1818.—Royaliste;
1824.—Royaliste libéral;
1827.—Libéral;
1828.—Libéral-socialiste;
1830.—Libéral-socialiste-démocrate;
1849.—Libéral-socialiste-démocrate-républicain.

(1968b, 9.1019–20)

[These are the successive phases through which my conscience passed—if I must say so myself—advancing inexorably, never once retreating, toward enlightenment:

1818.—Royalist;
1824.—Liberal royalist;
1827.—Liberal;
1828.—Socialist liberal;
1830.—Socialist-democratic-liberal;
1849.—Socialist-democratic-liberal-republican.]

Hugo tried to present his political metamorphoses as a deliberate yet disinterested evolution. Certainly one could, on the contrary, see these permutations as less systematic and coherent, and more calculated. In any case, the thorny question of exactly how and why Hugo's politics changed has been examined in detail elsewhere and is, for the most part, beyond the scope of this study (cf. Martine Rebérioux, Hugo dans le débat politique et social, in Georgel 1985, 196–245). We shall only deal at length with Hugo's political position-taking insofar as it relates directly to his pursuit of fame. In particular, in considering Hugo's exile, we shall develop the idea of his politics as largely "poetic" rather than pragmatic.

Hugo's successes of the 1820s and 1830s as a poet, dramatist, novelist, and leader of the French Romantic movement received substantial, official consecration by the early 1840s. Benjamin's 1841 caricature of Hugo is thus noteworthy not only for the complex ambivalence it displays toward his monumental renown, but also for the way it takes stock of his achievements to date, with its adoring crowds, swelling coffers, and stacked volumes of the new complete works. In 1840, Hugo succeeded Balzac as the president of the Société des gens de lettres; in 1841 he was elected to the Académie Française, as Benjamin's caricature indicates; and in 1845 he was named pair de France, an

event anticipated by the text beneath the drawing. Even the dismal failure of the play Les Burgraves in the spring of 1843—"le Waterloo du drame romantique" [the Waterloo of romantic theater] (Maurois 1954, 310)—could be explained away as further proof of Hugo's exceptional renown. The journalist Édouard Thierry, the same Hugo protégé who attacked Balzac's Lost illusions, "expliqua très bien, dans un article intitulé Aristide, cet ostracisme dont Paris, comme Athènes, punit les renommées qui durent trop" [explained quite well, in an article entitled Aristide, that ostracism with which Paris, like Athens, punishes renown that lasts too long] (1964, 1649). Still, the debacle of Les Burgraves affected Hugo, so much so in fact that he never again wrote openly for the theater.

In September 1843, Hugo's newlywed daughter Léopoldine and her husband Charles Vacquerie drowned in a freak boating accident. In an episode symptomatic of the growing role that the press played in the lives of famous persons, Hugo learned of the accident from a newspaper he found at a café in Rochefort, as he and mistress Juliette Drouet were returning together from a trip to Spain. The loss of his eldest daughter devastated Hugo. From this point onward moreover, his profound tristesse and admirable grandeur in the face of personal tragedy entered into the public's myth of Victor Hugo and came to figure prominently in his iconography, gaining new currency with each successive, wrenching loss: the deaths of his wife (1867), of his sons Charles (1871) and François-Victor (1872), and of Juliette Drouet (1883), or for that matter his daughter Adèle's insanity, for which she was interned from 1872 until her death in 1915.[8]

By the middle of the 1840s, Hugo entered into a sort of mid-glory crisis. A conjunction of personal and professional factors made this a transitional phase in his life, and moved him to cast about for another dimension to his fame. On the one hand, there was the shock of Léopoldine's death, aggravated by Hugo's guilt over his adulterous absence when it occurred; the cooling-down of Hugo's once-tempestuous relations with Juliette Drouet, confirmed in 1844 by the beginning of his affair with the young beauty Léonie d'Aunet, whose given name bore a morbid consonance to that of his deceased daughter; and the failure of *Les Burgraves*, signaling the presumed bankruptcy of Romantic drama, in which Hugo had been so heavily invested. On the other hand, presidency of the *Société des gens de lettres*, membership in the *Académie Française* and, above all, a seat in the *Chambre des pairs* offered the lure of, indeed seemed to authorize Hugo's aspirations toward, a larger public role.

From 1843 (*Le Rhin, Les Burgraves*) to 1853 (*Les Châtiments*), Hugo stopped publishing literary works, although he did not exactly stop writing, particularly poems mourning Léopoldine, others singing the pleasures of Léonie, as well as early drafts of what would become *Les Misérables*. As far as the general public could tell, though, during most of this period, Hugo seemed to turn away from literature and busy himself instead with social obligations and political involvement. From 1844–48, he frequented the court of Louis-Philippe, perhaps fancying that he would become the king's advisor. No doubt, there were at the time influential examples of writers who had traded in literary fame for political power:

faut-il voir dans Hugo un ambitieux qui, n'ayant plus rien à gagner en gloire littéraire, pensait la prolonger dans l'exercice du pouvoir, à l'exemple des grands aînés, Chateaubriand, ministre sous la Restauration, ou Lamartine, député depuis 1833? Ce n'est pas impossible. (Georgel 1985, 199)

[should Hugo be seen as a climber who, having nothing left to gain through literary fame, thought to prolong his glory through political power, like his predecessors Chateaubriand, who served as minister under the Restoration, or Lamartine, a deputy since 1833? It is quite possible.]

Amid the turmoil of 1848, Hugo flip-flopped ineffectually from one political stance to another: he first championed the Republic, then came out in favor of the Regency of the *duchesse d'Orléans*. As a member of the constituent assembly, he struggled for peace during the June Days, then supported Louis-Napoléon's candidacy for president. Hugo seems initially to have idealized Napoleon I's mediocre nephew, imagining that Louis-Napoléon's rise to power would offer him a unique opportunity:

Il entrevit un quatrième acte d'*Hernani*, un rôle romantique à jouer; une place, pour lui, de penseur guidant un empereur libéral; l'un de ses plus vieux rêves. Et puis l'autre Napoléon lui avait toujours inspiré ses plus beaux vers. Au-delà de ce grand nez, de ce regard vitreux, il voyait l'Arc de Triomphe, le dôme des Invalides et des strophes futures. (Maurois 1954, 354)

[He foresaw a fourth act of *Hernani*, a romantic role to play; a place for him, as a thinker guiding a liberal emperor; it was one of his oldest dreams. And the other Napoleon had always inspired his finest verses. Beyond this big nose, and glassy eyes, he saw the Arc de Triomphe, the Invalides dome, and stanzas to come.]

Ironically, at first Hugo did not see the smallness, the anti-monumentality of the man he would later ridicule as *Napoléon le petit*. Louis-Napoléon's reign would indeed raise Hugo to a higher level of glory, but not in the way he imagined initially. Soon after Hugo's election to the legislative assembly, relations between the poet and the *prince-président* soured. By the end of 1851, he would leave France in protest, for nearly two decades. In exile, he left behind his recent failures at finding a more conventional political role, to evolve a more creative—and ultimately much more successful one—in which he defined the terms.

Glorious Exile

Si je possédais par hasard
Une île déserte et tranquille,
Je me dirais, nouveau César:
Je suis le premier de mon île. . . .

Sur les rocs, témoins de ma gloire,
J'écrirais mon nom et mon sort,
Et je serais sûr qu'à ma mort
Les rocs garderaient ma mémoire.
　　—Victor Hugo, "Ce que je ferais dans une île déserte" (1818; 1964–67, 1.161–62)

[If perchance I possessed
A quiet desert isle,
I would call myself a new Caesar,
Number one on my island. . . .

Upon the rocks, witnesses to my glory
I would write my name and my destiny,

And be sure that when I died
The rocks would remember me.]
—Victor Hugo, "What I would do upon
a desert isle" (1818)

L'éloignement, excellent pour la gloire et le retentissement d'un homme vivant. Voltaire à Ferney, Hugo à Jersey, deux solitudes qui riment et semblent se faire echo.

[Distance is excellent for a living man's glory and impact. Voltaire at Ferney, Hugo on Jersey: solitudes that rhyme, and seem to echo each other]
—Edmond et Jules de Goncourt, *Journal*
(1989, February 5, 1868)

Paradoxical as it might seem at first glance, Hugo's long absence from France during the Second Empire would elevate his public stature to new heights, preparing his eventual apotheosis as the Third Republic's preeminent cultural hero.

The idea of exile—and especially of an island exile with all its Napoleonic resonances—had long appealed to him, as his 1818 poem "Ce que je ferais dans une île déserte" suggests. In the abstract, exile promised the sanctity of isolation, the privilege of rejection, and endless possibilities for lone heroism. In reality, however, it took substantial manuevering to make the most of this opportunity. Hugo had flourished in Paris over the past three decades and grown accustomed to shining in the social, cultural, and political spotlight. Now, wrenched from this propitious environment, he yearned to prove—to himself, to France, to the world—that he still mattered, indeed more than ever before. He constantly invited flattering parallels between himself and the great exiles of western civilization, from Moses and John of Patmos, to Dante and Voltaire, to Napoleon Bonaparte, whose banishment offered a heroic counterpoint to the reign of the current, ersatz Napoleon. He sought moreover to amplify and exalt his reputation by mobilizing both word and image in such diverse forms as political tracts, prose fiction, literary essays, poetry, photographs, postcards, even self-fashioning and home furnishing. Through such multifaceted efforts, Hugo strove to infuse his surroundings with significance and forge a supremely meaningful role for himself.

The events of Hugo's exile began to unfold with his vocal opposition to Louis-Napoléon and vain resistance to the coup d'état of December 2, 1851, which obliged him to flee, nine days later, to Brussels. Within the next six months, having abandoned plans for a comprehensive *Histoire du 2 décembre*, for which he lacked adequate documentation, Hugo wrote a brief, scathing indictment of Louis-Napoléon, entitled *Napoléon le petit*. Knowing that its release would mean expulsion from Belgium, Hugo left for Jersey, where he arrived on August 5, 1852, the very day the work was published. Printed on India paper, Hugo's tract was smuggled into France by all available means: sewn into the lining of clothes, launched paratrooper-like across the Channel as "balloon-books" (Robb 1998, 322), even stuffed into hollow plaster busts of Louis-Napoleon! *Napoléon le petit* was an immediate, brilliant success, both in France and abroad; translated into a number of languages, it sold a million copies throughout the world (Maurois 1954, 403). Hugo's achievement with *Napoléon le petit* exemplified both his own brand of conquering zeal and the broader compensatory bent in the nineteenth-century world of letters. In contrast with earlier military conquerers like Napoleon or his father the Napoleonic general, Victor Hugo in exile, and on the run, operated from a position of apparent weakness, all the better to launch his triumphant cultural assault on the Second Empire.

Louis-Napoléon's reaction, upon first seeing a copy of *Napoléon le petit*, was telling: "Lorsque Louis Napoléon le vit, il le prit, l'examina, un instant avec le sourire du mépris sur les lèvres; puis, s'adressant aux personnes qui l'entouraient, il dit, en leur montrant le pamphlet: 'Voyez, messieurs, voici Napoléon-le-petit, par Victor Hugo-le-grand'" [When Louis Napoleon saw it, he took it, examined it briefly with a disdainful smile upon his lips then, speaking to the people gathered round him, pointed to the tract and said, gentlemen, here is Napoleon the small, by Victor Hugo the great] (Hugo 1964–67, 1.67). "Napoleon the small" understood right away that the belittling comparison here was not only with his glorious uncle (as in Marx's *Le 18 Brumaire de Louis Bonaparte*, published the same year) but also, more importantly still, with Hugo himself, who sought to enhance his own *grandeur* by cutting the current French ruler down to size. In *Napoléon le petit*, moreover, Hugo pioneered a novel mode of defamatory writing, akin to classical satire, as Maurois observes, yet in other ways peculiar to modern fame culture, a mode that would grow to include such diverse texts as Zola's *J'accuse . . . !* (1988), Sartre's *L'Idiot de la famille* (1971–72), and (the defamer now defamed) Ionesco's *Hugoliade* (1982). In this defamatory mode, the author chooses as his subject a figure of authority, power, renown, toward whom he adopts a fiercely demonumentalizing, antihagiographic, and often antiestablishment stance. By assailing his subject—Napoléon III, the French military hierarchy, the great novelist or poet of an earlier generation—with a mix of irony, prosecutorial rhetoric, and documentary detail, the author defines his own agenda and, best of all, promotes his own celebrity.

As we have seen, a significant publishing hiatus preceded Hugo's exile. Once in exile, though, Hugo focused his energies on publishing partisan political writings: the soon-abandoned *Histoire du 2 décembre* (which later would become *Histoire d'un crime*), the caustic *Napoléon le petit* (1852), and then the virulently anti-imperial poetry of *Les Châtiments* (1853). In a journal entry from March 23, 1852, while in the thick of composing *Napoléon le petit*, Hugo commented tellingly on how he construed his efforts at the time: "J'ai écrit hier à ma femme: 'Je suis jusqu'au cou dans le cloaque du 2 décembre. Cette vidange faite, je laverai les ailes de mon esprit et je publierai des vers. Louis Bonaparte est mon essuie-plume'" [Yesterday I wrote to my wife, "I am up to my neck in the cesspool of December 2. Once that sewer is cleared up, I shall cleanse my mind's wings and publish poetry. Bonaparte is helping me clean my pen"] (Hugo 1972, 3.223). This is somewhat wishful thinking, for publishing *Napoléon le petit* did not completely "wash" Hugo clean and allow him, straight off, to write some kind of pure poetry. *Les Châtiments* are instead an intermediary point. Thematically, they still wallow in the same cesspool of the *coup d'état* yet, as a volume of poetry rather than a political pamphlet, they already herald Hugo's voluminous, varied, and for the most part less narrowly political literary production while in exile, including *Les Contemplations*, the first half of *La légende des siècles*, *Les Misérables*, *William Shakespeare*, *Chansons des rues et des bois*, *Travailleurs de la mer*, and *L'Homme qui rit*. In the largest

sense, 1852–53 marked a transition for Hugo: from his activity immediately before exile, when he cast about haplessly for a more conventional place in French political life; to his rapid success in exile as a mordant political polemicist; and toward a more exalted role as a transcendant poet, seemingly above the fray, all the better to prevail over his political adversaries.

The years 1853–55 saw Hugo, Delphine de Girardin, and a small circle of other exiles gathering at Marine Terrace, Hugo's residence on Jersey, to practice the new vogue from America: "spiritism." They conjured up the absent and dead with the help of a lively three-legged table that tapped out in code the answers to their persistent questions. It is tempting to explain away the episode of the "tables tournantes" as fadishness, foolishness, self-indulgence, or simply gullibility, yet a substantial body of criticism has argued for the role that Hugo's dabbling in spiritism played, not only in strengthening his spiritual and mystical predilections, but also in catalyzing his literary production in exile (cf. in particular: Viatte 1942, Barrère 1949–50, Levaillant 1954, and, most recently, Robb 1998, 331–41). In much the same way, I contend, this spiritist phase catalyzed his personal myth-making; occurring early on in Hugo's exile, it set the grandiose tone for the rest of the period. In Hugo's mind, at least, the evidence from the spirit world affirmed that he was a man of destiny, in a place of destiny.

The roster of disembodied visitors to Hugo's drawing-room was as long as it was impressive:

> The complete guest-list eventually included Cain, Jacob, Moses, Isaiah, Sappho, Socrates, Jesus, Judas, Mohammed, Joan of Arc, Luther, Galileo, Molière, the Marquis de Sade (whose comments have not survived), Mozart, Walter Scott, some angels, Androcles' Lion, Balaam's Ass, a comet, and an inhabitant of Jupiter called Tyatafia. There were also personifications—India, Prayer, Metempsychosis—and entities called the Iron Mask, the Finger of Death, the White Wing and the Shadow of the Tomb. (Robb 1998, 334)

Remarkably, as commentators including Maurois and Roy have observed, these distinguished spirits not only discoursed freely with Hugo and his companions, but spoke largely *in* Hugo's voice: "ils parlent (en vers et en prose) avec le style, les tics, le ton, les thèses et les antithèses de Victor Hugo" (Roy 1958, pref.). The grand themes that they discussed were also those that preoccupied Hugo at the time: freedom, justice, good and evil, redemption and retribution, mortality and immortality, and the extent of his own extraordinary renown. As Robb remarks cannily,

> Hugo's fame had spread further than anyone suspected. Dante announced himself with the words "*Caro mio*" and congratulated Hugo on his recent poem, "La Vision de Dante". When Napoleon I called, he was asked if he had read *Napoléon-le-Petit*. He had, and deemed it "an immense truth, a baptism for the traitor". Chateaubriand also left his island tomb and expressed a more poetic view: "My bones moved." (334)

Hugo's experiences with the "tables tournantes" helped foster his view of exile as a kind of geographical and temporal *medium*, a privileged realm from which his renown spread to the furthest reaches of space and time, and also where great spirits from distant lands and periods gathered to discuss the weightiest of matters, where even discordant precursors like Napoleon I and Chateaubriand, while mortal enemies in life, now sang in unison the praises of their glorious heir Victor Hugo. The séances of 1853–55 thus reaffirmed Hugo's long-standing sense of great destiny and reassured him that, while no longer in Paris, he was still at the center of the universe. This island refuge in Jersey, despite its humble appearance, was the monumental pulpit from which Hugo held forth to the ages, the vital crossroads not only of current world affairs, but of the entire history of civilization.

In late 1855, however, the earth's axis shifted slightly to the northwest. Hugo's solidarity with some local, agitating exiles caused his expulsion from Jersey, and he fled to the neighboring Channel island of Guernsey. Soon he purchased a home, called it first "Liberty House" then "Hauteville House" (the double "H" felicitously echoing the initial of his surname), and began appointing it as he wished (renovations would only be completed in 1862). These signs that he was settling in for a long stay displeased his family, particularly his children, who were all adults by now. Accustomed to the bustle and distractions of Paris and lacking their patriarch's sense of mission, Hugo's wife and children grew increasingly bored, stifled, and restless. Over the next two years they began to break ranks, to abandon Guernsey for ever-longer stays in Paris. For Hugo's family, notes Maurois, 1858 in particular was "l'année de la révolte" [the year of rebellion] (1954, 437).

Still, despite an offer of amnesty in 1859, Hugo chose to remain in exile until the fall of the Second Empire in 1870. Why exactly? Perhaps, as Robb contends, Napoleon III's offer was a trick, and Hugo understood the real danger of returning (373). Certainly, despite many hardships, especially the growing alienation of his family, exile was proving useful for Hugo. He was publishing again, prolifically and successfully. Exile had also freed him from the morass of everyday political life and was allowing him to evolve a more creative approach to politics. If Hugo had returned to France under amnesty, moreover, he would have been seen as acquiescing to Louis Napoleon and would have lost the considerable moral authority and public attention he enjoyed as the preeminent foe of the regime. Above all, from the moral high ground of exile, Hugo could best elaborate his own legend, best define his role as France's Great Writer, not only for the present, but for posterity. In short, Hugo was thriving in exile and, in many respects, even more so than he had in Paris. He even regretted not having been exiled sooner. As he wrote in his journal in 1864, "Quel dommage que j'aie été exilé si tard! J'aurais fait toutes sortes de travaux, peut-être utiles" [What a shame that I was exiled so late! I would have done all sorts of work, useful work perhaps] (Hugo 1972, 3.402).

In 1862, Hugo published *Les Misérables* and, of all the works he produced in exile, this probably had the greatest long-term impact on his reputation. The novel was important in so many ways: for its monumental proportions, for the massive advertising campaign that preceded and accompanied its publication, and for its instant popularity. Above all, it established Hugo's solidarity with the common people of France, a crucial bridge toward his Third Republic role as the republican poet *par excellence*.

In *William Shakespeare*, published in 1864, Hugo elaborated further his long-standing obsession with precursors. Intended originally as an introduction to his son François Victor's translation of Shakespeare's plays, the essay grew into a substantial work in its own right. The title is misleading, notes Robb, for rather than a work of literary criticism, this is "a vast development of the 1824 obituary of Byron in which Hugo had imagined the great names of literature forming a new family around him" (1998, 400). Here, this genealogy of greatness has become a realm of "Equals," incomparable geniuses—from Homer, to St. John, to Rabelais, to Shakespeare—whose "blatant resemblance" to Hugo prompted contemporary reviewers to say that Hugo should instead have entitled the volume "*Myself.*'"

From the mid 1860s onward, Hugo identified himself increasingly with famous literary exiles, particularly Dante and Voltaire. In 1865, in a letter read at the six-hundred-year celebration of Dante's birth, Hugo declared the Italian poet a "precursor" and illuminating "torch" for his nation and his time:

> il est bon qu'à cette heure éclatante, en plein triomphe, en plein progrès, en plein soleil de civilisation et de gloire, [l'Italie] se souvienne de cette nuit sombre où Dante a été son flambeau.
>
> La reconnaissance des grands peuples envers les grands hommes est de bon exemple. Non, ne laissons pas dire que les peuples sont ingrats. À un moment donné, un homme a été la conscience d'une nation. En glorifiant cet homme, la nation atteste sa conscience. (1964, 574)

> [in this hour of triumph and progress, as the sun of civilization and glory shines radiantly upon her, it is good for (Italy) to remember that dark night when Dante was her torch.
>
> Great peoples' gratitude toward their great men offers a fine example. No, let it not be said that the populace is ungrateful. At a particular time, one man was the conscience of an entire nation. By glorifying this man, the nation attests its own conscience.]

A "bon exemple" indeed. Here, as in his earlier funerary homage to Balzac, Hugo is speaking largely of himself. Dante, he contends, was a beacon of hope for a land in the depths of despotism, centuries before the current Italian republic. Similarly, he, Victor Hugo, would be the conscience of the great French nation during what he saw as the dark hours of the Second Empire, and he anticipates his own people's overwhelming gratitude upon their inevitable liberation.

"Six siècles sont déjà le piédestal de Dante" [Six centuries already form Dante's pedestal], he declares, invoking much the same pedestal and statue metaphor of fame that he had used fifteen years earlier in eulogizing Balzac. Moreover, "Les humanités futures continueront cette gloire" [future generations shall continue this glory] (1964, 574). Future generations will not only continue to honor Dante but, we infer, will honor Hugo for much the same reasons, and in a similarly monumental fashion.

In 1867, when *Le Siècle* opened a popular subscription to erect a statue to Voltaire, Hugo sent the newspaper a list of subscribers among the Guernsey expatriates, together with this note to the editor. It sounded a great deal like his earlier homage to Dante:

> Souscrire pour la statue de Voltaire est un devoir public.
> Voltaire est précurseur.
> Porte-flambeau du dix-huitième siècle, il précède et annonce la Révolution Française. Il est l'étoile de ce grand matin.
> Les prêtres ont raison de l'appeler Lucifer. (1964, 581)

> [Subscribing for Voltaire's statue is a civic duty.
> Voltaire is a precursor.
> He was the torchbearer for the eighteenth century, anticipating and heralding the French Revolution. He is our morning star.
> The priests are right to call him Lucifer.]

Hugo's characterization of Voltaire as "our morning star" also needs to be read against his own identification with the liberating, illuminating morning star in the poem "Stella," in *Les Châtiments*. Here, from the beach on Jersey, poet Hugo observes the morning star "Stella" in the predawn darkness and, like a good ventriloquist, listens attentively to the words he puts in her mouth. "Je suis l'astre qui vient d'abord" [I am the first star to appear], she affirms, for she heralds the arrival of "l'ange Liberté,... le géant Lumière!" [the angel Liberty,... the giant Light] (Hugo 1964–67, 2.179). Stella's role, moreover, is to identify, to shed light upon, those great men who will, in turn, lead their nations from darkness into light, oppression to liberty. "O nations!" she declares, "Je suis la Poésie ardente. / J'ai brillé sur Moïse et j'ai brillé sur Dante" [O, nations! I am the burning flame of Poetry. / I shone on Moses, and shone on Dante]. The star does not say so explicitly, but the poem's *mise-en-scène* makes it clear that she also now shines portentously on the poet ("Je m'étais endormi la nuit près de la grève. . . ." he begins, "J'ouvris les yeux, je vis l'étoile du matin" [I had fallen asleep at night near the shore . . . I opened my eyes and saw the morning star; 178]). Hugo thus places himself in an exalted lineage of illuminatory, emancipatory figures—and, more specifically, of exiled prophets and poets who rescue their nations through their shining example. In much the same way, Hugo's letter in *Le Siècle* inserts Voltaire into this lineage of visionary, national saviors, thus positioning Voltaire as his immediate precursor. Just as Voltaire heralded the Revolution, Hugo in turn heralds the Republic, understood here as the fulfillment of the Revolution's liberatory, enlightenment project.

In 1867, there was also a successful revival of Hugo's *Hernani* at the *Comédie Française*, and no battle over its merits this time. Far from it: the revival instead celebrated Hugo's long, brilliant career, and, coinciding with the 1867 *Exposition Universelle*, showcased Hugo as the great French writer for the entire world to admire. Along similar lines, in the same year, Hugo was honored as the voice of Paris itself for, despite his long absence, he was chosen to write the preface to a prestigious *Paris-Guide*, aimed at the crowds attending the *Exposition*.

It was no surprise that when the Second Empire fell in 1870, Hugo returned to Paris, triumphant.

HUGO   "Grand poète, quel dommage qu'il ait fait de la politique!"
  —Gustave Flaubert, *Dictionnaire des idées reçues* (1979)

HUGO   ["Great poet, what a shame he went into politics!"]
  —Gustave Flaubert, *Dictionary of received ideas*

The first pressing matter for Hugo to resolve in exile was to renegotiate his role in public life: to redefine his political stance and, making what military euphemists call a "victorious retreat," to return to literature. In the years before the *coup d'état*, Hugo had indeed tried his hand at conventional politics, but with little success. He was, as Priscilla Clark notes, "by temperament and by design an ineffectual legislator, lacking any notion of parliamentary

strategy and antipathetic to the compromises such strategy entails" (1987, 151). The ambiguities and murky machinations surrounding Louis-Napoléon's rise to power had especially baffled him: "Victor Hugo, esprit qui pensait en noir et blanc se perdit dans cette grisaille" [Victor Hugo, who saw things in black and white, got lost amid such grayness] (Maurois 1954, 354). Hugo's characteristic Manichaeism had indeed been ill-suited for practicing Realpolitik. In exile, though, he was removed from the daily complications and exigencies of actual political life. He could indulge in a "poetic politics" of sweeping gestures (e.g., refusing amnesty), memorable phrases (e.g., "Quand la liberté rentrera, je rentrerai" [When Liberty returns, I shall return; 1964, 551), and heroic poses (e.g., glaring back at France from the *Rocher des proscrits*). He could make bold pronouncements and demonize enemies with impunity, all the while glorifying himself and his cause.[9]

In the largest sense, Hugo's "poetic politics" in exile juxtaposed literary and political activity, at once joining and opposing them. Ultimately, "poetry" surpassed mundane politics as a vehicle both for effecting broader political change and for achieving lasting renown. To be sure, on a strictly practical level, Hugo's return to publishing was facilitated by his isolation from the distractions and obligations of Parisian life and necessitated by the burden of supporting a large household in exile. In addition, though, to these material imperatives, there were also larger, symbolic ones driving Hugo's literary production in exile. Hugo sought to shame Napoléon III and the regime he embodied, to shrink them into oblivion, not only through the counter-example of his personal heroism, but also through the mounting evidence of his own greatness as an author. Thus, after an initial attack with more narrowly political writings, Hugo lay siege to imperial France with a barrage of literary masterpieces. Works like *Les Misérables*, while too weighty to launch from his terrace as "balloon books," nonetheless provided substantial ammunition for Hugo's ongoing campaign to both dishonor the Second Empire and exalt his own reputation. As he wrote in his journal in 1863,

Vie politique, vie littéraire, deux côtés d'une même chose qui est la vie publique. . . .

On entre... plus profondément encore dans l'âme des peuples et dans l'histoire intérieure des sociétés humaines par la vie littéraire que par la vie politique. (Hugo 1972, 3.397)

[Political life, literary life, two sides of the same thing, of public life....

You enter... More profoundly into the soul of the populace, and into human societies' inner history, through literary rather than through political life.]

Hugo saw literature not only as the ultimate political weapon, but also as the royal road into the cultural memory of the nation.

A staging-ground for his multilayered assault on imperial France, Hugo's exile was also his stage. In the 1830s, Hugo had transformed the use of space in French classical theater, attacking the conventional *unité de lieu* or unity of place by creating elaborate, varied sets for his plays. Now, the Channel Islands became Hugo's stage, the laboratory for his fertile, spatial imagination. He evolved a powerful spatial drama of proximity and distance, presence and absence, inside and out, light and dark, a symbolic geography of exile in which his surroundings resonated with meaning. In particular, they echoed with historical precedent for, thanks in part at least to his *tables tournantes* experiences, Hugo also viewed his exile as a kind of metempsychosis that both reenacted and crowned the great exiles of the past.

From the outset, Hugo pitted exile's hallowed ground against the moral and political corruption within French borders. In the poem "La Société est sauvée" [Society is saved] which opens the first book of *Les Châtiments* (Hugo 1964–67, 2.19–20) and begins "France! à l'heure où tu te prosternes" [France! as you lie prostrate], Hugo foregrounds the figure of the exile standing heroically on the beach ("Le banni, debout sur la grève" [The exile, standing upon the beach]), at the border between land and sea, by extension the border of France itself : as Hugo would write in 1875, in "Ce que c'est que l'exil" [What exile is], "On regarde la mer, et on voit Paris" [You look at the sea, and see Paris] (1964, 514). This heroic figure of the exile hurls his potent words ("Ses paroles qui menacent") across the Channel, at his shameful homeland. Hugo elaborates upon this oppositional structure in another poem from *Les Châtiments*, with the

revealingly geographic title "Carte d'Europe" [Map of Europe]: "Où sont la liberté, la vertu?" he asks, answering "disparues! / Dans l'exil" [Where are liberty, virtue?... gone! / In exile] (Hugo 1964–67, 2.40). In "Ultima Verba," moreover, Hugo declares, "J'attacherai la gloire à tout ce qu'on insulte; / Je jetterai l'oppobre à tout ce qu'on bénit" [I shall assign glory to all that is insulted; / I shall cast shame upon all that is praised] (2.214). More than just the final poem in the collection, "Ultima Verba" is also a final reckoning. In the end, true glory shall accrue to the virtuous, if for now downtrodden champions of liberty; infamy, to the self-serving scoundrels who support the corrupt, current regime. The Second Empire's last shall be first; the margins, the center; and the exiled, national heroes.

As a locale, the Channel Islands might, at first glance, seem inauspicious, but they would prove a great strategic asset for Hugo in elaborating his symbolic geography of exile. Here, he could be just far enough outside French borders to remain "pure," uncontaminated, yet close enough to France to impose himself on the collective memory, as at once the stalwart voice of opposition and the great French poet. In a practical sense, he could stay in contact and stay in view, that is, correspond easily with editors and theatrical producers, receive Parisian visitors, journalists, photographers. He could assure his presence on both the literary marketplace and on the broader marketplace of fame. Paris, for the moment housing a despised regime, was nonetheless the long-standing seat of French greatness, and thus Hugo's guiding star. "[D]urant cette longue nuit faite par l'exil," Hugo wrote later on, referring to himself in the third person, "il n'a pas perdu de vue Paris un seul instant" [During this long night of exile, he did not lose sight of Paris for one moment] (1964, 514). His contribution to the 1867 *Paris-Guide* was emblematic both of this loyalty to Paris and of Hugo's broader presence-in-absence while in exile. Though he had not set foot on French soil, much less in the capital, for more than fifteen years, Hugo was chosen to write the volume's preface, the guide-within-the-guide. In an expository style that had, since *Napoléon le petit*, become more prophetic than polemical, Hugo expounded optimistically upon the simultaneous progress of science and reason, and affirmed his faith in the survival of Paris as the incarnation of France's greatness, despite the baseness of the current regime. Clearly, while physically absent, he considered himself—and was considered—spiritually present, absolutely and indispensably central to France and French culture. Who else, in short, but the greatest living French writer could reveal to the world the grandeur and continued promise of Paris?

Paradoxically, the relative cultural insignificance of the Channel Islands also worked to Hugo's advantage, providing a sort of cultural, as well as geographic, limbo. By staying here rather than in, say, London, Madrid, or New York, and refusing to make his way in a cultural center other than Paris, Hugo remained fundamentally French. He maintained his identity as France's leading literary figure and his unconditional allegiance, not to the current French government, but to the French nation and culture, and to their grandeur. It is emblematic that Hugo literally kept France in constant view, from the "lookout" where he wrote. Hauteville House's original lookout had faced the wrong way, so Hugo turned it into a bedroom and built another that offered the vista he preferred. From here, while at work, he saw the morning sunrise, a recurrent symbol of liberation in his work, as in "Stella"; the open sea, an image not only of the distance separating him from his homeland, but also of unfathomable genius, of the *homme-océan*, like Shakespeare or Cervantes, that Hugo aspired to be; the other Channel Islands, delimiting the purgatorial realm of exile; and beyond this all, visible in fair weather and veiled in foul, France, with all it meant for Hugo, all it embodied of passing evil and lasting good. From this floor of the house, moreover, Hugo did not just craft literary masterpieces and gaze possessively at the coast of France. He lodged the family's maids in two small rooms adjacent the lookout and, as his journals reveal, regularly sought carnal recreation there. In the space of the lookout, literary, territorial, and sexual conquest intertwined once again.

Jersey and Guernsey also provided Hugo with the setting he had long craved, the opportunity to elaborate upon the fantasy of exile he had sketched, decades earlier, in "Ce que je ferais dans une île déserte." Perched now upon an island of his own, he could, more readily than ever before, indulge in salutary isolation; cultivate a tragic, Napoleonic destiny; and frame prophetic, even apocalyptic visions. Like Napoleon in exile moreover, Hugo felt at once abandoned and watched. He was aware that, not only through his publications, but also through the eyes and ears of journalists and spies, France—and to some extent the world—was observing him. He developed a heightened self-consciousness, a keen sense that, despite his seeming isolation, his every act and utterance was a public one.

In particular, from the outset, Hugo and his circle understood and exploited the rich napoleonic resonances of an island exile. Auguste Vacquerie, in so many ways the high priest of *hugolâtrie*, as an 1872 André Gill caricature suggests (Georgel 1985, 89), accompanied Hugo in exile and, upon their arrrival in Jersey, he commented ponderously on the similarity between the names Saint-Hélier and Sainte-Hélène (Dhainaut 1980, 26; Heilbrun and Molinari 1998, 48). The Parisian literary world could not help but notice such comparisons, particularly after Hugo's self-consciously napoleonic heroics in *Les Châtiments*. More often than not, though, during the Second Empire, Hugo's literary peers did not take his emulation of Bonaparte too seriously, preferring to cast it in mock-heroic terms. For example, with a sense of irony Vacquerie lacked, Baudelaire wrote of Hugo, "il croit que, par un *fiat* de la Providence, Sainte-Hélène a pris la place de Jersey" [he believes that, through divine *fiat*, Saint-Helena has replaced Jersey] (Baudelaire 1975–76, 1.665), thus ridiculing the delusions of grandeur that would transform close, quaint Jersey into formidably remote Saint Helena, and Hugo into Napoleon. The French people, however, were generally more receptive to such an identification, for despite some negative coverage of Hugo in the period's popular press, "Pictures of Hugo were a common sight on the walls of workers' homes where they took the place once occupied by that other saviour-in-exile, Napoleon Bonaparte" (Robb 1998, 436). In the popular imagination, Hugo fulfilled the role, pioneered perhaps by Voltaire, but perfected by Napoleon Bonaparte, of France's great man, unjustly exiled. This role must have seemed all the more poignant in the context of the Second Empire, with real greatness appearing persecuted by enthroned ignominy—with Hugo as Napoleon Bonaparte's true heir, banished by the false, though for now triumphant one, Louis Napoleon.

In exile, as a self-appointed prophet, Hugo aimed increasingly at the future, both in his visionary literary production and in his more pedestrian pronouncements on Progress and the coming of the Republic. Particularly during his latter years in exile, after the earlier populist moment of *Les Misérables*, Hugo claimed that he was writing not for the present, but for the future. As he remarked in 1869, "Mes oeuvres actuelles s'étonnent, et les intelligences contemporaines s'y dérobent. . . . Si l'écrivain n'écrivait que pour son temps, je devrais briser et jeter ma plume" [My current works astonish, and contemporary minds get lost in them. . . . If the writer wrote only for his time, I would have to break my pen and throw it away] (Hugo 1972, 3.468). If only hypothetically, Hugo equates breaking the phallic pen with renouncing literary glory—invoking exactly the same metaphor as Balzac's pseudonymous alter-ego Horace de Saint-Aubin when he abandons literature, and with it his designs on posterity, to his successor, the author of the *Scenes of private life* (cf. above).

Not of his time, the figure of the prophet has also, traditionally, been seen as not of this earth, and throughout his Second Empire exile, Hugo cultivated this role. Speaking to his contemporaries, he located himself not only beyond the sea, but also beyond the grave, like his once-favorite precursor Chateaubriand, in the *Mémoires d'outre-tombe* [Memoirs from beyond the grave] (1976). While Hugo's posturing as prophet and phantom may at first have been scoffed at, over time these efforts did color the public's view of him, both during the Second Empire and into the Third Republic.

Already, during the "tables tournantes" experiments of 1853–55, Hugo communed with spirits of the departed who sounded a great deal like himself. He spoke from beyond through a mysterious kind of ventriloquy. By the period of the Crimean War, though (1854–56), Hugo was ready to forego such mediation and claim the voice of the dead as his own, "referring to himself in letters and 'declarations' as 'the voice from beyond the grave': '*Exul sicut mortuus*'" (literally, "An exile is like a dead man"

[Ovid, *Tristia*, qtd. in Robb 1998, 343]). Such pronouncements did not go unnoticed among Hugo's literary peers, although where he envisioned heroic martyrdom, they were more likely to see monumental pretension and yet another opportunity for them to take aim at a favorite target. Barbey d'Aurevilly, for one, appropriated Hugo's *outre-tombe* stance as a convenient way of trashing the poet's latest work. "[L]es *Contemplations*. . . . est un livre accablant pour la mémoire de M. Hugo. . . . À dater des *Contemplations*, M. V. Hugo n'existe plus. On en doit parler comme d'un mort" [*The Contempations*. . . . is a devastating book for M. Hugo's reputation. . . . From *The Contempations* on, M. V. Hugo exists no more. He is to be spoken of as a dead man.][10]

In 1859, publication of *La légende des siècles, Première série* [The Legend of the centuries, First series] marked another significant point in the development of Hugo's prophetic, otherworldly stance. The *Légende* was a series of fifteen shorter epic poems. Individually, the poems showcased Hugo's poetic virtuosity, whereas together, offering a synthetic view of human history, they "seemed to come from a vantage-point in space" (Robb 1998, 366). Beginning with a section entitled "D'Ève à Jésus" [From Eve to Jesus], the work ended with ones called "Le Temps présent" [The Present time], "Vingtième siècle" [Twentieth century] and—most ambitiously visionary of all—"Hors des Temps" [Beyond Time] (Hugo 1904–52, vol. 21) Reacting to the work's prophetic bent, the caricaturist Marcelin drew Hugo in Old Testament garb, upon a rocky promontory, with scenes from the *Légende* playing out in the void beyond him (fig. 48). These subjects sweep across the composition from upper left to lower right, and are labeled (e.g., "Jupiter," or "Charlemagne") with, in the bottom righthand corner, an "et coetera" surrounded by exclamation marks, conveying expansiveness, much as in the "Etc., etc., etc." capping the list of Dumas' works on the pedestal of Carrier-Belleuse's monument to him, or the "etc." continuing the abundant events of Rastignac's life beyond Balzac's brief exposition of them in the preface to *A Daughter of Eve* (cf. above). As a latter-day Moses, atop Jersey's famed "Rocher des proscrits" or Outlaw's rock rather than Mount Sinai, Hugo

Fig. 48. Marcelin, *La Légende des siècles!!! Par Victor Hugo!!!* (*The Legend of the centuries!!! By Victor Hugo!!!*). © Photothèque des musées de la ville de Paris.

appears ready to lead his troubled people out of the Imperial desert and into the Republican promised land. As if this were not grandiose enough, Hugo also holds tablets upon which he himself writes, making him poet, prophet, and ruler of the universe wrapped up in one. Double-edged like so many other images of Hugo, from Borel's "Hugoth" onward, Marcelin's caricature is at once a tribute to the great man's creative power and vision and a send-up of his megalomania and presumption. Hugo's exile invited a mix of earnest and ironic comparison with biblical *Exodus*, but also with *Revelation*. As a modern John of Patmos, Hugo was gazing out from his solitary island and prophesying the end: not of the world perhaps, but certainly of the Second Empire. Sniped the Goncourt brothers in a journal entry on April 11, 1864, "Hugo, à l'heure qu'il est, c'est saint Jean dans l'île du Pathos" [At present, Hugo is Saint John upon the island of Pathos] (1989), thus mocking not only Hugo's self-important, prophetic posturing, but also his pursuit of both contemporary sympathy and lasting grandeur through exhibitionistic, public suffering.

A few months before, his thoughts darkened by the flight of his daughter Adèle, Hugo had written in his journal, "La vieillesse arrive, la mort approche; un autre monde m'appelle" [Old age comes, death nears; another world beckons] (1964, 1401). Three years after this, another journal entry suggests that Hugo's prophetic, beyond the grave posturing was beginning to be echoed, beyond the ironic tones of his intellectual peers, in the broader public's more reverential view of him. He noted something that occurred during a visit to Brussels: "Minuit. Une femme, jeune, m'a arrêté dans la rue de Ligne sous un réverbère et m'a dit: 'Vous ressemblez à Victor Hugo; on dit qu'il est mort'" [Midnight. A woman, a young one, stops me beneath a street lamp on the rue de Ligne and says, "You look like Victor Hugo; they say he's dead"] (1411). Hugo left no other indication of amorous dalliance resulting from this chance encounter, but his awareness of the late hour, the woman's youth, and the appeal of his own celebrity status clearly give the lie to the great poet and notorious seducer being anything less than alive here. In the long run, however, as we shall see, his beyond the grave pose while in exile would evolve into the Third Republic's vision

of him as already immortal, and he would be transformed from a prospective visionary into a retrospective one, from prophet of the Republic into its spiritual ancestor.

EXILIUM VITA EST.
—Victor Hugo, inscription in the woodwork of his dining room at Hauteville House, Guernsey

Victor Hugo's decision to remain where he was dismayed his wife, who would have preferred to go elsewhere, London or Spain perhaps. She understood though his reasons for staying and, in particular, his strategic use of a place she had grown to abhor. In 1857 or 1858, she wrote to him, "j'admets qu'avec ta célébrité, ta mission, ta personnalité, tu aies choisi un rocher où tu es admirablement dans ton cadre" [I admit you've chosen a rock that provides an admirable setting for your mission, and your personality] (Dhainaut 1980, 25). The multiple senses of *cadre* point to the ways in which Hugo was making the most of his exile in the Channel Islands. In a narrow sense, *cadre* is an image's "frame," and while in exile, Hugo paid particular attention to his physical appearance, launching into circulation carefully composed portraits of himself as banished hero. As Georgel remarks, "Hugo travaille son personnage comme un acteur travaille son rôle, un graveur sa plaque de cuivre" [Hugo works on his image like an actor works on his role, or an engraver his copper plate] (1985, 74). *Cadre* also means "surroundings" and, as we have seen, Hugo took advantage of all that the Channel Islands offered as the general setting for his exile, from the heroic and poetic possibilities of an island location, to the practical and moral advantages of simultaneous proximity to and separation from France, to the illuminating contrast between these sleepy British islands and Hugo's distinctly French glory. Finally, in the largest sense, *cadre* means scope, limits, context, suggesting the overall process Hugo underwent of defining himself, and his legend, through his exile. He seemed to believe that his exile would provide the measure of his entire life, that his exile was his life, as one of his many inscriptions in the decor at Hauteville House proclaims. In order for his exile to sum up his life fully, though, Hugo needed, even more than before, to present himself memorably to the world. He did so through writing, of course, but some of his most revealing efforts at self-presentation took visual or at once visual and verbal forms, from the manipulation of his own appearance, to the composition of numerous *cartes de visite*, to the extensive refurbishing of his house on Guernsey.

While in exile, Hugo served up his own image in ways that would haunt his legend for decades, particularly during his apotheosis as the Third Republic's preeminent cultural hero. As Claude Roy remarks, "Victor Hugo . . . avait le sens très vif de sa légende; il organisait sa gloire en marchant. Il se photographiait lui-même dans les attitudes que son coeur et sa rouerie lui conseillaient de prendre. Il posait pour sa galerie avec un naturel inébranlable" [Victor Hugo . . . had a keen sense of his own legend, he fashioned his glory on the go. He photographed himself in attitudes that his own heart and cunning recommended. He posed for his gallery with unflappable naturalness] (preface). Hugo posed repeatedly for cameras, especially from 1853–56, the most active period for the "atelier de Jersey," consisting of pioneering amateur photographers Charles and François-Victor Hugo, and Auguste Vacquerie (cf. Heilbrun and Molinari). The pictures they produced display a self-consciousness at once typical of early photographic subjects, and particularly marked in Hugo, so aware of his own celebrity status, and convinced of the importance of his every gesture. As this period coincided with the exiles' experiments in spiritism, Hugo struck trance-like poses that suggested communion with the beyond, including one entitled "Victor Hugo écoutant Dieu" [Victor Hugo listening to God] (fig. 49).[11] Such images recall earlier "inspired" renderings of Hugo and look forward to abundant Third Republic representations of him as visionary, prophet, magus (Georgel 1985, 104–08). There were also many photos of the great man atop the islands' rugged cliffs, especially upon the *Rocher des proscrits* or outlaw's rock (fig. 50), a striking natural "monument" on Jersey which from this point on became associated with Hugo, much as the Cathedral of Notre-Dame had earlier. Indeed, these images were but the first in a long lineage—from caricatures, to monuments, on to plastic figurines—that would seize upon the *rocher des Proscrits* as the very incarnation of Hugo's heroic exile

and, more broadly, of his exemplary Republican virtue (Georgel 1875, 108). Such images of lone heroism amid barren surroundings also evoke Hugo's "Napoleonic" destiny, as do photographs from exile in which he emulates Bonaparte's characteristic hand-on-stomach stance (Georgel 1985, 94; Heilbrun and Molinari 1998, 67, 97, 103, 212, 216–17).

Hugo's Second Empire self-fashioning involved fashion as well. He shed the Parisian elegance he had cultivated before, in his roles as Romantic torchbearer, and then as parliamentarian and peer of the realm. He began to dress more like a laborer. On a practical level, work clothes were convenient for the Channel Island's rustic setting and for the vigorous outdoor activities in which he engaged. In a social and political sense, like his authorship of *Les Misérables*, this guise helped the common people identify with Hugo and lay the groundwork for the Third Republic's vision of him as the poet of the people—not a worker-poet, but a poet-worker, an incarnation illustrated, for example, by an image of him at his writing desk, on the cover for the circa 1880 musical score, "Les ouvriers de la pensée" [The workers of thought] (Georgel 1985, 200). This affectation of wearing work clothes, as Balzac had done in the 1842 daguerreotype (cf. chapter 2), not only alluded to his literary labor, but was also a transcendance of fashion and thus, in a larger sense, of the here and now. It was a useful way to dress for the kind of "time travel" Hugo sought increasingly to undertake as prophet, then as ancestor of the Republic. Still, as Georgel remarks, Hugo's real self-fashioning "coup de génie" [stroke of genius] (74) was his sudden growth of a beard in 1861. This, together with the concurrent whitening of his hair, lent Hugo a distinctly patriarchal, Old Testament air, consonant with the public image as prophet and demiurge that he was promoting at the time. As Robb observes,

This was the patriarchal Hugo who began to imprint himself on the French mind through the photographs which filtered into France. . . . The emergence of the beard would coincide . . . [with Hugo's description in *Dieu*] of "the monstrous sages of earlier times". . . .
Hugo claimed that he grew a beard to protect his chest from the cold, but it allowed a powerful confusion to germinate in the collective unconscious.

oyiendo a Dios

(X. H.

Fig. 49. Auguste Vacquerie, *Oyiendo a Dios* (*Listening to God* [photograph of Victor Hugo, with inscription in Spanish, from A. Alix's Marine Terrace souvenir album]). © Photothèque des musées de la ville de Paris.

Fig. 50. Anonymous, *Victor Hugo sur le rocher des Proscrits (Victor Hugo on the Outlaw's rock).* © Photothèque des musées de la ville de Paris.

In 1866, someone wrote to tell him that a fifteen-year-old boy had asked on his death-bed to be buried with a photograph of Victor Hugo: "for him you were almost a God." (1998, 351)

As this suggests, Hugo's new bearded look helped prepare a later vision of him as the Third Republic's wise, benevolent grandfather and as latter-day divinity.

Less obvious but just as revealing as a means of self-presentation were the dozens of *cartes de visite* that Hugo composed and sent to his friends back in France. As we have seen with Balzac, the proper name was commonly understood, in nineteenth-century France, as the quintessence of the self, and in many of Hugo's hand-drawn cards his name sprawls out, in giant letters, across largely imaginary architectural backdrops or landscapes, dominating the represented space (Georgel 1985, 90; Petit, Pierrot, and Prévost 1985, 42, 148, 197, 206) . Hugo's name is not simply incorporated into the landscape; rather, elements of the landscape are incorporated into Hugo's name, as in the drawing in which the cathedral of Notre-Dame becomes the "H" in Hugo (Georgel 1985, 90; similarly, Petit, Pierrot, and Prévost 1985, 279). His *cartes de visite* thus provide a model, a *mise-en abîme*, of his struggle to secure lasting fame by both setting the stage for and starring in a grand spatial drama, by amplifying and imposing his name—and, in the largest sense, his self—through a symbolic geography of exile.

Like the *cartes de visite*, Hugo's interior design work shows how he sought to transform the space of exile in his own image. Before this period, Hugo had decorated his quarters and made his own furniture, but never to this obsessive extent. He did so in part because now—freed from Parisian distractions and social obligations—he had time on his hands, but also because he had something to prove. Hugo worked tirelessly to set up his modest residence on Guernsey exactly as he wished. No corner of "Hauteville House" remained untouched by his decorating zeal. He tracked down, purchased, and arranged thousands of antiques, *bibelots*, and *chinoiseries*; mounted decorative tiles and ceramic plates in significant patterns, incorporated over fifty mirrors into the overall design, and carved furniture and massive wooden panels intricately, inscribing them with impressive names and phrases. Here, once again, Hugo invoked the authority of great "precursors": geniuses, prophets, cultural heroes, including Job, Isaiah, Moses, Homer, Aeschylus, Socrates, Lucretius, Christ, Dante, Columbus, Luther, Shakespeare, Molière, and Washington. Likewise, he designated an impressively sculpted armchair, emblazoned with the motto "Ego Hugo"—"I am Hugo"—as the "fauteuil des ancêtres." In this way, Hugo's décor situated him advantageously vis-à-vis both biological and spiritual lineages. Along similar lines, composing a huge "H" over the dining room fireplace, in faience tiles, he conjoined his identity with the hearth, focal point of the home, the center from which all radiates outward (fig. 51). While exile is by definition an eccentric state, Hugo strove to make it concentric: this hearth is emblematic of his larger campaign to relocate the Channel Islands, his residence there and, above all, himself, at the very center of Creation. Hauteville House is thus a richly suggestive study in word-image relations, a painstakingly crafted *Gesamtkunstwerk*, a self-made memorial or, as Hugo's son Charles said, "un véritable autographe de trois étages" [a veritable three-story autograph] (Grossiord 1994, 12)—a kind of monumental "signature piece," like the *cartes de visite*, in which Hugo invested himself massively. It is, ultimately, an elaborate *mise-en-abîme* of his efforts to bend the space of exile to his will and emerge as a transcendantly great man, for his nation, and for all time. As Hugo wrote in the dedication to *Les Travailleurs de la mer* [The Toilers of the sea], he fancied the Channel Islands "[s]on tombeau probable" [his probable tomb] (Hugo 1975, 619), and thus his exile a sort of mausoleum, a vehicle to carry his fame into the future—for the afterlife, or at least for a premature afterlife in the early Third Republic.

Preposthumous Apotheosis

La vieillesse couronne et la ruine achève.
Il faut à l'édifice un passé dont on rêve,
     Deuil, triomphe ou remords.
Nous voulons, en foulant son enceinte pavée,
Sentir dans la poussière à nos pieds soulevée
     De la cendre des morts!
          —Victor Hugo, "À l'Arc de triomphe"
               (1837; 1964–67, 1.937)

Fig. 51. Victor Hugo, *Salle à manger de Hauteville-House (Cheminée en forme de H.)* (*Hauteville-House dining room [H-shaped chimney]*). © Photothèque des musées de la ville de Paris.

[Old age is a triumph and ruin the finishing
    touch.
An edifice needs a past of which we dream.
        Mourning, triumph or remorse.
Treading upon its paved enclosure, we want
To feel, in the dust that our feet raise,
        The ashes of the dead!]
    —Victor Hugo, "To the Arch of Triumph" (1837)

Tu rentreras comme Voltaire;
Chargé d'ans, en ton grand Paris;
Des Jeux, des Grâces et des Ris
Tu seras l'hôte involontaire;

Tu seras le mourant aimé;
On murmurera dès l'aurore,
A ton seuil à demi fermé,
Déjà! mêlé de : Pas encore!
        —Victor Hugo, "Tu rentreras comme Voltaire"
            (*Toute la lyre*, 1888; 1904–52, 29.89)

[You shall return to your great Paris,
Like Voltaire, heavy with years;
Without willing it, you shall be the object
Of Festivities, Honors, and Jubilation.

You shall be loved as you die,
From daybreak shall it be whispered,
At your half-closed threshold,
Already! mixed with: Not yet!]
    —Victor Hugo, "You shall return like Voltaire"

Victor Hugo was an ideal hero for the early Third Republic, for in many ways he synthesized Carlyle's model of the sublime hero with Michelet's antiheroic but prorepublican stance. He was an exemplary republican to bolster a shaky republic and a transcendant French cultural figure at a time when France increasingly sought international prestige through cultural rather than military might. He was a figure around whom the French citizenry could rally and a paragon of French cultural superiority for the entire world to admire.

Perched atop nearly a century of short-lived regimes, with the First and Second republics among the shortest, the Third Republic was marked by a profound sense of its own tenuousness. Hugo's considerable moral authority, the fruit of his long exile, seemed to lend much-needed support to the fledgling republic. This is suggested retrospectively by Adolphe Willette's July 15, 1893, drawing from *La Plume*, "Victor Hugo et la jeune République" [Victor Hugo

and the young Republic] (Georgel 1985, 599) in which a powerful, determined-looking old man helps a feeble, hesitant young girl with a Phrygian cap carry a bucket of water: "Comme Jean Valjean aidait Cosette, Victor Hugo a aidé la jeune Marianne" [Like Jean Valjean helped Cosette, Victor Hugo helped young Marianne], glosses the caption in the 1902 Larousse *Victor Hugo en images* (61). This motif was used as well in Geoffroy's July 15, 1905, drawing in *L'Assiette au Beurre*, "Les premiers pas" [The first steps] (Georgel 1985, 599). Similarly, Hugo appeared in countless images—caricatures, calendars, playing cards, and so on—alongside other "pillars" of the republic, past and present, from Vercingétorix to Gambetta (Georgel 1985, 131–39, 152).

The early Third Republic's malaise over its solidity and future was deeply rooted in larger questions of French identity and, particularly, of how to justify France's claims to greatness in the world. From the defeat of 1815 onward the French had developed a collective inferiority complex—exacerbated by the debacle of 1870—in which they compensated for a dearth of military success with real or imagined cultural glory. The sort of resolute Frenchness Hugo had exhibited in exile (his unflinching Paris-centrism, his refusal to learn English) combined with his extraordinary international recognition and appeal to make him a perfect vehicle for such compensatory *rayonnement*, or cultural "radiance."

By the beginning of the Third Republic, material conditions were also ripe for the mass promotion of a figure like Hugo. The rapid expansion of the press at the time provided a convenient and powerful means for popularizing cultural heroes, as the massive coverage of Hugo's funeral, in particular, would demonstrate. Much the same was true of the educational system. From 1881 onward, the new free, secular schools mandated by *la loi Jules Ferry* needed textbooks appropriate for the Republican masses. Hugo's exemplary heroism in exile provided inspiring object lessons for civic primers, and selections from his work—particularly the more patriotic and didactic writings—made excellent material for a new kind of egalitarian literary study in French, rather than in the traditional, elitist Latin or Greek. In addition, it was now increasingly possible to mass-produce celebrity memorabilia, of which Hugo would become a favorite subject.

From the vantage point of the early Third Republic, Hugo's only potential shortcoming, as a celebrity, was that he was not actually dead. After all, capping a long Western tradition of canonizations, ascensions, and apotheoses, posthumous fame was seen as the ultimate achievement, and all the more so in the face of the increasing ease with which passing celebrity could be attained. Hugo's contemporary renown was so resplendent, however, that one could imagine him dead already, having achieved posthumous fame prematurely. To be sure, Hugo's eventual passing and monumental legacy had been a matter for speculation since he first achieved widespread fame, as in the anonymous 1830 lithograph "Une vue du Père la Chaise en 1930" [A view of the Père la Chaise in 1930] (Georgel 1985, 395): an atmospherically "Gothic" tomb, inscribed with the names of Hugo's works, dominating the cemetery that his contemporaries in early nineteenth-century France understood as the proving ground of fame *par excellence*, as it towers above the other tiny, scattered grave markers, including ones marked "A. de Vigny," "Ste Beuve," and "Dumas." In recent years, though, urged on by Hugo's beyond the grave stance in exile, this collective sense of anticipation had reached a new intensity, with the idea of his "immortality" becoming a commonplace during the Third Republic. Already in 1871, a Cham caricature that appeared on January 24, in *Le Charivari*, showed an admirably statuesque Victor Hugo passing a boy who attempts to sell him a bulletproof vest as an old woman exclaims, "Imbécile, pas à lui, Victor Hugo est immortel!" [Imbecile, not for him, Victor Hugo is immortal!] (Georgel 1985, 122). In the last decade and a half of his life—to use the terms with which Sartre would evoke his own boyhood fantasies of writerly renown, inspired largely by a Hugolian model of literary glory—Victor Hugo was already considered "tout à fait posthume" [completely posthumous] (Sartre 1964a, 165; 1964c, 199).

In particular, from the advent of the Third Republic until his death, Hugo participated often in events that in many ways anticipated his death, even rehearsed his unprecedentedly elaborate state funeral in 1885. Throughout the 1870s, tributes to precursors often featured Hugo as a speaker, honoring him as well by extension. In the 1880s, Hugo became ever more frequently the object of homages, ceremonies, and celebrations that honored him in much the same spirit as the period's tributes to his predecessors.

In 1874, when invited to a celebration in honor of Petrarch's five-hundredth birthday, Hugo did not attend, ostensibly because his grandson was ill, yet his absence probably stemmed more from his own lack of enthusiasm about Petrarch as a precursor. His letter of regrets, like his essay on William Shakespeare a decade earlier, was largely a pretext for talking about himself, his own time, and his own reputation, a way of positioning himself in history. He said little of substance about Petrarch and chose instead to expound upon such pet themes as republicanism, the nineteenth century as an age of Progress, or the coming of "les États-Unis d'Europe" [the United States of Europe] and, in conclusion, he even belittled Petrarch's greatness, in order to sing the praises of his preferred precursor Dante:

Il manque à Pétrarque cet on ne sait quoi de tragique qui ajoute à la grandeur des poëtes une cime noire, et qui a toujours marqué le plus haut sommet du génie. Il lui manque l'insulte, le deuil, l'affront, la persécution. Dans la gloire Pétrarque est dépassé par Dante, et le triomphe par l'exil. (1964, 735–36)

[Petrarch lacks the tragic element that adds a shadowy peak to poets' greatness, and that always marked the highest summits of genius. He lacks insult, affront, mourning, persecution. In glory, Petrarch is surpassed by Dante, and triumph by exile.]

Through his comparison of these two long-defunct Italian poets, Hugo defines genius itself as the lot of the accursed *poète maudit*, not of the complacent contemporary celebrity. Forever preoccupied with his literary posterity, Hugo had become wary of the Third Republic's voluble, demonstrative veneration and was reminding his public that while now adored, he too had been insulted, cursed, banished, and had mourned. Having suffered, he belonged, like Dante—or Napoleon—atop "the highest summit of genius." He, too, was a transcendant figure, a genius for all time.

Hugo pushed much the same agenda in a well-publicized speech commemorating the centenary of Voltaire's death, in 1878. While earlier, a younger, more politically conservative Hugo had kept his distance from Voltaire and the *philosophes*, he had begun their rehabilitation while in exile and now continued in this vein (in parallel with his rehabilitation of the Revolution, most notably with the publication of *Quatrevingt-treize* in 1874). His praise for them reached new heights of hyperbole with the centenary speech, and his enthusiasm was largely narcissistic. Once again, he invoked these precursors to talk about himself, beginning the speech with this portrait of Voltaire as Victor Hugo:

> Il y a cent ans aujourd'hui un homme mourait. Il mourait immortel. Il s'en allait chargé d'années, chargé d'oeuvres, chargé de la plus illustre et de la plus redoutable des responsabilités, la responsabilité de la conscience humaine avertie et rectifiée. Il s'en allait maudit et béni, maudit par le passé, béni par l'avenir, et ce sont là, messieurs, les deux formes superbes de la gloire. Il avait à son lit de mort, d'un côté l'acclamation des contemporains et de la postérité, de l'autre ce triomphe de huée et de haine que l'implacable passé fait à ceux qui l'ont combattu. Il était plus qu'un homme, il était un siècle. (1964, 766)

> [One hundred years ago, a man was dying, immortal in death. He went laden with years, with works, with the most glorious and frightful of responsibilities, to warn and amend human conscience. He went cursed and blessed, cursed by the past, blessed by the future and these, gentlemen, are the two greatest forms of glory. At his deathbed he had, on one side, the acclaim of his contemporaries and of posterity, on the other, that triumph of hatred and jeers that the past makes those who fought it endure. More than a man, he was a century.]

This is how Hugo wanted himself to be seen, upon the threshold of the hereafter: as already immortal, and as both the fertile creator of "works" and virtuous guardian of human conscience's sacred flame. He also wrestled once again with the potential liability of his overwhelming current-day renown. His earlier letter on Petrarch had inferred that contemporary celebrity was alright if you had suffered beforehand—that you could enjoy it and still

attain lasting fame if you had, as it were, paid your dues in advance. Here Hugo stretches this line of reasoning further, conflating present and future renown as equivalently "superb" forms of glory, that necessarily redound to those who have stood the test of jeering hatred in the past, "ce triomphe de huée et de haine." For the pre-posthumously immortal great man then—Voltaire in the 1770s, Hugo in the 1870s—the present is already conjoined with the glorious future. Much like the Emersonian "representative man" (Emerson 1930), the Hugolian *grand homme* embodies his time and place. Poised on the brink of posterity, triumphant over the objections of the past, and revered in old age as he promises to be forever after, the *grand homme* does not just speak for and span his century. Hugo, like Voltaire, *is* his century.

After such an opener, it is no surprise that Hugo's speech ended with great fanfare, both on his part, and on that of the listeners:

> Que le dix-huitième siècle vienne au secours du dix-neuvième; les philosophes nos prédécesseurs sont les apôtres du vrai, invoquons ces illustres fantômes; que, devant les monarchies rêvant les guerres, ils proclament le droit de l'homme à la vie, le droit de la conscience à la liberté, la souveraineté de la raison, la sainteté du travail, la bonté de la paix; et, puisque la nuit sort des trônes, que la lumière sorte des tombeaux! (*Acclamation unanime et prolongée. De toutes parts éclate le cri: Vive Victor Hugo!*) (1964, 769)

> [May the eighteenth century come to the rescue of the nineteenth; our predecessors the *philosophes* are the apostles of truth. Let us invoke these glorious phantoms. Before monarchies dreaming of war, may they proclaim the right to life and freedom of conscience, the sovereignty of reason, the sanctity of work, the goodness of peace; and, as the reign of night comes to an end, may light emerge from tombs! (*Unanimous and prolonged cheering. From everywhere bursts forth the cry, Long live Victor Hugo!*)]

More noteworthy than Hugo's Homais-like platitudes on progress is the interplay between his remarks and the public's spirited reaction for, in response to Hugo praising Voltaire, the public hails Hugo. Taking its cue from Hugo's long-standing, self-serving use of precursors, the audience automatically, reflexively substitutes him for his eighteenth-century counterpart. It is as if Hugo had said, "Long live the memory of the dead writer Voltaire," to which his public responded, "Long live Victor Hugo, the soon-to-be dead writer." In reality, though, the last words of Hugo's speech are "puisque la nuit sort des trônes, que la lumière sorte des tombeaux!" [as the reign of night comes to an end, may light emerge from tombs!] More than just an exhortation to "enlightenment," this is a message about Hugo's relationship to his enlightenment precursors. The light of "progress" emerges from the tomb, Hugo suggests, so that we may see the living in light of the dead. Much the same illuminatory effect is produced by the Daniel Vierge print of "Victor Hugo prononçant son discours à l'occasion du Centenaire de Voltaire, le 30 mai 1878" [Victor Hugo giving his speech on the occasion of Voltaire's Centenary, May 30, 1878] which accompanied the account of the speech in *Le Monde Illustré* of June 8, 1878 (Georgel 283). Hugo, seen only from waist up, stands statuesquely, flanked by a bust of Voltaire, inviting comparison between the great man of the past and the great man of the present, between the already and soon-to-be statufied. While precursor Voltaire remains in shadows, Hugo shines. In the print, as in the speech, the light that Voltaire and the *philosophes* cast upon the nineteenth century is not just that of "enlightenment." It is also the spotlight of fame, shining upon Victor Hugo, their self-proclaimed heir.

For the national celebration of Hugo's eightieth year in 1881, flowers and provincial delegations abounded, much as they would during his 1885 state funeral, and in a fitting tribute to the grand apostle of "l'ange Liberté" [the angel Liberty] (Hugo 1964–67, 2.179) and hero-to-be of Republican primers (Georgel 1985, 256–262), punishments were suspended by decree in French schools. The subsequent renaming of Hugo's street in his honor, a privilege once reserved for kings (Bournon 1909, 183–84), exemplifies the displacement of bygone royal glory onto the modern republic's great man. This vision of Hugo's grandeur is encapsulated as well by the circa 1904 playing card displaying Hugo on its face, accompanied by the notation, "REMPLACE LE ROI" [REPLACES THE KING] (Georgel 1985, 77; the suit to which the tender poet and notorious lady's man belongs is, of course, "hearts").

Not content to just rewrite geography and national history, Hugo's Third Republic contemporaries also revised literary history in his honor. *Le roi s'amuse* had premiered on November 22, 1832, but was banned after this one performance. Emile Perrin, director of the *Théâtre Français*, now launched the play's revival on November 22, 1882, the fiftieth anniversary of its ill-starred premier. Numerous dignitaries were there, including Jules Grévy, president of the Republic, who attended in an official capacity. In short, this was a full-blown, official consecration, designed to redress the original injustice done to the play and its author by an earlier regime. Time, like space, could be bent to Victor Hugo's glory.

This evolution from events honoring Hugo's precursors to ones honoring Hugo, together with an ever more widespread belief in Hugo's premature immortality, confirms that he had come to be seen as a "precursor" himself. Now that France had reached the great Republican future Hugo had so long heralded, he increasingly relegated himself, and was relegated by his contemporaries, to the regime's mythical past as its spiritual ancestor. For Hugo, this was the ultimate step in his longstanding manipulation of precursors. From a Third Republic viewpoint, it was at once a quest for sorely needed legitimacy and moral authority but also, in the manner of so much nineteenth-century genealogical fiction, an attempt to compensate for present inadequacies by appropriating a distinguished ancestry.

Increasingly then, Hugo was cast in the role of the collective ancestor and, specifically, of the new republic's virtuous grandfather. This transformation, which perhaps began when Hugo grew his impressively patriarchal white beard in exile, was urged on, during the Third Republic, by his frequent acts of self-conscious grandfatherliness, including appearances with his grandchildren at important public occasions. During the 1881 parade in honor of his eightieth year, for example, as the crowds passed by, he stood at his open window between young Georges and Jeanne, whom he called "de bons petits républicains" [good little republicans] (Maurois 1954, 551), the implication here being that little republican apples fall close to the republican family tree. The press, and popular culture generally, seized upon excellent material like this, spinning off endless visual, verbal, even musical variations on the theme (Georgel 1985, 306–07, Beuve and Daragon 1902, 129–47). Above all, though, it was Hugo's 1877 collection of poems, *L'Art d'être grand-père* [The Art of being a grandfather], that established him as the national ancestor *par excellence*. While this volume is somewhat forgotten today, excerpts from it played a prominent role in the Third Republic's school curriculum for several decades to come. Not surprisingly, this republican, didactic dimension already figured in Hugo's text. *L'Art d'être grand-père* begins with a reminder of his exile, a section called "A Guernesey" [On Guernsey], which in turn begins with a poem entitled "L'Exilé satisfait" [The Satisfied exile]; it ends with a section entitled "Que les petits liront quand ils seront grands" ["Which the little ones shall read when they are big"], which contains such inspirational poems as "Patrie," "Persévérance," "Progrès," "Fraternité," and "L'Âme à la poursuite du vrai" [Fatherland, Perseverance, Progress, Fraternity, and The soul in search of truth] (Hugo 1964–67, 3.577–698). Four years before *la loi Jules Ferry*, progressive-minded Hugo had already composed a model textbook for the new republican school system.

During the Second Empire, as a self-styled Republican prophet and visionary writer, Hugo strove to project himself out of the present into the future. Now, under the Third Republic, he carried on an analogous but largely opposite campaign. Continuing his long-cultivated beyond the grave stance, Hugo still tried to place himself elsewhere, but shifted direction: from *beyond the present in the future* to *beyond the present in the past*. This shift is what enabled Hugo to conflate himself so readily with the great men of earlier times. When, for example, in his 1878 homage Hugo characterized Voltaire as "ce grand mort, . . . ce grand vivant, . . . ce grand esprit" [this great dead man, . . . this great living man, . . . this great spirit] (1964, 768) he was, once again, speaking largely about himself. Voltaire's glory was an afterlife; Hugo's, for the moment, a predeath. This preposthumous apotheosis was a multifaceted phenomenon, encompassing not only Hugo's appropriation of precursors and efforts to become one himself, but also the period's many official,

prefunerary commemorative activities. By the time Hugo finally died, in 1885, the Third Republic had indeed—in so many ways, and with his blessing—been burying him triumphantly for fifteen years. Moreover, in anticipation of his passing, in a move that speaks at once to his exalted self-image, to his stature in the eyes of his contemporaries and, more broadly, to the evolution of the writer's status in society, Hugo bequeathed his manuscripts to the nation—the first major writer in France to do so. Before long, these would serve as the basis for his *Oeuvres complètes* in the *Imprimerie nationale* edition (1904–52).

From Monumentality toward Ubiquity

Aux héros du savoir plus qu'à ceux des batailles
On va faire aujourd'hui de grandes funérailles.
Lis ce mot sur les murs: 'Commémoration!'
 —Alfred de Vigny, "Une Bouteille à la mer"
 (1986–93, 1.158)

[Today, instead of war heroes, heroes of knowledge
Shall be given great funerals.
Read this word upon the walls: 'Commemoration!']
 —Alfred de Vigny, "A Bottle thrown to sea"

Et peut-être, en ta terre où brille l'espérance,
 Pur flambeau,
Pour prix de mon exil, tu m'accorderas, France,
 Un tombeau.
 —Victor Hugo, "Au moment de rentrer en
 France, 31 août 1870" (1964–67, 2.236)

[And perhaps, France, in your land where there
 shines the pure torch
 Of hope,
To reward my exile, you shall offer me
 A tomb.]
 —Victor Hugo, "Upon Returning to France,
 August 31, 1870"

Et je pénétrai dans une série d'étroites pièces dont les murs étaient garnis d'un nombre prodigieux d'Hugos de toutes matières, de tous formats, de tous aspects. Dans les temples de l'Inde, on ne voit que des Bouddhas. Ici, Bouddha c'est Victor Hugo;—Hugo souriant, Hugo pensif, Hugo avec barbe et sans barbe, Hugo avec cheveux ras et aux cheveux ondulés, Hugo en famille, Hugo seul

sur son rocher, Hugo formidable, Hugo paterne, Hugo écoutant chanter l'alouette ou lançant la foudre, Hugo sénateur, Hugo prophète, Hugo-Océan, Hugo-Soleil!
—Adolphe Brisson, "Préface," *Victor Hugo par le bibelot* (Beuve and Daragon 1902, viii)

[And I entered into a series of narrow rooms whose walls were adorned with a fantastic number of Hugos in all materials, in all formats, of all sorts. In the temples of India, you see only Buddhas. Here, Buddha was Victor Hugo—smiling Hugo, pensive Hugo, Hugo with and without a beard, Hugo with short-cropped hair and with wavy locks, Hugo with his family, Hugo alone on his rock, Hugo the prophet, Hugo the Ocean, Hugo the Sun!]
—Adophe Brisson, "Preface," *Victor Hugo through trinkets*

On May 22, 1885, Victor Hugo died of an inflammation of the lungs—the renowned orator and literary champion of *le Verbe* smitten, appropriately enough, at the physical source of his eloquence. The next day, the Senate and *Chambre des députés* voted, almost unanimously, for a national funeral. This was an opportunity not to be missed, to galvanize the French national consciousness and bolster the Republic while taking no real political risk. After the "pre-posthumous apotheosis" of the past decade and a half, the time had come for Hugo to be transformed definitively into a deceased *gloire*, and enter his long-awaited immortality.

But did this afterlife live up to expectations? Yes and no. In the years immediately following Hugo's death, roughly 1885–1902, revered by most though reviled by others, he was, above all, a preponderant force in French culture. To be sure, Hugo had had both supporters and detractors during his lifetime, but afterward, these tendencies polarized with new intensity. France split among Hugophiles and Hugophobes, as it would as well among Dreyfusards and anti-Dreyfusards—and along much the same ideological lines. Still, on either side of the divide, the French were so obsessed with Hugo that in retrospect, we might best combine *Hugophilie* and *Hugophobie* and talk instead of a generalized "Hugo*folie*," a collective neurosis in which, whether one approved of Hugo or not, he mattered inordinately all the same.

Most did approve, though, so much so that their veneration became a sort of "cult," both in a traditional, devotional sense, and already in the more modern sense of a "cult" of personality or celebrity—a curious mix, that is, of solemnity and jest, piety and commerce, monolithic hero-worship and proliferating memorabilia. Such a broad-based Hugo cult had, in some ways, been prefigured during his "pre-posthumous" apotheosis but began in earnest with his state funeral. An advertisement for a special "Victor Hugo" issue of *La Revue Universelle*, on the last page of the 1902 *Victor Hugo en images*, conveys the cult's expansive view of Hugo:

Le culte de Hugo, c'est à la fois le culte de la famille, le culte de la patrie et le culte de l'humanité. Le grand poète de *La Pitié suprême* et des *Châtiments* a en effet éloquemment exprimé tous les sentiments ressentis par l'être humain, sentiments de pitié pour les faibles, pour les opprimés, de haine pour les oppresseurs, d'amour pour les enfants et d'admiration pour les héros.

Il se penche avec tendresse sur les berceaux, glorifie la nature, exalte la vie et s'incline pieusement sur les tombes.

Hugo résume en lui et dans son oeuvre formidable toute l'humanité nouvelle.

[The cult of Hugo is at once the cult of the family, of the fatherland, and of humanity. Indeed, the great poet of *Supreme Pity* and of *Punishments* eloquently expressed all human feelings—of pity for the weak, for the oppressed, of hatred for the oppressors, of love for children, and of admiration for heroes.

He watches tenderly over cribs, glorifies nature, exalts life, and kneels piously over tombs.

Hugo and his prodigious work embody a new dawn for humanity.]

Between Hugo's death and the centenary of his birth, however, as numerous monuments were projected but few realized, his name and effigy appeared on or in an ever greater variety of articles, advertisements, souvenirs, trinkets, and products. While in one sense confirming Hugo's vast appeal at the time, these developments also heralded a profound shift, both in his fame and in fame itself, from a monumental vision of glory, to the beginnings of a modern mass-media, mass-market brand of celebrity: from monumentality, that is, toward ubiquity.

The proportions of Hugo's state funeral and its setting were appropriately monumental.

From 6:00 P.M. on Sunday, May 31, 1885, until nearly noon the following day, Hugo lay beneath a dramatically draped *Arc de Triomphe*. As Hugo's pursuit of glory had long been intertwined with libidinal yearnings, the massive orgy that apparently took place that night, in the vicinity of the Arch, added an appropriately Dionysian note to his apotheosis. At 11:30 A.M. on Monday, the procession began. His casket reached its destination at 2:00 P.M. When the last of the marchers had arrived—by 6:30!—Hugo entered his final resting place, the *Panthéon*, which had for this purpose been once more, this time definitively, deconsecrated as a church. In all two million spectators, more than the population of Paris at the time, watched Victor Hugo's funeral procession. Elsewhere, the capital seemed eerily deserted, with streets empty and stores closed, displaying signs that read, "Fermé pour cause de deuil national" [Closed for national mourning] (Beuve and Daragon 1902, pl. xii).

The ever-closer identification of writer and monument, flesh and stone, that characterized the evolving vision of literary greatness in nineteenth-century France, culminated in this ceremony marking Hugo's passage from the animate, into the inanimate. Lying in state beneath the *Arc de Triomphe*, then enshrined in the temple of the *Panthéon*, Victor Hugo seemed to be fused with the monument, seemed literally to become a *lieu de mémoire* or realm of memory. This was an elaborate, commemorative petrifaction, organized around two monumental structures charged with meaning, both for French culture in general and Hugo in particular.

The *Arc de Triomphe*, with its military and specifically Napoleonic resonances, had repeatedly been the subject of Hugo's heroic reveries, and its decoration for his funeral recalled how it had been arrayed, forty-five years earlier, for the "retour des cendres," the return to Paris of Napoleon I's remains. This time, the arch was decorated by none other than Charles Garnier, designer of the Paris Opera, and Napoleon III's favorite architect. The Garnier connection was an odd reminder of the Second Empire, but somehow emblematic of the way the events of the Second Empire had set the stage for Hugo's Third Republic apotheosis. Charles Garnier's *mise-en-scène* for the *Arc de Triomphe* was also, though, in his words, "un monument

d'un jour pour cette âme éternelle" [a one-day monument for this eternal soul] (Georgel 1985, 308). Contemporary commentators noted as well the curious impermanence of this "temporary" monument: as one journalist wrote of Hugo's apotheosis beneath the arch, "ceux qui ne l'ont pas vue, ne la verront jamais, et ceux qui l'ont vue ne la reverront plus" [those who did not see it, shall never see it, and those who saw it shall never see it again] (309). While Hugo's lying in state beneath the *Arc*, like his burial in the *Panthéon*, was in one sense the culmination of nineteenth-century France's vision of the writer as monument, the temporary nature of this "one-day monument" was perhaps already taking things in a different direction, toward a twentieth-century conception of fame as fleeting apotheosis.

The *Panthéon*, as Robb observes, was one of Hugo's least favorite buildings architecturally (525), yet in his introductory essay to the 1867 *Paris-Guide* Hugo did single it out for praise, as the temple and tomb of great men. This was a reflection not just on his likely final resting place, but also on the nature of the afterlife that awaited him there. In *Le 19e siècle à travers les âges* [The nineteenth century across the ages], Philippe Muray (1984) develops at length the idea that a secular cult of great men arose in nineteenth-century France, in opposition to traditional Christianity, and culminating in Hugo's "pantheonization."[12] It is within this context that we need to understand not only Hugo's burial in and deconsecration of the *Panthéon*, but also his earlier comments in the *Paris-Guide*. Hugo contends, in this essay, that in the modern world, "l'*urbi et orbi*" has moved from Rome to Paris, and that such a "mystérieux déplacement du pouvoir spirituel" [mysterious displacement of spiritual power] is embodied in the *Panthéon*:

Les clefs de Pierre, l'allusion décourageante à la porte du ciel plutôt fermée qu'ouverte, sont remplacées par le rappel perpétuel du bien qu'ont fait aux peuples les grandes âmes, et si Saint-Pierre de Rome est un plus vaste dôme, le Panthéon est une plus haute pensée. Le Panthéon, plein de grands hommes, et de héros utiles, a au-dessus de la ville le rayonnement d'un tombeau étoile (1964, 658)

[Peter's keys, that discouraging allusion to the closed rather than open gates of heaven, are replaced by the eternal reminder of the good that great souls have done for humanity, and if Saint Peter's in Rome has a larger dome, the Pantheon embodies loftier thoughts. Full of great men and useful heroes, the Pantheon shines over the city like a funerary star.]

Here, to use Muray's pascalian terms, Hugo trades "un pari sur la résurrection" [a wager on resurrection] for "le pari panthéonien collectif.... le pari des revenants" [the collective wager on the Pantheon ... the wager on ghosts] (Muray 1984, 108)—replacing the Christian afterlife, that is, with a vision of the *Panthéon* as a latter-day Elysian fields for humanity's great men. Muray contends, moreover, that Hugo's posthumous deconsecration of the *Panthéon* was prefigured a half-century earlier by his textual appropriation of *Notre-Dame*, also a symbolic desacralization of the edifice, which supplanted Christianity with a classically inspired, at once pre-and post-Christian spirituality: in the novel, "Hugo, dès la troisième ligne, débaptise l'édifice en graffitant sur lui son sépulchral ANANKÈ grec. Fatalité! Fatalitas! Fantômas! Irruption du Destin païen dans la cathédrale gothique. Hellénistico-gothique!" [From the third line, Hugo dechristianizes the edifice, by scrawling upon it, in Greek, a sepulchral ANANKÈ. Fate! Fatalitas! Phantomas! Pagan Destiny bursts into a gothic cathedral. Hellenistico-gothic!] (107). In the public's mind, Hugo's "claim" on *Notre-Dame* seemed to endure—still informing, for example, a 1907 invitation to the neo-pagan "Fête de l'arbre de Noël" [Christmas tree festival] sponsored by the *société des hugophiles*, emblazoned with a rendering of Hugo-as-classical-deity, enthroned upon *Notre-Dame*, apparently the rightful owner of a secularized, *hellénistico-gothique* edifice (Georgel 1985, 89). Hugo's burial in the *Panthéon* thus represented a triumph both for Hugo in particular, and for secular, Republican, anti-clerical forces in general—a triumph that had not only been prefigured by Hugo's dispossession of *Notre-Dame* and anticipated in the *Paris-Guide*, but anticipated widely as well by the public, especially as Hugo's death approached. In one emblematic Talp caricature from the cover of *La Comédie Politique* on March 8, 1885, God the father acknowledges that "L'Hugotianisme a remplacé le Christianisme démodé" [Hugotianism has replaced outmoded Christianity], and cedes his heavenly throne to Victor Hugo (Georgel 1985, 95); revealingly, in Talp's cover for the same paper published on the day of the funeral (May 31, 1885), Hugo instead replaces Napoleon, the century's other great, secular divinity ("Victor Hugo au Pont d'Arcole") [Victor Hugo at the Arcola Bridge] (Georgel 1985, 94). Along similar lines, on the day of Hugo's death, Edmond de Goncourt remarked, "Drôle de peuple que ce peuple français! Il ne veut plus de Dieu, il ne veut plus de religion, et vient-il de *débondieuser* le Christ, aussitôt, il *bondieuse* Hugo et proclame l'hugolâtrie" [How curious are the French! They want no more God, they want no more religion, and no sooner have they de-deified Christ, than they deify Hugo and proclaim hugolatry!] (1989, 2.1160).

Hugo's influence upon the *Panthéon* continued well beyond the funeral. In 1891, the government commissioned Auguste Rodin to design a monument to Victor Hugo to be placed in an empty space along the left transept of the *Panthéon*. The project was rejected on aesthetic grounds, but a few years later the state made amends to Rodin and instead, in 1906, placed his *Thinker* in front of the *Panthéon*, where it would remain until 1922. Significantly, the dedication ceremony for the statue paid tribute to Hugo as well: "Le 21 avril 1906, au cours de l'inauguration, une actrice en péplum lit du Hugo entre les colonnes" [On April 21, 1906, during the inaugural ceremony, an actress in a peplum read Hugo between the columns] (Muray 1984, 102). The actress's pagan costume conjured up Hugo's dechristianization of the building, and the reading of his work recalled the original project for a monument to him there. As Hugo long haunted *Notre-Dame*, so too, it seems, did he haunt the *Panthéon*.

At his death, Hugo had for over half a century cut a monumental figure, from his incarnations as the literary giant of the Romantic movement and dignitary of the later July Monarchy, to his grandiose posturing in exile, on to his "pre-posthumous" apotheosis as the fledgling Third Republic's great cultural hero and, finally, to his triumphant state funeral, framed by the *Arc de Triomphe* and the *Panthéon*. All this would seem to promise abundant monuments to Hugo after his death, but such was not the case. While many were envisioned, few were raised: "Après avoir tant agité de projets et annoncé de monuments à Hugo, la République en éleva fort peu, non sans peine et pour peu de temps" [After kicking about so many projects, and planning so many monuments to Hugo, the Republic raised but a few, with difficulty, and only for a short time] (Georgel 1985, 130). Why?

First, on a practical level, municipalities may have balked at funding a statue on a par with Hugo's stature: "Une statue coûte fort cher et d'autant plus celle dédié à Hugo 'qu'elle doit être ce qu'a été l'oeuvre du maître, c'est-à-dire colossal'" [A statue costs a great deal, and all the moreso one dedicated to Hugo "which must be colossal like the master's *oeuvre*"] (273). Municipal budgets were limited, and the funds available for such a project were stretched particularly thin in this period of "statuomanie":

A Paris même et à Besançon, on élève bien des statues en attendant de rendre hommage à Hugo. Paris érige 150 monuments entre 1870 et 1914.... Pendant ce temps trente-neuf grands hommes sont statufiés dans le Doubs, dont Pasteur à neuf reprises. C'est bien lui le héros local, pas Victor Hugo!

[Even in Paris and in Besançon, many statues were raised while waiting for the opportunity to pay tribute to Hugo. 150 monuments were raised in Paris from 1870 to 1914.... During this time thirty nine great men were statufied in the Doubs, including Pasteur nine times. He was the real local hero, not Victor Hugo!]

While lesser glories could simply be statufied and relegated to a square somewhere, Hugo's resplendent renown seemed to call for something more. Yet the fact that municipalities did manage to honor so many other figures suggests that "le vrai problème que pose la 'statufication' de Hugo n'est pas d'ordre financier" [the true problem posed by Hugo's "statufication" was not a financial one]. The true problem was instead that of the values Hugo was thought to embody: "le nom de Victor Hugo renfermant en lui-même deux personnes, un poète-écrivain et un porte-parole politique, le problème essentiel de cette statufication ... est de savoir à laquelle de ces deux personnes l'on souhaite rendre hommage" [as the name Victor Hugo harbored two personas, a writer-poet and

a political spokesman, the basic problem of this statufication ... is knowing which of these personas one wishes to honor]. Conflicting visions and interests, among committees and artists, aborted dozens of projects. Thus, in the years following Hugo's death, he was only commemorated to a limited extent through statuary, and also to a somewhat greater extent through less strictly monumental public tributes with such public spaces as streets, squares, and schools renamed in his honor. Increasingly, though, the commemorative energies that moved so many to dream of monumentalizing Hugo would be channeled elsewhere, evolving instead toward ubiquity.

Emblematically, for Hugo's funeral, the French people spent over one million francs on flowers alone—a commemorative yet paradoxically ephemeral gesture, repeated by a multitude of anonymous fans, that suggested not only an increasingly keen and widespread desire to "buy into" the compelling aura of the famous, but also the underlying slipperiness, the elusiveness of such transactions. Hugo's massive funeral, while in some ways recalling the pageantry of Renaissance *entrées royales*, in many important respects offered a novel kind of mass-cultural phenomenon and, as such, a departure from the period's monumental vision of literary glory. In particular, amid the monumental pomp and circumstance of Hugo's official funeral, the press and memorabilia emerged in force. Abundant, varied and pervasive, these were vehicles of a less monolithic, more ubiquitous mode of fame: modern celebrity rather than traditional glory.

To begin with, the newly liberalized press worked overtime to satisfy the public's voracious appetite for news of Hugo's passing:

pendant près de trois semaines, la maladie puis la mort, enfin les funérailles de Hugo, font 'la une' de centaines de journaux, tant nationaux que locaux, emplissent des milliers de colonnes, donnent lieu à une profusion d'images: dessins pris sur le vif, gravures, photographies, reproductions d'oeuvres d'art..., tous les moyens sont bons pour relater ces faits exceptionnels, les décrire, les donner à voir, les ancrer dans la mémoire. (Georgel 1985, 186)

[For nearly three weeks, Hugo's illness, then death, and finally funeral made headlines in

hundreds of newspapers, both national and local, filling thousands of columns and giving rise
to an abundance of images: sketches, engravings,
photographs, reproductions of artworks . . . , all
means were used to relate these extraordinary
events, to describe them, to make them visible, to
anchor them in our memory.]

Massive but not monolithic like the monument,
the press coverage recorded the event through a
proliferation of documentary material, a profusion and diffusion of word and image. Over the
next couple of decades, the press continued to
serve up a similar diet of Hugo caricatures, portraits, revelations about his life, reassessments
of his work, interviews with those who knew
him, and so forth.

Memorabilia followed much the same pattern. For Hugo's funeral, as for the earlier *fête
nationale* of 1881 but on a much larger scale,
souvenir ribbons, medals, and pins abounded
to help individual citizens commemorate the
occasion. Producers and merchants competed
briskly for this business, as suggested by one
Léopold Cerf who, in his advertising copy,
claimed to offer the only authorized souvenir,
"[le] seul emblème authentique Victor Hugo,
monté en épingles et en broches qui a été adopté
pour la grande manifestation populaire, lors des
funérailles de notre grand poète national" [the
only authentic Victor Hugo memento, available as a pin or brooch, issued for the great
public outpouring of sympathy for our great
national poet, at the time of his funeral] (Beuve
and Daragon 1902, pl. xii). After the funeral,
this trade by no means subsided; rather, it expanded and diversified, leading to an extraordinary production of objects. While such items of
Third Republic Hugo memorabilia might seem
one-dimensional at first, upon closer scrutiny,
we find in them complex webs of motivations
and desires on the part of both producers and
consumers, a jumble of commercial, devotional,
and ideological strands.

No doubt the most touching objects were the
unique, hand-fashioned ones, made by and for
the people, in the manner of pre-industrial or
"classical" popular culture objects: an unfinished needlepoint slipper bearing Hugo's effigy,
a pocket diary with a popular portrait of Hugo
pasted to the cover, or hairdresser E. Flaunet's
picture of the wake under the *Arc* (Georgel

1985, 146), imitated from a photoengraving in
Le Monde Illustré of June 6, 1885, but woven out of countless strands from a multitude
of anonymous heads, a curious juxtaposition
of handcrafting and mechanical reproduction,
as well as a powerful metaphor for the popular veneration of Hugo. Yet traditional popular culture objects were, for the most part,
exceptions, for items of Hugo memorabilia were
generally popular culture objects in a modern
sense, mass-produced, manufactured to fulfill
and further arouse the consumer's desire to
coopt Hugo's greatness (fig. 52). During this
period, Hugo's name was used to sell everything from tapioca to cigars, in advertisements,
on labels, or on posters for such products as
"le Savon des Muses, dédié à Victor Hugo"
[Soap of the Muses, dedicated to Victor Hugo],
the "Elixir Victor Hugo" (an *élixir de longue
vie*, perhaps?), and also "Victor Hugo" brand
ink (for both aspiring poets and civic-minded
schoolchildren?). His image appeared on everything from lapel pins to dinner plates, inkwells
to pocketwatches, commemorative plates to ceramic pipes, liquor bottles to andirons. Indeed,
with the possible exception of the writing paraphernalia, it was not Hugo's specifically literary
prestige, but rather his more general appeal as
a great man that these products appropriated
(Georgel 1985, 140–45).

While commercial, such objects had a devotional side as well. They in many ways continued earlier traditions of popular or "naive" religious paraphernalia, like saints' and pilgrimage
medals, woodcuts of the Virgin Mary, or relics
of the True Cross. The story of Paul Beuve,
an early collector of Hugo memorabilia, is particularly instructive in this respect. He came
to collect Hugo memorabilia through a miraculous conversion. Walking home after the poet's
funeral, Beuve "fut touché par la grâce" [was
touched by grace] (Beuve and Daragon 1902,
vi). He happened upon a clumsily modeled ter-
racotta dish bearing the great man's effigy and
felt compelled to purchase it immediately: "cette
acquisition décida de sa destinée. Dès lors il
ne vécut que dans l'espoir de réunir des objets où l'image de Victor Hugo, sous une forme
quelconque, serait reproduite" [this acquisition
determined his destiny. From this point on he
lived only in the hope of collecting objects reproducing the image of Victor Hugo, in whatever

Fig. 52. Paul Beuve and Henri Daragon, *Victor Hugo Memorabilia*. Photo M. Garval.

form]. Beuve's obsession apparently had little to do with Hugo's *oeuvre*, of which he was no particular connoisseur; rather,

> Il vénère Hugo comme on adore Dieu, par élan de foi et de modestie. Il ne le discute, ni ne l'explique. Il le subit. Et de même que les anachorètes ornaient l'autel du Seigneur—n'ayant pas d'objet plus précieuse à y déposer—de branches et de coquillages, de même Paul Beuve consacre à son idole de pauvres reliques. (v)

> [He reveres Hugo like one worships God, with faith and modesty. He neither discusses nor explains him. He submits to him. And just as holy hermits, having no more precious object to offer, lay branches and shells upon the Lord's altar, so Paul Beuve honors his idol with humble relics.]

Yet even before Beuve acquired such souvenirs, indeed from their creation, these were already sacramental objects in the broader public veneration of Hugo: "L'ouvrier qui en a conçu l'idée, qui les a construits de ses doigts, le camelot qui les a criés sur la voie publique, le passant qui s'en amusa une heure, étaient pleins de LUI, de son nom, de son génie, de sa gloire!" [The worker who had the idea, who made them with his own hands, the harker who hawked them on the street, the passerby who was amused by them for an hour, all were filled with HIM, with his name, his genius, his glory!] (xiv). In an extraordinary intermingling of the commercial and the devotional, as memorabilia was produced, sold, and consumed, all involved in the commercial transaction also participated in a religious experience, with collector Beuve as the final link in a chain of worship, beginning with the objects' producers.

Contradictory tendencies thus pervaded Hugo memorabilia. Hugo commemorative plates, for example (Beuve and Daragon 1902, 19–27, Georgel 1985, 148–49) (fig. 53), were on one level clearly commercial objects. They also had a devotional side, however, depicting Hugo as the virtuous grandfather caring for his sick grandchild, a representative episode in the exemplary life of Saint Hugo; or as a radiant beacon of light; or even as God the father straddling the globe. Yet such scenes had strong ideological resonances as well. A hagiographical vignette of Hugo holding Jeanne, labeled "pendant le siège" [during the siege], doubles as an illustration of the great man's personal involvement in the historical and political drama of modern France. Likewise, depicting Hugo as God uses conventional devotional imagery in the service of the republican cult of great men: religious iconography for secular, ideological ends. Much the same crossover occurs in another common type of Hugo memorabilia that would juxtapose the "immortal" poet with the inexorable passage of time. The very commonness of such objects as Victor Hugo pocketwatches and Victor Hugo calendars (Beuve and Daragon 1902, 71–74; Georgel 1985, 152) points to their commercial success at the time, yet they also posit Hugo as "l'image même de la pérennité" [the very image of posterity] (Georgel 1985, 152), an eternal verity filling in the void left by the decline of other lasting values, particularly Christianity. One "Grand Calendrier national et historique" [Great national and historical calendar], for example, has an unmistakable ideological ax to grind, with its gallery of republican and proto-republican heroes; Hugo occupies a privileged spot here, immediately to the left of a central bust representing the Republic, across from Vercingétorix and next to Gambetta. Other calendars seem quite different, however. With abundant floral motifs, ribbons, and fancy lettering, they recall the iconographic tradition of the ecclesiastical calendar; as one might expect, the days of the year are accompanied by the appropriate saints' names. Still, these calendars quote inspirational lines from Hugo rather than from scripture, much as the "Grand Calendrier national et historique" contradicts the very values it promotes by also including saints' names.

While just representative examples, these reveal a precarious balance at the time, an uneasy mix among powerful cultural cross-currents. For a brief time around the turn of the century, the monument and memorabilia did compete and complement each other as vehicles for literary renown, the singularity, grandeur, and gravity of the one contrasting with and enhanced by the multiplicity, humility, and insubstantiality of the other. Particularly within the period's extraordinary Hugo "cult," such divergent elements worked together to convey his vast appeal. But a strange hodge-podge like this could not endure. On the one hand, while at its apogee, the monumental vision of literary

Fig. 53. Paul Beuve and Henri Daragon, *Victor Hugo Commemorative Plates.* **Photo M. Garval.**

greatness would soon decline irrevocably, its monolithic ideal undermined by the emergent mass culture's impulse toward ubiquity. On the other hand, while the new mass-media, mass-market sort of celebrity at first seized hold of the day's cultural, and especially literary idols—the same ones venerated by statuemania—it soon would turn instead toward more suitably media-and market-oriented, show business type figures. Meanwhile, though, Hugo's influence remained preponderant. Over the course of the nineteenth century, Hugo's example had largely defined the period's grandiose vision of literary greatness; now, it was redefining this vision, leading the French public through a crucial transition and, ultimately, beyond the dream of stone.

Conclusion: The Dream Crumbles

On a beau multiplier les monuments et les statues, en l'honneur des médiocres heureux, rien ne demeure de ces constructions frêles et de ces fragiles images; le temps use les mauvaises pierres aussi vite que les mauvais talents, il efface sur les bronzes durs, ainsi que sur la molle mémoire des hommes, les noms qui y furent gravés par la routine et par l'ignorance.

—Octave Mirbeau, La Postérité, in *Les Écrivains 1884–1894* (1925–27)

[In vain do monuments and statues abound, honoring annointed mediocrities, for nothing remains of these frail structures and fragile images. Time wears away bad stone as fast as bad talent, erasing from hard bronze, as from man's feeble memory, names graven through habit or ignorance.]

—Octabe Mirbeau, Posterity, in *Writers 1884–1894*

Joy in Mudville?

It is challenging to examine a cultural phenomenon as rich, complex, and expansive as the dream of stone. It is yet more challenging to take stock of that dream's disintegration: disappearance is more mysterious than emergence, absence more elusive than presence, ruins more puzzling than the structures from which they have devolved. What exactly might be the *dénouement* to the vast cultural drama that the dream of stone had offered, that in many ways opened with Voltaire and Houdon's bust of him crowned at the *Comédie Française* in 1778, and that had played out so elaborately over the course of the nineteenth century? How, that is, did French literary culture evolve, not only from the ascension of "le Roi Voltaire" to Victor Hugo's replacing both the king and God almighty, but also on to the recent retreat from the television scene of "Le Roi Lire," the inimitable literary popularizer Bernard Pivot? There can, of course, be no single, conclusive

answer. Our approach to the dream's crumbling shall therefore be multiple, fragmentary, and largely speculative. Center stage, though, in much of this shall be the emblematic figure of Jean-Paul Sartre, France's premier public writer in the twentieth century, for like Voltaire the "philosophe" and Hugo the "prophet," Sartre the "intellectual" embodied the literary culture of his day (Clark 1987).

Sartre's *La Nausée* [Nausea], with its tortured pondering of the past, its will to modernity, and its young author's long-standing literary ambitions—to be dissected years later in his autobiographical *Les Mots* [The Words]— is probably as good a place to start as any. Toward the beginning of the novel, narrator Antoine Roquentin has been working in the Bouville library, trying in vain to write his life of M. de Rollebon. During a break, he contemplates the adjacent *Cour des Hypothèques*, focusing on its pathetic monument to a local *grand homme*. Much as Roquentin's abortive biography of Rollebon frames the broader impossibility of reconstructing any coherent vision of the past, this passage registers the irrevocable decadence of the great man statue and of the ideal it embodied:

A l'entrée de la rue Chamade et de la rue Suspédard, de vieilles chaînes barrent l'accès aux voitures. Ces dames en noir, qui viennent promener leurs chiens, glissent sous les arcades, le long des murs. Elles s'avancent rarement jusqu'au plein jour, mais elles jettent de côté des regards de jeunes filles, furtifs et satisfaits, sur la statue de Gustave Impétraz. Elles ne doivent pas savoir le nom de ce géant de bronze, mais elles voient bien, à sa redingote et à son haut-de-forme, que ce fut quelqu'un du beau monde. Il tient son chapeau de la main gauche et pose la main droite sur une pile d'in-folio: c'est un peu comme si leur grand-père était là, sur le socle, coulé en bronze. Elles n'ont pas besoin de le regarder longtemps pour comprendre qu'il pensait comme elles, tout juste comme elles, sur tous les sujets. Au service de leurs petites idées étroites et solides il a mis son autorité et l'immense érudition puisée dans les in-folio que sa lourde main écrase. . . . Les saintes idées, les bonnes idées qu'elles tiennent de leurs pères, elles n'ont plus la responsabilité de les défendre; un homme de bronze s'en est fait le gardien. . . .

Peut-être que cette place était gaie, vers 1800, avec ses briques roses et ses maisons. A présent elle a quelque chose de sec et de mauvais, une pointe délicate d'horreur. Ça vient de ce bonhomme, là-haut, sur son socle. En coulant cet universitaire dans le bronze, on en a fait un sorcier.

Je regarde Impétraz en face. Il n'a pas d'yeux, à peine de nez, une barbe rongée par cette lèpre étrange qui s'abat quelquefois, comme une épidémie, sur toutes les statues d'un quartier. Il salue; son gilet, à l'endroit du coeur, porte une grande tâche vert clair. Il a l'air souffreteux et mauvais. Il ne vit pas, non, mais il n'est pas non plus inanimé. Une sourde puissance émane de lui; c'est comme un vent qui me repousse: Impétraz voudrait me chasser de la cour des Hypothèques. (Sartre 1938, 47–48)

[At the entrance to the Rue Chamade and the Rue Suspedard, old chains bar the way to vehicles. Women in black. . . . cast ingénue glances from the corner of their eyes, on the statue of Gustave Impétraz. They don't know the name of this bronze giant. . . . He holds his hat in his left hand, placing his right on a stack of papers: it is a little as though their grandfather were there on the pedestal, cast in bronze. They do not need to look at him very long to understand that he thought as they do, on all subjects. At the service of their obstinately narrow, small ideas, he has placed the authority and immense erudition drawn from the papers crushed in his hand. . . . They no longer have the responsibility of standing up for their Christian ideals, the high ideals which they get from their fathers; a man of bronze has made himself their guardian.

This place might have been gay, around 1800, with its pink bricks and houses. Now there is something dry and evil about it, a delicate touch of horror. It comes from that fellow up there on his pedestal. When they cast this scholar in bronze they also turned out a sorcerer.

I look at Impétraz full in the face. He has no eyes, hardly any nose, and beard eaten away by that strange leprosy which sometimes descends, like an epidemic, on all the statues in one neighborhood. He bows; on the left hand side near his heart his waistcoat is soiled with a light green stain. He looks. He does not live, but neither is he inanimate. A mute power emanates from him: like a wind driving me backwards: Impétraz would like to chase me out of the Cour des Hypothèques.] (Sartre 1964b, 27–29)

The very name of the *place*, "la cour des *Hypothèques*" ("mortgages"), already suggests underlying instability and mutability, much like the name of the dreary town itself ("Mud-ville"). One wonders, moreover, how much longer the "old chains" here will still hold back cars, and with them—as would so often occur in early twentieth-century France—the modernization of the square, with the marginalization or outright elimination of its central great man monument. This particular statue, like others of its kind, is an archaism, a holdover ("as though their grandfather were there"), devoid of its erstwhile function, appeal, and symbolic value. For one thing, the Impétraz monument, no longer a locus of renown, has lost its commemorative power (passersby "don't know the name"), and its "authority" works only in the service of small ideas. Likewise, its manly vigor has waned, and only ladies of a certain age, dressed in widowly black and cowering in shadows, cast furtive "ingénue" glances its way, much as comparably faded flowers in Balzac might covet a "beau de l'Empire" like Sixte du Châtelet (CH 5:399). He is plagued moreover by leprous decay that afflicts in particular the distinguishing features of his face, and his heart, ostensible core of the writer's sensibility, thus doubly attacking his identity. Neither alive nor inanimate, but rather strangely "undead," the statue seems more like a zombie or vampire than the proud symbol of a great man's immortality.

Gustave Impétraz, as a man of letters, was also a paradigmatic late nineteenth-century great man, an embodiment—however shabby— of the bygone dream of stone. In the middle of Roquentin's reflection on Impétraz, he recalls what he learned about him in *La Grande Encyclopédie*:

il florissait vers 1890. Il était inspecteur d'académie. Il peignait d'exquises bagatelles et fit trois livres: "De la popularité chez les Grecs anciens" (1887), "La pédagogie de Rollin" (1891) et un Testament poétique en 1899. Il mourut en 1902, emportant les regrets émus des ressortissants et des gens de goût. (Sartre 1938, 47) [he flourished around 1890. . . . And wrote three books: *Popularity and the Ancient Greeks* (1887), Rollin's *Pedagogy* (1891) and a poetic Testament in 1899. He died in 1902, to the deep regret of his dependents and people of good taste.] (Sartre 1964b, 28)

Emblematically, Impétraz flourished around 1890, like statuemania itself, and died in 1902, the year of Hugo's centenary, in which multiple signs of the dream of stone's impending disintegration converged. Typifying the broader abuse and dilution of the great man ideal around the turn of the century, the figure honored by this Bouville monument was a minor man of letters in a provincial backwater, author of three particularly dull-sounding tomes and, perhaps worst of all, an academic. Although passersby no longer know his name, we do, and it is suggestive not only of the intermingled revulsion and fascination in Sartre's proxy Roquentin, but also of this monument's— and the monument's—decadence. "Gustave," for one, has a quaintly nineteenth-century ring, reminiscent in particular of Gustave Flaubert, the Sartrean exemplar of the nineteenth-century bourgeois writer. "Impétraz" resonates moreover with "impétrant," a legal term for a person invested with some authority, especially a diploma, precisely the sort of petty legalistic and scholastic authority so antipathetic to Sartre, and certainly not the formidable public authority to which figures like Hugo or Zola aspired and often achieved. At the same time, the negation "im-," combined with "pétr-" ("stone," as in "pétré" and "pétrifié") but also "pétri" (molded, formed), suggests the statue's inchoateness or, better yet, its disintegration.[1]

It seems that the only power remaining in the statue and, by extension, in the dream of greatness it represented, is the power to arouse vague nostalgic longings in narrow-minded old ladies and confirm their petty-bourgeois ideas, while inspiring nothing but disgust—nausea— in the forward-thinking contemporary intellectual. At least this is what Sartre would like us to believe. But if the monument and all it embodied were indeed so ripe for demolition, why take several pages to do so? Sartre it seems, like the square itself, was haunted by the specter of the ostensibly defunct great man ideal.

As the treatment of the Impétraz monument suggests, by the publication of *Nausea* in 1938, nineteenth-century France's literary dream of stone had, for the most part, crumbled, though vestiges remained. How had it come to this? To begin with, around the turn of the century, well before Sartre's novel, the dream of stone began to show multiple fault lines, including Auguste Rodin's emphatically phallic Balzac monument (1898); the divergent caricatural visions of Zola from before and after *J'Accuse . . . !* (1898); and, the tenor of Hugo's centenary year commemoration (1902), a far more narrowly literary event than his grand state funeral seventeen years earlier.

Rodin's Erection

Rodin's *Balzac* was completed in 1898, at the height of statuemania (fig. 54). The story of its creation—Rodin's five-year long struggle to evolve the statue to its final permutation, and his endless quarrels along the way with the *Société des gens de lettres*, the professional writer's organization that commissioned and ultimately rejected it—is a familiar one, and needs no further rehearsing here (cf. Elsen, Butler). For our purposes, it will be more useful to focus on the statue's form, the public's reaction to it, and the significance of all this to the period's phallic vision of literary greatness that was such an integral part of the dream of stone. To be sure, as rich and multifaceted a work as the *Balzac* cannot be reduced to just one interpretation. Already, Rodin's contemporaries were able to envision it in many ways, from masterpiece to flop, and even, among dissenters, from snowman, to scarecrow, to seal. Its openness to a plurality of interpretations also accounts for the continued keen interest in it today. Nonetheless, as we have seen, from at least the 1830s onward, nineteenth-century French culture persistently associated the great male writer with the phallus, through both word and image, urging us to consider Rodin's statue in light of this extensive visual and verbal tradition.

Albert Elsen has demonstrated that in an earlier nude version of the work, Balzac holds his erect penis in his hand, and that in the

A. RODIN

BALZAC

SALON DE 1898

Fig. 54. **Anonymous, photograph of Auguste Rodin,** *Balzac*. © **Photothèque des musées de la ville de Paris.**

final, draped version, the arms end up in the same position (fig. 55). Examining the finished statue, Elsen observes as well that

> The side views of the *Balzac* enforce its sexuality.... His head has become a fountainhead of creative power, and by a kind of Freudian upward displacement it continues the sexual emphasis of the earlier headless nude study. What more fitting tribute to Balzac's potency as a creator from the sculptor most obsessed with the life force! (Elsen 1963, 101)

Rodin's solution to the problem of representing Balzac's ungracious body heroically had been to cover it with the flowing monk's robe Balzac wore when he wrote. Beneath this authorial cloak, Balzac holds his penis instead of its standard writerly substitute, the pen. This is the phallus as pen, rather than the pen as phallus—and the superposition here of masturbation and writing recalls the way in which Grandville's *Balzac*, holding the phallic cane betwixt his legs, summons up the universe of *The Human Comedy* around him in an ejaculatory fit of literary creation (cf. chapter 1). By draping or sheathing his *Balzac*, moreover, Rodin has hidden the penis grasped furtively beneath the surface but, in turn, has made the entire statue look like a penis. Rodin thus plays with the conventional veiling of the writerly phallus in nineteenth-century France. He at once veils and unveils, concealing all the better to reveal. A canny 1898 Radiguet caricature takes this process yet a step further, turning the Balzac monument into a phallic statuette that rises out of the pubic hair-like curls of Rodin's beard, and that the sculptor grasps, suggestively, with his right hand—at once mirroring and exposing the masturbatory stance concealed by the statue's drapery (fig. 56).

What then was the public reaction to this statue? Its first exhibition, in the Salon of 1898, was met mostly with shock and outrage. The official pronouncement from the *Société des gens de lettres* rejected the statue on the grounds that it was unrecognizable—"Le Comité . . . a le devoir et le regret de protester contre l'ébauche que M. Rodin expose au Salon et dans laquelle elle se refuse de *reconnaître* la statue de Balzac" [The Committee . . . must regretfully protest the model that M. Rodin exhibited at the salon,

for it did not recognize this as a statue of Balzac] (Chincholle 1898)—leaving open the key question of what exactly they did see in it that was so objectionable. It seems that contemporary commentators struggled to come to terms with the frank association here between writer and phallus. Previously, the burden of veiling or attenuating such an association had been on the creator, whereas now the burden had shifted to the receptor, to the public, for Rodin had not employed the usual strategies for deflecting this potentially obscene identification. The context was not private nor confidential for, from the outset, this was designed as a public monument. The association between writer and phallus, far from indirect or oblique, was extraordinarily direct, given both the statue's general shape and what its hands appear to be doing. This was also not intended as a joke; Rodin was serious, indeed, he considered the *Balzac* to be his finest achievement as a sculptor. The fact that this was a public work could not be changed, so Rodin's contemporaries instead pursued attenuating strategies in the other two areas, characterizing the work as anything but a writer that looked like a phallus, and attributing a joke to Rodin where none was intended, or filling their own commentary with humor, irony, and innuendo. No less an art connoisseur than Bernard Berenson thus described what he called this "stupid monstrosity" in a letter to no less an art collector than Isabella Stewart Gardner: "Insofar as he has any form at all, he looks like a polar bear standing on his hind legs" (Butler 1993, 319). Along similar lines, a typical contemporary review, published in *Le Soleil* on May 5, 1898, suggests at one point that the *Balzac* was simply a joke on Rodin's part, "une fumisterie d'atelier" [a studio joke]; and at another, delights in recounting the reaction of a smartly dressed young women, "une intellectuelle," obviously turned on by how well the statue embodied such a great stud of letters: "C'est bien là ce taureau littéraire qu'était Balzac!" [Oh yes, there's that literary bull Balzac!] she pants.

Rodin's monument thus marked the culmination of nineteenth-century France's phallic vision of literary greatness. It took a long, increasingly clichéd tradition of great men brandishing phallic scepters, swords, as well as, more recently, paintbrushes or pens, and distilled this

Fig. 55. Auguste Rodin, *Balzac, étude de nu F, dite en athlète (Balzac, nude study F, in an athletic pose)*. 95.5 × 42 × 30.5 cm, in plaster, inventory number S. 178. Photo Adam Rzepka, courtesy of the Musée Rodin, Paris.

Nº 18 (*Nouvelle Série*). — 2ª ANNÉE. 13 Mai 1899.

5 Centimes (Etranger 10 Centimes).

LE PETIT
ILLUSTRÉ AMUSANT
JOURNAL HUMORISTIQUE PARAISSANT LE SAMEDI

Un an : PARIS, **2 fr. 50**
DÉPARTEMENTS, **3 fr.** — ÉTRANGER, **8 fr.**

Six mois : FRANCE, **1 fr. 50**. ÉTRANGER, **4 fr.**

M. ANTONIN RESCHAL, Rédacteur en Chef

Le Petit Illustré Amusant est en vente à Paris dans tous les kiosques, en province dans
toutes les gares et chez tous les libraires. A l'Etranger, dans les principales villes.

10, RUE DE PARADIS, 10
PARIS

*Les Manuscrits et dessins non insérés
ne sont pas rendus*

GALERIE DES ANTAGONISTES. — VIII.

Dessin de M. Radiguet.

RODIN — FALGUIERE

Fig. 56. M. Radiguet, *Les Balzac: Rodin—Falguière*. Photo M. Garval.

to its essence, with the mighty creator apparently holding phallus in hand. In a larger sense, it managed to frame a compelling portrait of Balzac that also seemed like a prodigious phallus. It thus went as far as a great man statue could go in associating the great writer and the phallus without collapsing the terms of the identification into obscenity or absurdity: that is, a portrait of the writer as public masturbator, or as Priapus. Likewise, while the work remained clearly representational—depicting a man, looking like Balzac, wearing what he used to wear—its radical streamlining of form, which seemed at once modern and primitive, flirted precariously with abstraction. It was, in these ways, "une oeuvre limite," a work at the very edge of the possible, a point of no return for the figurative great man monument. Indeed, it was to be Rodin's last attempt at a great man statue of this sort and, more broadly, it marked serious sculpture's turn away from what had become an exceedingly hackneyed form of commemorative statuary. Rodin's *Balzac* and the surrounding controversy heralded the decline of the great man statue in general, and particularly of the grandiose, monumental, and deeply phallic vision of the writer that it had come to embody.

Zola, Before and After

While Zola's involvement in the Dreyfus Affair marked a turning point in his evolution as a public figure, when images from before and after "J'Accuse . . . !" are considered in isolation, these "before and after pictures" can appear similar. When, however, we compare the corpus of caricatures from before with the corpus of caricatures from afterward, we discover an important shift occurring in the public's view of Zola as a writer and, more broadly, in the period's monumental vision of literary greatness.

From early on in his career, Zola's work as a critic revealed just how heavily he was invested in the literary "dream of stone." As we have seen, Zola's essay on Balzac in *Les Romanciers naturalistes* praises Balzac's *The Human Comedy* as a latter-day "tower of Babel" from which, over time, the interstitial mud and sand vanish, while structural marble remains; similarly, "Une Statue pour Balzac" condemns Dumas for his work's lack of "consistance" (Zola

1906, 88), predicting its imminent reduction to dust. Metaphorically speaking, for Zola enduring literary achievement was carved in stone, whereas forgettable literary mediocrity was no more solid and durable than sand, mud, or dust. But when Zola's contemporaries held him up to this monumental standard, he generally was seen as falling short.

Zola was also late nineteenth-century France's most broadly and viciously caricatured writer, lambasted for offenses to bourgeois propriety in his novels and, later on, for his involvement in the Dreyfus Affair. Taking a cue from Zola's own frank depictions of bestial impulses and bodily functions, contemporary caricaturists ridiculed him with more of the same: pigs and shit were their chief iconographical weapons.

A "before picture" Sapeck's ironically titled "La Haute-École de M. Émile Zola" ["M. Émile Zola's Haute École"] likens Zola to the pig he rides, both through his porcine features and the pig's Zolian *pince-nez* (fig. 57). The image

**Fig. 57. Sapeck, *La Haute-École de M. Émile Zola.*
Photo M. Garval.**

further debases the writer by surrounding him with a couple of large turds, one of which his porcine alter-ego seems eager to devour. Likewise, an "after picture," Alfred Le Petit's "Ah! Ah! Monsieur Zola, C'est vilain ce que tu fais là!" [Ah! Ah! M. Zola, What a nasty thing you're doing there!] displays a similar equivalency, indeed a fusion, between writer and pig; as usual, a copious turd is not far behind (fig. 58). In another "before picture," Zola emerges from a chamber pot, and the contents splash out, onto a manuscript of his novel *Nana* (fig. 59). The tip of the giant pen Zola holds is coated with filth as well, an example of the chamber-pot-as-inkwell motif so common in Zola caricatures. Similarly, it would seem, Zola's head sinks into a giant chamberpot, in a callous "after picture" from the front page of a right-wing paper, published a scant two weeks after Zola's death by asphyxiation (fig. 60). Studies of Zola caricatures, from John Grand-Carteret's 1908 *Zola en images* to Bertrand Tillier's 1998 *Cochon de Zola!*, have argued for the continuity that the preceding two pairs of images seem to suggest. As Tillier asserts, "Du monstre littéraire au monstre politique dreyfusard, la caricature de Zola exploite les mêmes clichés, sans véritable rupture" [No real break occurs from Zola the literary giant to Zola the dreyfusard political figure, as caricature relies upon the same clichés] (43). In other words, from pig to pig, turd to turd, and chamber pot to chamber pot, the more things change, the more they stay the same. The next pair of images, however, point up the shortcomings of such an assessment.

The "before picture," Albert Robida's "Le Triomphe du naturalisme" [The Triumph of naturalism] depicts a mock-heroic triumph, a burlesque apotheosis (fig. 61). Zola is hoisted atop a Vendôme Column on which the heroic bas-reliefs have been replaced by ones of Zola's characters in drunken debauchery; Zola also sits jauntily upon a pipe-smoking horse, an ironic remembrance of the equestrian statue of Louis XIV that preceded the column; and Zola is surrounded by his own cheering, proletarian characters, who frolic atop the column here as they do in a carnavalesque scene from the novel *L'Assommoir*. Meanwhile, lest we be duped by this fanciful *monde à l'envers*, the caricaturist shows the so-called "vile idealists," led by Victor Hugo, who disapprove of the seemingly exalted

naturalist's consecration, and whose presence reminds us to reverse the terms here, to return to the proper order of things, with exalted idealists prevailing over vile naturalists, Hugo over Zola, and enduring literary greatness over passing notoriety. This, as we shall see, is a far cry from Bobb's "J'Amuse!!," an "after picture" based upon Zola's departure, the preceding week, into self-imposed exile. Dressed as a postman, Zola strews his accusatory letters futilely on the ground as the amused French public behind him guffaws, and he mutters, "Ah! Les Français ne prennent plus mes petits papiers au sérieux . . . Eh bien! Je vais les distribuer à l'étranger!!" [Ah! The French no longer take my little papers seriously . . . Well, then, I'll just distribute them abroad!!] (fig. 62).

In what ways does the earlier "Triumph of naturalism" differ from this later image, and what change does this exemplify within the Zola iconography as a whole? In the earlier caricature, as in all caricatures of Zola from before "J'Accuse . . . !", Zola and his work are held to a standard of monumentality and found lacking. On the contrary, in the later caricature, as in all caricatures of Zola from after "J'Accuse . . . !", this standard no longer applies, signaling a shift in the period's conception, not only of Zola's fame but of literary fame in general. The "before pictures" fall moreover into two main categories, which can best be understood with reference to Zola's own writings on literary monumentality. As we have seen in Zola's divergent critical assessments of Balzac and Dumas, he praised all that is hard, enduring, and monumental, and condemned all that is soft, transitory, and insubstantial. Ironically, both categories of "before" pictures ridicule Zola's supposed shortcomings in precisely the terms he used himself. The first category depicts him as unworthy of the sort of praise he lavished upon Balzac, with images of Zola tilting at unassailable monuments and enjoying false apotheoses. The second category, by far the larger, questions Zola's literary merit and staying power with images of pigs, turds, chamber pots, and dung heaps.

In addition to "Le Triomphe du naturalisme," the first category of "before pictures" includes: Gill's Zola saluting Balzac from *Les Hommes d'aujourd'hui* (Frontis); his "Loisirs

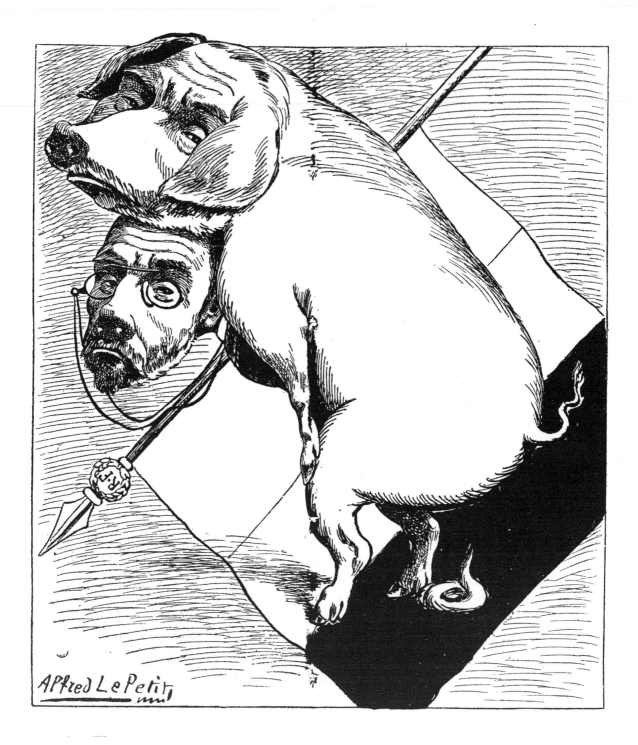

Fig. 58. Alfred Le Petit, *Ah! Ah! Monsieur Zola, C'est vilain ce que tu fais là!* ("*Ah! Ah! M. Zola, What a nasty thing you're doing there!*"). Photo M. Garval.

Fig. 59. Moloch, *Vignette of Zola for Touchatout's Le Trombinoscope*. Photo M. Garval.

Fig. 60. Zut, *Zola*. Photo M. Garval.

naturalistes: A quoi M. Zola perd son temps" [Naturalist pastimes: How M. Zola wastes his time], in which a tiny Zola tries in vain to pull Hugo from his pedestal (fig. 6); along similar lines, Pasquin's "À Balzac," in which Zola stands on his novels and on tiptoe to raise himself to the height of a Balzac bust (fig. 63); the latter's "Une Apothéose" (including a "Vive Zola" banner complete with steaming hot turd, an overturned chamber pot, a champagne-swilling Nana baring her breasts and, in the extreme foreground, an indignant Victor Hugo disapproving of it all) (fig. 64); a composition in which Zola holds the puny candle of Naturalism up to the formidable radiance of Victor Hugo, alias "le géant Lumière" (fig. 65); and the even more phallic image of impotent little dog Zola juxtaposed with Victor Hugo-as-tree in the 1881 caricature "La fête de Victor Hugo, L'ordre et la marche de la fête, Engueulade par E. Zola" (cf. chapter 1) (fig. 12).

Robida's "Zola, doux rêve" [Zola, sweet dream] is emblematic of the second, scatological category of "before" pictures (fig. 66). While there are no pigs here, at least not in sight, there is dung aplenty. The drawing, which appeared following the publication of Zola's agrarian novel *La Terre* [*The Earth*], portrays him as

Salve de 21 coups de canon, tirée sur le Pont des Arts par les académiciens valides.

Banquet à l'Ely-sée-Montmartre.

Retour de l' :lysée.

Inauguration de la statue d'Émile Zola.

Les vils idéalistes.

Fig. 61. Albert Robida, *Le Triomphe du naturalisme* **(***The Triumph of naturalism***). Photo M. Garval.**

a wheelbarrow-wielding peasant, laboring to build a mountain of manure. This, as the accompanying article explains, is an image of his literary production as a successive heaping on of dung. Perched atop the formidable pile he has already amassed—atop the "colossales Alpes de guano" [colossal Alps of guano] that are his work—Zola dreams of turning the entire planet into a "concrétion d'ordures, boule d'immondices" [agglomeration of filth, ball of refuse]. Zola's ambitions are perhaps monumental; the results, seen as anything but. In this characteristic example, then, as in the entire second category of Zola caricatures from before "J'Accuse . . . !", Zola and his work are denigrated through abundant porcine and scatological associations. On one level, this is simply a vulgar put-down—that is, "Zola's a swine; his novels, shit." On another, this is a way to

dismiss him and his work as antimonumental, to anticipate their impermanence. The weapons in his literary critical arsenal are thus turned against him: just as he relegates Dumas to the mortality of dust, Zola wallows here in his own literary detritus, destined for oblivion.

What remains, though, when the standard of monumentality drops out of the Zola iconography after "J'Accuse . . . !," and what—if anything—replaces it? The answer to the first part of this would appear simple, for hogs and droppings seem just as plentiful in caricatures of Zola from after "J'Accuse . . . !" as in those from before. Their meaning changes, however. Before, these base images signify Zola's baseness as a literary figure. After, the same iconographical elements are used in the service of contemporary nationalism, militarism, and antisemitism: emblematically, for example,

J'AMUSE !!

Feu Zola. — Ah ! les Français ne prennent plus mes petits papiers au sérieux... Eh bien ! je vais les distribuer à l'étranger ! !

Fig. 62. Bobb, *J'amuse!!* Photo M. Garval.

Fig. 63. F. Pasquin, *À Balzac*. Photo M. Garval.

the "naturalist caca" that once overflowed Zola's chamber pots and wheelbarrows becomes "caca international," as Zola-pig besmears a map of the Hexagon with "international," hence unfrench, antipatriotic filth (fig. 67). Thus, before "J'Accuse . . . !", the scatological panoply tells us that Zola is on the wrong side of literary immortality; after, that he is on the wrong side of the contemporary political fence.

In the post-"J'Accuse . . . !" corpus of Zola caricatures, posterity appears largely irrelevant; instead, it is contemporary popularity, even notoriety, that matters. At this point, it seems, Zola's appeal proceeded no longer from

Fig. 64. F. Pasquin, *Une Apothéose*. Photo M. Garval.

his monumental literary *oeuvre*, nor even for his ongoing heroism in Dreyfus' defense, but rather from his skillful maneuvering into the media spotlight. This is exemplified by the image of Zola sinking into a chamber pot (fig. 60). As his impending immersion, the reminders of his death by asphyxiation, the burning of his books, even the title of the newspaper—*Ta Gueul'* [*Shut yer trap*]—suggest, this illustration longs to silence troublesome Zola yet, paradoxically, his demise is also such big news that this reactionary publication features him in a

Armé d'une chandelle, au fond de sa boutique,
Zola croit rayonner d'un éclat sans pareil
Et, dans son fol orgueil, nous voyons ce critique
S'efforcer d'obscurcir les rayons du soleil.

Fig. 65. Alfred Le Petit, *Les Contemporains: Zola*. Photo M. Garval.

full, front-page spread. Similarly (fig. 62), in "J'Amuse . . . !!", postman Zola complains that his "petits papiers" are not getting taken seriously, yet *he* is getting taken seriously as a celebrity, looming in the foreground with, in back, the anonymous crowd of the *fin-de-siècle*'s emerging mass-media culture. The vision of monumental fame that informed Zola caricatures before "J'Accuse . . . !" is thus supplanted by a nascent preoccupation with media stardom, divorced from an earlier concern with achieving massive, heroic and, above all, enduring renown. This fascination with celebrity status for its own sake, which Rousseau already observed in the eager visits of people who had not read his books (cf. introduction), is compounded

at the *fin-de-siècle* by the rise of mass media, and would be compounded further in the twentieth century by the development of electronic media, and in the hands of such talented media manipulators as Sartre and Bernard Pivot.

Hugo at 100

During his lifetime and immediately afterward, amid unprecedented veneration for writers in general, Hugo achieved even broader appeal than any of his peers. By the centenary of his birth in 1902, though, there were already clear signs of his greater dominion waning. To be

Fig. 66. Albert Robida, *Zola, doux rêve* (*Zola, sweet dream*). Photo M. Garval.

sure, unlike Hugo's Parisian funeral, the centenary was celebrated throughout France and around the world, from Cambrai to Athens, Bucharest to Chicago. However, "à cet élargissement géographique correspond un resserrement intellectuel et sociologique. Toutes ces fêtes ont été organisées, à l'attention d'un public scolaire ou érudit, par des sociétés savantes ou par des sociétés d'instruction publique" [this geographic expansion was accompanied by an intellectual and sociological contraction. All these celebrations were organized for academic or erudite audiences, by scholarly societies or public education groups] (Georgel 1985, 292). Increasingly, Hugo was seen less as a broader cultural hero and more as just an important writer.

Along similar lines, in 1902 a curious, symptomatic little book was published: *Victor Hugo par le bibelot* [Victor Hugo through trinkets],

the annotated, illustrated catalogue of the Hugo memorabilia amassed by Paul Beuve since his miraculous conversion to "hugolâtrie" seventeen years earlier (cf. above). Since the poet's death, this "obscur bureaucrate" (Beuve and Daragon 1902, vi), "en apparence . . . un homme ordinaire" (v) [obscure bureaucrat . . . apparently . . . an ordinary fellow], had accumulated several thousand pieces of Hugo memorabilia, a sampling that attests to the extraordinary profusion of such objects during this period and the public's keen interest in them. With the publication of this book and, even more so with this collection absorbed into the permanent collection of the new *Musée Victor Hugo* (founded in 1903), Beuve's obsession was legitimated, and the humble objects themselves not only catalogued and commented, but also elevated and preserved. At the same time, the

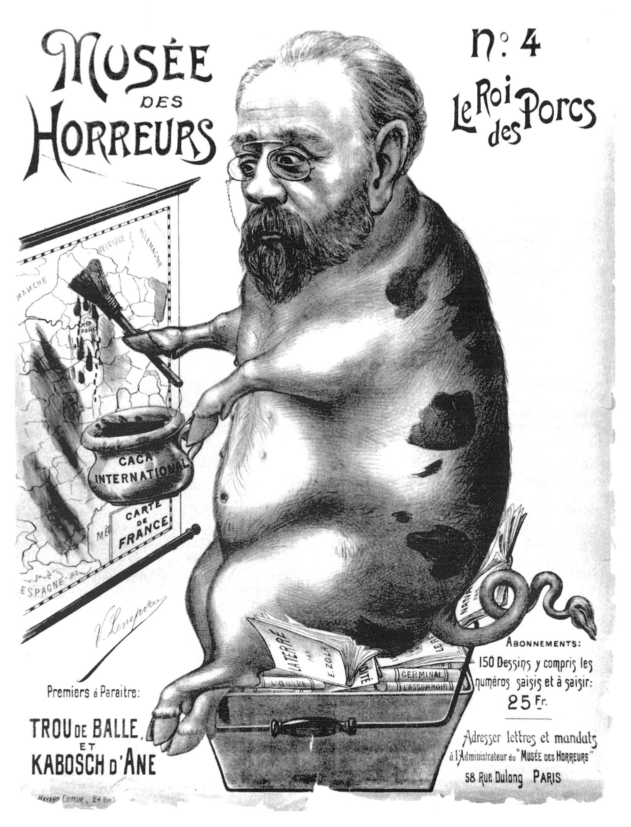

Fig. 67. V. Lenepveu, *Le Roi des Porcs* (*The King of Swine*). **Photo Musée Jean Jaurès, Castres.**

transfiguration of Beuve's diverse paraphernalia into a "collection," and of the individual knick-knacks into artifacts, confirmed that the wave of Hugo memorabilia was largely over. Hugo's appeal was no longer broad enough to inspire the memorabilia mill which, in the decades ahead, particularly with the rise of cinema, radio, and eventually television, would increasingly turn its attention toward entertainers instead.

The year 1902 was also when the Barrias monument was inaugurated (fig. 43). Erected on the *place Victor-Hugo*, it represented the writer as he would have looked during the early years of his exile. This most imposing monument, while not innovative aesthetically, was ambitious iconographically. Indeed, in a 1952 interview, over a decade after the monument's destruction, as Parisians still puzzled over what should replace it, Pablo Picasso recalled admiringly its abundant and grandiose commemorative features: "les gloires, les trompettes, les palmes ... et les bas-reliefs, ... tout cela fait un monument" [the glories, trumpets, palms ... and low reliefs, ... all that makes a monument] (Picasso 1952). Moreover it attempted, however uneasily, to represent different aspects of Hugo's legend through its sculptural program. Perched pensively atop a granite boulder—the *Rocher des proscrits*, once again—a bronze Hugo was flanked by lyric, dramatic, epic, and satiric muses, while the granite pedestal displayed four bronze bas-reliefs: *Victor Hugo à la tribune le 17 juillet 1851*, *Souvenir de la nuit du 4*, *Victor Hugo et ses personnages*, and *Victor Hugo reçu au Parnasse* [*Victor Hugo at the rostrum, July 17, 1851*; *Remembrance of the night of the 4th*; *Victor Hugo and his characters*; and *Victor Hugo entering Parnassus*]. While Barrias and the committee overseeing the monument's elaboration had quarreled extensively over these elements, the end result nonetheless synthesized both Hugo's political and literary legacies. However, the former was increasingly giving way to the latter, particularly in the monuments raised in his honor:

[Hugo] était de plus en plus présent dans les bibliothèques—mais sa gloire s'en trouvait transformée.... cette gloire, telle qu'on peut la saisir à travers le décor public, tout en semblant croître—parce que les hommages se sont multipliés—n'a en fait cessé de se rétrécir, car de nationale et même universelle qu'elle était, riche de la complexité du personnage, elle est devenue de plus en plus uniquement littéraire et donc de plus en plus à usage de groupes restreints: les associations littéraires (Georgel 1985, 280)

[Hugo was more and more present in libraries, but at the same time his glory was transformed ... Public art tells the story: while his glory seemed to grow—because tributes abounded—in fact it shrank continuously for, once national and even universal, embodying his complexity as a public figure, it became more and more exclusively literary and therefore more and more the concern of narrowly-defined groups, i.e., of literary clubs.]

By the time the Barrias was erected, the work's grand synthesis was already largely outdated. It had become increasingly implausible to think of Victor Hugo as much more than a literary figure and, from this point onward, he would matter mainly as a writer to other writers, readers, and critics. Unlike the erection of the Barrias monument, which still purported to serve up a universal figure for the general public's veneration, the founding the following year of the *Musée Victor Hugo* offered a different, narrower, yet more intense relation to the writer, far more indicative of how French literary culture would evolve from this point on. Converting Hugo's one-time residence on the *place des Vosges* into a museum established a shrine on the pilgrimage routes of modern literary tourism, which would grow to include Combourg (for Chateaubriand), Saché (for Balzac), Nohant (for Sand), Croisset (for Flaubert), Médan (for Zola), even Illiers-Combray (its real name now joined with that of Proust's fictional destination), sites visited by relatively modest numbers of zealous initiates.

The fate of the Barrias statue was also emblematic of important changes in the public's attitude toward great men in general and great writers in particular. Once up, it remained popular for a while, figuring frequently in pre-World War I postcards. But when the German occupiers melted down the monument for raw materials in 1941, other concerns loomed larger, and few seemed to care. Contrasting with the lively debate over its creation four decades earlier, this silence revealed a substantially different cultural context—much the same as that of *Nausea* in which, amid a general indifference to monuments, only a would-be famous writer might still care enough to ponder, in them, the posthumous destiny of illustrious predecessors.

The Decline of Statuemania

While Rodin's *Balzac*, Zola caricatures, and the events of Hugo's centenary year all pointed toward the dream of stone's impending decline, the clearest sign would be the decline of statuemania itself, the phenomenon that most tangibly and spectacularly embodied the dream of stone.

In a sense, statuemania and the dream of stone, so closely interrelated, were both doomed from the outset for basically the same reasons. They both arose out of uncertainty and change, out of a combination of rapid technological evolution, political instability, and broad societal transformation, against which they offered a compensatory vision of grandeur and permanence. Proceeding, in particular, from postrevolutionary democratization and secularization, the period's obsessive commemoration of cultural heroes and artifacts was a desperate, and ultimately futile effort to shift the center of lasting values onto a cultural field already troubled by its own internal revolutions. Monuments to Balzac or Delacroix took the place of ones to Henri IV or Louis XIV and, as Sartre wrote of his grandfather, "ce pasteur manqué" [that minister manqué], nineteenth-century French culture "avait gardé le Divin pour le verser dans la Culture" [had retained the Divine and invested it in Culture] (Sartre, 1964a, 147; 1964c, 177–78). However, with the ever-greater sway of avant-gardism in the arts, cultural movements came to seem as volatile as political regimes, and eventually a skeptical public would lose faith in the transcendent possibilities of culture, just as it had lost faith in Christian transcendance. Historian Maurice Agulhon connects the rise and fall of statuemania in particular to these shifts in values: "[Si] la statuomanie a connu la même courbe d'ascension, épanouissement et déclin, qu'un certain système de valeurs philosophiques, et dans les mêmes temps, c'est peut-être qu'elle lui était apparentée" [(If) statuemania went through the same pattern of rise, development, and decline, as a certain system of philosophical values, and at the same time,

perhaps it is because they were related] (1978, 152). These, too, were the liberal, bourgeois, positivist values underpinning the "dream of stone": an ideal of greatness, reverence for culture, belief in the immortality of great men and their works.[2] Change and impermanence had driven French culture, particularly French literary culture, to seek an antidote in monumentality, but ultimately, the forces of instability, whose gathering strength gave this quest its peculiar urgency, would triumph.

In the early years of the twentieth century, a mix of practical and aesthetic considerations also hastened the great man statue's demise. June Hargrove points out that with the invention of the automobile and corresponding increase in traffic, public thoroughfares could no longer be clogged with monuments (Nora 1997, 2.1876–77). Agulhon observes as well that the modern way of moving through the city does not allow for public statuary to be appreciated properly: "Les anciennes statues de carrefour ou de places publiques ne peuvent plus guère être regardées ni par l'automobiliste qui passe vite, ni même par le piéton qui, pour maintes raisons, n'est plus guère flâneur" [Old statues in intersections or public squares can no longer be looked at properly, either by drivers who pass quickly, or even by pedestrians who, for so many reasons, no longer stroll] (1978, 165). Furthermore, unlike the cluttered eclecticism that characterized the nineteenth century's use of space, a sparser style of architecture and urban planning came into favor in the twentieth. Picasso, in his retrospective reflection on the Barrias *Hugo*, links this modernist rejection of monuments to great men with contemporary "taste" and concern for urban "hygiene": "Il semble qu'aujourd'hui on craigne la représentation des grands hommes dans nos villes. On déguise cette crainte sous des prétextes de goût. Et peut-être d'hygiène, parce que c'est difficile d'enlever la poussière des petits coins" [Today we seem to fear representing great men in our cities. We hide this fear under the pretext of taste. And perhaps of hygiene, for it is hard to get the dust out of all the nooks and crannies] (Picasso 1952). Such ostensible concern for the cleanliness of statues' private parts, Picasso infers, belies the real concern for neatness of the city's public spaces: a new urban minimalism, a sort of reverse *horror vacui*.[3]

More problematic still would be the growing gap between the material reality of monuments and the ideal they were supposed to represent, as their increasing abundance and cliché-ridden execution clashed with their ostensible goal of transcendant distinction. By the 1880s and 1890s the French were becoming aware of the excesses and abuses of their commemorative predilection, as we can see in the writings of figures like Edmond de Goncourt and Octave Mirbeau or, for that matter, in the coining, ca. 1887, of the term *statuomanie*, with its humorous, even pejorative overtones (*Trésor de la langue française* 1971–1994). Between the turn of the century and the First World War, there arose substantial disillusionment with monuments, as suggested by the correspondence between André Gide and Paul Claudel, dealing with the projects for monuments to Verlaine and Rimbaud and with the publication of a fund-raising *Hommage à Verlaine*, similar in conception to the earlier *Tombeau de Baudelaire*:

Charles Morice m'a demandé une collaboration à un livre collectif appelé *Hommage à Verlaine*, et qui servira à payer l'affreux navet qu'on veut ériger à la mémoire de ce pauvre homme. J'ai d'abord refusé, en disant ce que je pensais des monuments, hommage hypocrite et dérisoire à des gens qu'on a laissé crever de faim. Il a insisté en invoquant l'autorité qu'il savait pour moi décisive de Mallarmé, initiateur, paraît-il, de l'entreprise. J'ai donc envoyé des vers, mais je ne sais s'ils feront plaisir à tout le monde. (Claudel to Gide, 17 June 1910; Claudel and Gide 1949, 140–41)
Pour l'hommage à Verlaine, j'ai fait comme vous aviez fait d'abord; le livre se passera de mon nom. (Gide to Claudel, June 1910; 143)
On m'a demandé de faire partie du Comité d'un monument pour Arthur Rimbaud. J'ai refusé. J'ai suffisamment de regrets d'avoir en quelque mesure que ce soit collaboré à l'érection de l'imbécile chose dernièrement dédiée à la mémoire de Verlaine. Je ne veux pas être complice d'une nouvelle profanation à l'égard de l'écrivain dont j'honore le plus la mémoire et que je considère comme un ascendant spirituel. On me dit que vous avez donné votre assentiment, mais je suppose que c'est sans enthousiasme et que vous n'aimez pas plus que moi les monuments. (Paul Claudel to André Gide, 21 June 1911; 180)

[Charles Morice asked me to collaborate on a collective volume entitled *Homage to Verlaine*, which will help pay for the horrid dud they want to erect in memory of this poor fellow. At first I refused, telling them what I think of monuments, hypocritical, pathetic homages to people who were let die of hunger. He insisted, by invoking Mallarmé, whose authority he knew would sway me, and who has apparently initiated this project. So, I have sent some verses, but don't know if everybody will like them.
As far as the homage to Verlaine is concerned, I have done as you had at first: my name shall not appear in the volume.
I was asked to be part of the Committee for a monument to Arthur Rimbaud. I refused. I have enough regrets about having to whatever extent contributed to the erection of that imbecilic thing recently erected in memory of Verlaine. I do not want to be accomplice to another profanation, this time targeting the writer whose memory I cherish the most, and whom I consider a kind of spiritual ancestor. I have heard that you have agreed, but I suppose that it is without enthusiasm, and that you like monuments no more than I.]

While deploring the inadequacy of monuments to embody a transcendant ideal, this exchange still does so without really questioning that ideal, as the use of such reverential terms as "profanation," "honorer la mémoire," and "ascendant spirituel" [spiritual ancestor] suggests. As we have seen, the ideal could—and did— exist independent of actual monuments, in such modalities as complete works, eulogies, street names, or writers' homes converted into museums (cf. above). But how much longer could such an ideal thrive amid the ongoing, public onslaught of "affreux navets" [horrid duds] and "imbéciles choses" [imbecilic things], of tributes to luminaries like Verlaine and Rimbaud alongside seemingly equivalent ones to Impétraz-like mediocrities? In the years ahead, more innovative sculptors would attempt to honor great men without actually depicting them: thus, Aristide Maillol's 1912–29 monument to Cézanne, a nude *baigneuse* figure, more a stylistic exercise in the female form than anything else; or Albert Bartholomé's allegorical monument to Jean-Jacques Rousseau, of 1907–12, for his tomb in the Pantheon (Chevillot 1990, 60–63). Paradoxically, to honor great men exceptionally could now mean banishing them from the pedestal—the aesthetic bankruptcy of the great man statue, as a genre, betraying the deeper ideological bankruptcy of the great man ideal.

According to Hargrove, it was the First World War, above all, that brought a definitive change, a turn away from the commemorative frenzy of the preceding decades:

la Première Guerre mondiale . . . avait . . . donné naissance à une réaction hostile contre une statuomanie qui avait accompagné la genèse de la tragédie. L'incapacité des pouvoirs établis à résoudre une crise internationale sans sacrificier des millions de vies humaines avait jeté le discrédit sur les valeurs traditionelles et terni la gloire des héros révérés. . . . Aux yeux des cyniques de l'après-guerre, les statues des hommes célèbres étaient devenues des anachronismes. (Nora 1997, 2.1877)

[the tragedy of the First World War gave rise to a hostile reaction against statuemania, which had coexisted with the events leading up to the war. The establishment's inability to resolve an international crisis without sacrificing millions of lives had discredited traditional values and tarnished the glory of revered heroes. For the cynics of the postwar period, statues of famous men had become anachronisms.]

With the catastrophic events of World War I, the earlier disillusionment with the genre of the great man monument spread to its philosophical underpinnings. The war's unprecedented slaughter and destruction shattered the widespread faith in progress through human agency that had been the cornerstone of the great man ideal. Emblematically, when the war was over, the French spurned great man monuments, choosing instead to raise far soberer "monuments aux morts" [monuments to the dead] commemorating the local war dead in municipal parks and town squares throughout the land (cf. Antoine Prost, Les monuments aux morts, in Nora 1.199–223). At about this time, moreover, the persistent monumental metaphor largely dropped out of literary discourse, and French literary culture indulged instead in iconoclastic movements like Dada and Surrealism with their delight in fortuitous juxtapositions, "automatic" writing, and the evanescence of dreams: a literature of the irreverent, of the fleeting; in short, of the antimonumental.[4] Today, at a century's remove from the commemorative frenzy of statuemania, a grandiose public statue to a celebrated

male writer like Nobel Prize winner Claude Simon seems no more plausible than one to a celebrated female peer like Marguerite Duras. In self-conscious counterpoint to statuemania's pervasiveness and bombast, contemporary literary monuments are rare and—like Roseline Granet's stubby, studious little Sartre in a courtyard at the old *Bibliothèque nationale* (1986) or Patrice Alexandre's metal fragments of text paying homage to Saint-John Perse in the *Jardin des Plantes* (1989)—seem excessive only in their modesty.

As this suggests, the monumentalizing impulse largely subsided, within the literary realm, in the early years of the twentieth century. But, assuming that such abundant commemorative energies could not just disappear, where did they go? Part of the answer would be that the great man monument endured a forced afterlife under various totalitarian regimes, its bankrupt aesthetic pressed into the service of other doomed ideologies, yielding so many allegories of the fatherland, heroic hammer-wielding model workers, or their colossal leaders, toppled with no regrets when the regimes that erected them fell. In France, moreover, in recent years, in contrast to the paucity and humbleness of new public statuary, Parisian *grands travaux* and other grandiose civic projects have provided other ways of flaunting French greatness to the world. In this sense, the *Grande Arche de la Défense*, the *Grand Louvre*, or the *TGV* (*Train à Grande Vitesse*)—their names all bespeaking a continuing, compensatory will to *grandeur*—would be the contemporary avatars of the great man ideal. Yet there also seems to have occurred a broader shift, in the focus of commemorative activity, from glory and creation to infamy and destruction. In our disabused, modern 'global village,' after the cataclysms of the twentieth and early twenty-first centuries, what could still seem so big that it would capture the monumentalizing imagination—that it might still inspire some sort of dream of stone? As cultural accomplishments and ideals have shrunk before the enormity of mass warfare, genocide, and terrorism, public interest has gravitated instead toward commemorative projects that plumb the depths of the abyss, like Shelomo Selinger's 1976 *Mémorial de la déportation du camp de Drancy*, or Maya Lin's 1982 *Vietnam*

Veterans Memorial in Washington, D.C. Most recently, debate has focused on how, if at all, to memorialize the September 11 attacks on the World Trade Center. For a month following the event's six-month anniversary, for example, the "Tribute in Light" offered a ghostly, immaterial, and of course temporary reconstruction of the destroyed towers. Meanwhile, New York-based architectural writer Fred Bernstein proposed a controversial "Twin Piers" project, paradoxically enormous yet prostrate, an antimonumental monument. More obscure, but just as intriguing, a Canadian organization (whose mailing address reads "c/o Therapy Nouvelle") has promoted a "Twin Towers of Love" monument—described with utopian, new-age zeal on its website—and solicited names electronically, to be inscribed on the structure ("The micro-second you choose to send us your name, the country you are from and your religion or spiritual belief to be inscribed on the Twin Towers of Love monument, you become part of this energy" [http:///www.twintowersoflove.org/]). This concern for spiritual "energy," like the debate over the inviolable sanctity of ground zero, reveals a transcendant dimension in the face of mass destruction that no longer seems to exist in our relation to cultural productions like art and literature.

Such observations should not suggest, however, that the dream of stone has disappeared entirely from French literary culture. While the dream did decline irrevocably in the early part of the twentieth century, vestiges have persisted in such typically French forms and institutions as the leatherbound *Pléiade* editions, the *Panthéon*, or the *Académie Française*, as well as in the unofficial ways that the French have continued to revere writers and their work, and that writers have continued to see themselves and serve themselves up to the public. In part, at least, this explains the success in France of television shows dedicated to serious discussion of good books. But the Pivot phenomenon also needs to be considered in light of other, and in many respects countervailing developments in the evolution of literary fame.

Literary Fame Amid the Ruins

In nineteenth-century France, ways of understanding renown were organized around two poles: transitory celebrity on one end, and enduring glory on the other, embodied respectively by caricature and the monument. Photography, however, would alter this balance. From its advent in the mid nineteenth century, photography began transforming society's understanding of celebrity. This is why Nadar's *Panthéon* is such an emblematic image, with caricature and sculpture acting out the period's understanding of fame, as photography waits in the wing (cf. introduction).

In *La chambre claire* [Camera lucida], Roland Barthes argues that photography replaces the monument as the locus of cultural memory in the modern world:

> Les anciennes sociétés s'arrangeaient pour que le souvenir, substitut de la vie, fût éternel et qu'au moins la chose qui disait la Mort fût elle-même immortelle: c'était le Monument. Mais en faisant de la Photographie, mortelle, le témoin général et comme naturel de 'ce qui a été', la société moderne a renoncé au Monument. (Barthes 1980, 146)

> [Earlier societies managed so that memory, the substitute for life, was eternal and that at least the thing which spoke Death should itself be immortal: this was the Monument. But by making the (mortal) Photograph into the general and somehow natural witness of "what has been," modern society has renounced the Monument.] (Barthes 1981, 193)

Eventually, photography would do what Barthes contends here, largely supplanting the monument, providing different ways of understanding our relation to time and memory. At first, though, like new technologies generally, the new medium was used as a substitute for or supplement to existing ones: as preliminary studies in the elaboration of Nadar's *Panthéon*; or, in such forms as deathbed and gravestone photography, that called upon the photographic image to perform much the same function as funerary busts and steles had earlier. Increasingly, though, photography would transcend existing modes, to create something new. Noticeable signs of such a paradigm shift underfoot appeared as malaise within the other modes of representing renown: the general freneticism of statuemania; the increasing pomposity of monuments, with their ever more complicated iconographical programs, and weird mixes of documentary and allegorical elements;

and the growing number of statues appearing within caricature, at first as more modest busts, then increasingly and more emphatically as full-length monuments—a curious phenomenon that, like photography itself, began to take hold in the early 1850s, and became a commonplace during the Third Republic. Such forms of malaise proceeded from the nature of the photographic medium. Through the photograph, writes Braudy, "The absent as well as the dead would be present again, and, in a manner only aspired to by writers and artists, the immediate and the eternal promised to be made one" (1986, 493). Photography conflated the presence and absence of the subject, the immediacy and durability of the image and, ultimately, helped collapse the older oppositions between caricature and monument, between passing celebrity and enduring fame, to frame a new vision of renown as a passing apotheosis, as something like Warhol's fifteen-minute fame for all.

But what impact did such a shift have upon the literary world? How, for example, did a figure like Sartre fit into this new context? To begin with, between his literary début in *La Nausée* (1938) and his autobiographical *Les Mots* (1964), Sartre had become tremendously famous, basking far longer in the media limelight than Warhol's hypothetical fifteen minutes. In 1964 as well, in a supreme gesture of reverse snobbery, false modesty, and clever media manipulation, Sartre refused the Nobel Prize for literature, refusal creating a far greater sensation than acceptance. Along similar lines, in a stunning understatement from the close of *Les Mots*, he concedes, "j'ai perdu mes chances de mourir inconnu" [I've lost the chance of dying unknown] (Sartre 1964a, 212; 1964c, 254).

In a sense, Sartre's literary fame picked up where Zola's left off in the drawing "J'Amuse!!!," with the famous writer celebrated as a media phenomenon, rather than as the immortal creator of immortal works. Yet Sartre remained haunted by the dream of stone. In *La Nausée*, he had already displayed his own ambivalence—crystallized in the Impétraz episode—toward an earlier, monumental vision of literary greatness, that at once fascinated and repulsed him. In *Les Mots*, having become extraordinarily famous himself, Sartre ponders the contradictions of his own position, of his shining celebrity amid the ruins of a monumental ideal. What did it mean to be and, more fundamentally, how could one be, a great writer within an antimonumental literary culture? Indeed, after enumerating the various embodiments of his childhood great writer fantasy (Pardaillan, Grisélidis, Strogoff), he puzzles over his descent from such a lineage: "Je ne relève que d'eux qui ne relèvent que de Dieu et je ne crois pas en Dieu" [I'm answerable only to them, who are answerable only to God, and I don't believe in God] (Sartre 1964a, 212; 1964c, 254). The larger question for Sartre here, as elsewhere, is what to make of transcendence—God's, or the writer's—if you do not believe in it, do not even think it still exists, but are obsessed with it all the same.

In *Les Mots*, Sartre's childhood dreams of becoming a writer form a compendium of heroic, reverential notions about literary greatness. "[J]e refilai à l'écrivain les pouvoirs sacrés du héros" [I palmed off on the writer the sacred powers of the hero] (Sartre 1964a, 139; 1964c, 167), he explains. Moreover, an assiduous reader of "le Grand Larousse et les notices nécrologiques" [the encyclopedia and the obituaries . . . in the newspapers] (Sartre 1964a, 139; 1964c, 168), he internalizes standard nineteenth-century narratives of literary glory: the writer is inevitably thanked, perhaps first by an anonymous letter, then, "ses compatriotes, après sa mort, se cotisaient pour lui élever un monument; dans sa ville natale et parfois dans la capitale de son pays, des rues portaient son nom" [his countrymen took up a collection after his death to erect a monument to him; in his native town and sometimes in the capital of his country, streets were named after him] (Sartre 1964a, 140; 1964c, 168). While neglected during his lifetime, he is certain of his future glory: "méconnu, délaissé, . . . sans me douter une minute que le Panthéon m'attend" [unappreciated, forsaken, . . . without suspecting for a minute that the Pantheon awaits me] (Sartre 1964a, 146; 1964c, 175–76). Whether fancying himself an "écrivain-chevalier" or "écrivain-martyr" [writer-knight or writer-martyr] (Sartre 1964a, 147; 1964c, 177), young Sartre longs to take the nondescript world around him, "de vains ramas de blancheurs" [idle heaps of whiteness] and give this "des contours fixes, un sens" [definite contours . . . a meaning]; in other words, he adds, "j'en ferais des monuments véritables . . . je dresserais des cathédrales de paroles sous l'oeil

bleu du ciel. Je bâtirais pour des millénaires. . . .
et, plus tard, dans les bibliothèques en ruines, [mes ouvrages] survivraient à l'homme"
[I would make real monuments of them. . . . I
would set up cathedrals of words beneath the
blue eyes of the word sky. I would build for
the ages. . . . and, later, in ruined libraries, [my
works] would outlive man] (Sartre 1964a, 152;
1964c, 183).

But this, alas, was no longer the nineteenth
century. While evoking boyhood dreams of himself as a monumental, Victor Hugo-like literary
figure, Sartre juxtaposes them with doubts that
this could ever be possible:

J'étais voué, illustre, *j'avais* ma tombe au Père-
Lachaise et peut-être au Panthéon, mon avenue
à Paris, mes squares et mes places en province,
à l'étranger: pourtant, au coeur de l'optimisme,
invisible, innommé, je gardais le soupçon de mon
inconsistance. (Sartre 1964a, 173)

[I was consecrated, illustrious. I had my tomb
in Père Lachaise Cemetery and perhaps in the
Pantheon; an avenue was named after me in Paris,
as were public squares in the provinces and in
foreign countries. Yet, at the core of my optimism
I had a sneaking feeling that I lacked substance.]
(Sartre 1964c, 208)

Similarly, as we have seen, he asserts with
tellingly sexual undertones that, while for a
long time he took his pen for a sword, he now
knows his own powerlessness or "impuissance"
—also the term for impotence in French (Sartre
1964a, 211; 1964c, 253–54). Like all of *Les
Mots*, such passages are written from a double perspective: that of the boy and that of the
grown man. On the one hand, there is the boy
of nine or ten on the threshold of the Great
War, at the tail end of a pervasively monumental literary culture, in which he had been
thoroughly inculcated by his grandfather, "un
homme du XIXe siècle qui se prenait, comme
tant d'autres, comme Victor Hugo lui-même,
pour Victor Hugo" [a man of the nineteenth
century who took himself for Victor Hugo, as
did so many others, including Victor Hugo him-
self] (Sartre 1964a, 15; 1964c, 24), a man who
"avait cessé de lire depuis la mort de Victor
Hugo" [had stopped reading since the death of
Victor Hugo] (Sartre 1964a, 51; 1964c, 65). On
the other hand, there is the grown man who

came of age intellectually during the twenties
and thirties and published his first works on
the brink of the Second World War. He cannot
help suspecting his own efforts of weakness,
flimsiness, fragility, even impotence. This is the
inconsistance of a literary culture that had, for
the most part, shed its monumental trappings.

Les Mots was Sartre's attempt to make sense
not just of what, as a child, he had imagined
he would become, but also of how such visions of grandeur, while essentially obsolete,
had nonetheless inflected what he had become:
"ce vieux bâtiment ruineux, mon imposture,
c'est aussi mon caractère: on se défait d'une
névrose, on ne se guérit pas de soi. Usés, ef-
facés, humiliés, rencoignés, passés sous silence,
tous les traits de l'enfant sont restés chez le
quinquagénaire" [that old, crumbling structure,
my imposture, is also my character: one gets rid
of a neurosis, one doesn't get cured of one's self.
Though they are worn out, blurred, humiliated,
thrust aside, ignored, all of the child's traits
are still to be found in the quinquagenarian]
(Sartre 1964a, 212; 1964c, 254). What does this
yield, though, finally? "Si je range l'impossible
Salut au magasin des accessoires, que reste-
t-il?" he asks at book's end. "Tout un homme,
fait de tous les hommes, et qui les vaut tous
et que vaut n'importe qui" [If I relegate impossible Salvation to the proproom, what remains? A whole man, composed of all men and
as good as all of them and no better than any]
(Sartre 1964a, 213; 1964c, 255). In one sense,
after the beautifully wrought prose of the preceding 200 pages, after such a superb literary
slight of hand—"rien dans les mains, rien dans
les poches" [nothing in my hands, nothing up
my sleeve] (Sartre 1964a, 212; 1964c, 255)—
this apparent profession of humility seems yet
another example of Sartrean bad faith. In another, this final assertion, cautiously prefaced
with "if," remains a hypothetical one. Perhaps
salvation, imaginary but persistent, cannot be
jettisoned, or perhaps Sartre is just not ready
to do so.

In *Les Mots*, while Sartre subjects himself
to considerable self-irony, he does so, nonetheless, in the service of careful self-justification—
assuming that the public would, even should
care how he came to be the writer he is. Published just a year earlier, in 1963, Boris Vian's
L'écume des jours [*Mood Indigo*] also probes the

literary phenomenon that Sartre had become at the height of his fame, but does so in a wickedly satirical vein, devoid of Sartre's self-indulgence. Vian's novel, in large measure also a paean to the spontaneity and irreverence of jazz, is a willfully hip, iconoclastic work, informed by an aesthetics of improvisation and kaleidoscopic fragmentation, at antipodes to any monumental ideal of literary creation. In particular, the character "Jean-Sol Partre," Jean-Paul Sartre's parodic double, appears at once hyperbolically famous and fundamentally hollow. Partre's lectures are outrageous "happenings" to which—in a description reminiscent of Flaubert's *Salammbô*—he arrives, like some eastern potentate, upon an elephant, in an armored howdah surrounded by ax-wielding bodyguards as the beast crushes innumerable bodies underfoot. Meanwhile, multitudes of fans arrive however they can, by parachute, through rat-infested sewers, hidden in coffins, risking their lives, with thousands literally dying to get close to their idol. The magnetic appeal of such an Elvis-like star, combined with the hysterical, swooning fans, and generally orgy-like atmosphere, make Partre's lectures reminiscent of a rock concert:

> Il émanait de son corps souple et ascétique une radiance extraordinaire, et le public, captivé par le charme redoutable qui parait ses moindres gestes, attendait, anxieux, le signal du départ.
>
> Nombreux étaient les cas d'évanouissement dûs à l'exaltation intra-utérine qui s'emparait particulièrement du public féminin, et . . . vingt-quatre spectateurs . . . s'étaient faufilés sous l'estrade et se déshabillaient à tâtons pour tenir moins de place. (Vian 1979, 101)

> [From his lithe, ascetic body there emanated an extraordinary radiance, and the audience, captivated by the formidable charm in which his every movement was clothed, waited anxiously for the signal for him to start.
>
> There were countless cases of fainting, due to the intrauterine exaltation which overcame the female members of the audience, and . . . twenty-four spectators . . . had wormed their way under the platform and undressed in the dark so as to take up less room.] (Vian 1968, 81)

The press coverage is massive as well: "Jean-Sol venait de débuter. On n'entendit, tout d'abord, que le cliquetis des obturateurs. Les photographes et les reporters de la presse et du cinéma s'en donnaient à coeur joie" [Jean-Sol had just begun. All one could hear to start with was the click of the camera shutters. The photographers and the press and newsreel reporters were working away to their heart's content] (Vian 1979, 102; 1968, 82). Media darling, Partre is also a cynical, greedy master of self-promotion. To be sure, these were critiques already leveled at Hugo. The difference lies though in the entirely different magnitude of media attention that had become available by the mid twentieth century. Emblematically, Sartre's *L'Être et le néant* [Being and Nothingness] becomes Partre's "*La Lettre et le Néon*, l'étude critique célèbre sur les enseignes lumineuses" [*La Lettre et le Néon*, the celebrated critical study on illuminated signs] (Vian 1979, 153; 1968, 124), the faddish existentialist philosophy of the time thus transformed into a reflection on, and of, modern advertising. Literary celebrity is indeed a lucrative business for Partre, whose main concern about dying is that he could no longer collect royalties (Vian 1979, 208; 1968, 170). Opportunistic booksellers also peddle Partre's books, his articles, recordings of his lectures, even old pants with pipe burns and old pipes with teethmarks, reputed to have been his, to fans like protagonist Chick, who ruins himself buying such paraphernalia.

While Jean-Sol Partre's celebrity is extraordinary, nothing about him is substantial or enduring. His travestied name, one of inveterate punster Vian's cleverest inventions, already evokes the partial, particular, and particulate rather than the whole, general, synthetic; it is redolent of soil, pasture, parturition, of all that is low, transitory, slippery, soft, organic; and it is further degraded through association with Vian's version of Simone de Beauvoir, the "Duchesse de Bovouard," the Bovouard-Partre pair recalling Flaubert's dim-witted Bouvard and Pécuchet, adding snide and perhaps misogynist insinuations of bovine obtuseness, reminiscent of the treatment George Sand received in Touchatout's *Trombinoscope* (cf. chapter 3). Equally revealing are the titles of his works: *Paradoxe sur le Dégueulis* [Paradox on Vomit], *Choix Préalable avant le Haut-le-Coeur* [Choice Precedent to Throwing-up], *Vomi* [Vomit], and

Encyclopédie de la Nausée [Encyclopedia of Nausea, twenty volumes, with photographs]. On the most obvious level, this is a repeated, parodic allusion to Sartre's *La Nausée*. More profoundly, though, this impugns the works' simultaneous abundance and lack of substance. Partre's production is implausibly copious: "Il publie au moins cinq articles par semaine" [He publishes at least five articles a week] (Vian 1979, 50; 1968, 39) and he writes nineteen of the projected twenty volumes of his encyclopedia of nausea in less than a year. Writing, for Partre, is an ongoing regurgitation, a scriptural bulimia, an endless cycle of ingestion and ejection:

> Partre passe ses journées dans un débit, à boire et à écrire avec d'autres gens qui viennent boire et écrire, ils boivent du thé des Mers et des alcools doux, cela leur évite de penser à ce qu'ils écrivent et il entre et sort beaucoup de monde, cela remue les idées du fond et on en pêche une ou l'autre, il ne faut pas éliminer tout le superflu, on met un peu d'idées et un peu de superflu, on dilue. Les gens absorbent ces choses-là plus facilement, surtout les femmes n'aiment pas ce qui est pur. (Vian 1979, 206)

> [Partre spends his days in a bar, drinking and writing with other people like himself who come to drink and write, they drink tea and sweet liqueurs, that saves them thinking about what they're writing and lots of people come in and out, that stirs up the ideas on the bottom and they fish one or another of them up, one mustn't cut out all the padding, you put in a few ideas and a bit of padding and dilute. People absorb that sort of thing more easily, especially women, who don't like it straight.] (Vian 1968, 169)

In the aqueous *débit* [bar], drinks and borrowed ideas flow in, all gets stirred up, pages interlaced with superfluities flow back out to get absorbed, in turn, by the reading public—especially women. This association of women with the soft, sloshy, impure mess of Partre's writing recalls, *in contrario*, the dream of stone, with its vision of literary creators and creation as hard, phallic, and fundamentally male.

Not surprisingly, what is said in his work does not matter to Partre, does not even interest him: "—Ça sera assez embêtant à lire," confesses Jean-Sol à propos his *Encyclopédie de la Nausée*, "parce que ça m'embête déjà beaucoup à écrire. J'ai une forte crampe au poignet gauche à force de tenir la feuille" [It'll be pretty tedious to read . . . because I've already found it very tedious writing it. I've got severe cramp in the left wrist from holding the paper] (Vian 1979, 207–8; 1968, 170). His spoken words are just as irrelevant; indeed, one cannot even hear what he says during his lectures, his mousy voice drowned out by the din of fans and press: "on n'entend rien, . . . Il ne fait pas plus de bruit qu'une souris" [you can't hear a thing here, . . . He makes no more sound than a mouse] (Vian 1979, 103; 1968, 82). Essentially the same picture is conveyed by the actual volumes containing Partre's works, for in describing them Vian indulges in an elaborate parody of the nineteenth-century's reverential binding and printing practices, with the inferiority of the material here betraying the true shabbiness of the work. Thus, collector Chick has "une édition du *Choix préalable avant le Haut-le-Coeur* de Partre, sur rouleau hygiénique non dentelé" [a copy of Partre's *Choice Precedent to Throwing-up*, on an unperforated toilet roll] (Vian 1979, 50; 1968, 38), unperforated toilet paper presumably being more prized by the connoisseur and, in any case, allowing an uninterrupted flow of worthlessness, the medium providing an image of the empty message it contains; or the master's latest work, "recouvert de peau de néant, épaisse et verte, le nom de Partre se détacha[n]t en lettres creuses sur la reliure" [covered in thick, green oblivion-skin, and Partre's name was picked out in hollow letters on the binding] (Vian 1979, 200; 1968, 164); or "[d]es tirages limités sur tue-mouches" [limited editions printed on flypaper] (Vian 1979, 201; 1968, 165)—limited editions with incapacitating physical limitations, the individual pages of ignoble fly-paper undoubtedly sticking together in an undifferentiated, unreadable mess.

After such excoriation of Partre and his work, the only thing left is to assassinate him, and this occurs at the hands of Alise, Chick's jealous girlfriend. She fears that, if the encyclopedia of nausea were completed, Chick would ruin himself purchasing a copy, so she goes into the Left Bank café where Partre is working, sits right down in the next seat and confronts him, exemplifying the electronic era's strange mix of distance and intimacy, in which celebrities seem both formidably unapproachable and cozily familiar. When he refuses to cancel or de-fer publication, she tears out his heart with a special tool. But, in this antimonumental age, death is no longer a portal into immortality, for either the writer or his work. After slaying Partre, Alise destroys his manuscript, then dispatches as well the booksellers peddling his books and souvenirs before she sets their inventories on fire. Nothing shall survive the destruction, not even the fan and his cherished relics: when Chick dies defending his collection from desecration by police agents, come to collect back taxes squandered on Partre memorabilia, his apartment is about to be engulfed in flames from the bookshop next door, torched by Alise. At the very instant of Partre's death, moreover, he appears stunned by the tetrahedral form of his extracted heart, a paradoxical minipyramid of bleeding flesh. This, too, is our last image of the famous writer, with the greatest of monumental structures and standard nineteenth-century metaphor for literary permanence (Flaubert envisioned books as pyramids) transformed here into the most sensitive and vulnerable of internal organs, ripped out of a living body and left sitting on the table like an unfinished piece of meat, soon to be tidied away by the café staff.

Fantastic, even hallucinatory at times, Vian's satire aims nonetheless at real developments within French literary culture, namely the rise of a media-driven model of the writer as public intellectual, and shift toward a vision of literary fame as passing apotheosis, best embodied at the time by Partre's prototype Sartre. Literary France had arrived at this juncture through a long process of cultural formation, leading out of the royal monopolization of renown during the *ancien régime*, into the ascent of Voltaire and the *philosophes*, through the nineteenth-century monumentalizing of cultural figures and accomplishments, and on toward an amnesiac modernity of fifteen-minute fame for all. The volatile state of affairs evoked in *L'écume des jours* would also, in a sense, become institutionalized a dozen years later, with the start of Bernard Pivot's televised literary talk show *Apostrophes*, which continued until recently as *Bouillon de culture*, and in which the latest cultural luminaries would be served up weekly to the hungry but forgetful *téléspectateurs*.

The names of Pivot's shows ring appropriately antimonumental. "Apostrophes" suggests plurality, volatility, even absence (designating the sign that marks the elision of a vowel). "Bouillon de culture" suggests a sloshy, inchoate, ephemeral creation, like its culinary analogue (and reminiscent of Vian's description of the *débit* as a sort of endless *pot-au-feu*, where ideas and superfluities flow in and out). Pivot himself is unassuming, disarming, even folksy. For Pivot books seem not dauntingly monumental *oeuvres*, but constant companions, which he holds, caresses, his finger tucked lovingly into their soft, welcoming folds. Far from the hard, phallic monumental tomes of the nineteenth-century imagination, Pivot's books are the soft, pliable, feminized objects of his affections. Pivot is a tell-tale lover, though, always ready to share his current book's charms with the multitudes as he spreads open the binding, runs his slender finger along the lines of text, and recites this or that choice passage, with exhibitionistic zeal, before the appreciative television audience.

In Pivot's universe, authors are as familiar and approachable as their books. Alive, not dead as in the nineteenth-century mortuary ideal of literary glory, and up for discussion rather than veneration, they generally appear grouped in lively round-tables rather than in the solemn, heroic singularity of the monument (even when an author appears by herself, like Margaret Duras in 1984, she is not alone, sharing the spotlight with Pivot, and dialoguing not only with him but also with the absent yet seemingly present television audience). As both self-promoter and promoter of the figures he selects, Pivot recalls Nadar, that groundbreaking impresario and midwife of renown, just as Nadar in turn anticipated Pivot, and all the more so because he foresaw the possibilities of Pivot's celebrity interview format, hoping to record sound to accompany the pictures of his interview with Michel-Eugène Chevreul, the famed chemist and centenarian (Barret 132). Yet, unlike the worthies in Nadar's mid nineteenth-century lithograph who march purposefully toward the everlasting glory of the public monument, Pivot's contemporary stars blaze for a brief, brilliant moment, in the intimacy of the television viewer's home, before fading into the darkness of the electronic night.

It is symptomatic of transformations in French literary culture, and of broader changes in the nature of fame, that Pivot is probably better known to the French public than many of the intellectual luminaries featured on his show. In a way, this is to be expected, as there is only one Pivot, who reappears every week while hosting different authors. This is, moreover, a dynamic with ample precedent in the nineteenth century, in impresarios like Nadar or P. T. Barnum who would bask in the reflected light of celebrities they served up to the public, or in the fame-making machinery of *The Human Comedy*, in which the popularity of the myriad fictional characters redounds to the greater glory of their creator. In a sense, Pivot's shows have taken the last, logical step in the long democratization of literary fame, bringing great writers into average citizens' living rooms, making each viewer feel part of the conversation. Thus, more than anyone else in contemporary France, Pivot has helped preserve the particularity of French literary culture—and, above all, its deep-rooted belief that writers and their books really matter, so much so that even cynical politicians might find it advantageous to appear on national television, analyzing Maupassant's work (as President Valéry Giscard d'Estaing did on "Apostrophes" in 1979).

But Pivot is a hard act to follow. Despite his success over the last quarter century, it is hard for anyone, least of all Pivot himself, to be sanguine about the prospects for such programming in future. As he remarks in a recent interview,

[J]e suis très pessimiste pour l'avenir du livre sur les grandes chaînes hertziennes, soumises à la loi de l'Audimat et à la frénésie parkinsonienne du zapping. . . . La multiplication des chaînes a inauguré une télévision ségrégationniste dont le livre fera les frais, cessant d'être l'élément fédérateur pour lequel je me suis tant battu. . . . [E]n 1975, en plus d'«Apostrophes», je proposais chaque soir de la semaine de courts entretiens avec des écrivains. Cela s'intitulait «le Livre du jour». Et ça passait à 18h45! À l'heure où aujourd'hui sont diffusés «le Bigdil» et «Loft Story», je recevais . . . Roger Caillois, André Siniavski, Roland Barthes, Michel Foucault, Michel Tournier, Jean-Loup Trassard, Leonardo Sciascia, Michel Butor, Maurice Clavel, Alejo Carpentier, Édouard Glissant . . . À vous d'en tirer une morale (Pivot 2001, 112)

[I am very pessimistic about the future of books on the big television stations, ruled by ratings and by the spastic frenzy of channel-surfing. The proliferation of channels has brought about a segmenting of television, which shall take its toll upon books, which shall cease to be the unifying element I fought so hard to establish. In 1975, in addition to "Apostrophes," I offered nightly short interviews with writers. It was called "The Book of the Day." And was broadcast at 6:45 p.m.! In the time slot now reserved for "le Bigdil" and "Loft Story" (American-style game and reality shows, respectively), I hosted . . . Roger Caillois, André Siniavski, Roland Barthes, Michel Foucault, Michel Tournier, Jean-Loup Trassard, Leonardo Sciascia, Michel Butor, Maurice Clavel, Alejo Carpentier, Édouard Glissant . . . Draw your own conclusions.]

Pivot is right to point to the recent, nefarious effects of the television audience's fragmentation, and of "lowest common denominator" American formats like game shows and reality tv. Yet perhaps there is also something inherently contradictory, even corrosive about promoting reading on television—a phenomenon best exemplified by American public television's Barney exhorting, with a cute, show-tune-like number, "Read a book, book, book, book, book / Read a book!" as his juvenile audience remains glued to the screen, mesmerized by his purple splendor. If we agree with Mc Luhan that the medium is the message, then perhaps Pivot's shows always contained the seeds of their own destruction. In the long run, television cultivates viewers, not readers.

Hugo at 200

Il n'est pas douteux que Victor Hugo a dominé le XIXe siècle, son siècle. Mais il n'a pas dominé le XXe siècle, et je ne peux vraiment pas imaginer ce qu'il en sera pour celui qui commence.
— Alfredo Bryce-Echenique, "Le trombone du XIXe siècle." *Le Nouvel Observateur*, February 7–13, 2002

[No doubt Victor Hugo dominated his century, the 19th. But he did not dominate the 20th, and I cannot really imagine what he will be for the century just beginning.]
— Alfredo Bryce-Echenique, "The trombone of the 19th century." *Le Nouvel Observateur*, February 7–13, 2002

Perhaps it is premature to take stock of Hugo's bicentenary at this point. But we can venture some thoughts both on Hugo's renown as he enters his third century and, more broadly, on the state of literary fame in France at the dawn of the twenty-first.

For an issue published in February 2002 to coincide with Hugo's birthday, the *Nouvel Observateur* offers a cover story on "Hugo, l'écrivain universel" [Hugo, the universal writer] for which six foreign writers and a French one (Mona Ozouf) were asked to provide their own, individual views on Hugo ("raconter 'leur' Hugo" [to tell "their" Hugo]). The resulting kaleidoscope is revealing, both in the individual perspectives expressed and in their diversity. For example, in a contribution with the suggestive title "Moi et le pachyderme" [The pachyderm and I], Belgian essayist Simon Leys asserts, "Étant immense et multiforme, Hugo séduit tout particulièrement chaque lecteur pour une infinité de raisons différentes" [Immense and multifarious, Hugo exercises a quite particular sort of fascination upon each reader, for infinitely different reasons] (56). Leys' remark seems to begin by confirming Hugo's continued immensity as a public figure, yet in the second half of the sentence we realize that "Hugo" designates not the man but his work which, no longer anchoring any sort of cultural consensus, pleases each reader for different reasons—with, in Leys' case, a predilection for Hugo's letters, journals, and graphic work. In "Hugo marche droit" [Hugo walks straight], Mona Ozouf focuses instead on *Choses vues* to argue for Hugo's moral rectitude in favoring clemency and opposing capital punishment. Turkish writer Orhan Pamuk also reflects on Hugo's political *engagement*, and on what has come of such activism since:

Nous devons en partie à sa passion pour sa propre gloire l'idée d'engagement, cette politisation du «grand écrivain» rangé du côté de la justice et de la vérité, si importante, depuis Zola jusqu'à Sartre, non seulement pour les intellectuels en France, mais pour les milieux de la culture dans le monde entier. . . . [L]a France est un pays qui a toujours vécu à l'avant-garde les expériences historiques de l'humanité. Aussi chauvins qu'aient pu se montrer, à une certaine époque, les grands écrivains français, il s'adressaient toujours non seulement à la France, mais à l'humanité. Cela n'est plus le cas aujourd'hui, et on sent, dans cette commémoration par la France de l'un de ses plus grands et fantasques ancêtres, un arrière-goût de nostalgie. (58–59)

[We owe the idea of engagement, in part, to his passion for his own glory. From Zola right up to Sartre, this politicization of the "great writer," champion of justice and truth, was so important—not only for intellectuals in France, but for the intelligentsia around the world. . . . France is a country that was always in the avant-garde of humanity's historical experiments. As chauvinistic as they might have appeared at a certain time, France's great writers always spoke not only to France, but to humanity. This is no longer the case today, and in France's current commemoration of one of its greatest, most mythical ancestors, one senses an underlying nostalgia.]

Peruvian author Alfredo Bryce-Echenique certainly feels no such nostalgia for Hugo, finding him "sensiblement moins cher et moins sympathique que Fontenelle" [considerably less dear and less sympathetic than Fontenelle] (57). Bangladeshi writer Taslima Nasreen takes a more positive but just as idiosyncratic tack, opening her remarks with, "Chaque fois que je pense à Victor Hugo, je ne peux m'empêcher de songer à Rabindranath Tagore, le grand poète, romancier, dramaturge et artiste bengali" [Each time I think of Victor Hugo, I cannot help thinking of Rabindranath Tagore, the great bengali poet, novelist, playwright and artist] (52). Nasreen's ensuing evocation of the resemblances and affinities between the two writers is compelling, even touching, yet it remains hard to imagine anyone but a Bangladeshi intellectual instantly thinking of Tagore whenever Hugo is mentioned.

These and the other perspectives offered are intriguing, but perhaps most helpful by being largely besides the point. It is characteristic, for one, that in its lead into the article, the unrepentently intellectual *Nouvel Observateur* qualifies Hugo as "l'auteur de 'la Légende des siècles'" [the author of *The Legend of the Centuries*] at a time when, in light of the recent, tremendously successful musical and film versions of Hugo's two most famous novels, the general public, even in France, increasingly knows Hugo as, above all, the author of *Notre-Dame de Paris* and *Les Misérables*. At Hugo's centenary, his dominion had waned since his state funeral, and he was seen ever less as a crucial public figure and more as just an important writer. Now, at Hugo's bicentenary, there seem to be ever fewer serious readers of Hugo's work—like those featured in the *Nouvel Observateur*—yet ever more casual, or even nonreaders, particularly of these two novels. Moreover, while Hugo has for a long time not been revered widely as a "great man," his work, or at least a particular part of it, looms large in the public imagination.

Of the three main authors considered in this book, Hugo is the one who, during his lifetime and immediately afterward, most fully achieved the sort of fame he had sought—as a monumental writer—yet as this ideal of the writer has faded over time, so too has Hugo's luster as such. On the contrary, while George Sand's example remained largely unparalleled during her lifetime, over time, and particularly with the recent feminist rehabilitation of her life and work, it has opened up a significant new cultural space, in which women can be taken seriously as important writers. Likewise, while Balzac set up *The Human Comedy* as a preposthumous *oeuvres complètes* and set into motion its monumental fame-making machinery, this has also proven most effective over time. In large measure, Hugo's fame today, much like Balzac's, has little to do with his personal appeal, and is rooted instead in the popularity of his work. Of *l'homme et l'oeuvre*—the twin pillars of nineteenth- century France's literary dream of stone—it seems the work that has proven most enduring. Nonetheless, the *Nouvel Observateur* bills Hugo as "the universal writer," yet this is only true insofar as one can assemble a collection of erudite, professional writers from around the world who can find provocative things to say about their great French precursor. Considered more broadly, this label seems an oxymoron. In western and western-style liberal democracies over the course of the twentieth century, there has been a distinct loss of authorial authority, a general lowering of the stakes concerning writers, no longer seen to pose as great a potential threat, nor to offer as great a potential benefit to society. Indeed, it takes an extreme ideological context, like the collapse of the Iron Curtain or Muslim fundamentalist rule, for a writer to take on the extraliterary importance that figures like Hugo, Zola, or even still Sartre once enjoyed: thus, Vaclav Havel's rise to power in the Czech Republic or the *fatwa* pronounced against Salman Rushdie in Iran.

Ultimately, France may be witnessing the end of its distinctive literary culture, of the original and long-standing "exception culturelle" that held sway from Voltaire through Bernard Pivot. In particular, the homogenizing, leveling influence of American popular culture is providing aftershocks that may damage the dream of stone's ruins beyond recognition. This is perhaps nowhere as evident as in the worldwide success of films like Disney's 1996 *Hunchback of Notre-Dame*—well worth looking at in some brief detail for what it tells us both about Hugo today and about broader cultural transformations.

With the formidable publicity surrounding it, and its merchandising tie-ins in particular (soundtrack, lunchboxes, Quasimodo action figures, and so on), this animated marketing extravaganza might recall the earlier vogue of Hugo memorabilia. Yet, whereas Hugo's image was once ubiquitous, it is now completely absent, albeit massively supplanted by Hollywood versions of his fictional creations—notably, singing, swinging "Quasi," a sort of junior Marty Feldman who, with his soft bulging eyes, lilting limp, and flopsy hairstyle, is so ugly as to be cute, and like the American schoolkids he so obviously emulates, just longs not to be an "outcast" (fortunately, in an age before automatic weapons); or, Esmeralda, strutting her cartoon stuff in a sinuous red dress, her voice provided by Demi Moore, who feigns the same righteous indignation as always, in the same husky monotone as always. Hugo's celebrated name, once triumphantly assigned the former *avenue d'Eylau* as part of his eightieth-year celebration, does not fare much better than his image. Attribution of the story to Victor Hugo is relegated to the final credits, along with the names of the innumerable character designers, layout assistants, background artists, visual effects animators, color stylists, dialogue editors, technical production support staff, and so forth, who worked on this particular Disney feature. Specifically, after the names of the directors and that of the producer, it appears on the screen:

ANIMATION STORY BY
TAB MURPHY
From the Victor Hugo Novel
Notre-Dame de Paris

Victor Hugo is thus subordinated to Tab Murphy, and the novel to animation. Hugo's name is also recast as a modifier qualifying the kind of novel, or rather the brand of entertainment product—a now familiar corporate formulation, as in "a Walt Disney animated classic."

Within the film there is, however, an ironic remembrance of the story's original creator. Quasi's only pals are three gargoyles who, like the toys in Disney's *Toy Story* movies, are only animated when the "kid" is around. There is dignified "Victor," with his fake British blueblood accent. Victor's sidekick, vulgar "Hugo" with his "big, fat, stupid mouth," alternately stuffs his stone face with snack foods and belts out show tunes like some Gothic lounge singer. The mighty cathedral as the embodiment of Hugo's monumental stature is reduced to these pitiful fragments—perhaps alive, perhaps just a figment of Quasimodo's imagination. This is an interesting twist, with Victor Hugo existing only in the imagination of the character he imagined, and one cannot help but wonder if this vision of little dancing gargoyles is all that remains of the dream of stone.

There is also a third gargoyle pal, "Laverne" —but whence this invented name, nowhere to be found in the novel? Perhaps it is simply Hollywood tokenism to include a female gargoyle in the trio. Or perhaps, amid myriad other American pop culture allusions in the film, it recalls the 70s "buddy" sitcom, "Laverne and Shirley," suggesting the comic relief that this "Laverne, Victor, and Hugo" show, embedded in Disney's "Hunchback," is supposed to provide. Or perhaps it is a suggestion of Jules Verne, that other nineteenth-century French writer with significant name recognition for the American public, particularly among the juvenile audience that this film targets. In any case, ostensibly the oldest and wisest of the three foolish gargoyles, Laverne plays a key role at the end of the film when of course, after all, everything works out for the best (a nonindigenous concept the French call "une fin hollywoodienne," or simply "un happy ending"). Unlike in the novel, Quasimodo lives on; indeed, little Quasi gets to hang out with the popular kids Phoebus and Esmeralda and is celebrated with a final curtain call on the square before Notre-Dame, amid the crowd's acclamation—"Three cheers for Quasimodo!"—the kind of popular adulation

once accorded his creator. Still, not content to finish with this feel-good moment, the filmakers try for one more laugh. While perhaps a vague remembrance of Hugo's chapter "Paris à vol d'oiseau" [A Bird's eye view of Paris], this is certainly part of the Disney version's heavy-handed leitmotif of birds symbolizing Quasimodo's quest for freedom, and also the final instance of a kitschy shtick that punctuates the film. As the camera fades away from the cathedral and Quasimodo's apotheosis beside it, birds beset Laverne's head one last time. "Don't you ever migrate?!" she shrieks. Hollywood, not Hugo, would seem to have the last word.

Yet perhaps this is too pessimistic, too cynical. If so, how might we still assess Hugo's once-transcendant fame, two centuries after his birth, and one century after the *Maison Victor Hugo* was founded? The true measure of Hugo's stature today must lie between the *Nouvel Observateur* celebrating him as "the universal writer," and his near total absence from the Disney *Hunchback*. Part of the answer might be found in a suggestive ad for the literary websites www.auteurs.net and www.lire.fr, published in the French business magazine *Newbiz* in June 2001. Exhibiting a black and white photo of Victor Hugo clutching a colorful surfboard, it exclaims, "Si vous aimez la littérature, mettez-vous au surf!" [If you love literature, go surfing.] Singling out Hugo as the very symbol of literature, and assuming him instantly recognizable (he is not identified by name), the ad would seem to confirm Hugo's continued prominence, at least for a French audience. Still, most French people would also recognize Mickey Mouse, underscoring just how radically the French cultural context has changed in the past 100 years.

Back in an age of fervent Hugomania, collector Paul Beuve did not choose his miraculous conversion. He was chosen. Now, amid infinite consumer options, not on any such road to Damascus, but along the information superhighway, you can gaze at every imaginable perversion, rant and rave with fellow neo-Nazis, shop for Disney action figures, or visit a literary website. Online, in the privacy of your own home—far from the public realm staked out by statuemania—you can indulge what the ad calls a "passion," in this case a comparatively innocuous one for writers and their work. That once monumental edifice, France's long-standing literary dream of stone, in so far as it persists at all in an age of virtual evanescence, has drifted away from collective consensus, and toward a culture of *zapping* (i.e., channel-surfing). What Bernard Pivot calls the "spastic frenzy"of the remote control (Pivot 2001, 112) is also that of the mouse click: the fickle flicker of individual choice.

Notes

Introduction

1. In French, Baudelaire's phrase resonates with the biblical word-play on *Pierre* (Peter) and *pierre* (rock): Jesus declares to his disciple Peter, "Tu es Pierre, et sur cette pierre je bâtirai mon Église, et la Puissance de la mort n'aura pas de force contre elle. Je te donnerai les clefs du Royaume des cieux" (Matthew 16:18–19). *Pierre/pierre* is thus linked with the monumental construct of the Church (at once Saint Peter's in Rome, and all of Christianity), as well as with the prospect of eternal life. With all this cultural baggage clearly in mind, Hugo's introductory essay to an 1867 *Paris-Guide* works through Saint Peter, and Saint Peter's basilica, to contend that in the modern world, the *"urbi et orbi"* has moved from Rome to Paris, and that such a "mystérieux déplacement du pouvoir spirituel" [mysterious shift in spiritual power] is embodied in the *Panthéon* (cf. 199 above). As Philippe Muray contends, Hugo promoted and was in turn promoted by the secular cult of great men that flourished in nineteenth-century France, in opposition to traditional Christianity, and that replaced the Christian afterlife with a vision of the *Panthéon* as a latter-day Elysian fields for humanity's great men—culminating, of course, in Hugo's spectacular "pantheonization."

2. Nadar planned originally to produce four lithographs: one with literary celebrities, another with theatrical celebrities, another with artistic celebrities, and another with musical celebrities. Only the first of these was produced. Despite the stir caused by its publication, Nadar's literary pantheon was not a commercial success, so he abandoned plans for the others. Instead, when he published a revised *Panthéon* in 1858, he included some of the figures, like the composer Rossini, who would have figured in the other three lithographs.

While Nadar does not seem to have used photography for documenting his *Panthéon* before 1854, "il est certain qu'en janvier 1854, Nadar a recours à la photographie au moment où il rassemble les portraits de femmes de lettres qui apparaîtront, non caricaturés, dans son *Panthéon*" [it is certain that in January 1854, Nadar relied upon photography as he gathered together the portraits of women writers who would appear, not caricatured, in his *Pantheon*] (Chotard 81). His brother Adrien, who had been dabbling in the new medium since 1853, was apparently the photographer here. Nadar himself began experimenting with photography between February and April 1854 (Chotard 82); the *Panthéon* was published in March.

3. "Augustus founded two public libraries, among the earliest in Rome, one connected with the Temple of Apollo on the Palatine Hill (close to his house) and the other on the Campus Martius, perhaps connected with the Temple of Mars the Avenger. Each contained a collection of Greek or Roman authors housed in rooms decorated with busts and medallions of the great writers—the first hall of fame. In the earliest Roman public library, founded by Pollio the historian a few years before, only one living author was so honored, and Horace notes with satisfaction that Augustus had included many" (Braudy 119).

4. Examples include: Alexandre Dumas *père*'s *Les Crimes célèbres* [Famous crimes] (original edition 1839–40) and *Les Grands hommes en robe de chambre* [Great men in their dressing gowns] (original edition, 1855–56), as well as Maurice Alhoy's *Les Brigands et bandits célèbres* [Famous brigands and bandits] (1845).

5. Cf. Morel, *Achille Devéria, témoin du romantisme parisien, 1800–1857* [Achille Devéria, a witness to parisian romanticism, 1800–1857]; Guillaume and Le Men, *Benjamin Roubaud et Le Panthéon Charivarique*; Chotard, *Nadar: Caricatures, photographies* 44–48; 144–149 below, on Durat's *Photobiographies*; and McCauley, *Industrial Madness: Commercial Photography in Paris*, 1848–71, on Disdéri and the *carte de visite*.

While Roubaud prefigured Nadar the caricaturist (cf. Guillaume and Le Men, and Chotard), Devéria was an important precursor of Nadar the photographic portraitist:

Les portraits les plus réussis de Devéria . . . Nous donnent une impression d'aisance, de naturel qui vient sans doute des relations familières que l'artiste entretenait avec ses modèles; Devéria a su rendre sans affectation aucune, mais avec beaucoup d'élégance, la spontanéité de leurs attitudes et de leurs poses. Son grand mérite est d'aller à l'essentiel, de savoir résumer en quelques traits une silhouette. . . . Le décor reste secondaire et n'est qu'à peine esquissé. . . . L'attention de Devéria se concentre sur les traits du visage, sur les expressions. . . . Au milieu du siècle, lorsque la photographie détrônera la lithographie, comme mode de représentation à bon marché, les portraitistes professionnels avec en tête Nadar, n'oublieront pas les leçons de Devéria. (Morel 11)

[Devéria's most successful portraits . . . Give us an impression of ease, of naturalness that comes, no doubt, from the familiar relations that the artist maintained with his models; Devéria knew how, with no affectation but a great deal of elegance, to render the spontaneity in their attitudes and poses. His great gift is to go right to the heart of things, to be able to capture a silhouette in a few lines. . . . The background remains secondary, and is just scarcely sketched out. . . . Devéria's attention concentrates on facial features, on expressions. . . . At the middle of the century, as photography outstripped lithography as an inexpensive means of representation, professional portraitists, and most notably Nadar, would not forget Devéria's lessons.]

6. Joan of Arc is a particularly interesting, polyvalent figure: at once masculine and feminine, and appropriated as both Catholic and secular, republican exemplar.

7. In her correspondance, Sand equivocated tellingly on her identification with the latter: in 1833, she wrote, "Je ne me convainquis pas assez d'une chose, c'est que j'étais absolument et complètement *Lélia*. Je voulus me persuader que non, j'espérai pouvoir abjurer ce rôle froid et odieux" [I could not convince myself enough of one thing—that I was absolutely and completely Lélia. I wanted to persuade myself of the contrary, I hoped to be able to renounce this cold, odious role] (Corr. 2.374); in 1836, "Lélia n'est pas moi. Je suis meilleure enfant que cela; mais c'est mon idéal" [Lélia is not me. I'm nicer than that, but that's my ideal] (Corr. 3.403).

Chapter 1. The Dream of Stone

1. This work remains a touchstone for intellectuals on the left: the 1977 edition features a preface by François Mitterrand.

2. Symbolism diverged somewhat from this tendency, however, through its involvement in *vers libre*.

3. Even when transformed into a church bell, though, the bronze continues to cast its evil spell on the village where it was unearthed.

4. Cf. André Fermigier, "Mérimée et l'Inspection des monuments historiques" [Mérimée and the Inspection of historical monuments], Nora 1.1599–1614.

5. Cf. Bruno Foucart, "Viollet-le-Duc et la restauration" [Viollet-le-Duc and restoration], Nora 1.1615–43.

6. Along similar lines, Flaubert's *Dictionnaire des idées reçues* offers this definition: "PYRAMIDE: Ouvrage inutile" [PYRAMID: Useless work] (Bouvard et Pécuchet 548).

7. This was written in the margin, beneath the last lines of the poem "Claire"; while the poem is dated 1846—when Juliette Drouet's daughter Claire Pradier, for whom it was written, died—the manuscript is marked "27 Xbre 1854" (*Oeuvres poétiques* 2: notes, 755, 853), which is probably when both the poem and this fragment were written. Here it seems, as elsewhere in *Les Contemplations*, Hugo manipulated dates for effect.

8. Paris: Librairie Joseph Gibert, n.d. 493.

9. Il y a deux espèces de livres rares: premièrement, ceux qui sont dignes d'êtres réimprimés, et l'imprimerie y pourvoira, si elle n'y a pas pourvu; secondement, ceux dont la rareté fait tout le prix, et que la *litho-typographie* reproduirait à cent mille, sans atténuer la valeur de l'édition originale, parce que cette valeur consiste dans l'identité de la chose et non pas dans sa figure. [There are two types of rare books: first, those worth reprinting, and the publishing industry shall provide for that, if it has not done so already; secondly, those whose value resides entirely in its rareness, and which litho-typography would reproduce in one-hundred thousand copies, without affecting the value of the original edition, for this value consists of the thing's identity, not its appearance] ("La *litho-typographie*," 238–39)

10. Cf. "La *litho-typographie*" 241–42 for some interesting considerations on how the development of lithographic facsimiles might affect the value of older versus newer bindings.

11. Albert-Ernest Carrier-Belleuse (1824–87) made the bronze statue of Dumas, which stood in Villers-Cotterêts until being destroyed during World War II. Its terra cotta model, from about 1883, is preserved in the Getty Museum.

12. Toward the end of his life, Ménard (1822–1901) campaigned vigorously for orthographic reform, and against vivisection (Peyre 449–51).

13. Abel Hermant, in his inaugural speech for the Falguière Balzac monument, covers much similar ground:

L'auteur de ce monument national a eu, messieurs, une fortune unique dans l'histoire des lettres: presque tous les inventeurs traînent à leur suite une queue d'imitateurs encombrante et compromettante—Balzac a laissé une lignée. Il n'a pas créé que son oeuvre—il a créé une littérature.
Il est exceptionnel de se survivre, il est plus rare de se continuer : Balzac se continue et il se propage. Sa race, voilà le vrai monument de sa gloire. Mais nos imaginations positives en exigeaient un plus matériel, la personnalité d'une effigie, la trompeuse permanence du marbre. C'est pourquoi notre piété filiale s'est obstinée à lui élever ce socle et cette statue; et maintenant les voilà en place pour ce que durent les édifices humains. (60–61)

[Gentlemen, the author honored by this national monument had a unique destiny in the history of letters: nearly all inventors drag along in their path a cumbersome and compromising crowd of imitators; Balzac left a lineage. Not only did he create his work—he created a new literature.
It is exceptional to survive, it is rarer to be continued. Balzac has been continued, and propagated. His lineage is the true monument to his glory. But our positive imaginations required a more material one, an effigy's embodiment, marble's deceptive permanence. That is why our filial piety drove us to raise this pedestal and this statue, and now here they are, in their place, for as long as human edifices endure.]

Chapter 2. Honoré de Balzac

1. Ambitious Bernard-François Balssa was born in 1746 to a peasant family of eleven children. Burning to succeed in the world, he appropriated the name of a once prominent but by then defunct local family, the aristocratic Balzac d'Entragues. His eldest son was named simply Honoré Balzac, but in 1802, with the birth of a second daughter—and with Napoleon firmly in power, authorizing such pretensions by example—he dared add the nobiliary particle, which the family used intermittently from then on.

2. On the extraordinary diffractions of identity in Stendhal's writing, see Gérard Genette, "'Stendhal,'" *Figures II*.

3. The murder may instead have been committed by a local notary named Albar, relative of yet another local Maître Albar, Bernard-François Balzac's first employer.

4. Cf. for example the saga of Lucien de Rubempré in *Lost Illusions* and *Harlot High and Low*.

5. "Mar" was his nickname among the "Berrichon" group (including Belloy, George Sand, and Jules Sandeau); "Mar O'C" was not only a bad word play on "Maroc," but also reminiscent, with its fake anglo-Irish consonance, of his earlier literary pseudonym "Lord R'Hoone."

6. Pierre Barbéris emphasizes quite rightly the way in which, through the elaboration of "biographies mythiques"

(21), "ces pseudonymes . . . vont devenir des personnages, de plus de présence et de plus de réalité, souvent, que les 'héros' dont ils sont censés transmettre l'histoire" [these pseudonyms . . . would become characters, often with more presence and reality than the "heroes" whose stories they were supposed to be transmitting] (13–14).

7. Balzac thus incorporates the nobiliary particle into his definitive literary signature at the same time he assumes his public role as novelist. His imagination would in fact continue to link "novels" and the dubious possession of the nobiliary particle, as a revealing oversight in *La Cousine Bette* suggests: Crevel refers to a certain "Mlle de Romans" although, as the Pléiade editor notes, "la demoiselle Romans n'avait . . . pas droit à la particule dont B. la gratifie" [Miss Romans had no right to the particle which Balzac accorded her] (cf. note, 8.64).

8. As Nicole Mozet observes, "il y [a] un péril très relatif à avouer une oeuvre à succès, et dont la paternité n'était plus un secret" [there is a very relative danger in avowing a work that was a success, and whose authorship was no longer a secret] (*Balzac au pluriel* 14).

9. Within the romantic imagination, and especially for Balzac, signing—putting the very core of one's being *on the line*—is glorified as a deeply heroic act. As José-Luis Diaz notes, "l'héroisme romantique va mettre une prédilection particulière à idéaliser, dans tous les événements de la vie collective et surtout littéraire, le courage du signataire, palladin de ces temps où—refrain connu—la plume a remplacé l'épée." [romantic heroism would have a particular predilection for idealizing, in all facets of public and especially literary life, the courage of the signer, that warrior for these times in which—familiar refrain—the pen has replaced the sword] (27).

10. Already in 1825, for example, he had signed "Honoré de Balzac" for the first time in his correspondence in a letter to the duchesse d'Abrantès, which deals with authors who conceal their true identities:

> Plus que personne, je vous jure, je connais les exigences et la pudeur des auteurs, et je ne suis pas homme à déchirer le voile dont vous couvrez vos écrits, comme ces fleuristes qui jettent un[e] gaze sur leurs guirlandes commencées.
> [More than anyone, I swear, I know the needs and modesty of authors, and I am not one to tear the veil with which you cover your writings, like those florists who throw gauze upon the garlands they have begun.]
> (22 July 1825, 1.267–71; editor Roger Pierrot notes here the "[p]remière apparition de la particule dans la signature de Balzac" [first appearance of the particle in Balzac's signature].

This crucial rehearsal of Balzac's future literary signature thus takes place under the sign of authorial pseudonymity. In much the same way, Balzac's most fervent apology of his signature, in the 1836 *Historique du procès du Lys dans la Vallée*, ends by invoking the examples of Voltaire and Molière, the most famous pseudonyms in french literature! In attempting to assert the legitimacy of his identity, Balzac inevitably points up its spuriousness.

11. To be sure, "Honoré de Balzac" is not a pseudonym from a strictly juridical point of view, for without the particle, this name already figures on the author's birth certificate, and the adoption of the particle has many precedents in his family. From a less legalistic standpoint,

however, "Honoré de Balzac" must be seen as profoundly pseudonymous.

12. This obsession with name and signature, particularly striking in Balzac's case, was typical of his day as well. Amid the dislocations of identity in the wake of the Revolution, there arose a correspondent, cratylistic desire for name and person to match. Eusèbe Salverte's influential *Essai sur les noms*, for example, begins, "Notre nom propre, c'est nous-mêmes" [Our proper name is ourself] (1), a line which Balzac quotes in *La Peau de Chagrin* (CH 10.199). Indeed, this view finds particular resonance with Balzac, both in defense of his own name and in commentary on his characters' names, as in the novella *Z. Marcas*.

What is true for the name is even more so for the signature, the most extreme form of the name, the mark of identity at once most elusive and illusory, yet also most heavily invested with meaning. The signature becomes radically dislocated from its signer as it is swept up into the complex textual systems of the period's burgeoning legal, economic, political, and literary institutions. Post-structuralist theory has advanced essentially the same conception of the signature as a fundamentally unstable, "undecidable trait" (Kamuf 13), yet failed to recognize that in the nineteenth century, this view coexisted with its antithesis. In his 1850 "Physiologie de quelques signatures" ["Physiology of some signatures"], for example, Auguste Vitu celebrates this mystical token of a person's essential being:

> La signature, c'est un emblème, un chiffre cabalistique, un chiffre maçonnique, un monogramme physiologique où se réfugient la passion et ce qu'il y a de plus fugitif dans l'expression suprême de l'individualité. (*Livre des 400 auteurs* 58)
>
> [The signature is an emblem, a cabalistic cipher, a masonic cipher, a physiological monogram in which there resides passion, and all that is hardest to capture, within the supreme expression of individuality.]

José-Luis Diaz explains that the signature constitutes "le mode romantique privilégié d'affirmation, d'intensification et d'appropriation du nom propre" [the preferred romantic mode for affirmation, intensification and appropriation of the proper name] (27). If in the romantic imagination the name serves as nucleus for the author's persona, the signature serves in turn as nucleus for the name: within concentric circles of identity, the innermost circle would be the signature, focal point of an "insularité individuelle irréductible" [irreducible individual insularity] (27).

13. This has sometimes been called the "Notice Sandeau-Balzac," since Balzac used Sandeau's name to sign it, as he did with Félix Davin's for the "Introduction aux études philosophiques."

14. Namely: Albar, the name of both the *notaire* under whom he began his career and the one who may have committed the murder for which Louis was condemned; Joseph d'Albert, *maître des requêtes*, to whom Bernard-François served as secretary; and Albi, the Balssa's home town, where his brother was executed.

15. It is the antithesis of the name "Scribonius," deriving from "scribe," which Balzac bestowed upon himself in

a text with the suggestive name, *Les Martyres ignorés*. In this study dating from 1837, "Balzac s'est mis en scène lui-même, comme auditeur, sous le nom de Scribonius (remplacé par celui de Raphaël sur les épreuves)" (Bardèche, *Balzac* 101). Replaced by "Raphaël," "Scribonius" had itself replaced the pronoun "Moi" (cf. 12.719–51), betraying Balzac's ongoing desire to appropriate a "writerly" name.

16. Cf. Dugas de la Boissonny, particularly chapter 1, 'L'Histoire de l'état civil.' For clarity's sake, I shall use the term "secular" *état civil*, although this risks redundancy (secular = civil); furthermore, speaking of an *état civil* before the Revolutionary period is an anachronism. One would in fact need to distinguish between a "proto-" *état civil* before the Revolution and a true *état civil* after.

17. According to the article on "État" in *La Grande Encyclopédie,*

> La naissance, en effet, n'est pas un fait purement naturel: une autre vie physique commence avec elle, c'est la vie civile; elle fait du nouvel être, en même temps qu'une individualité morale et juridique, une entité de droit; elle en fait en un mot une personne civile. . . . Sans l'*état civil* . . . l'homme ne serait rien; il n'aurait ni nationalité, ni famille; il serait dans ce que l'utopiste appelle l'état de nature.

> [In effect, birth is not a purely natural thing: another physical life begins with it, namely civil life; it makes the new being not only a moral and juridical individual, but also a legal entity; in a word, it makes him a civil person. . . . Without the *état civil* . . . man would be nothing; he would have neither nationality, nor family; he would be in what the utopianist calls the state of nature.]

Similarly, in *De l'état civil en France*, we find,

> Sans l'État civil, vous êtes étranger dans votre patrie, ou plutôt vous n'avez point de patrie: vous êtes sans nom, sans parents, sans héritage; vous n'avez nul droit à exercer comme membre du corps social, nulle répétition à faire, nul avantage à prétendre.

> [Without the État civil, you are a foreigner in your own country, or rather you have no country: you are without name, without heritage; you have no right to exercise as a member of the citizenry, no role to play, no advantage to enjoy.]

18. "Jusque vers 1880, l'individu astucieux peut changer de peau à son gré: pour se procurer un nouvel *état civil,* il lui suffit de connaître la date et le lieu de naissance du camarade dont il a décidé d'usurper l'identité: la rencontre, assez improbable, d'un témoin pourra seule déjouer le subterfuge; encore la reconnaissance, fondée sur la seule mémoire visuelle, pourra-t-elle aisément être contestée. On comprend mieux dès lors la terreur inspiré par le monstre ou le vengeur qui se dissimule sous une fausse identité. Les métamorphoses de Jacques Colin [sic], le destin de Jean Valjean, la stratégie d'Edmond Dantès ne devaient guère paraître invraisemblables aux lecteurs de ce temps" (Perrot 4.429–30).

[Up until around 1880, a clever individual can change skin at will: in order to procure a new *état civil*, he needs only to know the date and place of birth of an acquaintance whose identity he has decided to usurp: only the fairly unlikely meeting of a witness could uncover the subterfuge; and still, such recognition, based on visual memory alone, could easily be contested. One therefore understands better the terror inspired by the monster or revenge seeker hidden beneath a false identity. Jacques Collin's metamorphoses, Jean Valjean's destiny, Edmond Dantès's strategy would scarcely have seemed improbable to readers of the time.]

19. This has apparently continued to hold true in France, for in the "affaire des prénoms bretons" [breton given names affair], six children "nondéclarés devant l'*État civil* étaient considérés comme inexistants" [not declared before the *État civil* were considered as nonexistent] (Marquant 79). Between the late 1950s and early 1960s, "L'officier d'*État civil* auquel ces . . . naissances furent déclarées, refusa de les enregistrer, au motif que les prénoms donnés par la mère à ses enfants ne figuraient pas sur le manuel d'*État civil*" [The *État civil* officer to whom these births were declared refused to record them, on the grounds that the names the mother gave to her children did not figure in the *État civil* handbook] (Marquant 78).

20. True to a legend about his Renaissance namesake, Raphaël de Valentin dies of an excess of desire. Vasari claims that the amorous painter, always ready to pursue carnal pleasures, "on one occasion indulged in more than his usual excess" (Giorgio Vasari. "Raphaël," in: *The Great Masters* [selections from *The Lives of the Artists*]. New York: Hugh Lauter Levin Associates, 1986, p. 202) and thus returned home with a "violent fever" from which he soon died. As the story goes, it was his uncontrollable passion for his cherished mistress, *La Fornarina* (the similarity between the names "Fornarina" and "Foedora" is striking), which killed him. Likewise, Raphaël de Valentin, overwhelmed by "un de ces désirs furieux" [one of those furious desires] (357), dies clinging to his beloved Pauline. One of the salient features of the renewed interest in Raphael ushered in by the Romantic movement was precisely a fascination with the Fornarina legend: Ingres, for example, painted four versions of *Raphael and the Fornarina* over a period of almost fifty years (John Pope-Hennessey. Raphaël: *The Wrightsman Lectures*. New York: New York University Press, 1970, p. 11.) Balzac was also well aware of the legend, referring to it in several texts (including *Splendeurs et misères des courtisanes* and *Secrets de la Princesse de Cadignan*; 6, 475 and 964, respectively). In *La Peau de chagrin*, Raphaël muses, "Vieux guerrier, une phtisie vous dévore; diplomate, un anévrisme suspend dans votre coeur la mort à un fil; moi, peut-être une pulmonie va me dire: 'Partons!' comme elle a dit jadis à Raphaël d'Urbin, tué par un excès d'amour" [An old warrior is devoured by consumption; an aneurism leaves a diplomat's heart hanging onto life by a thread; me, perhaps lung disease will tell me: "Let's go!", much like Raphael of Urbino who, long ago, died of amorous excesses] (10, 198)

"Valentin" is the name of an illustrious Christian martyr who, for obscure reasons, became the patron saint of lovers. In the name of the martyred "sweetheart's saint," Eros and Thanatos meet; appropriately, Raphaël de Valentin's death, like Raphael Sanzio's, is precipitated by his sexual impulses. Dying in a paroxysm of lust, Raphaël is destroyed by desiring—reënacting the destiny of his renaissance namesake and fulfilling the narrative program of the peau itself ("A chaque vouloir je décroîtrai comme tes jours" [With each wish I shall shrink like your days; 10, 84]).

The Faustian overtones in *La Peau de chagrin* are obvious—the Mephistophelian antiquary, the fatal contract, and so on—and indeed several explicit references to Goethe's *Faust* are made in the text (cf. p. 44 and 259). In this play moreover, the character named Valentin, Gretchen's brother, appears on stage in one brief but dramatic scene: he laments his sister's disgrace, meets Mephistopheles and Faust, and engages in a duel with the latter. Mephistopheles makes the young soldier's hand go lame, allowing Faust to wound him mortally. Before dying, Valentin makes a long speech cursing his sister for her sins. There are several parallels with Raphaël de Valentin. Raphaël also engages in a duel whose outcome is determined by supernatural intervention. In Raphaël's case, his adversary's weapon is stymied by occult forces, a reversal of terms which can be explained through antiphrasis, in so many ways the dominant figure in this text. Like his Faustian namesake, the young de Valentin addresses a small group of listeners with a "death sentence"—that of the *peau*—hanging over his head. The young soldier seems only to appear on the scene to die; his death is delayed, however, by his speech, much as the textual moment of Raphaël's death is by the narration of his "autobiography."

21. Félicien Marceau suggests as much in considering "la revue des invités chez les Nucingen" [the listing of guests at the Nucingen's] in *Splendeurs et misères des courtisanes*. For readers familiar only with this novel, the names listed simply evoke "une brillante assemblée" [a sparkling get-together]; however,

Pour les autres, c'est un éblouissement. En quelques lignes, voici . . . quinze destins, quinze perspectives, quinze fenêtres . . . voici l'amour de Louise de Chaulieu, les passades de Mme de Maufrigneuse, les intrigues de Mme d'Espard, le charmant mariage de Mme Firmiani, le lâche abandon d'Ajuda, le drame du *Lys dans la vallée*, le génie de Félicité des Touches. [27–28]

[For others, it is a revelation. In a few lines, here are fifteen destinies, fifteen perspectives, fifteen windows . . . Here is Louise de Chaulieu's love, Mme de Maufrigneuse's affairs, Mme d'Espard's machinations, Mme Firmiani's charming marriage, d'Ajuda's cowardly desertion, the drama of the *Lily in the valley*, Félicité des Touches's genius.]

22. Pugh describes recurring names as containing "overtones" or carrying a certain "weight of association" (464), and characterizes the technique as a sort of "shorthand" (223). In much the same way, Butor characterizes the technique as "une ellipse romanesque" [a novelistic ellipsis] or as "un principe d'économie" [an economizing principle] (252).

23. This question is posed from the beginning. The same clerk who calls Chabert "notre vieux carrick" (a type of overcoat, already outmoded at the time) reproaches the *saute-ruisseau* for throwing a piece of bread at the old man: "Quelque pauvre que soit un client, c'est toujours un homme, que diable!"[However poor the client, it's still a man, damn it!] Recognizing the incoherence of the clerk's position, the *saute-ruisseau* remarks, "Si c'est un homme, pourquoi l'appelez-vous vieux carrick?" [If it's

a man, why do you call it an old overcoat?] (3.311–12). Similarly, Chabert is described as a dog (3.315, 330).

24. "Suis-je mort ou suis-je vivant?" [Am I dead or am I alive?] Chabert asks Derville (3.333).

25. Significantly, this is also described as a space in which people can be buried beneath piles of legal paperwork: Boucard's face remains "ensevelie dans un monceau d'actes" [buried in a pile of documents].

26. His "naturalness" is underscored by his given name, "Hyacinthe," and by the fact that in French, an illegitimate child is an "enfant naturel," and a foundling can be called a "champi," that is, a child of the fields, as in George Sand's *François le Champi*.

27. At one point, Chabert says to his wife, "Les morts ont donc bien tort de revenir?" [The dead are quite wrong to come back?] (3.360).

28. "ce crâne était épouvantable à voir. La première pensée que suggérait l'aspect de cette blessure était celle-ci: 'Par là s'est enfuie l'intelligence!'" [this skull was horrible to see. The first thought that the appearance of this injury suggested was, "From there his intelligence fled!"] (3.222).

29. The key difference though between this work and a true *conte fantastique* is that the reader, assured from the outset of the old man's identity as Chabert, is not made to hesitate between these competing versions. Paradoxically moreover, the "reasonable" version of the story casts the old man as a *revenant*: not an actual "ghost" though, but rather "one who has come back." The alternate version of the story delves into the abyss of insanity, of an old beggar fancying himself a Napoleonic war hero.

30. Particularly in the work of Mérimée (cf. "La Vénus d'Ille" and "Lokis").

31. Balzac typically refers to Hoffmann as "le Berlinois" (e.g., 5.359).

32. "Vous étiez chez la" suggests that Mme Ferraud was simply a *fille* in a bordello, and not a more glamorous *courtisane*.

33. Cf., for example, *Illusions perdues*: "L'exemple de Napoléon, si fatal au dixneuvième siècle par les prétentions qu'il inspire à tant de gens médiocres, apparut à Lucien qui jeta ses calculs au vent en se les reprochant" [Napoleon's example, so fatal to the nineteenth century through the pretentions it inspires in so many mediocre people, appeared to Lucien who threw his plans to the wind while reproaching himself for doing so] (5.178).

34. An isolated enclave on the fringes of society, the Bicêtre asylum might as well be St. Helena.

35. The words "biographie" and "biographe" first appeared in French in 1721; the adjective "biographique" made its debut just over a half-century later, in 1762 (*Petit Robert*). In English, Dryden was apparently first to use "biography" in 1683, Addison to use "biographer" in 1715, and Oldys to use "biographical" in 1738 (*Oxford English Dictionary*).

36. Cf., for example, James Olney, *Memory and Narrative: the Weave of Life-Writing* (Chicago: University Chicago Press, 1998) or Suzette A. Henke, *Shattered Subjects: Trauma and Testimony in Women's Life-Writing* (New York: St. Martin's, 1998).

37. "Le lexicographe du XIXe siècle touche . . . au mythe de Babel: il construit un monument, image de la totalité

du monde; et un monument de papier aussi durable que le monument de pierre. . . . Larousse écrit dans sa préface, . . . à propos de *L'Encyclopédie* de Diderot: 'Salut à cette oeuvre immortelle; découvrons-nous, inclinons-nous devant ce monument de l'esprit humain, comme nous le ferions au parvis du Panthéon, de Saint-Pierre de Rome ou de Notre-Dame de Paris, que nous contemplerions pour la première fois'" [The nineteenth-century lexicographer flirts with the myth of Babel: he constructs a monument, image of the world's totality; and a monument of paper as durable as one of stone. . . . Larousse writes in his preface, a propos Diderot's *Encyclopedia*, "Hail to this immortal work, let's tip our hats, let's bow before this monument of the human mind, as we would upon the square before the Pantheon, Saint Peter of Rome, or Notre-Dame de Paris, were we to contemplate them for the first time"] (Savy and Vigne 34)

38. To wit: *Biographie universelle classique, ou dictionnaire historique portatif, par une société de gens de lettres* [Universal classical biography, or portable historical dictionary, by a literary society]. Paris: Charles Gosselin, Libraire-Éditeur, 1829; *Biographie universelle et portative des contemporains, ou dictionnaire historique des hommes vivants et des hommes morts depuis 1788 et jusqu'à nos jours, qui se sont fait remarqués par leurs écrits, leurs actions, leurs talents, leurs vertus ou leurs crimes* [Universal and portable biography of contemporaries, or historical dictionary of men living and dead from 1788 and until our day, who have become known for their writings, their actions, their talents, their virtues or their crimes]. Rabbe, Vieilh de Boisjolin, and Sainte-Preuve, eds. Second edition. Paris: Chez l'éditeur, rue du Colombier, 21, 1836 (according to the "Avertissement des éditeurs," the first edition was out of print by 1830, but the revolution stalled plans for its reissue); *Biographie universelle et portative des contemporains* [Universal and portable biography of contemporaries]; *Biographie universelle des hommes qui se sont fait un nom* [Universal biography of men who made a name for themselves]; *Biographie universelle des hommes qui se sont fait un nom par leur génie, leurs talents, leurs vertus, leurs erreurs ou leurs crimes* [Universal biography of men who made a name for themselves through their genius, their talents, their virtues, their errors or their crimes]. Par F.-X Feller; revue, classée par ordre chronologique, continuée jusqu'en 1845. Paris: Poussielgue-Rusand, Libraire, 1845 (based on Feller's earlier *Dictionnaire historique*); and, *Nouvelle biographie universelle depuis les temps les plus reculés jusqu'à nos jours* [New universal biography from the most distant past until our day]. M. le docteur Hoefer, ed. Paris: Firmin Didot frères, éditeurs, 1852.

39. This is the world of Mme de Bargeton and Lucien de Rubempré, her "grand homme de province," in Balzac's *Illusions perdues*.

40. Alexandre Dumas père was not only a prolific writer of fiction; he was probably the most prolific biographer among nineteenth-century novelists as well: in addition to memoirs of Talma and Garibaldi, and biographies of Leonardo da Vinci, Michelangelo, Raphael Sanzio, Joan of Arc, Louis XIV, Louix XV, Louis XVI, and Napoleon, he also wrote a pair of biographical anthologies, *Les Crimes célèbres* [Famous crimes] and *Les Grands hommes en robe*

de chambre [Great men in their dressing gowns], particularly interesting in their treatment of fame.

41. "Brillat-Savarin," p. 93. As far as I have been able to tell, the first dictionary to include an entry on Balzac is Firmin Didot's *Nouvelle biographie universelle* (1852): the overall tone is laudatory, albeit with many qualifications and reservations.

Chapter 3. George Sand

1. Quoted in Germaine de Staël, *Dix années d'exil* [Ten years of exile] (Paris: 10/18, 1966): 253.

2. Cf. Erica Cocke, "Corinne and Consuelo: Women Artists in Dialogue with the World," 247–52, David A. Powell, ed., *Le Siècle de George Sand* (Rodopi, Amsterdam, and Atlanta, 1998).

3. The image thus condemns Sand's "prolixité dépréciative" [degrading prolixity], argues Czyba: "non gauchère, la romancière écrit pourtant ici de la main gauche, sans surveiller du regard ce qu'elle écrit, machinalement, pour ainsi dire, comme si lui importait seulement le nombre de volumes sur lesquels prendre assise" [while not left-handed, the novelist writes here however with her left hand, without keeping an eye on what she writes, mechanically as it were, as if it only mattered to her how many volumes she managed to fill] (1995, 15).

4. "La vie de George Sand et son talent passent par les mêmes phases et les mêmes aventures [que ses héroïnes]," argues Jacob in his preface. "Comme il arrive à propos de tous les artistes prédestinés, sa vie est écrite dans ses livres" [George Sand's life and talent pass through the same phases and adventures as her heroines . . . As it happens with all predestined artists, her life is written in her books] (i).

5. Cf. Michael D. Garval, "Visions of the Great Woman Writer: Imagining George Sand through Word and Image," *Le Siècle de George Sand*, David A. Powell, ed., Amsterdam: Rodopi, 1998, 213–24.

6. I am indebted to my colleague Afroz Taj for this clarification.

7. There do not, however, seem to be any significant connections between Pictet's narrative and Sand's *Laura, Voyage dans le cristal* [Laura, Voyage in crystal], published in the *Revue des deux mondes* in January 1864 and, the following year, in the collection *Laura: Voyages et impressions*. This is a text whose affinities lie instead with the work of E. T. A. Hoffman and Jules Verne (cf. Pearson-Stamps).

8. Commending Sand for having said little of her own life in her autobiography (unlike in "l'histoire de très mauvais goût de: *Elle et Lui*" [that story in such bad taste, *She and He*]), the *Trombinoscope* notes, "Les hommes—et surtout les femmes—de génie sont en général de pauvres malades dont la vie privée est pleine d'étrangetés" [Men—and especially women—of genius are in general poor sick creatures whose private life is full of strange things].

9. By now, printing technology had evolved to allow the reproduction of photographs in large-circulation periodicals such as *L'Illustration*. This portrait of Sand, almost identical to the pose featured forty years earlier in the same publication, is captioned simply "George Sand grand'mère."

10. This is the case, notably, of David d'Angers: "Au cours de sa carrière, le sculpteur applique une classification qui peut paraître naïve: les hommes morts ont droit à une statue, les grands génies bénéficient d'un buste et les simples talents d'un médaillon" [Through his career, the sculptor applied a classification that can seem naive: dead men are entitled to a statue, great geniuses are accorded a bust and simple talents a medallion] (Huchard et al.12).

11. Ernest Legouvé (1807–1903), poet, novelist, playwright and musicologist, was the author, notably, of *Le Mérite des femmes* [Women's merit], an *Histoire morale des femmes* [Moral history of women], and *La Femme en France au XIXe siècle* [Women in 19th-century France].

12. "L'architecte du piédestal est M. Genuys.... Sur la face de droite est une liste de ses ouvrages: *Valentine, André, Simon, Mauprat, François le Champi, le Meunier d'Angibault, la Mare au Diable, le Péché de M. Antoine, la Petite Fadette*, etc. liste qui se continue sur les autres faces du piédestal" [M. De Genuys is the pedestal's architect.... On the right face is a list of her works: *Valentine, André, Simon, Mauprat, François le Champi, The Miller of Angibault, The Devil's Pond, M. Antoine's Sin, Little Fadette*, etc. a list that continues on the pedestal's other faces] ("La Statue de George Sand" 87).

13. Unlike Millet, Sicard is virtually forgotten today. In his time, however, he enjoyed relative success as a 1891 prix de Rome recipient and creator of such works as the *Monument de la Révolution* in the Pantheon, *Le bon Samaritain* in the Luxembourg Gardens, the *Monument de Clémenceau* in Saint-Hermine (Vendée), the *Archibald Fountain* in Sydney, Australia, and the graceless 1926 monument to Sarah Bernhardt (cf. E. Bénézit, *Dictionnaire critique et documentaire des peintres, sculpteurs, dessinateurs et graveurs*; the *Grove Dictionary of Art* 2.769; and, Hargrove 288–89 and 295).

Chapter 4. Victor Hugo

1. "Victor Hugo" was later changed to "Canalis" as Balzac developed the recurring character of Canalis the poet (cf. chapter 1).

2. This is how Hugo is portrayed as well in Eugène Ionesco's *Hugoliade*.

3. The twin banners atop the cathedral, inscribed waggishly with "Orientales" and "Occidentales," allude not only to Hugo's work (he published *Les Orientales* in 1828), but also to the split between "orientalizing" romantics and "occidentalizing" classics which persisted, like the historical rupture between the eastern and western churches, despite "papal" efforts at reconciliation.

4. The entry for "CÉLÉBRITÉ" reads,

Dénigrer quand même les célébrités, en signalant leurs défauts privés.
Musset se saoulait.
Balzac était criblé de dettes.
Hugo est avare. (496)

[Denigrate celebrities anyway, pointing out their personal faults.
Musset got drunk.

Balzac was in serious debt.
Hugo is a miser.]

5. *Essais. Livre 3*. Paris: Garnier Flammarion, 1979, p. 327

6. Along these lines, Claude Roy asserts that Hugo could be considered "le Barnum de la poésie" [the Barnum of poetry] (preface).

7. Hugo's journals provide a wealth of information about his sexual conquests, often written in Spanish. After his encounter with Mme Baà, for example, he noted, "La primera negra de mi vida" (Maurois 515). The last "act" recorded in his journal dates from April 5,1885 (Maurois 563, Escholier 628); he died May 22.

8. For example: Gustave Staal's full-page illustration of Victor Hugo at his son Charles' deathbed, entitled "La douleur d'un grand poète" [The sorrow of a great poet], on the cover of *La Chronique Illustrée*, March 26, 1871 (Georgel 121).

9. Clark sees exile as the culmination of what she calls Hugo's "political poetics":

[Hugo's] political poetics was nowhere more clearly marked, or more magnificent, than in his self-imposed exile.... Characteristically, Hugo's finest hour was the most dramatic, the exile during which he spoke to France as a Frenchman—from a distance.... From the rocky promontory facing the coast of France, Hugo hurled anathema upon his errant homeland and called upon the chosen people to forswear false imperial gods and return to the paths of republican virtue. (151–52)

The term "political poetics" is useful because it characterizes Hugo's political stance as imaginative rather than pragmatic; however, it is not clear whether Clark means poetic feelings and utterances or a poetic system. The term "poetic politics" has the advantage of suggesting not a systematic approach, a specific *modus operandi*, but more of a general attitude, orientation, or state of mind.

10. From *Le Pays*, 19 June 1856, qtd. in *Poésies choisies de Victor Hugo* (Paris: Larousse, 1975): 165.

11. "Ce titre est la traduction d'une inscription en espagnol de cuisine de la main de Victor Hugo sous une des épreuves connues (Oyiendo a Dios)" [This title is the translation of an inscription from Spanish doggerel, in Victor Hugo's hand, upon one of the known proofs (Oyiendo a Dios)] (Heilbrun and Molinari, 108).

12. Muray goes so far as to see Claudel's conversion to catholicism as a reaction against Hugo's funeral the year before:

Je fais l'hypothèse que sa conversion à Notre-Dame, son pari sur Notre-Dame, s'élabore contre le pari panthéonien collectif. Un pari sur la résurrection contre le pari des revenants.
1885, perdu dans la foule bouleversée, Claudel assiste aux funérailles de Hugo sur la montagne Sainte-Geneviève.
1886, à Noël il se convertit à Notre-Dame.
Ensuite, il commence le bilan, c'est-à-dire sa vie d'écrivain....
Ce qui lui a valu son procès, de la part du Panthéon et des héritiers du Panthéon. Un écrivain 'catholique' au 20e siècle, et c'est toute l'histoire religieuse, politique, littéraire, qui se retrouve en lignes brisées. (Muray 103)

[My hypothesis is that his conversion in Notre-Dame, his wager on Notre-Dame, takes shape against the collective wager on the Pantheon. A wager for resurrection against a wager for ghosts.

1885, lost in the mourning crowd, Claudel watched Hugo's funeral upon the Sainte-Geneviève hill.

1886, at Christmas he converted in Notre-Dame.

Then, he began to take stock of things, began his life as a writer that is.

Which earned him condemnation from the Pantheon camp and its heirs. A "catholic" writer in the twentieth century, and all of religious, political, literary history is in shambles.]

Significantly, Claudel's response to Hugo's funeral, and especially to the definitive deconsecration of the *Panthéon* took place

à l'intérieur même de ce dont Hugo est encore à l'époque pour tout le monde le légitime propriétaire: *Notre-Dame de Paris* . . . Son roman, bien entendu. Qu'il suffit d'ouvrir pour voir que Hugo, dès la troisième ligne, débaptise l'édifice en graffitant sur lui son sépulchral ANANKÈ grec. Fatalité! Fatalitas! Fantômas! Irruption du Destin païen dans la cathédrale gothique. Hellénistico-gothique! (Muray 107)

[right inside what everyone at the time saw as Hugo's legitimate property: *Notre-Dame de Paris* . . . His novel, of course. It suffices to open it to see that, from the third line, Hugo dechristianizes the edifice, by scrawling upon it, in Greek, a sepulchral ANANKÈ. Fate! Fatalitas! Phantomas! Pagan Destiny bursts into a gothic cathedral. Hellenistico-gothic!]

Conclusion

1. As Rebecca Pauly notes, the Impétraz statue also recalls Sartre's maternal grandfather: "Le parallèle avec le grand-père dépeint dans *Les Mots* est saisissant. Une fois de plus, l'héritage lourd de la culture bourgeoise positiviste étouffe la lumière de la pensée authentique. Le grand-père avait aussi le goût des poses, de 'se pétrifier; il raffolait de ces courts instants d'éternité où il devenait sa propre statue.'" [The parallel with the grandfather depicted in *The Words* is striking. Once again, the legacy of bourgeois positivist culture weighed heavily, extinguishing any spark of authentic thought. His grandfather also liked to strike poses, "to turn to stone. He doted on those brief moments of eternity in which he became his own statue"] (Pauly 1987, 630; Sartre 1964a, 16; Sartre 1964c, 24).

2. Cf. Schopenhauer on the end of positivism, in *The World as Will and Representation*.

3. More recently, the rise of nonfigurative art has led to the installation in public spaces of a new kind of sometimes large-scale sculpture, yet often with no commemorative or symbolic function whatsoever, aside from signaling the aesthetic refinement and enlightened largesse of those funding it: in short, so many giant cubes in corporate plazas.

4. In 1928, in the preface to *Nadja*, surrealist ringleader André Breton remarks, "Je prendrai pour point de départ l'hôtel des Grands Hommes, place du Panthéon, où j'habitais vers 1918" ["My point of departure will be the Hôtel des Grands Hommes, Place du Panthéon, where I lived around 1918"] (Breton 1964, 24; 1960, 23). This would suggest leaving behind the dream of stone with its reverence for the great man, as would comments several pages earlier, on Hugo's pettiness in his dealings with his long-term mistress Juliette Drouet (Breton 1964, 12–13; 1960, 13–14). Breton would seem to be distancing himself from the monumental pretensions of his literary predecessors: "J'envie (c'est une façon de parler) tout homme qui a le temps de préparer quelque chose comme un livre" ("I envy [in a manner of speaking] any man who has the time to prepare something like a book"; Breton 1964, 173; 1960, 149). Paradoxically, though, he places this thought beneath a flattering photograph of himself, a portrait of the great artist, *à la Devéria*, with the subject's forehead bathed in light and piercing eyes looking beyond the frame, as if into eternity. One finds similar ambivalence as Breton comments, "Si je dis qu'à Paris la statue d'Étienne Dolet, place Maubert, m'a toujours tout ensemble attiré et causé un insupportable malaise" ("When I say that the statue of Etienne Dolet on its plinth in the Place Maubert in Paris has always fascinated me and induced unbearable discomfort"; Breton 1964, 26; 1960, 24), thus anticipating Sartre's mix of attraction and revulsion for the Impétraz statue in *La Nausée*, published a decade later.

Bibliography

Agulhon, Maurice. 1975. Imagerie civique et décor urbain dans la France du XIXe. *Ethnologie française*: 33–56.

———. 1978. La "statuomanie" et l'histoire. *Ethnologie française*: 145–72.

———. 1979. *Marianne au combat, l'imagerie et la symbolique républicaine de 1789 à 1880*. Paris: Flammarion.

Alhoy, Maurice. 1841. *Les Brigands et bandits célèbres*. Paris: Guiller.

———. 1845. *Physiologie de la Lorette*. Paris: Aubert.

Apgar, Garry. 1995. *L'art singulier de Jean Huber: Voir Voltaire*. Paris: Adam Biro.

Ariès, Philippe. 1977. *L'homme devant la mort*. Paris: Seuil.

Arnason, H. H. 1975. *The Sculptures of Houdon*. New York: Oxford University Press.

Audebrand, Philibert. 1876. Courrier de Paris. *L'Illustration* (June 17): 386–87.

Ausseur, Christine. 1992. *Guide littéraire des monuments de Paris*. Paris: Hermé.

Baldwin, Gordon, and Judith Keller. 1999. Catalogue. *Nadar, Warhol: Paris, New York*. Los Angeles: The J. Paul Getty Museum.

Balzac, Honoré de. 1839. *Galerie de la presse, de la littérature et des beaux-arts*. Paris: Aubert (signed "A-D").

———. *Oeuvres complètes*. 1955–1963. Edited by Maurice Bardèche. 28 vols. Paris: Club de l'Honnête Homme.

———. *Correspondance*. 1960–1969. Edited by Roger Pierrot. 5 vols. Paris: Garnier.

———. 1967–1971. *Lettres à Mme Hanska*. Edited by Roger Pierrot. 4 vols. Paris: Les Bibliophiles de l'Originale.

———. 1965–1976. *Oeuvres complètes*. Edited by Jean-A. Ducourneau. 30 vols. Paris: Les Bibliophiles de l'originale.

———. 1976–1981. *La Comédie humaine*. Edited by Pierre-Georges Castex. 12 vols. Paris: Gallimard, Bibliothèque de la Pléiade.

———. 1990. *Oeuvres diverses*. 2 vols. Paris: Gallimard, Bibliothèque de la Pléiade.

Bann, Stephen. 2001. *Parallel Lines: Printmakers, Painters and Photographers in Nineteenth-Century France*. New Haven: Yale University Press.

Barbéris, Pierre. 1985. *Aux Sources de Balzac: Les Romans de jeunesse*. Geneva-Paris: Slatkine Reprints.

Barbey d'Aurevilly, Jules. 1850. "La Mort de M. de Balzac." *La Mode* (August 24).

———. 1972. *Articles inédits (1852–1884)*. Edited by Jacques Petit and Andrée Hirschi. Besançon: Annales littéraires de l'université de Besançon.

Bardèche, Maurice. 1943. *Balzac romancier*. Paris: Plon.

———. 1980. *Balzac*. Paris: Julliard.

Barrère, Jean-Bertrand. 1949–50. *La Fantaisie de Victor Hugo*. 3 vols. Paris: Corti.

———. 1984. *Victor Hugo: l'homme et l'oeuvre*. Paris: SEDES.

Barrès, Maurice. 1988. *Les Déracinés*. Paris: Gallimard.

Barret, André. 1989. *Nadar: 50 photographies de ses illustres contemporains*. Paris: Diffusion Inter Forum.

Barthes, Roland. 1970. *S/Z*. Paris: Seuil.

———. 1980. *La chambre claire*. Paris: Éditions de l'Étoile, Gallimard, Seuil.

———. 1981. *Camera Lucida: Reflections on Photography*. Translated by Richard Howard. New York: Hill and Wang.

Les bas-bleus. 1839. *Aujourd'hui, journal des ridicules* (October 15): 1–2.

Baudelaire, Charles. 1975–76. *Oeuvres complètes*. Edited by Claude Pichois. 2 vols. Paris: Gallimard.

———. 1991. *The Flowers of Evil and Paris Spleen*. Translated by William H. Crosby. Brockport, NY: BOA Editions, Ltd.

Baudouin, Charles. 1972. *Psychanalyse de Victor Hugo*. Paris: Armand Colin.

Baudson, Pierre. 1979. Les Romans de Zola et la Caricature de leur temps. *Gazette des Beaux-Arts* (September): 69–72.

Beizer, Janet L. 1986. *Family Plots: Balzac's Narrative Generations*. New Haven: Yale University Press.

Bell, David Avrom. 2001. *The Cult of the Nation in France: Inventing Nationalism, 1680–1800*. Cambridge, MA: Harvard University Press.

Bellet, Roger, ed. 1982. *Femmes de lettres au XIXe siècle: autour de Louise Colet*. Lyon: Presses universitaires de Lyon.

Bellos, David. 1976. *Balzac Criticism in France, 1850–1900: The Making of a Reputation*. Oxford: Clarendon Press.

Bénichou, Paul. 1973. *Le sacre de l'écrivain, 1750–1830: Essai sur l'avènement d'un pouvoir spirituel laïque dans la France moderne*. Paris: José Corti.

Benjamin, Walter. 1969. "The Work of Art in the Age of Mechanical Reproduction." In *Illuminations*. New York: Schocken.

Bergman-Carton, Janis. 1995. *The Woman of Ideas in French Art, 1830–1848*. New Haven: Yale University Press.

Bernheimer, Charles. 1989. *Figures of Ill Repute*. Cambridge: Harvard University Press

Bersaucourt, Albert de, ed. 1912. *Les Pamphlets contre Victor Hugo*. Paris: Mercure de France.

Beuve, Paul and Henri Daragon. 1902. *Victor Hugo par le bibelot*. Paris: H. Daragon, Libraire.

Bibliophile Jacob [Paul L. Jacob]. 1843. *Galerie des femmes de George Sand*. Paris: Aubert.

Bibliothèque historique de la ville de Paris (BHVP). *Dossier "Actualités" George Sand*. (Collection of press clippings on Sand's life, work, and reception.)

Biet, Christian, Jean-Paul Brighelli, and Jean-Luc Rispail. 1986. *Alexandre Dumas ou les aventures d'un romancier*. Paris: Gallimard.

Biographie contemporaine ou histoire de la vie publique et privée de tous les hommes, morts ou vivants, qui ont acquis de la célébrité depuis la Révolution française jusqu'à nos jours. 1837. Paris: Louis Babeuf.

Biographie des femmes auteurs contemporaines. 1836. Edited by Alfred de Montferrand, illustrated by Jules Boilly. Paris: Armand-Aubrée.

Biographie universelle, ancienne et moderne, ou Histoire, par ordre alphabétique, de la vie publique et privée de tous les hommes qui se sont fait remarquer par leurs écrits, leurs actions, leurs talents, leurs vertus ou leurs crimes. Nouvelle édition. 1843. Edited by Louis-Gabriel Michaud. Paris: A. Thoisnier Desplaces, éditeur.

Biographie universelle classique, ou dictionnaire historique portatif, par une société de gens de lettres. 1829. Paris: Charles Gosselin, Libraire-Éditeur.

Biographie universelle des hommes qui se sont fait un nom par leur génie, leurs talents, leurs vertus, leurs erreurs ou leurs crimes. Par F.-X Feller; revue, classée par ordre chronologique, continuée jusqu'en 1845. 1845. Paris: Poussielgue-Rusand, Libraire.

Biographie universelle et portative des contemporains, ou dictionnaire historique des hommes vivants et des hommes morts depuis 1788 et jusqu'à nos jours, qui se sont fait remarquer par leurs écrits, leurs actions, leurs talents, leurs vertus ou leurs crimes. 1836. 2d ed. Edited by Rabbe-Vieilh de Boisjolin and Sainte-Preuve. Paris: Chez l'éditeur, rue du Colombier, 21.

Bird, Stephen. 2000. *Reinventing Voltaire: The Politics of Commemoration in Nineteenth-century France*. Oxford: Voltaire Foundation.

Blondel, Madeleine and Pierre Georgel. 1989. *Colloque de Dijon: Victor Hugo et les images*. Dijon: Ville de Dijon.

Bonnet, Jean-Claude. 1998. *Naissance du Panthéon: essai sur le culte des grands hommes*. Paris: Fayard.

Borel, Pétrus. 1836. *L'Obélisque de Louqsor, pamphlet*. Paris: Chez les marchands de nouveautés.

Borges, José Luis. 1999. "Kafka and his precursors." In *Selected Non-fictions*. Edited by Eliot Weinberger. New York: Viking.

Bournon, Fernand. 1909. *La Voie publique et son décor*. Paris: Librairie Renouard.

Boussel, Patrice, and Christian Galantaris. 1971. Catalog, *Les Portraits de Balzac connus et inconnus*. Paris: Ville de Paris, Musée de Balzac.

Bouteron, Marcel. 1934. *Muses Romantiques*. Paris: Plon.

Braudy, Leo. 1986. *The Frenzy of Renown*. New York: Oxford University Press.

Brault, Joseph. 1848. *Une Contemporaine. Biographies et intrigues de George Sand*. Paris.

Bredin, Jean-Denis. 1983. *L'Affaire*. Paris: Julliard.

Brétecher, Claire, and Jean-Louis Mourier. 1990. Catalog, *Rodin et la caricature*. Paris: Musée Rodin.

Bricard, Isabelle. 1995. *Dictionnaire de la mort des grands hommes*. Paris: Le Cherche-midi.

Brillat-Savarin, Jean-Anthelme. 1982. *La Physiologie du goût*. Paris: Flammarion.

Brown, Frederick. 1973. *Père Lachaise—Elysium as Real Estate*. New York: Viking.

Burette, Théodose. 1840. *La Physiologie du fumeur*. Illustrated by Alcide Lorentz. Paris: E. Bourdin.

Butler, Ruth, ed. 1980. *Rodin in Perspective*. Englewood Cliffs, NJ: Prentice Hall.

———. 1993. *Rodin: The Shape of Genius*. New Haven: Yale University Press.

Butor, Michel. 1959. "Les deux univers de Balzac, II: Le réel." In *Balzac*. Paris: Hachette.

Campo, Roberto E. 1998. *Ronsard's Contentious Sisters: The Paragone between Poetry and Painting in the Works of Pierre de Ronsard*. Chapel Hill: University of North Carolina Press.

Canfield, A. G. 1961. *The Reappearing Characters in Balzac's Comédie humaine*. Chapel Hill: University of North Carolina Press.

Carlyle, Thomas. 1993. *On Heroes, Hero-Worship, & the Heroic in History*. Berkeley and Los Angeles: University of California Press.

La Carmagnole des muses: l'homme de lettres et l'artiste dans la Révolution. 1988. Paris: Armand Colin.

Castille, C. Hippolyte. 1848. "Romanciers contemporains: George Sand." *La Semaine* (November 1): 18–19.

Cate, Curtis. 1975. *George Sand*. Boston: Houghton Mifflin.

Cayla, J. M. 1854. *Célébrités européennes: George Sand*. Paris: H. Boisgard.

Cellier, Léon. 1954. *L'Épopée romantique*. Paris: Presses universitaires de France.

"Le Centenaire de George Sand." 1904. *L'Illustration* (July 9): 20–21.

Le Centre canadien d'architecture and *la Caisse nationale des monuments historiques et des sites en France*. *Le Panthéon, symbole des révolutions*. 1989. Paris: Picard.

Cerfberr, Anatole, and Jules Christophe. 1925. *Répertoire de la Comédie humaine de H. de Balzac*. Introduction by Paul Bourget. Paris: Calmann-Lévy.

Chabert, Noëlle. 1996. Catalog, *Monument et modernité*. Paris: Mairie de Paris.

Champfleury [Jules Fleury]. 1871. *Histoire de la caricature moderne*. Paris: Dentu.

Champsaur, Félicien. 1879. *Les Hommes d'aujourd'hui. Émile Zola*. Paris: A. Cinqualbre, éditeur.

Chateaubriand, François-René de. *Mémoires d'outre-tombe*. 1951. Edited by Maurice Levaillant and Georges Moulinier. 2 vols. Paris: Gallimard.

———. 1976. *Mémoires de ma vie*. Edited by J. M. Gautier. Geneva: Droz.

Chevillot, Catherine. 1990. *La République et ses grands hommes*. Paris: Hachette/Réunion des musées nationaux.

Chincholle, Charles. 1898. "La Vente de la statue de Balzac." *Le Figaro*, May 12.

Chotard, Loïc. 1987. La Biographie contemporaine en France au dix-neuvième siècle. Autour du Panthéon Nadar. Ph.D. diss., Paris IV.

———. 1990. Catalog, *Nadar: Caricatures et photographies*. Paris: Paris-musées.

Chouelon, Bernadette. 1984. George Sand et la Comédie Française. *Présence de George Sand* 19: 35–40.

Citéra, Frédérique. 1989. Visages anonymes et pseudonymes d'Honoré de Balzac. *Anonymat et signature*. Edited by Jean Cuisenier. Paris: La Documentation française.

Citron, Pierre. 1986. *Dans Balzac*. Paris: Seuil.

Claudel, Paul, and André Gide. 1949. *Correspondance, 1899–1926*. Edited by Robert Mallet. Paris: Gallimard.

Clark, Priscilla Parkhurst. 1987. *Literary France: The Making of a Culture*. Berkeley and Los Angeles: University of California Press.

Clark, T. J. 1984. *The Painting of Modern Life. Paris in the Art of Manet and His Followers*. Princeton: Princeton University Press.

Clébert, Jean-Paul. 1992. *Les Hauts lieux de la littérature à Paris*. Paris: Bordas.

Colton, Judith. 1979. *The Parnasse françois: Titon du Tillet and the Origins of the Monument to Genius*. New Haven: Yale University Press.

Condorcet, Marquis de. 1994. *Vie de Voltaire*. Preface by Elisabeth Badinter. Paris: Quai Voltaire.

Crone, Rainer, and Siegfried Salzmann, eds. 1992. Catalog, *Rodin: Eros and Creativity*. Munich: Prestel.

Czyba, Luce. 1995. George Sand et la caricature. *Les amis de George Sand* 16: 5–20.

Dällenbach, Lucien. 1996. *La Canne de Balzac*. Paris: J. Corti.

Dantan jeune. 1838–1839. *Musée Dantan—Galerie des charges et croquis des célébrités de l'époque*. Paris: Delloye.

Daudet, Léon. 1922. Victor Hugo ou la légende d'un siècle. In *Les Oeuvres dans les hommes*. Paris: Nouvelle Librairie Nationale.

Daumier, Honoré. 1974. *Intellectuelles (Bas-Bleus) et femmes socialistes*. Paris: Éditions André Sauret.

David d'Angers, Pierre-Jean. 1958. *Les Carnets de David d'Angers*. Edited by André Bruel. 2 vols. Paris: Plon.

De Caso, Jacques. 1988. *David d'Angers: l'avenir de la mémoire*. Paris: Flammarion.

Decaux, Alain. 1984. *Victor Hugo*. Paris: Librairie Académique Perrin.

Delacroix, Eugène. 1923. *Oeuvres littéraires*. Edited by Élie Faure. 2 vols. Paris: G. Crès.

De l'État civil en France, depuis l'origine de la monarchie jusqu'à nos jours; et examen des changements qu'on propose de lui faire subir, en le remettant dans la dépendance du clergé. Par un ancien officier de l'État civil. 1826. Paris: Sétier, Imprimeur-Libraire.

Deraismes, Maria. 1980. *Ce que veulent les femmes: articles et conférences de 1869 à 1891*. Edited by Odile Krakovitch. Paris: Syros.

Desbordes-Valmore, Marceline. *Les Oeuvres poétiques. Édition complète*. Edited by M. Bertrand. 2 vol. Grenoble: Presses universitaires de Grenoble, 1973.

Descombes, Vincent. 1983. Who's who dans *La Comédie humaine*. In *Grammaire d'objets en tous genres*. Paris: Minuit.

Deslandes, André-François. 2000. *Réflexions sur les grands hommes qui sont morts en plaisantant*. Paris: Honoré Champion.

Desnoiresterres, Gustave. 1970. *Iconographie voltairienne*. Geneva: Slatkine Reprints.

Dhainaut, Pierre. 1980. *La Demeure océan de Victor Hugo*. Paris: Encre Editions.

Diaz, José-Luis. 1980. Balzac et la scène romantique du nom propre. *34/44* 7: 19–30.

———. 1990. Balzac et ses mythologies d'écrivain. *La Licorne* 18: 75–85.

Dictionnaire des monuments de Paris. 1992. Paris: Éditions Hervas.

Discours du citoyen Lejeune, curé de Clerey, à ses paroissiens, sur l'exécution de la Loi qui détermine le mode de constater l'état civil des Citoyens. 1792. Troyes: Sainton, Imprimeur.

Drohojowska, Comtesse. 1850. *Les Femmes illustres de la France*. Paris: P-C. Lehuby.

Duchet, Claude and Jacques Neefs, eds. 1982. *Balzac: l'invention du roman* (Colloque de Cérisy). Paris: Pierre Belfond.

Ducourneau, Jean A., ed. 1962. *Album Balzac*. Paris: Gallimard.

Dugas de la Boissonny, C. 1987. *L'état civil*. Paris: Presses Universitaires de France.

Dumas, Alexandre, père. 1840. *Napoléon*. Paris: Delloye.

———. 1851. *Les Crimes célèbres*. Paris: Librairie théâtrale.

———. 1866. *Les Grands hommes en robe de chambre*. Paris: Michel Lévy.

Dumas, Roland. 1987. *La propriété littéraire et artistique*. Paris: Presses Universitaires de France.

Dumesnil, Henri. 1891. *Aimé Millet, souvenirs intimes.* Paris: Al. Lemerre; Rapilly.

Dupriez, Bernard. 1984. *Gradus: Les procédés littéraires.* Paris: Union générale d'Éditions.

Ecalle, Martine, and Violaine Lumbroso, eds. 1964. *Album Hugo.* Paris: Gallimard, Pléiade.

Elsen, Albert. 1963. *Rodin.* New York: Museum of Modern Art.

Emerson, Ralph Waldo. 1930. *Representative Men.* Boston: Houghton Mifflin.

Escholier, Raymond. 1953. *Un amant de génie: Victor Hugo.* Paris: Fayard.

État. [1892.] *La Grande Encyclopédie.*

État civil des citoyens ou analyse sommaire du décret du 20 septembre 1792, et celui du 21 [sic, should be 31] janvier dernier, avec des formules de différentes Actes de Naissances, Mariages et décès, pour en faciliter la rédaction aux Officiers Municipaux, Juges de Paix, Commissaires de Police et leurs Greffiers, etc. 1793. Paris: Krapen.

Fagel, André, et al. 1904. "Courrier de Paris." *L'Illustration* (May 28): 354–55.

Farwell, Beatrice. 1989. Catalog, *The Charged Image: French Lithographic Caricature, 1816–1848.* Santa Barbara, CA: Santa Barbara Museum of Art.

Femmes de lettres françaises contemporaines. 1844. *L'Illustration* (June 22): 264–67.

Fermigier, André. 1976. Préface. In George Sand, *François le Champi.* Paris: Gallimard.

Ferry, Gabriel. 1902. La popularité de Balzac au seuil du Xxe siècle. *La Revue* 20 (October 15): 201–10.

Flaubert, Gustave. 1973. *Correspondance.* Edited by Jean Bruneau. 3 vol. Paris: Gallimard.

———. 1979. *Bouvard et Pécuchet, avec un choix des scénarios, du Sottisier, L'Album de la Marquise et Le dictionnaire des idées reçues.* Paris: Gallimard.

———. 1989. *Voyage en Bretagne.* Brussels: Éditions Complexe.

Fortunatus. 1842. *Le Rivarol de 1842, dictionnaire satirique des célébrités contemporaines.* Paris: au bureau du feuilleton mensuel.

Fosca, François. 1941. *Edmond et Jules Goncourt.* Paris: Albin Michel.

Foucault, Michel. 1966. *Les Mots et les choses.* Paris: Gallimard.

———. 1975. *Surveiller et punir.* Paris: Gallimard.

———. 1984. "What is an Author?" In *The Foucault Reader,* edited by Paul Rabinow. New York: Pantheon.

Fourny, Jean-François, and Charles D. Minahen, eds. 1997. *Situating Sartre in Twentieth-Century Thought and Culture.* New York: St. Martin's.

Frey, John Andrew. 1999. *A Victor Hugo Encyclopedia.* Westport, CT: Greenwood.

Fusco, Peter, and H. W. Janson. 1980. Catalog, *The Romantics to Rodin: French Nineteenth-Century Sculpture from North American Collections.* Los Angeles: Los Angeles County Museum of Art.

Galerie des dames françaises distinguées dans les lettres et les arts. 1843. Paris: Dussillon.

Gamboni, Dario. 1997. *The Destruction of Art.* New Haven: Yale University Press.

Gardes, Gilbert. 1994. *Le Monument public français.* Paris: Presses Universitaires de France.

Garnier ["Membre du Tiers-État"]. 1789. *Moyens d'établir un ordre propre à consigner, conserver & transmettre à la postérité, dans toute leur pureté et intégrité, les noms de familles, afin que désormais il n'y ait plus d'incertitude, ni par conséquent de contestations & plaintes à ce sujet; ce qui est de la plus grande importance pour faire régner la justice & la concorde dans la société.*

Garval, Michael. 1998a. "The Rise and Fall of the Literary Monument in Post-Revolutionary France." In *The Pictured Word. Word & Image Interactions 2,* edited by Martin Heusser et al. Amsterdam: Rodopi.

———. 1998b. Visions of the Great Woman Writer: Imagining George Sand through Word and Image. In *Le Siècle de George Sand,* edited by David A. Powell. Amsterdam: Rodopi.

———. 2003. "A Dream of Stone": Fame, Vision, and the Monument in Nineteenth-Century French Literary Culture. *College Literature* 30.2 (Spring): 82–119.

Gautier, Théophile. 1966. *Le Roman de la momie.* Paris: Garnier-Flammarion.

———. 1970. *Poésies complètes.* Edited by René Jasinski. 3 vols. Paris: Nizet.

———. 1981. *Récits fantastiques.* Paris: Flammarion.

Genestier, Philippe. 1990. *La Monumentalité: sens et non-sens d'un concept. Architecture, symbolisme et pouvoir.* Nantes: Laboratoire théorique des mutations urbaines/ Bureau de la recherche architecturale.

Genette, Gérard. 1969. "Stendhal." In *Figures II.* Paris: Seuil.

———. 1976. *Mimologiques: Voyage en Cratylie.* Paris: Seuil.

Genlis, Madame de. 1811–12. *Examen critique de l'ouvrage intitulé "Biographie Universelle."* 2 vols. Paris: Maradan.

———. 1826. *De l'influence des femmes sur la littérature française.* Paris: Lecointe et Durey.

Georgel, Chantal, ed. 1994. Catalog, *La Jeunesse des musées. Les musées de France au XIXe siècle.* Paris.

Georgel, Pierre, ed. 1985. Catalogue, *La gloire de Victor Hugo.* Paris: Réunion des musées nationaux.

George Sand. 1954. *Bibliothèque Nationale, Exposition organisée pour le cent cinquantième anniversaire de sa naissance.* Paris: Bibliothèque Nationale.

George Sand. 1982. Spec. section of *Magazine littéraire,* 295: 16–56.

George Sand. 1992. Spec. issue of *Revue des sciences humaines,* April–June.

George Sand. 1977. *Visages du romantisme.* Paris: Bibliothèque Nationale.

Gielly, Louis. 1948. *Voltaire: documents iconographiques.* Geneva: Pierre Cailler.

Girardin, Delphine de. 1946. *La Canne de M. de Balzac.* Paris: Bateau ivre.

Goncourt, Edmond de. 1989. *Journal: mémoires de la vie littéraire.* Paris: R. Laffont.

Gourriet, Jean-Baptiste. 1819. *Les charlatans célèbres.* Paris: Lerouge.

Graham, Victor E. and W. McAllister Johnson. 1974. *The Paris Entries of Charles IX and Elisabeth of Austria, 1571.* Toronto: University of Toronto Press.

———. 1979. *The Royal Tour of France by Charles IX and Catherine de' Medici: Festivals and Entries, 1564–6.* Toronto: University of Toronto Press.

Grand-Carteret, John. 1888. *Les Moeurs et la caricature en France.* Paris: À la Librairie Illustrée.

———. 1893. *XIXeme siècle en France.* Paris: Firmin-Didot.

———. 1908. *Zola en images.* Paris: Juven.

Grossiord, Sophie. 1994. *Hauteville-House: guide général.* Paris: Paris-Musées.

Groupe International de Recherches Balzaciennes. 1993. *Balzac, Oeuvres complètes: le "moment" de la* Comédie humaine. Saint-Denis: Presses Universitaires de Vincennes.

Guillaume, Valérie, and Ségolène Le Men. 1988. Catalog, *Benjamin Roubaud et le Panthéon charivarique.* Paris: Maison de Balzac.

Guise, René. 1984. Balzac et 'Le Charivari' en 1837. *L'Année balzacienne*, 1984.

Hambourg, Maria Morris, Françoise Heilbrun, and Philippe Néagu, eds. 1994. Catalogue, *Nadar, les années créatrices: 1854–1860.* Paris: Réunion des musées nationaux.

Hamon, Philippe. 1989. *Expositions: littérature et architecture au XIXe siècle.* Paris: José Corti.

Hanoosh, Michele. 1992. *Baudelaire and Caricature: From the Comic to an Art of Modernity.* University Park: Penn State University Press.

Hargrove, June. 1991. "Shaping the National Image: The Cult of Statues to Great Men in the Third Republic." *Studies in the History of Art* 29: 48–63.

———. 1990. *The Statues of Paris: An Open-air Pantheon.* New York: Vendome Press.

Haskell, Francis. 1993. *History and Its Images: Art and the Interpretation of the Past.* New Haven: Yale University Press.

Heilbrun, Françoise, and Danielle Molinari. 1998. Catalog, *En collaboration avec le soleil: Victor Hugo, photographies de l'exil.* Paris: Réunion des musées nationaux.

Heine, Heinrich. 1872. *Lutèce, lettres sur la vie politique, artistique et sociale de la France.* Paris: Lévy.

Hermant, Abel. 1903. *Honoré de Balzac.* Paris.

Heuvel, Jacques van den. 1983. *Album Voltaire.* Paris: Gallimard.

Hollier, Denis. 1989. "Egypt in Paris." In *A New History of French Literature.* Cambridge, MA: Harvard University Press.

Horace. 1964. *The Odes and Epodes.* Translated by C. E. Bennett. Cambridge, MA: Harvard University Press.

———. 1993. *Satires I.* Edited by P. Michael Brown. Warminster (England): Aris & Phillips.

Houssaye, Arsène. 1878. *Le roi Voltaire.* Paris: Dentu.

———. 1884. *Inauguration de la statue de George Sand.* Saint-Germain: D. Bardin.

———. 1893. "Les Dernières heures de Balzac." *Le Figaro,* August 20.

Huchard, Viviane, et al. 1990. Catalogue, *Aux Grands hommes, David d'Angers.* Saint-Rémy-lès-Chevreuse: Fondation Coubertin.

Hugo, Victor. 1904–52. *Oeuvres complètes.* [l'Édition de l'Imprimerie Nationale.] Edited by P. Meurice, G. Simon, and C. Daubray. 45 vols. Paris: Ollendorff; Albin Michel.

———. 1964. *Oeuvres politiques complètes, oeuvres diverses.* Paris: Jean-Jacques Pauvert.

———. 1964–1967. *Oeuvres poétiques.* Paris: Gallimard, Pléiade.

———. 1965. *Quatrevingt-treize.* Paris: Flammarion.

———. 1965–1969. *Les Contemplations.* Paris: Livre de poche.

———. 1968. *Cromwell.* Paris: Garnier Flammarion.

———. 1968. *Oeuvres complètes. Édition Chronologique.* Edited by Jean Massin. Paris: Le Club Français du livre.

———. 1972. *Choses vues.* Edited by Hubert Juin. 4 vols. Paris: Gallimard.

———. 1974. *Notre-Dame de Paris.* Paris: Gallimard (Folio).

———. 1975. *Notre-Dame de Paris, 1482. Les Travailleurs de la mer.* Edited by Jacques Seebacher. Paris: Gallimard.

———. 1979. *Les Châtiments.* Paris: Garnier-Flammarion.

———. 1985–90. *Oeuvres complètes.* Jacques Seebacher, ed. 15 vols. Paris: Robert Laffont.

Ionesco, Eugène. 1982. *Hugoliade.* Translated by Dragomir Costineanu. Paris: Gallimard.

Jacob, Paul [*le Bibliophile*]. 1843. *Galerie des femmes de George Sand.* Paris: Aubert & Cie.

Jacques, Annie, and Jean-Pierre Mouilleseaux. 1989. *Les Architectes de la liberté.* Paris: École nationale supérieure des Beaux-arts.

Janson, H. W. 1976. *The Rise and Fall of the Public Monument.* New Orleans: The Graduate School, Tulane University.

———. 1977. *The History of Art.* 2d ed. New York: Harry N. Abrams.

Jeannot, André. 1986. *Honoré de Balzac: le forçat de la gloire.* Paris: Geigy.

Joly, Henri. 1883. *Psychologie des grands hommes.* Paris: Hachette et cie.

Kahn, Maurice. 1904. "George Sand à Nohant. L'Art d'être grand'mère." *L'Illustration* (July 2): 6–7.

Kamuf, Peggy. 1988. *Signature Pieces: On the Institution of Authorship.* Ithaca, NY: Cornell University Press.

Kleeblatt, Norman L. 1993. "MERDE!: The Caricatural

Attack against Emile Zola." *Art Journal 52/3* (fall): 54–58.

Kselman, Thomas A. 1993. *Death and the Afterlife in Modern France*. Princeton: Princeton University Press.

Lacambre, Geneviève. 1994. *Maison d'artiste, maison-musée: Le musée Gustave-Moreau*. Paris: Éditions de la Réunion des musées nationaux.

Laffont, Achille. 1853. "Un jeune homme de lettres." Illustrated by Gustave Doré. In *Le Journal pour rire* (December 24): 1–6.

Lanfranchi, Jacques. 1979. Les statues de Paris. Ph.D. diss., Paris I.

Lanson, Gustave. 1981. *Manuel illustré d'histoire de la littérature française*. Paris: Hachette.

Laster, Arnaud. 1984. *Victor Hugo*. Paris: Belfond.

Lebas, Jean-Baptiste-Apollinaire. 1839. *L'Obélisque de Luxor*. Paris: Carilian-Goeury et Vᵣ Dalmont, éds.

Leith, James A. 1965. *The Idea of Art as Propaganda in France, 1750–1799*. Toronto: University of Toronto Press.

———. 1991. *Space and Revolution: Projects for Monuments, Squares, and Public Buildings in France, 1789–1799*. Montreal and Kingston: McGill-Queen's University Press.

Lemoine, Bertrand. 1989. *La Tour de Monsieur Eiffel*. Paris: Gallimard.

Le Normand-Romain, Antoinette. 1995. Catalogue, *Mémoire de marbre. La sculpture funéraire en France 1804–1914*. Paris: Agence culturelle de Paris.

Lepape, Pierre. 1994. *Voltaire le conquérant: naissance des intellectuels au siècle des Lumières*. Paris: Éditions du Seuil.

Levaillant, Maurice. 1954. *La Crise mystique de Victor Hugo*. Paris: Corti.

Lichtenthäler, Barbara. 1988. *Balzac als Jurist: das Recht-Strukturelement der "Comédie humaine."* Bonn: Romantischer Verlag.

La Litho-typographie. Lettre du Docteur Néophobus au Docteur Old-Book. 1839. *Revue des Deux mondes*, (July 1): 235–43.

Le Livre des 400 auteurs. 1850. Paris: aux bureaux du magasin des familles

Lloyd, Rosemary. 1981. *Baudelaire's Literary Criticism*. Cambridge; NY: Cambridge University Press.

———. 1999. *Mallarmé: The Poet and His Circle*. Ithaca: Cornell University Press.

Loménie, Louis de. 1840–1847. *Galerie des contemporains illustres*. 10 vol. Paris: au Bureau central.

Lotte, Fernand. 1947. *En marge de la "Comédie humaine": la vie du docteur Horace Bianchon, grand consultant de la Monarchie de juillet*. Cairo: Éditions de la Revue du Caïre.

———. 1961. Le Retour des personnages. *L'Année balzacienne*, 227–82.

———, ed. 1963. *Armorial de la* Comédie humaine. Paris: Garnier.

Loyrette, Henri. 1985. *Eiffel—Un ingénieur et son oeuvre*. Fribourg: Office du Livre.

Lubin, Georges. 1967. *George Sand en Berry*. Paris: Hachette.

———. 1973. *Album Sand*. Paris: Gallimard.

———. 1981. George Sand et l'Académie Française. *Les Amis de George Sand* 1: 3–5.

———. 1986. Les portraits de George Sand. *Présence de George Sand* 27: 4–14.

Maigrot, J.-B. 1837. *Illustrations littéraires de la France, ou galerie anecdotique de nos principaux auteurs peints par leurs actions et leurs écrits*. Paris: Lehuby.

Malhotra, Ruth. 1980. *Horror-Galerie: Ein Bestiarium der dritten Französischen Republik*. Dortmund: Harenberg Kommunikation.

Mallet, Françoise. 1981. *George Sand*. Paris: Grasset.

Marceau, Félicien. 1970. *Balzac et son monde*. Paris: Gallimard.

Marcelin. 1853. "Les romans populaires." *Le Journal pour rire* (September 10): 1–3.

Marini, Marcelle. 1974. "Chabert mort ou vif." *Littérature* 13: 92–112.

Martin, Michel. 1986. *Les monuments équestres de Louis XIV, une grande entreprise de propagande monarchique*. Paris: Picard.

Marquant, Robert. 1977. *L'état civil des personnes*. Paris: Masson.

Mathély, Paul. 1984. *Le droit français des signes distinctifs*. Paris: Libraires du journal des notaires et des avocats.

Maurois, André. 1952. *Lélia, ou la vie de George Sand*. Paris: Hachette.

———. 1954. *Olympio ou la vie de Victor Hugo*. Paris: Hachette.

———. 1965. *Prométhée ou la vie de Balzac*. Paris: Hachette.

McCall, Anne E. 1999. Monuments of the Maternal: Reflections on the Desbordes-Valmore Correspondence. *L'Esprit Créateur* 39, no. 2 (summer): 41–51.

McCauley, Anne. 1983. Caricature and photography in Second Empire Paris. *Art Journal* 43 (winter): 355–61.

Mémoires de l'Obélisque de Louqsor, écrits par lui-même, et dédiés aux Parisiens. 1836. Paris: chez tous les principaux libraires.

Menu, Bernadette. 1987. *L'Obélisque de la Concorde*. Paris: Éditions du Lunx.

Mérimée, Prosper. 1982. *La Vénus d'Ille et autres nouvelles*. Paris: Flammarion.

Meyer-Petit, Judith. 1991. "Le Balzac de Grandville: un éventail de lectures." *Année Balzacienne*, 455–61.

Miller, D. A. 1988. *The Novel and the Police*. Berkeley and Los Angeles: University of California Press.

Mirbeau, Octave. 1925–27. *Les Écrivains, 1884–1894*. 2 vols. Paris: E. Flammarion.

————. 1989. *La Mort de Balzac*. Tusson (Charente): Du Lérot.

Mirecourt, Eugène de. 1856. *George Sand*. Paris: Gustave Havard.

Mollier, Jean-Yves. 1992. "Balzac et la propriété littéraire internationale." *L'Année Balzacienne*, 145–73.

Monselet, Charles. 1852. *Statues et statuettes contemporaines*. Paris: D. Giraud et J. Dagneau.

————. 1971. *La lorgnette littéraire. Augmenté du complément, Dictionnaire des grands et des petits auteurs de mon temps*. Geneva: Slatkine.

Morel, Dominique. 1985. Catalog, *Achille Devéria, témoin du romantisme parisien, 1800–1857*. Paris: Paris-Musées.

Mozet, Nicole. 1984. "La femme-auteur comme symptôme." *34/44* 13: 35–41.

————. 1990. *Balzac au pluriel*. Paris: Presses universitaires de France.

Muray, Philippe. 1984. *Le 19e siècle à travers les âges*. Paris: Denoël, L'infini.

Nadar, Félix. 1979. *Nadar*. Edited by Philippe Néagu and Jean-Jacques Poulet-Allamagny. 2 vols. Paris: A. Hubschmid.

Naginski, Isabelle Hoog. 1991. *George Sand: Writing for Her Life*. New Brunswick: Rutgers University Press.

Nicole, Eugène. 1983. "L'onomastique littéraire." *Poétique* 54: 233–53.

Nisard, Désiré. 1844–61. *Histoire de la littérature française*. Paris: Firmin Didot frères.

Nodier, Charles. 1808. *Dictionnaire des onomatopées françaises*. Paris: Demonville, Imprimeur-Libraire.

————. 1835. Des artifices que certains auteurs ont employés pour déguiser leurs noms. *Bulletin du bibliophile* 24 (December).

————. 1835. Des nomenclatures. *Bulletin du bibliophile* 24 (December).

Nora, Pierre, ed. 1997. *Les Lieux de mémoire*. 3 vols. Paris: Gallimard.

Nouvelle biographie universelle depuis les temps les plus reculés jusqu'à nos jours. 1852. Edited by M. le docteur Hoefer. Paris: Firmin Didot frères, éditeurs.

"L'Olympe démocratique et social, Grand festival à l'occasion de l'élection de Me Jules Favre." 1849. *Le Caricaturiste, revue drolatique du dimanche*, July 22, 4–5; 7.

Parent, Françoise. 1981. *Lire à Paris au temps de Balzac*. Paris: Éditions de l'ÉHÉSS.

Patte, Pierre. 1765. *Monumens érigés en France à la gloire de Louis XV*. Paris: Chez l'auteur.

Pauly, Rebecca M. 1987. *Huis clos*, *Les Mots* et *La Nausée*: le bronze de Barbedienne et le coupe-papier. *The French Review* 60, no. 5 (April): 626–34.

Pearson-Stamps, Pauline. 1992. *Journey Within the Crystal: A Study and Translation of George Sand's* Laura, Voyage dans le cristal. New York: Peter Lang.

Périgois, E. 1906. *George Sand. La Bonne déesse de la pauvreté, ballade. Illustré de 16 grandes lithographies par Albert Robida*. Paris: A. Mariani.

Perrot, Michelle, ed. 1987. *De la République à la Grande Guerre. Histoire de la vie privée*. Edited by Philippe Ariès and Georges Duby. Vol. 4. Paris: Seuil.

Pessard, Gustave. 1912. *Statuomanie parisienne. Étude critique sur l'abus des statues*. Paris: H. Daragon.

Petit, Judith, Roger Pierrot, and Marie-Laure Prévost. 1985. Catalog, *Soleil d'encre, manuscrits et dessins de Victor Hugo*. Paris: Paris Musées/Bibliothèque nationale.

Petit dictionnaire critique et anecdotique des enseignes de Paris par un batteur de pavé. 1826. Paris: Imprimerie H. Balzac.

Peyre, Henri. 1932. *Louis Ménard. Yale Romanic Studies* 5. New Haven: Yale University Press.

Picasso, Pablo. 1952. "Picasso propose de faire le monument Hugo." Interview in *Tous les arts*, March 20–27.

Pictet, Adolphe. 1838. *Une course à Chamounix. Conte fantastique*. Paris: Librairie de Benjamin Duprat.

Pingeot, Anne, ed. 1986. Catalogue, *La Sculpture française au XIXe siècle*. Paris: Réunion des musées nationaux.

Pivot, Bernard. 2001. "La Confession du Roi Lire." Interview by Jérôme Garcin. *Le Nouvel observateur*, June 7–13.

Planté, Christine. 1987. "Un monstre du XIXe siècle, la femme auteur." *Sources. Travaux historiques* 12.

————. 1989. *La Petite soeur de Balzac: essai sur la femme auteur*. Paris: Seuil.

Poisson, Georges. 1988. "La statuaire commémorative parisienne sous le Second Empire." *Gazette des Beaux-Arts* (January–February): 93–102.

Porter, Dennis. 1995. *Rousseau's Legacy*. New York and Oxford: Oxford University Press.

Porterfield, Todd B. 1998. *The Allure of Empire: Art in the Service of French Imperialism, 1798–1838*. Princeton, NJ: Princeton University Press.

Powell, David. 1990. *George Sand*. Boston: Twayne.

Prendergast, Christopher. 1978. *Fiction and Melodrama*. London: Edward Arnold.

————. *The Order of Mimesis*. 1986. Cambridge: Cambridge University Press.

Proudhon, Pierre-Joseph. 1939. *Du principe de l'art et de sa destination sociale. Oeuvres complètes de P.-J. Proudhon*. Edited by C. Bouglé and H. Moysset. Vol. 15. Paris: Rivière.

Pugh, A. R. 1974. *Balzac's Recurring Characters*. Toronto: University of Toronto Press.

Queffélec, Lise. 1989. *Le Roman-feuilleton français au XIXᵉ siècle*. Paris: Presses universitaires de France.

Quillenbois, ill. 1849. "Grande revue des grotesques, passée par le Caricaturiste." *Le Caricaturiste, revue drolatique du dimanche*, June 3.

Ragon, Michel. 1981. *L'espace de la mort*. Paris: Albin Michel.

Raynaud, Jean-Michel. 1983. *Voltaire, soi-disant*. Lille: Presses Universitaires de Lille.

Réau, Louis. 1964. *Houdon: sa vie et son oeuvre*. Paris: Centre national de la recherche scientifique.

Renard, Jules. 1965. *Journal 1887–1910*. Edited by Léon Guichard and Gilbert Sigaux. Paris: Gallimard.

Reybaud, Louis. 1846. *Jérôme Paturot*. Illustrated by J.-J. Grandville. Paris: J. J. Dubochet, Le Chevalier et Cᵢₑ.

Ribner, Jonathan P. 1993. *Broken Tablets: The Cult of the Law in French Art from David to Delacroix*. Berkeley: University of California Press.

Riegl, Alois. 1982. "The modern cult of monuments: Its character and its origin." *Oppositions* 25: 21–51.

Robb, Graham. 1998. *Victor Hugo*. New York: W.W. Norton & Co.

Robin, Ch. 1848. *Galerie des gens de lettres au XIXe siècle*. Paris: V. Lecon.

Rolland, Romain. 1952. "Le Vieux Orphée." *Europe* (Feb.–Mar.).

Ronsard, Pierre de. 1914–75. *Oeuvres complètes*. Edited by Paul Laumonier, Isidore Silver and Raymond Lebègue. 20 vols. Paris: Hachette.

Rousseau, Jean-Jacques. 1968. *Les Confessions II*. Paris: Garnier-Flammarion.

Roy, Claude. 1958. *La vie de Victor Hugo racontée par Victor Hugo*. Paris: Club des éditeurs.

Saint-Paulien. 1979. *Napoléon Balzac et l'empire de la Comédie humaine*. Paris: Albin Michel.

Sainte-Beuve, Charles Augustin. 1839. "De la littérature industrielle." *Revue des Deux mondes* (August 15): 675–91.

———. 1859. *Galerie des femmes célèbres, tirées des "Causeries du lundi" par M. Sainte-Beuve, ill de 12 portraits*. Paris: Garnier Frères.

———. 1876. *Portraits contemporains*. 5 vols. Paris: Calmann-Lévy.

Salverte, Eusèbe. 1824. *Essai historique et philosophique sur les noms d'hommes, de peuples et de lieux, considérés principalement dans leurs rapports avec la civilisation*. 2 vols. Paris: Bossange Père, Libraire.

Sand, George [Aurore Dupin]. 1865. *Laura: Voyages et impressions*. Paris: Michel Lévy frères.

———. 1964–1991. *Correspondance*. Edited by Georges Lubin. 25 vols. Paris: Garnier.

———. 1970. *Oeuvres autobiographiques*. 2 vols. Paris: Gallimard.

———. 1981. "Pourquoi les femmes à l'Académie." In *Les femmes et l'Académie Française. Une polémique du XIXe siècle avec une réponse de George Sand*. Paris: Éditions de l'Opale.

Sandeau, Jules [Honoré de Balzac]. 1948. "Vie et malheurs d'Horace de Saint-Aubin." In *Oeuvres oubliées d'Honoré de Balzac*. Vol. 1. Paris: Pressédition.

Sarment, Jacqueline. 1980. *Maison de Balzac*. Paris: Musées de la ville de Paris.

Sarment, Jacqueline, and Laurence Bardury. 1983. Catalog, *Dessins d'écrivains français du XIXe siècle*. Paris: Maison de Balzac.

Sartre, Jean-Paul. *La Nausée*. Paris: Gallimard, 1938.

———. 1964a. *Les Mots*. Paris: Gallimard.

———. 1964b. *Nausea*. Translated by Lloyd Alexander. New York: New Directions Publishing.

———. 1964c. *The Words*. Translated by Bernard Frechtman. New York: George Braziller.

———. 1971–72. *L'Idiot de la famille*. 3 vols. Paris: Gallimard.

Savy, Nicole, and Georges Vigne. 1987. Catalog, *Le siècle des dictionnaires*. Les dossiers du Musée d'Orsay 10. Paris: Réunion des musées nationaux.

Schehr, Lawrence. 1997. *Rendering French Realism*. Stanford, CA: Stanford University Press.

Schopp, Claude. 1981. "Le Tombeau d'Honoré de Balzac." *L'Année balzacienne*: 244–53.

Schor, Naomi. 1993. *George Sand and Idealism*. New York: Columbia University Press.

Segal, Naomi. 1998. *André Gide: Pederasty and Pedagogy*. Oxford; NY: Clarendon Press.

Serres, Michel. 1980. *Le Passage du Nord-Ouest*. Paris: Minuit.

Sgard, Jean, and Catherine Volpilhac-Auger. 1999. *La Notion d'oeuvres complètes*. Oxford: Voltaire Foundation.

Shattuck, Roger. 1958. *The Banquet Years; The Arts in France, 1885–1918*. New York: Harcourt Brace.

Slama, Béatrice. 1980. "Femmes écrivains." In *Misérable et glorieuse: la femme au XIXe siècle*. Edited by Jean-Paul Aron. Paris: Fayard.

Sorel, Philippe. 1989. Catalog, *Dantan Jeune, Caricatures et portraits de la société romantique*. Paris: Paris-Musées.

Soulié, Frédéric. 1841. *Physiologie du bas-bleu*. Illustrated by Jules Vernier. Paris: Aubert.

Statue de Honoré de Balzac à Tours, sa ville natale. Souscription nationale ouverte pour la municipalité. 1887. Tours.

La Statue de George Sand. 1884. *L'Illustration* (August 9): 87.

Stendhal [Henri Beyle]. 1962–68. *Correspondance*. Edited by Henri Martineau and Victor Del Litto. 3 vols. Paris: Gallimard.

Stewart, Philip. 1969. *Imitation and Illusion in the French Memoir-Novel, 1700–1750*. New Haven: Yale University Press.

Texier, Edmond. 1864. "George Sand." *L'Illustration* (March 26): 203–4.

Tilllier, Bertrand. 1984. George Sand au Panthéon . . . Nadar. *Les amis de George Sand* 15: 26–31.

———. 1993. *George Sand chargée*. Tusson (Charente): Du Lérot.

———. 1998. *Cochon de Zola!* Tusson (Charente): Du Lérot.

Titon du Tillet, Evrard. 1971. *Le Parnasse françois, suivi des Remarques sur la poësie et la musique et sur l'excellence de ces deux beaux-arts avec des observations particulières sur la poësie et la musique françoise et sur nos spectacles*. Geneva: Slatkine Reprints.

Tocqueville, Alexis de. 1967. *L'ancien régime et la Révolution*. Paris: Gallimard.

Todorov, Tzvetan. 1970. *Introduction à la littérature fantastique*. Paris: Seuil.

Le Tombeau de Charles Baudelaire. 1979. New York: AMS.

Touchatout [Léon Bienvenu]. 1873. *Le Trombinoscope* 103.

Trésor de la langue française. 1971–1994. Edited by Paul Imbs. Paris: CNRS.

Turquet, ["pour ses collègues"]. 1792. *Réflexions des commissaires de police de la ville de Paris, relativement aux registres qui constituent l'état des hommes*. Paris: Imprimerie Cl. Simon.

Ulbach, Louis. 1844. *Gloriana*. Paris: W. Coquebert.

———. 1869–71. *Nos Contemporains*. Paris: Armand Le Chevalier.

———, ed. 1867. *Paris-Guide par les principaux écrivains et artistes de la France*. Paris: Librairie Internationale.

Valéry, Paul. 1960. "La conquête de l'ubiquité." In *Oeuvres*. Vol. 2. Paris: Gallimard.

Van Heuvel, J. 1983. *Album Voltaire*. Paris: Gallimard.

Van Tieghem, Philippe. 1985. *Victor Hugo, un génie sans frontières*. Paris: Larousse.

Vernay, Jules. 1876. George Sand. *L'Illustration* (June 27): 90.

Verne, Jules. 1994. *Paris au XXe siècle*. Paris: Hachette.

Vian, Boris. 1968. *Mood Indigo*. Translated by John Sturrock. New York: Grove Press.

———. 1979. *L'écume des jours*. Paris: Éditions G.P.

Viatte, Auguste. 1942. *Victor Hugo et les illuminés de son temps*. Ottawa: Éditions de l'Arbre.

Vigny, Alfred de. 1986–93. *Oeuvres complètes*. Edited by François Germain, André Jarry, and Alphonse Bouvet. 2 vols. Paris: Gallimard.

Villiers de l'Isle-Adam, Auguste. 1986. "La Machine à gloire." In *Oeuvres complètes*. Vol. 1. Paris: Gallimard (Pléiade).

Victor Hugo en images. 1902. Paris: Librairie Larousse.

Vovelle, Michelle, and Régis Bertrand. 1983. *La ville des morts. Essai sur l'imaginaire urbain contemporain d'après les cimetières provençaux*. Paris: CNRS.

Waller, Margaret. 1993. *Male Malady*. New Brunswick: Rutgers University Press.

Walsh, Théobald. 1837. *George Sand*. Paris: Hivert.

Ward, Patricia. 1975. *The Medievalism of Victor Hugo*. University Park, PA: Penn State University Press.

Warner, Marina. 1985. *Monuments and Maidens: The Allegory of the Female Form*. New York: Atheneum.

Watt, Ian. 1957. *The Rise of the Novel*. Berkeley and Los Angeles: University of California Press.

Weber, Eugen. 1986. *France Fin de Siècle*. Cambridge, MA: Harvard University Press.

Wechsler, Judith. 1982. *A Human Comedy: Physiognomy and Caricature in 19th-Century Paris*. London; New York: Thames and Hudson.

Wilde, Oscar. 1909. "The Decay of Lying." In *The Works of Oscar Wilde*. Vol. 10. New York: Lamb Publishing.

Wright, Gordon. 1987. *France in Modern Times*. 4th ed. New York: W.W. Norton.

Yriarte, Charles. 1864. *Les Célébrités de la rue*. Paris: Dupray de la Mahérie.

Zola, Émile. 1888. Une Statue pour Balzac. In *Une campagne. 1880–1881*. Paris: Charpentier.

———. 1906. "Balzac." In *Les romanciers naturalistes*. Paris: Charpentier.

———. 1988. *J'Accuse . . . ! La Vérité en marche*. Brussels: Éditions Complexe.

Zweig, Stefan. 1979. *Balzac*. Frankfurt am Main: Fischer Taschenbuch Verlag.

Index

Numbers in italics indicate illustration pages